275

Acting Games: Connected

A comprehensive workbook of theatre games for developing acting skills

Gavin Levy

mp

MERIWETHER PUBLISHING
A division of Pioneer Drama Service, Inc.
Denver, Colorado

Meriwether Publishing
A division of Pioneer Drama Service, Inc.
PO Box 4267
Englewood, CO 80155

www.pioneerdrama.com

Editor: Theodore O. Zapel
Cover Design: Jan Melvin

Library of Congress Cataloging-in-Publication Data

Levy, Gavin.
    275 acting games : connected : a comprehensive workbook of theatre games for developing acting skills / by Gavin Levy
        p. cm.
        ISBN: 978-1-56608-274-7
1. Acting—Juvenile literature. 2. Improvisation (Acting)—Juvenile literature. I. Title. II. Title: Two hundred and seventy-five acting games.
    PN2061.L3885 2010
    792.02'8—dc22

                                                        2010003841

5   6   7   15   16   17

With special thanks to Freda Kosmin for going the extra mile. Your hard work and dedication is very much appreciated.

Table of Contents

Introduction

Welcome to *275 Acting Games: Connected.* Moving to Los Angeles had a profound effect on me. I continued working with actors of all ages. The exercises I used worked on the actors' instrument and we also explored the purpose and potential benefits behind each exercise. The challenge was that the actors wanted to know how each exercise could be applied to the industry. They were right. We were living in Hollywood, and everything is related to the industry in some way or other. I realized that by adding an industry connection, the actors became more motivated in their desire to excel. Working with my colleague Paul Gleason, at the Paul Gleason Theatre in Hollywood, went a long way towards helping me make these connections. In this book you will find that every exercise contains an *Industry Connection* section. The industry connections are not untapped discoveries. They are observations that as instructors we simply need to point out. You may live far away from Los Angeles, London, New York, Paris, or Madrid, but your actors still want to know how what you are sharing with them relates to the professional world. It will grab their attention and compel them to work even harder. It is up to the student to apply these observations to any relevant situation.

This book contains 275 acting exercises, activities, and games. The premise of this book is to give you ample choice should you require it. The purpose of this book is to give acting teachers the tools they will need, not just a game to play or an exercise to teach. This book will also enable acting teachers to hold group discussions when necessary and guide them on how to ask students leading questions. If you are looking for something that delves deeper into exercises and their purpose, read on.

Acting teachers, directors, and instructors at all levels will find many uses for this book. In *Inside the Actors' Studio,* Frances Ford Coppola said he likes to use many theatre games with his actors. I have discovered that many of the activities included here are just as effective with intermediate students as they are with novices. A variety of exercises presented in this book lend themselves to group work and teamwork. In this sense, they are ideal for instruction in the classroom, as well as other coaching environments. Also, bear in mind that the information and instructions in this book are not to be understood as hard and fast rules. You are free to adapt any exercise to suit your needs. If you disagree with my suggestions, you are under no obligation to borrow them. In fact, if I can encourage you, the instructor, as well as the students, to initiate activities, I have doubly served my purpose. I would, however, ask that before you discard a suggestion or an idea, you make sure you thoroughly understand what is being asked, or what is being said. There are instructors, and then there are good instructors. If you want your students to become good actors, then I hope you are the latter.

Many of these exercises have multiple names. I did not invent any of them. I may have adapted and molded some of them, but they lend themselves to this kind of treatment, and you should feel free to do the same. As teachers, we must aim to stretch our students in every possible direction and empower them with skills and knowledge — that is the task of this book. Some of these exercises are popular in improvisation circles, while others are used in industry-type workshops. Their benefits are only limited by where we choose to lead them.

You will see me refer to "the stage," "the performance space," and "the audience." If you are working in a classroom, any area you designate can be the stage. The audience is wherever you decide to put them. The terms are reference points, since you will not always have the parameters of a formal theatre within which to work. This should be taken as another opportunity for you to improvise.

Again, I did not invent these exercises. I have discovered them over many years, mainly from workshops I have run and attended. Notice I did not say *acting* workshops. I have utilized activities from all walks of life and adapted them to the needs of actors. I have also included activities I was taught as a child. Whether these activities were originally intended for actors or not, it has been my mission to make them relevant to the student of acting.

You will notice that when I describe the participants, I use various terms. This is because I want you to get a taste of how applicable these exercises are to a wide variety of people. Although I wrote these activities with actors in mind, they can be used in many fields. A theatre director who is using a game before rehearsals might say, "I need two actors to come up on-stage," whereas a business employer who uses a selection of these activities to enhance team spirit in his or her company might say, "I need two volunteers to come to the front of the room." An English teacher who uses a character exercise to help the class understand the characters in a book they are reading might say, "I need three students to come forward and demonstrate this situation." We constantly need to ask ourselves, "Who is my audience?" By this I mean, "Whose attitude are we trying to affect by using these activities?" I find it beneficial to use terminology appropriate to any particular target audience.

I have divided the book into thirty-three chapters to give you some idea of how and where the activities can be used. Again, these categorizations are not set in stone. An activity I have put under *Concentration and Focus* might fit just as well under *Imagination*. These labels are just guidelines to help you get on track. Incidentally, you will notice that I have cross-referenced several chapters, linking an activity in one chapter to an activity in a different chapter. This may at first seem redundant. However, the subject matter is so important that I chose to approach some areas again from different angles.

With regard to the information under the *Purpose* and *Industry Connection* subheadings, you may notice there is a certain amount of repetition. It is important for actors to train and retrain their skills until they become second nature. Dancers do not learn the basics and then forget about them, they constantly go back to them. The point is to encourage readers to live outside the box. Look at the suggestions I've given and add your own. You will also see a *Note* subheading that is used throughout the book. This section does not always apply specifically to the exercise it is listed under, but rather to the bigger picture of acting as a whole. Remember, much of what you want to teach will also be picked up through performance of the activity.

You will find that I use the terms "actor," "he," and masculine pronouns consistently throughout the book. This is not because I am sexist, but simply because it is less combersome than saying "actor/actress" or "he/she."

Break a leg and enjoy!

Note to reader:

Throughout the text, Mr. Levy makes reference to his other books, *112 Acting Games*, *Acting Games for Individual Performers*, and *Acting for Love & Money*. These books are available from Meriwether Publishing Ltd. at www.meriwether.com.

Chapter 1
Warm-Up, Balance, and Homeostasis

1. Facial Frantic

1. Have your actors stand in a circle, shoulder width apart. Have everyone relax their arms by their sides and shake everything out. This should be everything from their feet, arms, legs, head, toes, and tongue. In other words, shake out the whole enchilada.
2. Now, have them take in a nice big yawn. As they do this, they should open their mouths nice and wide. Have them do this two or three times, in whatever way they choose. Now have them do this two or three more times. Next, ask them to vocalize the yawn as they breathe out. This should not be a yawn, but more of a sigh. It is the exhalation and letting go of breath.
3. Have your actors swing their arms loosely by the sides of their body. Swing their arms side to side in an almost uncontrolled fashion. Tell them, "As you swing your arms to the right, allow your left foot to also pivot to the right, with your heel lifting from the ground, but the tip of your shoe stays. Your left knee and hip will also want to turn to the right side. As your arms swing to the left, follow the same procedure." Have them do this exercise for the next minute or so.
4. Ask your actors to scrunch up their eyes as tightly as they can and hold this expression for five seconds. Each time they release, their eyes should remain closed, but not so tightly. Have your actors repeat this exercise three times.
5. Have your actors scrunch up their entire face and hold it for five seconds. This should include every muscle of their face. Each time they release, their eyes should remain closed. Allow the eyes and all facial muscles to soften. Have your actors repeat this exercise three times. At the end of the third time have the actors open their eyes as they release.
6. Have your actors do diaphragmatic breathing for one minute. This means there should be very little tension in the neck and very little lifting of the shoulders. Have the actors put one hand just above their belly, if they need to.
7. Have your actors use the tip of their tongue to count every tooth in their mouth. Ask them to start from the upper left tooth and work in a clockwise direction. When they have finished, ask them to repeat the exercise, only this time they should go around their teeth counterclockwise. It is important to remind the actors that they are to count every single tooth as opposed to most of them.

5

Purpose

To connect the body to the voice

This exercise allows the actor to connect the body to the voice. While some of the exercises are very specific to the voice and face, others engage the entire body. These exercises encourage the actors to connect and entwine the two. The actors' voices will not want to be separate from the rest of their body, but be embraced by it. In order to use their full voice, they have to use their full body. Some actors are very good in voice class, under a controlled environment. The challenge comes when they are in the middle of a scene where they have to engage their entire body. It is at this point that their voice gives way, because they have gotten used to doing one of the two. They have not yet developed the skills to link their body and voice as a whole unit. The trained actor knows how to do this, and so must you. A caveat to this exercise is to tell your actors to take whichever character they are playing that week into their voice lessons with them.

Industry Connection

If the actors cannot understand you, they cannot hire you! As Michael McCallion says in *The Voice Book,* "All speech faults can be summed up in one generality: they impede the wish for communication by drawing our attention to the speech process rather than to that which we wish to communicate."[1] Whenever actors are told they need accent reduction there are those who will fight it or protest it. They say, "It will rob me of who I am!" There may be a degree of truth to this, but accent reduction is not accent annihilation! It still allows the actors to keep the flavor of who they are, while allowing them to become a more marketable commodity. Casting agents close all of the lines of interpretation down to selling the actor as a product. One of the most legendary actors of the golden age was Mickey Rooney. His real name is Joseph Yule. His name was given to him by a publicity man at Universal. Some actors become movie stars before they become an actor. There are well-packaged products who also have charm and charisma. These same actors will point to well-known stars and say, "I can hardly understand them and they're famous!" They can usually name you two or three actors like this. In almost all cases, even if this were true, those actors gained their fame in their own countries first. This means that they were very well understood in their native tongues. If you watch their movies, once they move stateside, you will almost always find that there is noticeable accent reduction if you watch them in chronological order. They do not totally lose their accent. They have learned to reduce it. Developing an accent is a challenging task. It is not simply changing the voice, but creating a whole way of being. If you still find protests, explain in the following way:

INSTRUCTOR: If you are not looking to be a working actor, then everything that has just been said need not apply to you, except that is not quite true. Every actor is a storyteller. How can you communicate a story if no one can understand words coming out of your mouth? The smart answer would be, "nonverbal communication," but we are talking about your voice, and the words, shapes, and sounds it produces.

---

1. Michael McCallion, *The Voice Book* (London: Faber and Faber, 1988), 187.

6

2. Warm-Up

Choose five actors to come forward into the performance space. Do not ask who would like to come forward, but select the actors randomly. Tell each one that in a moment you would like them to show the rest of the group a gentle mobility exercise or a gentle stretch. They are going to talk us through the exercise. Have the rest of the group perform the exercise or mobility exercise. They will also need to talk us through the purpose behind the exercise.

Here are a couple of examples of mobility exercises:

1. Swinging the arms from side to side.
2. Taking the arms out horizontally, so that they are in line with the shoulders, make small circles rotating forwards (palms down) and backwards (palms up).

Give the actors a few minutes to come up with these exercises before beginning. Finish up with a group discussion. If an actor who is demonstrating performed an exercise incorrectly, it should be raised in the group discussion. If an actor says he des not know any warm-up exercises, this is a major challenge. In the foundation course, this may be acceptable. At this stage, however, the actors have to be walking the walk. Ask the actors to avoid strenuous exercises. We are always looking at safety first, to avoid potential injuries. A warm-up exercise may be something they bring from football or volleyball training. It does not even have to be something that you have necessarily given them.

Purpose

To warm up the actor's instrument

This exercise asks the actors to have a basic understanding of warm-up exercises for their body. Before a play, the actors will want to warm up their vocal chords and their physical body to free it of unnecessary tension. They will want to feel free to explore whatever it is their character wants to explore. If at this stage the actors still do not know how to do this, then they are not using their instrument effectively. Actors, before a show, may do a vocal warm-up with a diction exercise. If this is the case, they know that it is for diction, so that they can be understood. If an actor shows everyone a calf stretch but does not understand that it is to loosen up the calves, then they don't understand the function of the exercise. It is not enough that the actors are *doing*. The actors have to understand *why* they are doing what they are doing!

Industry Connection

Actors who loosen up their body before meeting with a potential agent have an advantage. They can walk into the room physically relaxed with a body that feels at ease. The person after them may feel physically tight and in some degree of physical pain. The way people's bodies feel will not only read on their faces, it will also come out in their emotional responses. If their muscles are feeling tight, they will probably come across as more edgy, angry, and nervous. If muscles are tight, the actor may not be able to think clearly. This is fine if these are the signals they want to send. I doubt it, though. They need to give themselves every possible advantage in this industry and not take them away before they even begin.

7

3. Tense and Release

Have your actors form a circle in which the actors are about shoulder width apart. Ask one actor to go into the middle of the circle. At this point tell the actor in the center to tense all his muscles. Ask the actor to become as a stiff as a board. The actor needs to make a mental note of how this feels. Now tell the actor to relax all the muscles in his body, so that he is as floppy as a rag doll. The actor should be so relaxed that he flops to the ground. Again, ask the actor to make a mental note of how this feels. Now, let the actor experiment by moving between various degrees of tension and relaxation in one continuous motion. This will probably get some laughs from the audience as the actor's body will form all kinds of physical contortions. Ask the actor to do this at a rapid pace. Instruct the actor to rejoin the rest of the circle. The whole class should repeat the exercise while standing in the circle. Now ask your students to find their own space in the room. Give them three to five minutes to move around the room, allowing their bodies to experience various degrees of tension and relaxation. Bring the whole group back together into a circle. Watch two or three more actors work separately in the center of the circle. Finish up with a group discussion. Have the students talk about their observations, understandings, and personal discoveries in relation to the exercise.

Purpose

To understand the difference between tension and relaxation in the muscles

Some actors are told that the aim is to have no tension whatsoever in their bodies. This is somewhat of a misleading statement. When the actors totally relax their bodies, they begin to move like a rag doll. While it is true that their muscles are relaxed, it is also true that they have virtually no control over their body or muscles at this point. The actors will always want to garner a degree of control over their instrument. Ballet dancers appear perfectly relaxed while keeping a minor degree of tension in all their muscles. When the actors tense everything up, they discover that to move with ease is virtually impossible. They also discover that their ability to think clearly is affected. Some actors are unaware of the high degree of tension they are carrying in their bodies. Famous actors have commented that they feel they are working with varying degrees of nervous tension on-set. This exercise helps the actors to discover that their bodies need just the right amount of tension and release for every performance.

Industry Connection

Remind your actors that the camera picks up everything. It is able to get under the characters' skin and literally behind their eyes. The camera is able to invade on the privacy of the characters' lives. Let us say an actor is feeling nervous and tense. The same actor is in a close-up and his muscles are so tight that the muscles in his face are twitching, his fists are clenched, the veins in his neck are popping, and he begins sweating profusely. This particular shot is of his college or high school graduation. The director is looking for the actor who will move the audience to tears of joy. The challenge is that everything the tense actor's body is doing is failing him. The director does take after take because he cannot get what he is looking for. Actors have to learn to let go of the vast majority of tension in their body. As Eric Morris points out in his book *No Acting Please,* "Half the battle in conquering a human problem is to first recognize that it exists. Too many actors deny the existence of tension in themselves."[2] This does not mean becoming as loose as a rag doll, but finding a point of balance from which to work.

4. Human Puppet

Bring four actors into the performance area. Have the audience give them a scene suggestion that involves two actors. The scene is going to be performed in the following way: Two of the actors are going to be the performers and are able to talk, the other two are going to be literally moving the actors around the stage — like a puppeteer would move a puppet. For this to work effectively, the two performers are going to have to remain loose, free, and open. If a puppeteer picks up an arm, that arm has to be loose. Notice I did not say totally relaxed. If performers are totally relaxed, they may simply collapse and fall to the floor. Have the puppeteers stick to their puppet. If they want to have their puppet walk across the room and it is not feasible to lift them up, have the puppeteer put a hand on the small of the back of the performers they want to move and guide them to the intended place. They can gently halt them when they want them to stop. It is going to be a challenge for the performers not to start laughing, but the scene is more powerful if they can stay fully engaged in it. It is obviously not possible for the puppeteers to be invisible. As much as possible, tell them to look down or away from the audience. We need to form a barrier between the actors (puppets) and the puppeteers. Follow up with a group discussion then follow on with another group.

Variation

Have it so that the puppeteers are not confined to one puppet. Allow the puppeteers to move between puppets. It could be interesting to have four actors but only two puppeteers.

Purpose

To free up the body

If the actors (puppets) tense up their muscles, the puppeteers will not be able to move them effectively. For the puppeteers to do their job, the actors have to be able to stay free and loose. This is not so easy to do when they are being manhandled. An actor on-stage has to be able to be free within their body. If they are moving around full of tension, not only will it restrict their movement, it will also restrict their ability to think. Pain is the ultimate form of tension. When people are in pain they often say, "I can't think straight." While a little tension is necessary, the actors want to be able to keep the greater part of tension out of their body. Actors will want to aim to be freer, less in control, and more susceptible.

---

2. Eric Morris, *No Acting Please* (New York: Spelling Publication, 1979), 32.

Industry Connection

An actor may sometimes feel like a puppet that is being controlled. Actors can be quite coddled in the entertainment business. This feeling applies just as much to well-established stars as it does to aspiring actors. Movie stars in the black-and-white era were practically owned by the studios. They would commit to a five- or ten-year deal and were pretty much the property of the studio. This was not all negative, but it did mean that someone else was making major decisions with regard to their career. This still happens today in terms of agent, casting agents, directors, producers, and so on. With the rise of reality TV and internet sites, some people have become famous overnight. What is worth noting is that there are people who immediately jump on the bandwagon and take over the handling of the actor's career. Advise your actors to be cautious about whom they allow to pull the strings with regard to their careers.

5. Shaken, Not Stirred

Ask your actors to stand in a circle. Tell someone to make a movement that involves shaking, such as wiggling his left leg. After a few moments, have the whole group shake their left leg. It is very important that the students isolate the specific body part. Now go back to the original person and ask him to mime throwing that body part to someone else in the circle. The next person will want to act as if he caught the vibration and then shake a different body part, such as his right hand. The whole group should then shake their right hand. Continue in this way. This is a great warm-up exercise and you should be able to get around to everyone. If an actor has already had a vibration thrown to him, he should ask the person throwing to choose someone else. Finish up with a group discussion.

Purpose

Character development through isolation

The isolation of body parts leads the actors to become familiar with their body in a more specific manner. If an actor is playing a character with a limp, he is going to have to learn to isolate certain muscles of the leg. If an actor hangs around a shopping mall, he will notice that many people move in different ways. The actor will notice that some people appear to have one shoulder higher than the other. Other people appear to have shoulders that roll forward, or a head that appears to thrust too far forward. These challenges can be the result of muscle disuse or muscle atrophy. Certain muscles start to isolate themselves from engagement in movement. It is important for the actors to understand that they themselves do not necessarily move, stand, or sit in the same way as the character they are playing. Dance training can be of great benefit to actors. Dance instructor and choreographer Catherine Wilkinson told me in conversation, "Freedom of movement is important for actors. The best way to acquire this is through dance. Dance lessons help develop coordination, good mind-body connection, and a sense of rhythm that enhances movement, while speaking on the stage in front of the camera. If an actor is comfortable with the movement of their body through dance, they can follow any blocking direction without it interfering with their acting technique." The more familiar actors are with muscle and joint isolation, the more they will be able to use that awareness to their advantage.

10

Industry Connection

When actors throw their action across the circle, they have to clearly indicate the intended recipient. Only half doing this leads to confusion so that the actors are not sure with whom the thrower is communicating. Actors engaged in the industry have to become experts in terms of communication. This is not only true in terms of performance, it is also necessary in their day-to-day lives. When they are interviewed as a guest on a show, they have to communicate what they want to say. Actors are constantly communicating with their fans and they need to make sure they communicate accurately. Actors constantly have to communicate with directors, producers, casting agents, other actors, technical crews, and so on. It is not enough for the actor to be OK at communicating. The actor has to become an expert in the art of communication.

6. Stand-In

Have your actors sit as the audience. Bring two actors into the performance space. They will want to be facing one another, standing on marks on the stage. Have them hold these positions for two minutes. Tell them to keep eye contact, but ask them not to talk to each other. Now ask one of them to sit in a chair, and have the other actor stand behind the chair. Have them freeze in these positions for another two minutes. If you want to, you can work with three or four actors. You can instruct them to sit around a table, looking at one another without moving. All of these are examples of what a stand-in does on a set. You can also change the positions you wish the actors to hold. An example would be, "Simon, can you lean in, and put your hand on the cup, and hold this?" Only give instructions once. This will allow you to see how well the actors are focused and paying attention. Follow up with a group discussion.

Purpose

To become comfortable with stillness

The actors are asked to stand or sit very still. They are asked not to fidget or talk to the other actors. When the crew is lighting a shot they need to know exactly where the actors will be. It is no good if one of the stand-ins goes wandering off to get a cup of coffee. If he does, then someone will tell him to get back to where he needs to be. Remember that wasted time is wasted money. If they are fidgeting, it is going to be hard to light accurately. Your actors may find it harder to stand still than they thought. This exercise is not as easy as it first appears. Of course, there are times when the stand-ins can talk softly to one another and move slightly. They have to be completely alert so that they are ready for any new instructions they are given. It is also important to note that stillness can be important in terms of character work. Powerful people tend not to move very much. There is still a lot going on behind the eyes. An actor has to be comfortable to peel off and throw away as much as possible.

Industry Connection

The role of the stand-in is not a particularly glamorous one. They have to stand around in various positions to help the crew light the scene. They do the work that can be considered tedious, which most actors are not required to do. This may not be the case on a low-budget project. Sometimes, they are also asked to move around to show the camera crew the blocking. The stand-in may also walk the blocking of the scene to help the crew discover what is going to happen and when.

The stand-in is an important part of the set. They are considered part of the crew. Some of your actors may say, "I will never be a stand-in!" This may well be the case, but it is also worth noting that many stand-ins are aspiring, or working, actors. Being a stand-in can be an invaluable experience. They get to see everything that happens behind the scenes. They get a firsthand look at all the technical aspects of being on-set. This exercise may appear boring to the actors. It is nevertheless a real job that takes place every day in Hollywood. It is not the aim of every exercise to be fun and entertaining. The actors are being given real experience of the world they are entering.

7. Walking

Instruct half your actors to sit as the audience. Tell the other half to go into the performance space. Ask the students in the performance space to "walk around the stage normally." Have the audience observe this. Have the students do this for two or three minutes. Afterwards, have the actors who were walking around sit facing the audience. At this point, have the audience make observations of what they saw. They may say things like:

"You appeared stiff and self-conscious."

"You kept scratching your head as you moved around the room."

"Your walk appeared forced and confused."

"Your legs looked really stiff as you moved."

After one group has worked, change over and let the other students walk around the room. This exercise is profound in that it highlights to the students that the most basic tasks, such as walking, can appear forced and contrived when tensions are present in the body. Follow up with a group discussion. It is also important that your students make objective comments, as opposed to personal attacks, about another student's walking. The actor has to learn how to become comfortable having others talk about them.

Purpose
To highlight self-created tensions

What is fascinating is that it seems as if some of the actors have forgotten how to walk. This is partly because they become self-conscious when they are being watched by the audience. Many actors have moments of insecurity. It is as if they have forgotten how to do the simplest things. This is a challenge that numerous actors face on-stage. The nerves of performing in front of a live audience create spasms, tension, and tightness throughout their bodies. This in turn causes the most basic movements to appear forced and unrealistic. We use an automatic function such as walking to highlight this point. You can also work this exercise by asking your actors to "breathe naturally" while they are being scrutinized by their peers. Remind your actors that tension is the enemy of the actor. The actors have to find ways to create balance in their body. From this place, they can move in any direction, mental or physical.

Industry Connection

Walking is an automatic process. We don't think about our walking; we just do it. However, it can happen that the actors suddenly become self-conscious and start thinking about their walking. An actor on-set may be asked to do the most basic of tasks. The director may say, "When you say 'Hi, Stan,' pick up the teaspoon." Picking up a teaspoon does not take a great deal of thought. It is something we have all done on many occasions. The challenge is that we have not all done it with an entire crew and cast looking over our shoulder. Suddenly, the actress becomes so self-conscious that she drops the teaspoon or she fumbles with it. She can hardly pick up the teaspoon. She asks herself, "What is wrong with me?" The challenge is that it is costing the producer more money for every take she messes up. It is one thing to know how to pick up a teaspoon, but an entirely different matter to do this on a multi-million-dollar film budget in front of hundreds of pairs of eyes. There are some actors that very few directors are willing to work with because they are considered unprofessional. Even if a director is interested, they can rarely find the financial backing from producers for actors that are considered a high risk. Good actors prepare their instrument to be ready for the challenges of their chosen profession. They may go in-depth in their preparation and then have to wait until sound, lights, wardrobe, and the director is ready to shout, "action." They are aware that when there is an intrusive sound on-set they should pause until it goes away. In one of the most famous movies ever made the director was filming an over-the-shoulder shot. One of the actors had to leave and the other actor filmed the scene with the continuity guy. He had to use every bit of talent he had for the scene. By being professional he saved the director time and the producer money. Good actors are always willing to go back to preparation. Some actors are so dedicated to their work and to their craft, they will heighten the experience and make other actors' performances stronger just by being near them. Good acting is not about lying, it is about telling the truth.

8. Body Warm-Up

Ask your students to find a space in the room and remain standing. This is a warm-up and isolation exercise.

Tell everyone to make figure eight circles with their big left toe.
Now tell them to make figure eight circles with their right big toe.
Tell them to make figure eights with their left foot.
And then they should make figure eights with their right foot.
Tell them to make figure eights with their left knee circling to the left and right.
Let them do the same thing with the right knee.
The students should now make figure eights with their left thumb.
And then they should make figure eights with their right thumb.
Have students make figure eight movements with their left hand in each direction.
Let them do the same thing with their right hand.
The students should make figure eights with their pelvis/waist going to the left.
And now they should do the same thing going to the right.
Come up with more figure eight movements that isolate other body parts.

Purpose

To warm up the instrument

The actors need to warm up their instrument in the same way that a musician fine-tunes his guitar or violin before every performance. A person who works in an office may use a computer to do the vast majority of his work. When actors go to work, they are using themselves. They have to make sure that their instrument is working at its optimal level. The good thing about a warm-up, such as the figure eight, is that it can be done anywhere. It is also practical and not particularly distracting to others. An actor can use it to warm up before going on-stage or just before an audition.

Industry Connection

At its core, this is an isolation exercise. The actors have to pinpoint specific body parts and work with them, one at a time. In the same way, actors have to pinpoint specific elements of their career to work on. To say, "I am going to be a working actor" is OK, but it is very general. The actor has to be able to isolate the ingredients that go along with this statement. He has to isolate technique, headshots, resumés, agents, marketing, auditioning, and networking, to name but a few. He then has to isolate even further when getting into each of these subcategories. Finding a photographer is one thing, to find a good photographer who knows how to work with actors is quite another story.

9. Eights

This is an excellent warm-up activity that really gets the blood pumping. Instruct your actors to stand in a circle. Explain in the following way:

INSTRUCTOR: Take your left hand and shake it eight times with some energy. Take your right hand and shake it eight times. Take your left arm and shake it eight times. Take your right arm and shake it eight times. Take your left foot and shake it eight times. Take your right foot and shake it eight times. Take your left leg and shake it eight times. Take your right leg and shake it eight times.

Now tell your actors to repeat the whole process, but this time they are going to shake everything four times. Once they have done this, tell them to shake everything twice, then finally to shake everything once. You should find everything crescendos so that it goes faster and faster. The key to this activity is to get your students to isolate particular body parts. It is also important that they are able to follow the process repeatedly. Tell them to use some really invigorating energy for this exercise, though this does not mean to say that they will want to overtly tense the muscles.

Purpose

To invigorate the body

This exercise is excellent at really getting the blood pumping around the body. It is excellent for waking up your actors when they are feeling physically drained. One reason for this is that getting everything moving at a rapid pace invigorates the body. The blood also becomes oxygenated to a greater extent, which increases the individual's energy level. If an actor is about to give a three-hour performance, it does not serve them to go on-stage drained and fatigued. The actor has to use the tools at his disposal to counter this lethargy. A tired actor will also be unfocused, which can lead to a performance that is par, at best. There are many ways in which actors can reenergize their body, including breathing exercises.

Variation
See the exercise Warm-Up on page 7. These two exercises go very well together.

Industry Connection
An actor may be on-set for two hours. They may be on-set for twelve hours, or more. The challenge for the actor is that there is no standard eight-hour work day. There is the occasional director who works in this way, but that is unusual. The actor has to find a way to stay physically and mentally alert. They can drink coffee and energy drinks, but while these will stimulate highs, they will also create lows. There is also the question of a healthy lifestyle. Actors have to have a toolbox that enables them to use their own body to invigorate and reenergize themselves at a moment's notice. Once the director says, "It's in the can," it is in the can! If the actor has given a lethargic and lackluster performance, it is there for the whole world to see.

10. Facial Warm-Up

This activity is a facial exercise warm-up. There are many ways of working the muscles of the face. Have everyone stand in a circle. Explain in the following way:

INSTRUCTOR: I would like everyone to stick out their tongue, then withdraw it. Stick it out as far as you can. Repeat this in and out motion ten times. Really stretch out your tongue.

Now, I want you to put out your tongue and point it up, to the right, down, and to the left. Do not put it back in your mouth this time. Do this three times. Repeat this three times in a counterclockwise direction.

I would now like you to make three tongue circles going in a clockwise direction. Again, the tongue does not need to go back inside the mouth. Repeat this same motion going in a counterclockwise direction.

I would now like you to blow raspberries for the next twenty seconds. You will want to feel your lips vibrating the entire time. Allow your lips to stay loose and relaxed.

I would now like you to make your vowel sounds, except that you are not going to say them out loud. You are going to silently mouth them in the most exaggerated way you can.

I would now like you to scrunch up all the muscles of your face as tightly as you can. Really scrunch everything up as tight as you can, and release it. Repeat this action three times.

Make your face as small as you can, and now make it as big as you can with your eyes wide open. Repeat these actions three times.

These exercises are an excellent way of warming up the muscles of the face. These are a few examples of how you can do this with your students.

Purpose

To warm up the muscles of the face

In a performance, actors are going to rely on their facial muscles in a variety of ways. They are going to use them in terms of articulation and enunciation. They are also going to use their facial muscles to portray the facial expressions and reactions of their character. If their facial muscles are not warmed up or flexible enough, the actor may find themselves restricted in both these areas. Pound for pound, the masseter (jaw muscle) is one of the strongest in the human body. To ignore the facial muscles is detrimental to the actor's instrument.

Industry Connection

What I like about these exercises is their practicality. If an actor is waiting for an audition, they could pop into the hallway and do these warm-up exercises without anyone noticing. This is the case for all but the raspberry blowing exercise. It is good for the actors to have practical exercises that they can use as and when they are needed. If actors have to sit in heavy traffic on their way to the audition and become somewhat stressed, they are going to need to find a way to let that go in an efficient manner. They will want to find a way to go with the flow. The actor who mumbles and becomes tongue-tied at an audition may find it costs him the job.

Chapter 2
Body Awareness

11. Don't Blink

In order to utilize this exercise to its fullest degree, you will want a number of your students to have monologues already learned. In this exercise you do not want your students to be looking down at a script.

Bring one or two actors into the performance space. Have the rest of the class sit as the audience. This exercise is beneficial especially for film work. If you have a video camera in your class, you may choose to film the actor performing. Another approach would be to have the actors work with a monologue that requires less movement. By working in this fashion, the stage monologue is able to represent a camera close-up.

INSTRUCTOR: Claire, I am going to have you work with me on this exercise as you already have a monologue prepared. The only added challenge is that as you perform your monologue for the class, you are not allowed to blink.

CLAIRE: I cannot blink at all?

INSTRUCTOR: You got it. While you do this I am going to use the audience as blink monitors. Each member of the audience is going to count silently to the number of times you blink during the monologue. Please note that no one is to count out loud. We are doing it this way so as not to interrupt the flow of Claire's monologue.

VERONICA: What should Claire do if she starts to notice that she is blinking?

INSTRUCTOR: This may well happen. We would still like to see a performance from Claire although she has an added challenge to deal with.

You could also do this exercise by having two students work in a close-up scene together and repeat the exercise in this fashion. If you prefer a more aggressive approach, you can have the students call out loud every time a student blinks. If you use this approach, it may be better to just choose one or two monitors.

Purpose
To understand how the body is functioning

By not blinking, this exercise demands that the actors have control of their bodily functions. Blinking is, generally speaking, an automatic response that we don't even think about. Nothing should be happening that they do not want to be happening. If they fidget in even the slightest manner, the audience will think there is a meaning to it. They will rightly or wrongly take the fidgeting to be part of the character's makeup. Being aware of something as subtle as blinking allows your actors to understand what their body is doing at any give moment. The actor must learn how to control the use of their body.

Industry Connection

This exercise is not to make your students' acting more believable, or to make them better actors. It is purely a technical exercise for film and television work, and yet your students may appear to be better actors to the camera once they have mastered it. As Michael Caine explains, "Blinking makes your

17

character seem weak. Not blinking will make you appear strong on screen."[3] Now a director or producer watching might say, "That actor has good stage presence. I want to work with her again." You see, as students practice and grow in all aspects of their acting, not only are they becoming stronger actors, they are also becoming a more marketable product that people will want to hire and work with. As you begin to make these links with your actors, you will find their enthusiasm to learn and work hard grows. It is also worth noting that a better actor is not necessarily a good actor.

12. Awareness

Tell your actors to walk around the room at a regular walking pace. As they do so, their arms and fingertips should be stretched up towards the sky. They should also be on tiptoe as they walk around the room. Everything should be stretched up, up, up! To avoid injury, tell the actors to do this in a safe and controlled fashion. Allow this to continue for a minute or two then ask the actors to form a circle.

Tell the actors that they are now going to focus on diaphragmatic breathing. Remind them of this, if need be, by putting their hand just above their belly button. Remind them that as they breathe in, they should be able to push their hand outwards with the breath. (See the Ten Steps exercise, page 70, for further clarification on diaphragmatic breathing.) Explain in the following way:

INSTRUCTOR: What I would like you to do next is to pant like a dog. As you're breathing diaphragmatically, you need to keep your shoulders still. Notice how your stomach bounces in and out. This is because as you take in a breath, your lungs are filling with air. The diaphragm is then pushed downward by the lungs and the stomach expands. I would like you to do this for the next minute when I will say stop. If for any reason you get dizzy, feel free to stop. What I would like you to do next is allow your arms to hang loose by the sides of your body. Swing your arms from side to side, in an almost uncontrolled fashion. As you swing your arms to the right, allow your left foot to also pivot to the right. Your left knee and hip should also turn to the right side. As your arms swing to the left, follow the same procedure. I'm going to have you do this exercise for the next two minutes.

Make sure there is enough distance between you and the next person. What I would like you to do next is pick up a book or your notepad and find a comfortable space somewhere in the room. Lie on your back and place a book on your stomach, just above your belly. Watch it rise and fall as you breathe. If it is hardly moving, then you are not practicing diaphragmatic breathing. Refocus the breath so it goes deep down the lungs and into your stomach. At this point, I want you to stop focusing on the breath and just continue breathing as you are. Take the next two minutes to lie there in absolute silence, apart from your inner thoughts.

---

3. Michael Caine, *Acting in Film* (New York: Applause Books, 1990), 61.

Purpose

To explore body awareness

These exercises explore body awareness in the actors' own way. In their day-to-day life, actors may not notice unnecessary tension. When they are on-stage, their audience will scrutinize every move they make, as if it has meaning. If their voice suddenly trails off because of lack of oxygen, their audience will wonder if they did it on purpose. Is it supposed to be part of their character? If their neck muscles are tightening through nerves, their audience may interpret this to mean anger in terms of the scene. Notice I said unnecessary tensions, because, of course, some tension in the body is necessary. Actors have to be able to control their body and their breathing. They have to be able to manipulate them in any way they desire, and in any way their character dictates. It is true that if an actor spent an entire performance focusing on the breath, there would be little room to focus on anything else. This is why it is so important that an actor has good technique, so that he can allow the technical aspects of his acting to be virtually automatic. With technique comes structure. As my colleague Paul Gleason says, "There are only three things you can do with any technique: you can stretch, strengthen, and coordinate." As the world-famous social psychologist Erich Fromm explains, "True freedom is not the absence of structure, but rather a clear structure that enables people to work within established boundaries in an autonomous and creative way."[4] Each actor will want to become an explorer of the craft. This can only happen when an actor has developed a fully-functional instrument.

Industry Connection

A close-up is not called a close-up for nothing. Nothing escapes the lens of the camera. In some movies, an actor will talk to the camera and bring the audience into his world. The camera lens watches human behavior and all it wants to do is watch. If you watch a certain well-known commercial, you will see a lady smiling. Unfortunately, her smile looks more like a grimace. It may be because she has done the same take fifty times. It may be because the director just snapped at her to get the shot right. It may be because after thirteen hours her feet are getting tired. Film is about stamina. It may be because rather than understanding her body, she is its servant. Instead of controlling her facial muscles through technique, she is going with blind faith. In the specific instance I am thinking of, the end results backfired. Instead of looking like a happy, confident woman, she looks like a neurotic, tense woman with a nervous disposition. She is nonverbally sending totally the wrong message for the product she is selling. While a number of the exercises in this warm-up are vocal in nature, they are really about understanding placement and technique. It is great that an actor is a natural actor and wants to let everything happen naturally, but what is he going to do when nature fails?

---

4. Erich Fromm, *TLC Handbook*-Volume 17 (Austin: 2005), 1.

13. Big Fish, Small Fish

This is an exercise that is often used in improvisation courses. Have your actors form a circle. The first person in the circle says "big fish." At the same time, he holds his hands a couple of inches apart. The next person to his right says "small fish," as he holds his hands at least one foot (twelve inches) apart. Keep going around the circle in the same fashion. If a player says "big fish" but keeps his hands open too wide, he is out. To make this more interesting, you can have him die a dramatic death or choose a forfeit. Do not tell him the forfeit until he has made his choice. A forfeit might be, "Perform a monologue for us right now." Each time you get all the way around the circle, reverse the order and start going the other way. At the end of the exercise, only one person should be left in. If the exercise is lasting too long or they are finding it too easy, have them speed it up. The faster they work this activity, the more challenging it becomes. When an actor dies, if the group does not buy into it, have him do it again. Don't let him get away with a sloppy death with no believability. Do not allow your students to give a weak and unjustified performance. Holding your students accountable will stand them in good stead for everything they do in their lives.

Purpose
To highlight contradictory behavior

This exercise forces the actors to be contradictory. They tell the group the fish is big and yet their physical action tells the group it is small. Ask your actors to think about how their characters contradict themselves all the time. Actors will want to get a handle on their character. A character might tell her husband she loves him, while really she hates his guts. A character might tell their mother-in-law, "Thank you for all your advice," when really they are thinking, "I wish you would mind your own business!" An actor will want to look for the dichotomy in each and every role. We live in a contradictory society and so do our characters. Politicians tell people to obey the law, while they break all the rules. A character may be written as hard as a bed of nails, but it is also up to the actor to find the character's more gentle side. If the actors stop short of this, they will never truly find the character they are searching for. This in itself may appear to be a contradiction. What it is saying is that none of us are one-dimensional people. Actors will want to be more interested in the character they are playing than they are as themselves playing the character. Actors have to know what is underneath the mask of every character they play.

Industry Connection

An actor's career is going to be full of contradictions, just like this exercise. They are going to go for an audition and the director will say, "I loved your work. Great job!" The actors will leave and tell their friends they booked the job. The next day, their agent calls them up and tells them the director gave it to someone else. This is not necessarily a lie. The director may have really liked the actor, but he just happened to like the next person even more. Here is a little scenario you can tell your actors they will probably run into at some point in their future if they have not already:

INSTRUCTOR: People will ask you, "What do you do for a living?" You say, "I am an actor." You will walk away with a slight feeling of uncertainty in the pit of your stomach. You are an actor, only you don't make the majority of your income from acting — or maybe you do — so you feel like a liar. You feel like you are not really telling the truth. So you decide to stop saying you're an actor. You start saying you're a waitress at the pizza joint instead. Now you feel guilty and confused because you don't feel like a waitress. In your heart and soul you are an actor. You are going to have to find what works for you. You are going to have to find what sits comfortably with you. The accessible actor is very human.

Note
Most movies that come out of Hollywood are made in English. These movies are sent all over the world and yet the first language of many of these countries is not English. In some of these countries there are still audiences who prefer to watch a movie that has been dubbed. Some actors have been the "dubber" for the same movie star for over thirty years. In many cases they have never met the actor whose work they are interpreting.

14. Dead Lions
This is a well-known children's activity that we are going to use for our purposes. Explain in the following way:

INSTRUCTOR: What I would like you to do is take off your shoes and put them somewhere at the side of the room and out of the way. If you have any gum in your mouth, please take it out and dispose of it. In a moment, I am going to ask you to lie down on your back and find a comfortable position. I will also ask you to close your eyes. When I say "dead lion," you will need to stay absolutely still. I will then begin walking around the room. If I see you flinch or move, I will tap you on the shoulder, which will mean you are out. At this point you will join the observer team and walk around the room looking for those who are moving in any way. If you see anyone moving, gently tap them on their shoulder, as previously explained, and they will also join the observer team. There is no talking or verbal communication of any kind during this activity. The aim is to be the last "dead lion" left. I want to clarify that there is a difference between breathing and moving. The person is out only if they flinch or actually move in any way.

Purpose
To experience stillness
In this exercise the actors have to stay as still as possible. This is easier said than done. Once they are told they cannot move, they are going to find the desire to fidget and move more intensely. Sometimes you will hear a person say, "That actor is so wonderful. They are so still." If actors emulate this literally, then they may give a wooden and stiff performance. What they are saying is that this actor knows how to move with the economy of effort. He does not move for the sake of moving, or throw his arms around with every gesture. He learns to do less. If an actor were playing a member of the British aristocracy, then the use of stillness would be very important. Some actors say the hardest thing to do is nothing. Sometimes stillness can be so powerful it will capture and snare an audience.

Industry Connection

If actors fidget in this exercise, they are out. They do not have a second chance. The reason I am saying it like this is because, in an audition, the actor will get treated in exactly the same way. Some actors will twist their foot, pick their nose, play with their hair, scrunch up their nose, scratch their knee, and wonder why they don't get a callback. The casting director cannot see the actors if the actors do not know how to get out of their own way! The reason we do exercises on body awareness is so that the only time the actor's body is doing anything is because he wants it to. Your actors have to thoroughly understand their instrument so that they can take it in any direction they choose. Some actors say, "They want to see me so I won't bother to train." It is true that they want to see the individual. What they want to see is the best and most talented version of that individual.

15. Walking Tall

Have your actors spread out around the room so that each one has his own space. Explain in the following way:

INSTRUCTOR: In a moment I would like you to start walking around the space. As you do so, I am going to ask you to imagine different textures. You will walk on these terrains and adjust your movement accordingly.

Start by walking around the space and imagine you are walking in mud. As you walk through it, your feet sink further into the mud and there is some give in your knees. Your legs feel a little heavier and you have to guard yourself from slipping. The mud is sticky, and at times it becomes quite difficult to lift your legs.

This is an example of how you might start to describe the mud they are walking through. Do not write these descriptions down, use your imagination to talk your actors through it as they are doing the exercise.

Some other examples of textures are:

Sand
Honey
Two feet of snow
Eggshells
Wet cement
Hot coals
Six inches of snow
A crater on the moon

Do not stop between each texture. Instruct the actors to move from one terrain to the next. The actors should complete this exercise without conversing with each other. Follow up with a group discussion.

Purpose

To connect mind and body

In this exercise, the actors have to connect their imagination to their body. If they are asked to imagine they are walking on hot coals, then they also have to experience this through their bodies. The intense heat and the potential fear and excitement should all be seen as they walk across those hot coals. In a play, good actors will use their imaginations on a constant basis. If they do not use their imaginations, then the audience will not use theirs. It is their imaginations that the audience will find so illuminating. Children live in a world of make-believe — that is why they are such convincing actors.

Industry Connection

This exercise is about working through different terrains. It is not always easy, yet by adapting, each actor will find a way. An acting career can flourish in much the same way. There will be many changes that happen when they are least expected and least desired. An actor can prepare for some, but not for all. In order for actors to stay one step ahead, they are going to have to be willing and able to adapt to the challenges that come their way. Some people think that famous actors have no challenges. Ask one and find out! In this exercise, the actors are asked to move across different surfaces and adapt to each one. The actors who cannot adapt will find themselves sinking in quick sand ... literally!

16. Sardines

This is a well-known game that has been played and enjoyed for many years. You will need a good amount of space for this exercise. It works best if you have a number of rooms in which it can be played. Explain in the following way:

INSTRUCTOR: Today, we are going to play a well-known game, which I think you will all enjoy. In a few moments, I am going to ask Travis to hide somewhere in this building. He is going to go off by himself. Travis, you are going to have to find a space that has the potential to hide a large number of people. I will give Travis a two-minute start. After two minutes, everyone else is going to go off. Your aim is not to find a hiding place for yourself, but to hide with Travis. In order to do this, you are going to have to find Travis. If you find him, you should hide with him. Eventually, everyone should be hiding with Travis, except for one person. The game ends when there is only one person left who is still searching.

CLAIRE: What happens if no one finds Travis?

INSTRUCTOR: I have actually never experienced that before. However, it is a good question. If, after ten minutes, no one has found Travis, we will declare him the winner. We will then start a new round with someone else going off to hide. Obviously, if you are hiding with Travis, you are going to have to keep quiet.

I suggest your actors should hide in a confined space, such as the building, school, theatre, or studio you are working in. You know your space better than anyone, so it is up to you to decide what works best. Working outside can be challenging, unless you set boundaries. It can also be of concern in terms of safety issues.

Purpose

To engage all the senses

The purpose of this exercise is for the actors to engage their senses. As they move around the building, they may not be able to see the actor who is hiding. They may have to rely on their other senses. They may hear them move or breathe. They may actually smell them. As odd as this sounds, it is a possibility, for instance, if they are wearing cologne or perfume — or forgot to brush their teeth. It is also possible that an actor may sense the presence of others in the room. This may sound strange, but we do it all the time. If you walk into a party, you can often sense the energy as you walk into the room for the first time. You

275 Acting Games: Connected

may walk into a room and sense that two people were just talking about you. Your actors are probably well aware of the importance of their senses in terms of acting. If you have not touched on this, then now may be a good time to do so.

Industry Connection

Nobody wants to be the last person who is left searching on his own. Even if it is just fun, there will be a feeling of failure or defeat. Every aspiring actor wants to become a professional, working actor. Working actors may also discover that they are always working with little free time to call their own. Unfortunately, the statistics show that only a tiny percentage of actors will ever achieve their dream. A number of actors become jaded about their acting career. There is no reason why actors cannot join this tiny percentage if they're willing to continue to work towards it. They may fail a number of times, but if they keep going, they will eventually find a way to live out their dreams. Each actor has to remind himself of why he wants to be an actor in the first place. Eventually, the hook is set somehow. As John Gielgud points out in his book *An Actor and His Time*, "But I do not think we actors should complain. Ours is one of the few creative professions in which artists get a personal reward during their lifetime. If we have a success, we have an audience that applauds and cheers and the critics write nice things about us. We actually have the immediate pleasure of any success we may achieve."[5] If at some point an actor decides he wants a different career, that is by no means to be considered a failure. It is worth pointing out to your students that many people don't even attempt to live out their dreams for fear of failing. The worst thing that can happen to them is that they fall flat on their face. In his book, *Think and Grow Rich*, Napoleon Hill talks about how Thomas Edison handled failure when he says, "Thomas Edison dreamed of a lamp that could be operated by electricity. He began to put his dream into action, and despite more than *ten thousand failures*, he stood by that dream until he made it a physical reality. Dreamers do not quit!"[6] Actors can learn a lot by their failures. Remind them that if they fall down, they can always get back up.

17. Electric Shock!

Ask your actors to stand in a circle holding hands. Pick one actor to stand in the middle of the circle. Tell this student to close his eyes. You should then point to one actor in the circle. Going in a clockwise direction, that actor is going to squeeze the hand of the actor next to him. Once the rhythm has started, ask the student in the center to open his eyes. He now has three guesses as to where the squeeze or *electric shock* is. He must identify the actual person whose hand was squeezed. The people in the circle should squeeze hands around the circle at a rapid pace. They must keep this going without stopping. Even when the person in the middle is guessing, they still should not stop the squeeze operation. The only time they will want to stop is if the person guesses correctly. They should also attempt to squeeze hands in a subtle manner so as to make it more challenging for the person in the middle. These are not strong squeezes. No one should be injured from this exercise. If the person in the middle guesses correctly in three guesses or fewer, he wins. If he cannot identify the right person, the

5. John Gielgud, *An Actor and His Time* (New York: Applause Books, 1997), 176.
6. Napoleon Hill, *Think and Grow Rich* (Hollywood: Melvin Powers Wilshire Book Company, 1966), 39.

group wins. Start another round by changing the person in the middle and repeating the process. (See Time Bomb in *112 Acting Games*)

Purpose

To understand and work with the subtleties of touch

If the actors in the circle squeeze each other's hands without any thought or consideration, the person in the middle will be able to guess in a heartbeat. The actors are going to have to use the subtlest actions to fool the actor in the middle. They have to squeeze so gently, that it is almost untraceable to the human eye. They have to do so while still conveying the message, "I just squeezed your hand. Please pass it on." Actors have to get used to the power that a touch conveys. A handshake can convey a thousand meanings. Perhaps an actor is in a scene where his handshake tells a friend, "I have lied to you." Maybe in another play, a wife hugs her husband in a way that says, "I no longer love you." In another scene, a mother strokes her baby's cheek in adoration. Not only are the characters portraying these feelings to each other, they must also convey the messages to the audience. An actor will want to discover the best and the worst of the human condition.

Industry Connection

As the squeeze is being passed around the circle, it does so at a rapid pace. The actor in the middle has to guess at precisely the right moment to identify the right person. If he is one second off, it will either be too soon or too late. Exact timing is the key to this exercise. An actor who is in a commercial will be expected to have the skill of exact timing. Let us say the commercial is thirty seconds long. The actor is asked to take a bite out of a peanut butter sandwich — the product — on the sixteenth second. Unfortunately, he keeps biting into the sandwich too soon or too late. The director makes him do the same take repeatedly to get the timing right. This may sound redundant or even petty, but is not uncommon. If you think about the potential cost of a commercial, it makes perfect sense. Every second of airtime could be costing the producers a small fortune. They are not going to want to break their budget because the actor cannot work within the correct time frame. It is true that the request is a technical one and has nothing to do with acting, yet it is a necessary skill with regard to commercials. Product placement is a key part of the commercial market. This exercise will help the actors to sharpen their sense of timing.

18. Contradiction Catch

You are going to need a soccer ball for this activity. If you like, you can use a lighter ball or even a tennis ball. Explain in the following way:

INSTRUCTOR: Everyone make a circle. Jim, come and join me in the middle of the circle. Jim is going to be the ball keeper. His job is going to be to throw the ball to various individuals around the circle. He can throw it to anyone and in any order. If the ball comes towards you, Jim will give you one of two instructions. He will say "head" or he will say "catch." The challenge is that you have to do the opposite of what he says. If Jim says "head," then you have to catch the ball. If he says "catch," you have to head the ball. Obviously, Jim, if you throw the ball toward their feet, they are not going to be able to head it. If you perform an incorrect action, you take Jim's place in the middle.

DANIEL: What happens if we find it too easy?

INSTRUCTOR: If it is too easy, I will ask Jim, or whoever is in the middle, to work faster.

RICK: When does the person in the middle call out the action?

INSTRUCTOR: This is an excellent question. Of course it makes no sense to throw the ball and then shout the instruction. It may have arrived before the person receiving the ball knows what to do. The instruction must come simultaneously with the ball being thrown. This gives both the receiver and the thrower only a split second to react.

Purpose
To highlight contradictions in a physical sense

If the actor is asked to catch the ball, he has to head it. This is obviously a pure contradiction in itself. It may seem that it has no purpose in the real world, yet it has a good deal of relevance. A boyfriend may tell his girlfriend, "I love you," and give her a hug and a kiss. The next day he may break up with her. A manager may shake an employee's hand and say, "You are the best worker I have." The next month he might lay her off. We live in a world that is full of contradictions. This is not only true of what we say, but also in what we do. That is why the fact that this activity has a physical aspect to it makes it so relevant. Raise the idea of contradictory behavior with your actors. People who contradict themselves are not always "bad" people. It all depends on the given circumstances, and every situation must be judged on its own merit. When actors play comedy they should look for the tragedy in the situation.

Industry Connection

The fact that this activity is in the form of a contradiction means it fits in nicely as an industry connection. An actor meets an agent and is told, "We really like you. We will definitely be in touch." The actor waits and waits, but never hears from the agent again. An actor goes to an audition where the casting agent is laughing throughout his performance. The actor feels sure that he has got the part, or at the very least a callback. The actor never hears from the casting director again. An actor rents an apartment because the landlord says, "A nice quiet neighborhood." Shortly after moving in the actor finds this not the case at all. The industry and contradictions go hand in hand. The actor who attempts to analyze each contradiction will probably become a nervous wreck. It is better for actors to accept that contradictions are part of their chosen profession and move on. I am not making this observation to be flippant. Some of the contradictions are based on such subjective reasoning that even if the actor had all the facts, they would still be of little use to him. It is better for actors to put their energy where it can do more good than wasting it on futile worrying.

Note

The casting directors may do the initial callbacks, but that does not mean they will make the final decisions. Once a part has been narrowed down to a small number of potentials, the director, producer, and others will most likely sit in. If an actor wants a part, he has to do the work that will give him the best possible shot. He may have to convince a whole array of people that he is made for the part and no one else. Sometimes a director will fight for the actor he wants to get the part. He will put everything on the line with the financial backers. An actor will want to make sure his instrument is prepared for such a leap of faith.

19. The Power of Words

Tell your actors to sit as the audience. Bring one actor into the performance space and explain in the following way:

INSTRUCTOR: Anna, thank you for volunteering for this exercise. In a moment I am going to announce a word representing an emotional state, and I want you to tell me where you feel it in your body.

ANNA: I'm not quite following.

INSTRUCTOR: I am going to mention an emotion, and I want you to say where you feel it in your body. Don't *think* about your reaction, *feel* it. Anger.

ANNA: I feel it in my head.

INSTRUCTOR: Fear.

ANNA: I feel it in the back of my neck.

INSTRUCTOR: Joy.

ANNA: I feel it in the pit of my stomach.

INSTRUCTOR: Very good. Thank you for demonstrating the exercise. We are all familiar with emotional states, because we have all experienced them from time to time. Each word is like a computer program that sends messages to our brain. What I would like you to do now is separate into pairs and work on this exercise. One of you is going to call out a word that is an emotional state and the other will tell you where they feel it in their body. Please remember not to spend too long analyzing and thinking. I want you to react with what you *feel*. Some other possible emotion words are: greed, suspicion, and hate. I want you to go through ten words with your partner and then change over.

Once the students have worked as pairs, bring them all back together to sit in a circle. Invite some of the groups to share their discoveries from the exercise. It may be a good idea to introduce a list of ten words and emotions for the students. Allow them to work with these words or come up with their own, if they prefer. Today's actors are at an advantage over actors from centuries past. "In 1878, the French Academy recognized the concept of 'pessimism.'"[7] The word optimism had only been recognized about one hundred years before. Numerous descriptive words, that can indicate clues with regard to a character's personality, have only come to exist in relatively recent times.

Purpose

To work on preparation

There has always been a heated discussion in the world of acting. Some people say that you can use an emotion to create the moment. Other people say that it is only through "action" that you can find the emotion. We are simply looking for a gut response. The second the actors hear a word or an emotion, they are asked where they feel it in their body. Their reaction is based on stimuli from past experiences. They have felt fear, anger, and joy before, and their body knows how to summon a response simply by hearing the word. This is pretty powerful information for the actor to have. If an actor states the emotion that his character is feeling at that precise moment, it will give him a physiological place

---

7. Rolf Fjelde, *Ibsen*. (New Jersey: A Spectrum Book, 1965), 82.

from which to begin. It is to understand how our body and mind work and how the actor can utilize this connection. It enables the actor to begin to discover the driving force behind the character. An actor is not playing an evil person but an individual. This is still the case even if a character indulges in his darkness. It is worth noting that no one thinks that he is purely evil, and an actor would therefore do well to avoid absolutes.

Industry Connection

This exercise can help actors in their preparation. When actors are on-set, they are going to be expected to produce the goods immediately. They may film a thirty-second scene. If the director is not happy with it, he may say, "Try something else." He is not going to give the actor an hour to go and prepare. Never forget that time is money. The director will want to get to the point of the scene. He is going to want the actor to do it immediately. If he still doesn't like what he sees, he is going to say, "Try something else." Again, the actor is going to have to find a way to work efficiently and effectively. Anything that helps actors to prepare is going to be of value to them. I am a firm believer in an actor developing a fully-functional instrument. From this foundation, actors can work and create at their optimal level. You cannot build a good actor on a bad foundation. In terms of exercises for the instrument, Augusto Boal, author of *Games for Actors and Non-Actors,* says, "I use the word exercise to designate all physical, muscular movement: respiratory, motor, vocal, which helps the doer to better recognition of his or her body."[8]

---

8. Augusto Boal, *Games for Actors and Non-Actors* (London: Routledge, 1992), 60.

Chapter 3
Observation

20. The F Word

Have the actors take a seat and hand out this short paragraph. It must be given to them exactly as it is typed out here. Ask them to put their name at the top of the page. The entire group should do this exercise at the same time.

FEATURE FILMS ARE THE RE
SULT OF YEARS OF SCIENTI
FIC STUDY COMBINED WITH
THE EXPERIENCE OF YEARS.

Ask them to look over the paragraph by themselves and to write at the bottom how many Fs there are. Give them one minute to do this. Have them do this without talking. Have the actors sit in silence while you walk around and collect the papers. Once you have all the papers collected, browse through them and separate them into groups of those who found two Fs, three, four, five, and so on. This should only take you a couple of minutes. Now ask those actors who said there were three Fs to defend their position. Get them to give their reasons. Next, you can ask the same question to those who said four, five, six, and so on. At no point should you bring out the paragraph again. Now see if you can get a group discussion going. Get the actors to defend their point of view. Once this has been exhausted, you can bring out the paragraph again. Show the actors all of the Fs, of which there are six.

Purpose
To look for what doesn't always appear to be there

This exercise highlights the fact that sometimes it is difficult for us to see what is right in front of us. In order to get the right answer, an actor is going to have to use a very specific form of concentration. Even though every actor who takes part in this exercise appears to be concentrating to their full ability, the results beg to differ. Only by breaking this paragraph down will they find the answer they are looking for. If the actors look at this paragraph as one big chunk, then they will most likely find the wrong answer, no matter how hard they concentrate. Let us say an actor is playing a character who's a villain. He knows this because it says so at the beginning of the play. He decides to play him as a villain through and through. What he may be missing is all the in-betweens. Perhaps there is a moment when the character sniffs a flower because he loves roses. Perhaps he is full of certainty and insecurity. Perhaps there is a moment when he stands over his father's grave and pays his respects. Look for all the in-betweens that make up the character, rather than just the overarching picture.

Industry Connection

Suppose that every time an actor goes for an audition he says, "No, thank you." He cannot understand what he is doing wrong and why he is never cast. The answer he is looking for might be staring him right in the face. In order to find it, he really has to be willing to look. He may actually know all the reasons, but not be willing to face them or confront them. Getting the part is a state of mind that embraces everything the working actor does. When your actors first looked for the Fs they may have been absolutely convinced that there were only three. I have seen actors check four or five times and still give this number with absolute conviction. Once it was pointed out that there were six, they couldn't believe that they missed them. Some of them still could not see more than three. This is in part because they are so blinded by their conviction that nothing else computes. Actors have to be careful that this does not happen or continue to happen in terms of their career.

21. The Rhythm Exercise

Have all of your actors sit in a circle. You are going to start this exercise with a demonstration. Start off by clapping a rhythm and having all the actors clap along with you. Change from clapping to snapping your fingers, and again have all the actors join in with you. Now start patting your hand on your knees and have all the actors join in with you. Send one of your actors out of the room. Point to one of the actors in the circle, but don't mention his name. To make sure everyone knows who he is, have him raise his hand for a moment. This actor is now going to become the leader. He will start a rhythm such as clapping his hands and everyone else will follow. Every so often, he should change the rhythm to something else, and everyone else will again follow. Have him start the rhythm while the actor is outside of the room. The actor who is outside the room will come in to the center of the circle. His job is to try to work out who is changing the rhythm. He is allowed up to three guesses in order to do so. The group should try not to look directly at the actor who is changing the rhythm, to make it more difficult for the guesser. Provided they can see the leader, they should be able to do this. Once the leader is discovered, or the three guesses are up, you can switch the leader. If the actor in the middle guesses the leader very quickly, ask him, "What gave it away? What made it so easy for you to guess who was changing the rhythm?" For instance, perhaps the leader is changing the rhythm too fast and the other actors cannot keep up. Perhaps some actors are not focused. Perhaps some actors are staring directly at the person who is changing the rhythm and giving it away. See how the group can problem solve to make it more challenging the next round.

Purpose

To work with the power of observation

The actor in the center really has to use his power of observation for this exercise. Observation is a powerful tool that the actor will want to develop at all times. Let's say you are out walking your dog and you see a couple arguing across the street. They are shouting at each other at the top of their lungs. All of a sudden, they stop shouting and start hugging and kissing each other. Things you see in everyday life will sometimes seem unbelievable to you. The fact that you see them with your own eyes reminds you they are real. As Uta Hagen says in her book *Respect for Acting*, "Our sense of reality is limited. We look at our daily lives for convenient, recognizable behaviorisms to transfer to the stage. Yet, every day some incident occurs that causes us to say: 'Wow! If you saw that on stage you wouldn't believe it.'"[9] Most people will ignore much of what is going on around them. It is the actors' jobs to observe and process that information for later use. Ask your actors to think of a character they have played and how they might react in a given situation.

Industry Connection

If the person in the middle continues to guess the leader too quickly, there is a problem. It means the actors have to discuss and problem solve what is going wrong. They have to see how they can make it more challenging in the next round. If you are on-set, you may often hear a director say, "We have to get this shot before we wrap!" Perhaps there is an issue with lights and so they have to get the shot in the next thirty minutes or they will lose it. So the story goes in the last scene of *Breakfast at Tiffany's,* for some reason they only had one chance to get the shot. If they didn't get the shot in one take, they would lose it. Audrey Hepburn did it in one take. It is perhaps the most famous scene in the entire movie. It is not only the crew that has to know how to problem solve, it is the actors. They are being hired because they are a professional. Ibsen is considered to be one of the greatest playwrights of all time. In describing Ibsen's background, P. Tennant says, "It is a matter of considerable importance to remember that Ibsen's development as a dramatist was intimately connected with his practical association with the stage. His years of apprenticeship were spent first as a salaried dramatist and instructor at the Bergen National Theater (1851-1857) and then as 'artistic director' of the Cristiania Norwegian Theater. You have to have the training and experience of a professional."[10] A degree in acting does not guarantee an acting career. It is experience and training that count for a lot. The actor must be willing to begin at the beginning. In regards to the importance of training, Dorothy Barret, the director of the American National Theatre of Performing Arts, told me, "An audience wants to see what you are thinking. In real life you don't always see what people are thinking as they hide behind a mask. Through the actor's mask the audience is able to let go of theirs. Saying the words isn't half as important as thinking the thoughts. I want to see what you are thinking. You have to train in order to develop the ability to react to the situation." Many working actors still go to class to stretch themselves and to extend their range.

Note

An actor may ask, "What type of training should I have?" I will retort, "Good training." There are many coaches teaching different techniques. The best acting coaches are the ones who work best with you. If you are becoming a stronger actor, then you are moving in the right direction. If they are helping your scene become better, but your acting stays the same, this has a very limited benefit to you and your career. A good acting coach will most likely come to you through trial and error. In an acting class, an actor may learn a great deal from watching another actor fail. An actor should be willing to try anything to find the one thing that works. In regards to acting, the legendary Tyrone Guthrie said, "There is no right or wrong way of acting or directing a play anymore than there is a single

---

9. Uta Hagen, *Respect for Acting* (New York: Macmillan Publishing Company, 1973), 24.
10. Rolph Fjelde, 29.

right way of hammering a nail or boiling an egg. But some of the many possible ways are righter than others and some are more wrong."[11] In the nineteenth century, French musician and teacher Francois Delsarte tried to approach acting scientifically. After observing numerous people in everyday life, his system called Science Applied Aesthetics was developed. It was taught all over the world but misinterpreted by unqualified teachers. They often missed the emotional connectivity Delsarte taught in his work. It was, however, the first major attempt to condense the actor's work into a training method.

22. Totally Tangled

To start this exercise, have two of the actors leave the room.

INSTRUCTOR: What I would like you to do is to hold hands in a circle. Everyone should now be holding hands with the person on either side of them. Without letting go, I want you to tangle yourselves up with everyone around you. You can do this by going over and under and through each other. Remember that you must do this without letting go of the hands you are already holding. Please do this carefully and cautiously. (At this point, bring the other two actors back into the room.) Your challenge is to work together to untangle the entire group. The only way the group can help you is by following your instructions. If your instruction is not correct, the group should still follow them. This may mean that the group becomes more tangled. The only people who should be talking are the two actors who are giving the instruction. Make sure that your instruction takes into account the safety aspects of this exercise.

Variation

If you want to make this exercise more challenging, you can impose a time limit on the actors. Another way to vary this exercise is to have two tangled circles. One actor has to untangle one circle, and the other actor works on the other circle. This then becomes like a mini competition.

Also see Arm Tangle in *112 Acting Games*.

Purpose

To communicate clearly

The two actors who are untangling the circle need to work together. They also have to find a way to communicate their instructions clearly to the other actors. If they are not able to do so, then the group is likely to become more, rather than less, tangled. On-stage, it is the actor's responsibility to communicate the story clearly. The actors have chosen to make storytelling their trade. They will want to become the consummate storyteller. Let us say that an actor is mumbling on-stage and the audience cannot hear him clearly. They will probably switch off and tune out of the performance. A Broadway audience is going to be savvy and will not suffer a mediocre performance. Once an actor loses an audience, it can be hard to get them back. In the theatre, there are often a lot of physical gestures, which communicate the story clearly to all parts of the theatre. Each gesture still has to be justified and motivated by a thought, otherwise it is pointless.

---

11. Andrew Brown, *Drama* (New York: Arc Books, 1962), Introduction.

Industry Connection

In order to get results from this exercise, the actors have to take it seriously. In order to get any results from an acting career, they are going to have to take it seriously. There are numerous people in Hollywood who say, "I am an actor." There is nothing wrong in this, except for the fact that they do virtually nothing to back up this fact. To be a working actor takes an incredible amount of drive, hard work, sacrifice, and commitment. Notice I did not say a *good actor*. That requires even more of everything I have just mentioned and a whole array of other elements. None of this is said to burst an actor's bubble. The problem is that many people do not want to *be* an actor, they are only in love with the *idea* of being an actor.

23. The Nose Knows

This is a really fun game, but it needs some preparation. It will require two or three blankets or sheets — this depends on how many students you have. You will need a few pairs of scissors. You will also need enough brown paper bags for one between two people. Tell your actors to find a partner with whom they have not often worked. Make one of them an A and the other one a B. Give the As two minutes to really study their B's noses. They have to look at them from every angle. After two minutes, tell the As to wait outside the room. Do not give them any further instruction at this stage. Now give all the Bs a paper bag. Tell them they need to cut a hole that is just big enough for their entire nose to be visible. Nothing but their entire nose should be seen. Instruct them to lie on the floor with their paper bag secure. They need to get under the blankets or sheets so that their entire body is covered, including their feet. Everyone should be under the blankets or sheets, which should go all the way up to the bottom of their paper bag. Nothing should be visible except their noses. Tell them that in a moment their partners will be coming back into the room to identify them. Explain that if any player talks or gives any kind of clue, their team will be disqualified. Go back outside and tell the As that they are going to receive three minutes to identify their partners. Explain to them that the only things that will be visible are their noses. They are not allowed to talk or touch the Bs in any way. When they think they know who their partner is, they should go and stand behind that nose. It is possible that three players will stand behind one nose, because they all believe that that person is their partner. When the three minutes are up, everyone should be standing by a nose. At this point, Bs can remove their masks so the group can see who got it right. Repeat the same process by switching players. Ask the Bs to give their paper bag to their partners. When it is their turn, As can simply turn the bag around to the other side and cut out their nose. The previously cut side will then be on the floor. This is a good way to waste less paper and conserve the environment. When the entire exercise is finished, follow up with a group discussion.

Purpose

To discover and create specific detail

The purpose is to encourage the actors to search for the finest detail. The only thing they have to go on is their partner's nose. They have to look at all the contours of their partner's nose. Perhaps their partner's nose has a small scratch or a freckle on the left hand side. They have to use any clue that will help their partner's nose to be memorable. Actors who know their character's birthday have come up with detail. Actors who know the day of the week their character was born have come up with specific detail. Actors who know their character is divorced has to come up with detail. Actors who know why their character is divorced and how it came about has come up with specific detail. Remind your actors that this information is not always given in the script. It may be up to them to create more specific detail around what they are actually given. They may need to use creative license to do what they need to do. Good acting is in the details. Some actors are so unbelievably believable. They enable their audiences to cry, think, and laugh. The actor will want to be willing to do anything to enhance his performance.

Industry Connection

In the lineup, the actors are covered with masks. It becomes difficult to know who they are. Once the masks are taken off, it easy to recognize the actor. Actors who move to major acting hubs sometimes forget who they are. They spend all their time trying to be what they think someone else wants them to be. In the end, they become a kind of surreal caricature of themselves. They cannot be completely blamed for behaving this way. They are told, "Be this," "Do that," "Wear this," "Wear that," "Talk like this," and so on. Many actors are expected to change, but that does not mean they need to pretend to be someone else. I am referring to their day-to-day life here. They are expected to become the best version of themselves. This is actually difficult. They are going to have to have the best posture they can possibly have. They will want to develop the best voice they can possibly have. They will want to have the most heightened senses they could possibly have and so on. Actors who are always looking to become the best versions of themselves have the potential to create any role. We are not looking for actors who hide themselves behind a mask. We are looking for sincere, heartfelt individuals who have the ability to move their audiences. After all, it is the audience who is the co-author of every performance. If you buy a Mini, you are not going to turn it into a Jaguar. You want it to be in the best possible condition that a Mini can be in. Actors will want to look at themselves in much the same way. A Mini is never going to be a Jaguar and there is absolutely no reason why it needs to be.

Note

I have seen a multi-million-dollar movie where a gun, which under normal circumstances can fire six bullets, is miraculously able to fire eleven. It is this lack of attention to detail that takes a potentially good movie and turns it into something mediocre at best.

24. Run Away Model

You will need two pencils and two pieces of paper for this exercise. Explain in the following way:

INSTRUCTOR: I am going to divide you into two teams. (The STUDENTS split into two teams.) I am going to give each team a piece of paper and a pencil. In a moment, I am going to ask you to come up with an order for your team. You are going to want to think about your order with special consideration. What each team is going to do is try to guess the other team's shoe sizes. You heard me correctly, I said shoe sizes. Simone, would you come and join me for a moment? Simone, I would like you to walk around the performance space for me, as if you were a fashion model. I am going to ask you to pause when you reach the front area to do a foot pose. (SIMONE does this and everyone has a little chuckle. It is OK for the students to laugh *with* each other, as opposed to *at* each other.) What the opposing team is going to do is write down the name of the person and their shoe size. You are going to attempt to guess each other's shoe sizes. Choose one person from your team to be the recorder. You will have to come to a group consensus when you are deciding on each shoe size. Everyone will take a turn at having their shoe size assessed by the opposing team.

DAVE: Does the team that gets the most shoe sizes correct win?

INSTRUCTOR: It is not a foregone conclusion. If a team guesses the shoe size exactly, they will get three points. If they are one shoe size off on either side, they will receive one point. The team with the most points wins. Your aim is also to confuse the other team by mixing up the order in which you send up team members. Each team has yet another card to play. Both teams are allowed to play one joker card. This means that as people share their shoe sizes and points are tallied, one person from each team has to exaggerate by three shoes sizes. I will need to receive the names of these two team representatives before we begin. If the other team can name the person who is lying, they will receive five points. If they get it wrong, the other team will receive five points.

CORY: What do you mean by mix up the order?

INSTRUCTOR: That is a good question, Cory. I mean you will want to mix up the order in terms of shoe sizes. If you send up everyone with similar shoe sizes, the other team may begin to fall into a rhythm. You want to make it as challenging for them as possible by varying who you send up and when. Remember to have fun when modeling on the catwalk, and show us some flare. Make sure you pause at the end to do your foot pose.

Don't let the students get away with just generally walking around the room. Have them really strut their stuff like a catwalk model.

Purpose

To look at the complete picture

The purpose of this exercise is for the actors to complete all aspects of the exercise. The only way they will be able to achieve this is to work as a team. The main objective is to guess the shoe sizes of the other group. This may be the only thing an actor chooses to focus on. They are also asked to walk on the catwalk like a model. This is the part that some actors may forget to focus on. Sometimes actors are excellent at the technical aspects of acting. They have a great voice, they know their lines, they know their blocking, and they know their entrances and exits. In their eyes, they have gone for the goal and accomplished their task. An audience may cheer them and call their performance entertaining, but nothing more. The actors have ignored the many textures, layers, and facets that make up their character. They have chosen not to put in the work that will enable them to discover who their character really is. It is the subtle nuances, the idiosyncrasies, the habit-forming behavior that allow us to see who the character really is. An actor will want to be aware of the potential flaws of human nature. Anyone can potentially entertain an audience. Few actors will ever move their audiences.

Industry Connection

When the teams first look at an actor's shoe, they may make an immediate assumption about the shoe's size. However, they may be wrong. They have to remember to take into account the type of shoe. A jazz or ballet shoe is going to look different from a running or basketball shoe. The style of the shoe may also make the shoe appear bigger or smaller. The clothes the actors are wearing may also draw more or less attention to their feet and influence the apparent size. The team that makes immediate assumptions will probably find itself running into trouble. There are many auditions, acting workshops, managers, agents, casting directors, directors, and producers who make certain verbal statements. Sometimes these statements sound too good to be true. If they sound too good to be true, they probably are. A few unscrupulous agents will tell actors that for a small fee they will make them a star. Sometimes they tell a parent they will do this for their child. Remind your actors that when the agent asks them for money, they should run a mile. Some of these agents never ask the actors to perform anything or show a demo reel. Why would a person invest in a product they know nothing about? If it sounds like a scam, it probably is.

Of course, your actors will want to be aware that there are many good agents out there. They just have to put in the time, effort, patience, and persistence to find them. It sometimes takes knocking on doors asking to audition and campaigning for the part. In the old days an actor may have to trudge up and down Sunset Boulevard touting agents and looking for work. Today an actor might email his headshot and resumé but he still has to be willing to do the work. Some actors just love to make the deal. Some aspiring actors take workshops with casting directors to be discovered. Most casting director workshops are not cheap. There may be a good reason to take a workshop with a specific casting director, but being discovered is not one of them. Some acting coaches will tell actors that they must stay with them for a number of years or they will learn nothing. They tell them that they must never study with anyone else because it will harm their work. There may be a degree of truth in what they are saying, or there may not. The bigger question is: What is the prime motivator for what they are saying? Is it a firm belief in guiding the actor in his work? Is it the continued income that each actor is providing? Of course an acting coach has to be paid. Again, the key question is: What is the prime motivating factor for why they say these things? The actors have to step back before making their decision. Actors have to learn to constantly step back and look at the bigger picture in terms of their acting careers.

Note

A number of actors suffer at school in terms of their achievements. They find that they are not able to get into the academic swing of things. When they find something that they are good at and love, they grab onto it with both hands.

25. Switcheroo

You are going to need a table, two sets of twenty different items, and two sheets. You will want to set this up ahead of time. Put the first twenty items on the left hand side of the table. There can be some common things as well as some more obscure items. Some examples are a roll of tape, a toothbrush, a tennis ball, a postcard, a postage stamp, and so on. Organize the items in any way you want and cover them with a sheet. The items on the right hand side are the same twenty items, but you are going to organize them in a different way. Once this is done, cover up these items as well. When your students arrive, tell them to sit as the audience. Show them the left hand objects, and ask them to make a mental note of the position of the items. Give them one minute to do so. Cover the left hand side again. Now take the sheet off the right hand side and see if the students can work out which items are incorrectly placed. You can let the actors come up and move the items. Only when there is consensus, or majority agreement from the audience, can an item be moved. When the audience believes that the right hand side is identical to the left, you are going to take the sheet off the left hand side. The students will now be able to see if they have made the two sides identical. I like working with two sets of items because the students receive visual confirmation of what they got right and what they missed. It seems to stimulate a more powerful response than having them just take your word for it. To play another round, simply have all your students turn around to face the back wall. At this point, select a student to shuffle all the items on the left and then on the right. You are now ready to play another round with your students.

Variation

Set up twenty items and show them to your students. The students need to close their eyes. At this point, you will want to take away five of the items. Tell the students to open their eyes and see if they can work out which five items you took away. You can also do this exercise by adding five new items instead of taking some away.

Purpose

To create compelling arguments

Let us say an actor wants to move the ketchup bottle to the left hand corner of the table. He is absolutely convinced that that is where it is supposed to go. If he cannot get others to go along with him, he is not going to be able to move the bottle. In other words, he is going to have to state his case and give a convincing argument. When actors are playing a character, they have to do the same thing. They have to clearly state the case of their character to the audience. They have to know their character intimately between the lines of dialogue. They will want to invite their audience to participate. Their character might be saying, "I stole the loaf of bread, but it was only so that I could feed my family. I am a good man." It is the actors who are going to have to convince us of this. If they are not able to, we will leave feeling that the character deserves the misery and suffering that enters their life. Remind your actors that they have to create compelling arguments on behalf of the character they are playing.

Industry Connection

The actors have to use a specific form of memorization. They are not being asked to memorize the twenty items, since there are the same twenty items on each side. They are being asked to remember the positioning of the items. They are being asked to use a specific form of visual memorization. This may sound petty, but it is far from being so. An actor in Hollywood, New York, Paris, or London is going to be meeting numerous people. They may be a person who is very good at remembering faces. This means they are very good at visual memorization. They may be poor at remembering names. This means they need to work on their auditory memorization skills. If an actor meets a casting director for the third time and calls him by the wrong name, there is going to be a big mark against the actor. You may not believe this, but people like it when you remember their name and are unimpressed when you do not. Some actors have changed their names in the hope that it will open up doors for them. If an actor was out shopping and he bumped into a producer he has met before and just said "hi," the producer may not remember the actor. If the actor meets the producer in a professional setting three months later, the producer's memory may be nudged. The actor has now scored points. Memorization is important and must be approached from all angles.

Note

Memorization is a basic tool for actors. It is also a muscle to which they have to keep retuning and strengthening. If not continually exercised, the memorization muscle will become weak and unreliable. This is unacceptable for the professional actor.

26. Action Mirror

This exercise is very similar to the exercise Mirroring in *112 Acting Games*. Ask everyone in the class to find a partner, and designate one partner as A and the other as B. Once all the students have paired up, tell the pairs to spread to different parts of the room so that they have some space. Explain the exercise as follows:

INSTRUCTOR: In a moment, A will start to move very slowly, and B, you will try to mirror their movements. During this time, I will intermittently call out actions. A is going to have to create the action that I call out. For instance, I may call out, "brushing your teeth." At this point, As will create the action for brushing your teeth and Bs will mirror the action. It is imperative that your movements are slow and flowing so that your partner can really follow them. The idea is not to trick your partner, but to help them. There is no talking during this exercise. I am only calling out actions intermittently. The rest of the time, As, you will have to keep the movement going with Bs mirroring.

Some other possible actions:
Drinking a cup of coffee
Buttoning up your coat
Brushing your hair
Peeling an orange
Putting on lipstick

Once As have led for a while, allow Bs to become the leaders. Do not allow the term "leader" to confuse you. The students are aiming to move at exactly the same time, but the leader inspires the movement. Follow up with a group discussion.

Purpose
To learn to cooperate with others
What an excellent exercise for cooperation and teamwork. Students have to work with their partners for this exercise to be a success. Cooperation is of vital importance to actors. If two actors are in a scene and one believes he is the star and tries to outshine the other actor, there is nothing authentic to watch. Actors must work together — act and react. You cannot react if you are too into yourself, with the result that you have no idea what the other person just said. Working together in the mirroring exercise will get your actors on the right track. Focus and concentration go without saying. Each actor will want to be able to focus, see, and assimilate. Also, the actors are again becoming more aware of their bodies and how they work as they strive to enhance their motor skills — their hand-eye coordination. Some actors have a real sensibility in their work.

Industry Connection
In this activity, there is a leader and a follower. The trick is that it must appear as if the actors are moving as one. In other words, the actors are creating a form of illusion. In its own way, film is also an illusion. When we watch a movie, it appears that a continuous flow of action and thought is taking place. This is an illusion. The director and editor take numerous shots that are piecemeal and shot out of sequence. They slice and dice them together so that is appears to be continuous — and that is the challenge. The actor must still know how to create a line of thought throughout each and every scene shot.

Chapter 4
Memorization

27. Name Evolution

This exercise is best suited to the first session the students have together.

Step 1: Have the actors form a circle. Go around the circle and have everyone say their name. Do not comment on it or tell the other actors they have to memorize the names. The actors' responses have to work subconsciously and become second nature.

Step 2: Have the actors stand in a circle. Go around the circle and have each person say his or her own name twice. As they do so, have them use a distinctive and unusual voice and put an action with it.

Step 3: Go around the circle again and have each person repeat their name and action twice, only this time, the other actors should join in. They can join in on the first or second beat and repeat the name and action of the other actor.

Step 4: Have one of the actors say the name and action of any other actor, with the same unusual voice and the action that goes with it. The person whose name and action they mention will then repeat this process for a different actor.

Step 5: See if any other actors can go around the entire group and repeat the other actors' names and actions.

Purpose
Memorization

In this exercise we have utilized the necessary ability of memorization. We have done so through visualization and utilizing the body — a kinesthetic response. The actors engaged their sense of sight, sound, and touch. Not only did they engage these senses, but they also heightened them. Think about how you memorize your lines for a play or a scene. Perhaps there is a more effective and creative way of doing it. Actors can sit down in a chair and memorize their lines by going down them with a piece of paper, but this might prove totally ineffective. Think about how fully engaging your senses may increase your efficiency in terms of memorization.

Industry Connection

Raise the following point with your actors:

INSTRUCTOR: You are at an audition and the director gives you some direction for the scene. You are nervous and you forget some of what is being said to you. You need your memorization skills to become second nature to your instrument and to be automatically built into your hardware. He calls you back the following week to audition for the network. He says, "I loved what you did last week. We would like to see you do exactly the same thing today." What if you cannot remember what you did last week? Even though you have the sides in your hand, if you cannot produce the goods and you might miss out on an opportunity. At some point the actor has to achieve a professional coming of age. They have to be able to take their work beyond formula.

This exercise gives the actor the opportunity to start the memorization process. It gives the actors the opportunity to exercise a different set of muscles.

If they pick up on this they will be ahead of the game and if they don't, they won't. In an audition there may be no second chances.

Note

You may wonder why industry links are necessary for beginning actors as well as professional. If actors understand why they are doing an exercise, they are more prone to do it. If they see how it links to their professional career, then ten or twenty years from now they may still be doing it. It is discipline and dedication that defines the actor. The aim is not just to see working actors but good actors with longevity in their careers — to see actors who can create a portrait in their craft. It is the actor's responsibility to make sure the arts live. In this regard I want to make a reference to the *Harry Potter* movie series. People who have seen these movies all over the world may not recognize many of the actors. This is not the case for English audiences. Many of these actors have been on British television for ten, twenty, or even thirty plus years. There is a point in each working actor's life when he realizes he has to take personal responsibility for his acting career.

I want to mention one more thing about memorization techniques here. There is a whole plethora of ways to memorize lines. It is the actors' responsibility to find an approach that works best for them. Another example is to record their cue lines into a recorder. They are the lines that are said to the actor by another character in the scene. Record their lines and then leave a gap in between each one. Actors will want there to be enough of a gap to allow them to say their line silently to themselves and then out loud. Your actors may find this technique useful or they may not. You are simply expanding their horizons by offering another example of a memorization approach.

28. Sound Bites

Have seven of your actors stand up and spread out around the room. Each actor will need a piece of paper and a pencil. The rest of the actors should find a place to sit as the audience. Tell the seven actors to each come up with their own sound. Some examples: a cow, a train whistle, a car engine, an owl, a creaking door, an airplane. Give them one minute in which to do this. It is important that the actors make sure their sound is recognizable. At no point should the actors discuss their sounds with each other or with the audience. For the next minute have the seven actors move around the room making their sound. The seven actors have two objectives in this exercise: to make their sound as convincingly as possible and when the minute is up, the seven actors have to write down all the sounds made by the other six actors. Give them one minute in which to do this.

The actor who remembers the most sounds wins. There is another challenge to this exercise. If anyone in the audience can truly explain why one of the seven actors was not convincing in his own sound, he can be disqualified. In order to do this, at least half the audience has to agree. An example would be, "Fred spent his whole time listening to the other actors without making his own sound." If the audience member can prove this and get enough support, Fred will be disqualified.

Variation

You can vary this exercise in a couple of ways. You can have the actors choose their own sound or you can whisper a sound to them. You might even choose to give two actors the same sound. You can also vary the number of actors who participate. You may choose ten or even fifteen to make it more challenging.

Purpose

To entwine concentration and memorization

This exercise demands that the actors enhance their ability to multitask. They have to make their own sound while making a mental note of everyone else's. This takes a good deal of focus, concentration, and memorization on their part. In any role an actor plays, they are going to have to utilize their skill to multitask. In a play, they have to know their lines, their cues, their blocking, and their motivations. They also have to be aware of the technical aspects of their performance. These will include areas such as nonverbal communication and vocal projection. The challenge is they may need to be doing virtually all these things, and maybe more, at the same time. When an audience watches a novice actor work, they sometimes laugh at his clumsy behavior and non-believable acting. This is in part because the actor is trying to do everything at a conscious level. As an actor develops, he is able to use technique for most of the tasks so that he can acutely focus on the rest. He develops tools to take away the self-imposed barriers that get in the way of his performance. As Robert Westrom explains in regards to vocal technique, "If some of your words come out slurred, or muffled, or your voice tone is monotonous, then it means you are trying to speak all the sounds through a one-size mouth opening. Practicing with the vowels will help end this."[12] Great actors don't have to think about their voice. They have a voice! When they act it appears so effortless that everybody says, "I can do that." If your actors are willing to do the work now, it will pay them back tenfold later on. If a student sees a great performance in a play or in a movie, it can feel like being in acting class in that he can learn so much.

Industry Connection

In this exercise, the actors have to follow the directions given. If they focus on listening to the other actors' sounds while ignoring their own, they will be disqualified. In an audition situation actors may be very nervous when they enter the room. They may have sat in the waiting room and gone over their lines a thousand times. When they walk into the room, all they can think about are their lines. As they enter the room, the molecular activity has changed. The director gives them some specific directions of how he wants them to play the part. Because they are so focused on remembering their lines, they don't hear what the director said. They do their audition and think they have done a great job. As the actor leaves the room the director turns to the cameraman and says, "Can't follow direction." Actors have to be fully aware of everything that is going on around them. Selective hearing should only be used for a specific purpose. A good actor works very hard to create a fully-functional instrument.

---

12. Robert Westrom, *Speech for the Actor* (Los Angeles: The Westrom Company, 1978), 62.

Note

When an audience member aims to disqualify another actor, you have to make sure his argument is justified. There is no official rulebook on how to do this. You are going to have to use judgment and finesse. The fact that other actors have to agree with him should help qualify his arguments. In regards to sound, it is important to note the transition from the silent movie era to the talking picture. Buster Keaton, Harold Lloyd, and Charlie Chaplin saw their heydays in the silent movies. This ended in the early 1930s. This meant that the actors who took over had the field to themselves. In the silent movies, actors avoided talking unless it was absolutely necessary. In the early days of talking pictures, the actors seemed to talk nonstop even when the material did not justify any dialogue. This meant that technology and the talking picture greatly affected the actors' world.

29. Matter of Fact

To start this exercise, tell your students to find a partner. Have them work with someone they do not know very well. Each member of the pair should share two facts about themselves with their partner. They will also want to share one lie with their partner. Their partner should be told which facts are true and which is the lie. Give each pair five to ten minutes. Once both the partners have done this, the whole group will come back together. Send up one pair at a time to introduce each other and present the three facts. They have to sound equally convincing when explaining each statement. It is the audience's job to guess which one of the three facts is false. Invite them to say which fact they believe is false and why. You can also do this by having them vote on it. Let each pair repeat the process. It is important to inform the students that the facts about them should be rather obscure. For instance, if a student said, "Delilah's birthday is March 18," all her friends in the group would already know if this is true or false. If the true fact was that Delilah found a hundred dollar bill on the beach when she was seven, this would be more challenging for the audience to work out.

Purpose

To focus on memorization

While there are many benefits to this exercise, one that might be overlooked by the actors is that of memorization. Players share with the audience two facts and one lie about their partner. If they are not focused in their memorization, it will be easy to forget what they had been told. Not only do they have to tell the audience, but they have to do so in a clear and convincing manner. They will not be able to do this unless they have memorized their partner's answers clearly and concisely. The aim is not just to tell the audience the facts, but rather to actually convince them. An actor on-stage who is fumbling through his lines will not be in a position to give a convincing performance. The actor's job is always going to be one of multitasking. When actors reach a point at which they can turn some of the technical aspects over to the subconscious, then there will be potential for their work to grow.

Industry Connection

It is not what is being said that will give the audience the answers, but what is left unsaid. It is the nonverbal clues being sent that contain the answers. If an actor shakes his foot, or looks up at the ceiling, or sways from side to side, these can all suggest nerves. This may help the audience to work out when the actor is lying. When actors move to LA, London, or New York, they will come across many aspiring actors. They will be given plenty of advice, whether they ask for it or not. Some of the advice will be good and some will be really bad and some simply misinformation. When actors hear this advice, it is important for them to read the nonverbal clues that come with it. The saying "talk is cheap" is not always true for actors. If they take the wrong kind of advice, they can be involved in a costly error. These exercises enable you to connect the work to the bigger picture of the acting world. It does not matter if your actors are in junior high, high school, college, or are working actors. What you are doing with these exercises is planting a seed.

30. Belly Laugh

Before starting this exercise, have everyone take off their shoes and put them somewhere out of the way. Also, if anyone is wearing necklaces, rings, or bracelets, have them remove these items too. Explain in the following way:

INSTRUCTOR: In a moment I am going to ask Marissa to lie on the floor. If you want to use something as a cushion to support your neck, that is fine. The cushion part only applies to the first person. Neil, you are then going to lie down on the floor at a right angle to Marissa, and carefully and slowly rest your head on Marissa's stomach. (Make sure this is below the sternum and breast area.) Sandy, you are then going to come and lie down, putting your head on Neil's belly. You are going to lie down at a right angle to him. We are going to repeat this until every member of the group is lying down with their head on another student's belly. The only person who does not have their head on another person's belly is the first person. In our case, this is Marissa. When everyone is lying down, there is going to be a lattice shape. (A hand goes up with a question.) Daniel, I know your hand is up, but I am going to hold off answering questions until I have explained further. (Sometimes it is important to go through the entire exercise before answering questions. Quite often, the students will find that their original question has then been answered.) I am now going to come around the room to number you. We have twenty-two people here today so I am going to number you from one to twenty-two. I am going to start with Marissa, who is going to be number one. Neil is going to be number two, and so on. When I say begin, Marissa is going to make one *ha* sound. This is a sound to replicate laughter. Once she has done this, Neil will make two *ha* sounds, "ha, ha." In other words, you will make the number of *ha* sounds corresponding to your number. Remember that it is only your turn when the person before you has completed their turn. Person sixteen cannot go until person fifteen has finished. There should only be one person at a time making any sounds. That brings me to my next point. There should be no talking or noises of any sort, except from the person whose turn it is. If anyone else starts to laugh, the whole thing has to start again from the first person. The aim for the group is to get as high as it can without anyone laughing. You also have to make sure you *ha* the right number

44

of times. You need to *ha* clearly and audibly. If you are number eight and you only *ha* seven times, the whole group starts again. Sounds easy, but believe me, it is quite a challenge. Daniel, I know your hand was up for a question earlier. Thank you for your patience. Do you still have a question?

DANIEL: You already answered it. Thanks.

NICKY: Can we not just continue from where we left off? People at the higher numbers might not get to participate.

INSTRUCTOR: Nicky makes a good point. Unfortunately, you have to start again each time, because that is part of the exercise. You raised another important point. Let me ask you, Nicky, in what way are you already participating?

NICKY: Oh, I see what you are getting at. By being quiet and not laughing, we are already involved in a big way.

INSTRUCTOR: Excellent response, Nicky! Potentially, anyone can be the cause for making the whole group start again. This means you are all going to have to work together on this exercise.

Purpose

To work with a multifaceted approach

The purpose behind this exercise is for the actors to work in a multifaceted scenario. At first, they may think that all they have to do is say "ha" when it is their turn. They then start to realize they cannot talk or laugh. They then find that they have to know when it is their turn. This means they have to really focus. Of course, they will also be able to feel the vibrations of the next person on their stomach. They also have to make sure they *ha* the right number of times. This means they have to remember their own number and use their memorization skills. It sounds simple, but you will be surprised how many actors *ha* the wrong number of times. What starts off as a simple, fun exercise becomes something a lot more challenging with many layers. When the actor plays a role he may feel his character is one-dimensional. Perhaps the breakdown says, "Ron is a thug." This is one aspect of the character. Even if being a thug is a big part of Ron's life, it is not the whole picture. There are many facets to Ron that the actor has to discover. You cannot judge a character on one dimension. Developing a character is like peeling an onion. As the actor does so, he will discover many layers beneath. Actors will want to wear the cloak of their characters while knowing when and how to take it off.

Industry Connection

If an actor talks or laughs or makes any kind of error, the whole cycle starts from the beginning again. This may feel unfair or frustrating, and yet this is the exercise. Actors pursuing their Hollywood or New York dreams may feel at times that things are unfair. They get an agent, only to realize their agent gets them no auditions. They are cast in a pilot show, only to find the pilot does not get picked up by a network. Very few pilots ever make it to become a series. For every step the actors take forward they may feel they are taking two steps back. The important lesson is that something is learned every step of the way. Actors may forget how many times they are supposed to make the *ha* sound. Their lack of focus and memorization will cost the whole group. If they learn from this, they can correct the situation. If they do not learn, they are doomed to repeat the same errors. The aspiring Hollywood actors, who learn and grow from their challenges, have the potential to achieve everything. The actors who do not learn will eventually be packing their bags.

Note

You often hear me talk about having the students remove items such as rings, bracelets, etc. Many of these exercises contain a lot of movement where arms and legs are waving around. We want to take out as much potential risk of injury as we can. Instructing the students to remove these objects is just common sense. Creating a safe environment for your students is as important as the work itself.

31. Instant Replay

This exercise is very popular in improvisation and sketch comedy circles. Its premise also inspired a well-known movie. Have your actors sit in the audience space. Pick three actors to come into the performance area. Two of the actors are going to act out a scene. Have the details decided beforehand by the audience. Allow the scene to run for one to two minutes. The third actor has a remote control — imaginary or real. They can make a number of choices. They can point their remote control and say, "Rewind thirty seconds." At that precise moment, the actors have to back up in the scene thirty seconds. Not only do they have to back up, but we have to see them go through all the reverse steps at an ultra-fast speed. The actor with the remote control may also call out things such as, "Fast-forward ten seconds," or "Freeze." Anything that a remote control can do, the actor with the remote can tell the actors to do. If you like, they can also take suggestions from the audience. The only rule is that if they want the actors to do something, they have to use or point the remote control at them. Change over and work with other actors.

Purpose

To enhance the actors' memorization

The actors may be asked to rewind a scene and replay it. The actors will obviously already need to have good memorization skills. If they are asked to fast-forward a scene by a minute, they will also need good memorization skills. It may take the actors a moment or two to realize this. In order for them to create what is to come, they are going to have to remember what came before. If they are being asked to create what happens a minute later, they are going to have to fill in the missing minute in their imaginations. Sometimes in a movie the scenes skip around. They can skip around in terms of time structure. One scene can be set in 1925 and the next scene may be set in 1940. The same character is now fifteen years older. It may be just the next day in terms of filming for the actor, but for the audience, it is fifteen years later. There are fifteen years of events and memories that the actor is going to have to recreate for the audience in order to convince them that fifteen years have in fact passed. If actors disconnect from their character's memories, there is no possibility for this to happen.

Industry Connection

The actors have to be able to work precisely, with specific detail. Let us say they are asked to rewind a scene thirty seconds and replay it. They are going to have to remember what they did and do it again in exactly the same way. This may sound simple enough, but it is not an easy thing to do. For continuity reasons, an actor on a film set has to be able to recreate certain scenes with a good deal of accuracy. This is especially true if the director is working with a number of different takes. If an actor is not able to recreate a scene with a degree of accuracy, it is going to be a nightmare in the editing room. If an actor is drinking a cup of coffee in one take, it will be illogical if he forgets to drink the coffee in the following take. Some directors shoot an enormous amount of film because they know that it takes some actors a while to get going. Great moments don't necessarily happen in an instant. The challenge here is that it can cost a great deal of money. A good actor has to know how to work comfortably with all the specific details. In a play it is important to note that it is all one take.

32. Traffic Light

Have your actors spread out around the room and explain in the following way:

INSTRUCTOR: In a moment I am going to begin to call out the traffic signals to you. If I say "green," I want you to start walking around the room. If I say "red," I want you to immediately stop walking. If I say "yellow," I want you to sit down on the floor or on a chair. I am going to be giving these orders at a rapid pace. It is a bit like Simon Says in that if you do the wrong thing you are out. So if I say "green" and you stop walking or sit down, you are out.

PAUL: Where do we go when we are out?

INSTRUCTOR: When you are out, I would like you to move to a side of the room. You can also help me by seeing who makes the wrong movement when I call out a signal. The last person left in is the winner.

Once you have played a round, you can let one of your actors take over as the caller. You can change the caller a number of times in one round. You can pick them from the people who are already out. This allows you to still engage those who are out.

Purpose

To be able to maintain focus and concentration

At the beginning of this game the actors may focus very well. As it goes on, some will tire and lose a degree of concentration. It will be at this moment that they make an error and will most likely be out. Many actors on-stage know how to concentrate during a performance. The challenge is that their concentration is not necessarily fluid throughout the entire performance. There may be a moment when they think about what they are going to eat after the show. They think that no one noticed, but some members in the audience will notice the break in concentration. They read the fact that the actor was mentally removed from the scene, even if only for a moment. When this happens the magic is broken, and the audience is brought down to reality. By this, I mean the audience may stop believing in the characters as they are abruptly reminded by the technical performance of the actor. To focus and concentrate throughout an entire performance is a challenge that all actors need to overcome. Actors do not always know where their performance is going to come from. It is focus that allows the actors to present themselves in the scene.

Industry Connection

There is one winner and then there are a lot of people who are out. Some coaches do not like activities that have winners and losers. I agree that there is no place for competition in acting. However, as far as the industry connection goes, it can be quite beneficial. If there is only one part available, only one actor is going to get it. Everyone else who tries out for that part is not going to get it, no matter how good they are. In crude terms, there is one winner and a lot of losers. I am not saying this mockingly. When an actor does not get the part, he will sometimes feel as if he has lost. An actor has to learn to embrace not getting a part, learn to shrug it off, and move on. An actor who can do this will be just fine. Actors who lament and anguish over every part they did not get is going to end up tying themselves in knots. This will lead to a career that is not productive and does not serve their long-term goals.

Note

It can feel pretty abrupt for an actor to be told, "You're out!" It is good to look for ways to keep your actors engaged, even if they are out in one part of the game, look for other ways to include them in a different way. They can be asked to become observers and see who else is out during each round.

33. Sandwich to Go

This is a basic memorization exercise that is a lot of fun. Instruct your students to sit in a circle on the floor. Choose one person to start the game. He will start by saying, "I would like a to-go sandwich with lettuce." The next person is going to repeat what was just said, but add one more ingredient to the sandwich. An example would be, "I would like a to-go sandwich with lettuce and tomatoes." The aim is to see how high the students can build the sandwich without making a mistake. If a student forgets an ingredient, the next person in the circle has to start a new round. Of course, the ingredients in the next sandwich may be quite different.

Variation

You can vary this exercise by putting limitations on the ingredients. An example would be to say, "I would like you now to make a vegetarian sandwich." Also see exercise This Is Jane in *112 Acting Games*.

Purpose

To work out the memorization muscle

The main thrust of this game is to memorize the previous ingredients before adding your own. As the game continues, the memorization muscle is increasingly called into use. Without memorization technique, an actor will only last a short time. Memorization is not acting, yet it is a vital part of the actor's work. This exercise works on the memorization muscle. There is line learning, and then there is learning lines. An actor may be in a play in which he knows all his lines. The challenge is that he has weak memorization technique. He knows his lines, but he has to put all his energy into remembering them. As a result, the actual meaning behind the lines suffers. Actors have mastered their memorization when they know their lines without having to think about them. When actors can do this, they can react in the moment. They are able to react from a planned lack of self-control. They do not have to rely on a false sense of security to remember their lines. Actors must work their memorization muscles.

Industry Connection

Memorization is a very important part of an actor's lifestyle. This is in part because the actor does not work a nine-to-five job. Actors' lives often come from eclectic backgrounds. They do not have a job in which they follow the same routine every day. They need their memorization skills to remember all the different things they need to get done in a particular day. For instance, perhaps they met a producer in a restaurant last month who gave the actor his card and said, "Stay in touch." The actor has to remember to drop the producer a card every few months letting him know what they are up to in terms of acting. The actor might also want to congratulate the producer on his success in one project or another. Actors will only do this if they remember to keep in touch. The producers are involved in choosing the directors, the locations, the aesthetics of the show, and shaping the story. They are engaged in many aspects of the production and not to be taken lightly. In the early westerns, some of the sponsors were cigarette companies. They didn't want the bad guys smoking in the movies because they thought it would send a negative image about smoking. Those pulling the purse strings can have tremendous influence over a project.

An agent may arrange for an actor to attend seven auditions in one week. It is up to the actor to know when he is going to each audition and what he needs to prepare. If he doesn't remember that he has seven auditions, he will probably miss one of them, or even more. If this happens, he is going to ruffle some feathers. Professional actors cannot afford to appear in an amateur light, or that is where they will stay.

Note

Sometimes a studio might blame an actor for not knowing his lines when arriving on-set. There are times when this is a fair criticism. There are also occasions where this is misleading. If a script is not ready, an actor may receive a different version. It may not be until the night before that he receives the final version of the next day's shooting. This is the only script that is going to matter. If the actor does not know his lines the next day, he is the one left with egg on his face. If he stays up all night, he still may not know all his lines in time. It may not sound fair, but then no one ever said an acting career was based on being fair.

Chapter 5
Bare Essentials

34. Acting

Two actors are chosen or volunteer to go in front of the other actors. They are then told, "I want you to 'act' for the class." If they ask for any further clarification, none is to be given. Allow them to struggle with this exercise in any way that comes up. Perhaps a forced, superficial conversation begins with unjustified actions. Perhaps the actors appear to be reaching for the emotion. Do not say anything, and allow the scene to continue. After five or so minutes, stop the scene and ask them to begin again, only this time, "I want you to strip away any falseness and simply have a conversation with the other actor." It may start off forced and false, but if left alone long enough you should see the beginnings of an everyday conversation. This may take two minutes or ten minutes to get to this point. It is also going to depend on the maturity level and the focus level of the rest of your students. If some members of the class start to giggle or become unfocused, the value of the exercise will be lost. This is where the power of the entire group comes into play. The class is going to have to work as an ensemble for this exercise to be effective. It is going to have to become familiar for them. They are going to have to create an extraordinary chemistry in what they do. The continuation point would be a group discussion on what has been observed. This is not an exercise that is to be repeated, nor is it one which other members of the class should attempt. If it is worked with one pair, and only one, a strong message will have been sent to the whole group, and that is enough.

Purpose
To strip away the unnecessary

This exercise highlights how easy it is for the actor to fall into clichés and tricks. It is based on an exercise that was sometimes used by Strasberg. A seasoned actor may know how to cry on cue, but the audience will most likely feel nothing. If the actor pushes a little less, perhaps the audience will be able to empathize a little more. The audience is the actors' barometer for whether they are telling the truth or not. The actor will want to feed the audience a really electric performance. The audience will want to feel like the actor is having an honest, intimate conversation with them. If an audience watches a good movie on numerous occasions, they will most likely have a different experience each time. In theatre they share the experience together. The theatre is the actor's original medium. It is very good for the actor to come face to face with a live audience. Some actors believe that theatre is like walking on a razor's edge in that there is no take two. Actors will want to celebrate eccentricity and diversity. They will want to embrace a progressive and flexible outlook on life. This exercise highlights that there are no tricks, only doing the work will lead the actors to the results that they and the audience are looking for. It also allows the actors to strip away everything to a bare minimum. An actor has to be willing to reach inside himself to a place that is raw. Technically, this probably should not work, but it allows the actor and the audience to see that very little is needed in his work, outside of honesty and truthfulness. An audience traditionally goes to the theatre to hear the truth. There is nothing worse than an actor selling the integrity of the moment down the river. Getting to this point on a consistent basis is what takes the work.

Industry Connection

Make the following observation with your actors:

INSTRUCTOR: In any Hollywood production there will be hundreds of things happening around you and yet it is up to you to cut through all of this. Most of what is happening around you is of no immediate concern. Everything around you contributes to the overarching result of the project but not necessarily to what you are doing in that precise moment. Stanislavski talked about the actor working within a small area of focus, and this will be of great importance to you here. If we take away the green screen or blue screen, the lights, the grips, the assistant director, the makeup, wardrobe, set, background, and so forth, all we are left with is the lone actor.

Note

If we accept the premise that "we are the sum of all our experiences," then perhaps it is fair to say that who you are as an actor is a sum of all your experiences. You may move out to Hollywood and find a great acting coach. You may say you owe everything to that coach for making you a great actor. What about your acting teachers before that? Are you saying that they taught you nothing? Did you learn nothing from them? Hopefully over the years you have been growing as an actor and making new discoveries. Look at all the experiences in your life that have contributed to this. When an actor says, "I owe it all to so and so," I doubt this is accurate. If we are a sum of all our experiences, then we owe "it all" to "everyone" and "everything" we have ever come across in our life. We are an amalgamation of thoughts and ideas that have influenced us. Today's actors are also indebted to those that have gone before them. Sophocles was a prolific playwright. He was born in 496 BCE and wrote over one hundred plays in his lifetime. Many of his plays are still influential today including *Antigone* and *Oedipus the King*. He was also the first to introduce three actors into a performance rather than only two. When your actors feel ready, encourage them to go do some shows. If you are a schoolteacher or a college professor, you have a great responsibility. Your work with your actors is going to be laying the building blocks for a foundation they will pull from for the rest of their lives.

35. Bare Essentials

Do not use this exercise in the first couple of weeks of class. As you read on you will see why it is better to wait at least five or six sessions. Explain in the following way:

INSTRUCTOR: Joshua, I would like you to come forward and join me in the performance space. What I would like you to do now is lead the rest of the group in a warm-up exercise. (Pick one of the actors to lead a warm-up. This should happen without prior warning and without any coaching. If they ask what type of warm-up they should do, tell them it is their choice.) The only stipulation is that it is a warm-up exercise of some sort.

Ask him to go through the exercise and explain it to the other actors. Once the warm-up is complete, you may choose to have another actor lead the group in a different type of warm-up. So if the first actor worked on tension in the body, ask the second actor to contrast this somehow. An example would be that if the first actor worked with the body, the second actor may want to do a vocal warm-up or perhaps something that is mentally stimulating. Again, there is no need to give them these examples, let them figure it out for themselves. You may find that the actor stands there for five minutes twiddling his thumbs. This is absolutely fine as any pausing or uncertainty becomes part of the exercise. Do not help them; let them struggle through on their own. You will not be doing them any favors by giving them an easy way out. If there is absolutely no way they can come up with an exercise, then at this point you may want to intervene. Still have the same student lead, but perhaps you could get suggestions from the group to help the student.

Purpose

To work specifically

As you teach and explain to the others, you are able to hone in on your own skills. If you are not able to explain an exercise concisely to others, then perhaps you are not doing it in the most efficient way yourself. If you kind of, sort of, know an exercise, then you are only kind of, sort of, getting results. Because each actor is working specifically on his own instrument, he should want to be able to use each exercise to its full potential. If actors are cast in a play, their characters are individuals. They are individuals that have their own individual wants, needs, and desires. They cannot play them as a "teenage girl" or a twenty-something "football player." There is nothing specific about those characters and it would lead them to playing stereotypes and clichés. They have to get detail oriented in their work. They have to learn to fall in love with the details. They must get specific in terms of their character so that their character becomes more real to them. It is also important that your actors are not in too much of a hurry to know everything about their characters. If they think they know everything, there will be nothing left to discover.

Industry Connection

When you pick an actor to lead this exercise, it is not to pick on him or embarrass him. The reason is to see if he is really walking his talk. If the actor is not able to lead the warm-up, then it is a good wake-up call for him. By this stage he will have seen and performed a number of warm-up exercises in class that he can select from. If he is not able to do so, he will know it is because he is slacking off and will be able to go away and correct this. Having more than one actor lead a warm-up gives you more leverage. By this, I mean you can choose to make a generalized statement without referring to anyone specifically. And this is still getting the point across. You don't have to do this. I am simply saying you can. Think about how many times an actor is on-set and he is asked to do something he was not originally told to do. As long as it is not against his contract, he will just have to get on and do it. The actor will want to be at the peak of preparedness at all times.

36. All the World's a Stage

Tell the actors that in a moment you would like one of them to go on-stage or in front of the room and take a seat. Then the actor is to imagine the curtain has just gone up, or the camera is rolling, and everyone is watching him just sitting there doing absolutely nothing. After a time, you will say "curtain close" or "cut" and he is to finish. This is based on an exercise by Stanislavski. Have one or two other actors do the same exercise.

Discussion

Ask the actors what they thought was happening. What is the purpose of this exercise? Did they believe the actor who was up on-stage, or were they signaling through gestures and superficial movements and actions?

Purpose

To get comfortable with stillness

Remind your actors that there will be numerous times when they are on-stage where they are seen but not heard. This may be when they are part of the atmosphere. This may also be because their character is listening to another character and a whole slew of other possibilities. Sometimes what is required of actors is stillness, allowing their characters to be engulfed in their thoughts. Some actors find their thoughts are more interesting than anything they could possibly read in a book. Your actors have to learn to get comfortable with stillness. They have to learn to get comfortable in their own skin before they can get comfortable in the skin of others. They have to learn to inhabit themselves. As you may find in this exercise, a number of actors will find the need to gesture or use external actions in order to feel comfortable in front of an audience. The actor will want to learn to love the sound of nothing. This exercise aims to help the actor strip away all that is unnecessary.

Industry Connection

In this exercise you will most likely see examples of superficial movements and actions. You will most likely see at least one actor looking uncomfortable and not knowing which way to turn. By looking this way, they are probably feeling the need to perform. If an actor is in a scene and a close-up is being filmed, then even the slightest flicker of an eyelash will register. If the actor contorts his face and performs all kinds of unnecessary actions, they will show and the actor will look ridiculous and lacking in credibility. Even if the actor is asked to do nothing at all, he must know exactly why he is doing "nothing."

37. Primal Sounds

This is an excellent warm-up exercise. Have your actors form a circle in which everyone is at least shoulder width apart. Have one actor step into the circle and make a very freeing sound with a complementary freeing movement. He should do this by holding nothing back. Now have him step back and join the main circle. At this point, have the entire group take a step forward and repeat both the movement and sound of the first actor. If they only half do this, have them do it again. The exercise is called "primal," so we want to see primal instincts here and not intellectual ones. Make sure you start with a big enough circle so that when the actors step forward, they do not bump into each other. Continue the same process until you have gone around the entire group.

Purpose
To let go of preconceived ideas
This exercise encourages the actors to let go of any preconceived ideas and just react. If actors inhibit or censor themselves, there will be nothing primal about their movement or sound. Let us say someone curses, then this is not a primal sound. This is an intellectual choice. You are not looking for actual words, but sounds that come from the actor's gut. When you see a performance that holds you, it is in part because the actor you are watching is uninhibited. The actor is able to reveal and unburden himself. He doesn't say, "I can't do that. I'm scared what people might think. It's embarrassing." The actor throws himself into the role and embraces it. This is not so much an intellectual thing as it a visceral response. This is a simple exercise, and yet when it is done correctly, it is extremely powerful.

Industry Connection
In this exercise, the actors have to throw themselves in completely. If they hold themselves back, then they are not completing the exercise. Actors may move to Los Angeles or London and say, "I'm going to give it a try and see how it goes." If this is their approach, they might as well just pack up and leave. If they are not willing to throw everything they've got into being an actor, then they are just wasting their time. Actors often move to New York, Los Angeles, or London due to drive and ambition. They have a certain focus and true passion. Professional actors do not have a "job," they have a "life style." They have a burning ambition. This means that at all times of day or night, acting is somewhere on their minds. It is as if they have creativity running through their veins. Sometimes they are working on a script, at other times they are talking to their agent, while at other times they are auditioning for a part. The professional, working actors know how to throw themselves in completely. They are creatively and entirely reliable. The amateur actor does not even consider this possibility. By amateur I do not mean an unpaid actor, but a state of mind.

38. To Train or Not to Train
For this exercise you will need access to enough computers for your students to break into groups of no more than three or four. Explain in the following way:

INSTRUCTOR: In a moment I am going to ask you to break into groups. Each group is going to pick an actor, past or present. The only stipulation is that the actor you choose has won an Oscar at some point in their career. I want you to go on the Internet and do some research on them. What I want each group to do is discover as much as they can about the actor's training background.

MARCUS: Is it just the training they are doing now?

INSTRUCTOR: That is a good question, Marcus. I actually want you to look at any training they have had relating to acting throughout their life. This means drama school, high school, private coaches, basically anything you can find.

CLAIRE: Does voice and singing training count?

INSTRUCTOR: Voice training is definitely one to look for, including accent reduction classes. Singing may at first appear unimportant to the actor, and yet you will be surprised how many actors have starred in musicals or actually sung at some point in their careers. Let's include all types of vocal training in our search. I want you to use your imaginations in doing this research. There are many search engines and resources to help you on the web. You are going to be given twenty minutes to complete this task and then you will present your findings. You are going to have to work efficiently, effectively, and brainstorm as a team.

You may want to formulate a list of all of the Oscar winners to help your actors see who they can choose. This list should be fairly easy to come by. Do not start the twenty minutes until all the groups have chosen their person. Make sure each group chooses a different actor. If you have a longer period, you may choose to give the students more time. Because each group only has one computer, it is necessary to make sure that everyone is participating fully. Perhaps while two people are searching online, another can prepare a list of questions and the fourth person can read out the facts. The fifth member of the group might write down the answers. Tell each group to make sure that each member of their team is to be used. If students have Internet on their phones, and you are comfortable with them using these as well, this can be used as an extra computer for the group.

Purpose

To see the value of training

The premise of this exercise is that, "Great actors have a degree of training." As your actors pursue this assignment, you might discover that this is not always the case. The aim of this exercise is to encourage your actors to train as actors. For example, Meryl Streep earned her MFA from Yale School of Drama. Russell Crowe intended to apply to the National Institute of Dramatic Art. He was talked out of it, but went on to become an Oscar winner. Sally Field was already a famous sitcom star when she decided to go to New York to study with Lee Strasberg. I mention this because despite the fact that I believe actors will want to train, whenever we use absolutes in acting we will find ourselves being contradicted. Your actors will probably find in their research that the vast majority of the Oscar winners have had some sort of training. The importance and significance of this will be up to you and your class to decide.

Industry Connection

Tell your students to turn on their televisions and watch some commercials. They will discover that in the vast majority of cases the actors speak clearly and enunciate their words. The producers know that in order to sell the product, every word said by the actor has to be understood by the audience. Does this mean that everyone in commercials has had vocal training? Probably not, but in the vast majority of cases they probably have had some degree of it. Ask your students to watch their favorite dramas on television. Have them research actors who have been on television for ten years or more. Ask them to see what type of training these actors have received. The reason I mention ten years is because it gives the students the opportunity to look at actors who have longevity in their careers. Numerous actors prefer never to watch their own performances. If they compare themselves to actors who did one show or one episode, this is not a good measuring stick. Some individuals are good-looking kids with loads of hair and they believe this makes them an actor. We are looking at good actors and groundbreaking actors with longevity in their careers.

Note
The word training can be somewhat deceiving. We have all heard world-famous actors who have said they never trained in any acting school or program. However, what stands out is the caliber of actors and directors they had the opportunity to work with throughout their careers. In other words, they were in acting school almost every day of their lives; they just called it by another name.

39. Newspaper Nightmare
You will need to have done some preparation ahead of time for this activity. Split your actors into teams of five or six. In front of the actors there should be separate piles of old newspapers, two pairs of scissors, masking tape or regular tape, coloring material, and an envelope. Each group has to pick a pile. Once they take the pile back to their corner, they can open their envelope. The envelope is going to name a famous character.

Some examples of characters are:
The Hulk
Harry Potter
The Wizard of Oz
Peter Pan
Tigger
Darth Vader
Snow White
Pocahontas

Each team will get twenty minutes to make a costume based on the character named in their envelope. The material they will use is the newspaper with which they were provided. One member of each group must volunteer to be the model. The costume must be made to fit him. Give each group twenty to thirty minutes to complete the task. At the end, have each group present their character and costume. You can make this into a mini competition with prizes, but you do not have to. I have found it is more fun when the groups also have colors to work with. Please remember that each group should have two pairs of scissors. If any of the cutting is to happen near the model, ask the person to be extra careful when cutting. Please make sure to recycle the newspaper!

Purpose
To make something out of nothing
One of the profound aspects of this exercise is that the groups attempt to make something out of nothing. It is true that they do have materials to work with, but everything else comes from their creativity and imagination. They will want to have an instinct for drama. Actors have to be able to draw on so many layers of emotion. They have to be able to unleash themselves. If actors lose their sense of wonder, they lose everything. Actors in a play have material to work

with. They are given the words of the play, but little else. If they do not find a way to lift the words off the page, the play will become meaningless in terms of performance. This is part of the reason why the same play performed by two different casts can be considered a success or a failure at the same time. When actors pick up a play, they have a book to work with. It is up to the cast and crew to turn it into something truly wonderful. While the play itself is of great help, it is not enough. It is the actors who must take those words and do something with them.

Industry Connection

There is a degree of delegation involved in this exercise. Not everyone can be cutting at the same time. Only one member of the group can be the model. There is only one roll of tape that can be shared, but is likely to be mainly used by only one or two people. If the group does not clearly delegate roles to its members, they may have trouble completing the task successfully. Making a play or movie is as much about delegating responsibilities as anything else. There is a lot of waiting around in between scenes on a set. Let us say an actor is in his trailer waiting to do his next scene. He is not going to head to the set until he is called. It is the personal assistant's responsibility to go and get the actor. This responsibility will have been delegated to a specific personal assistant. The crewmember in charge of lighting may have delegated three crewmembers to light a car that is involved in the next scene. There is a lot of shop talk that happens on a set. A film set is the combination of many forms of delegation, all happening at once. When the chain is broken, it usually means that either something was communicated incorrectly, or a task was not completed. This will most likely lead to time wasted, with a financial price tag attached. This information is important for the actor to know. A movie is a production. That means someone has to pay to produce it. There are a lot of personalities that have to be negotiated. A good movie set can end up feeling like a family. To make a good movie takes an unimaginable amount of work, focus, money, teamwork, and cooperation, to say the least.

Chapter 6
Sensory Awareness

40. Energy Hands

Have the actors stand in a circle. Have them bring their hands up, scrunch them, and then open them to their full flexibility. On opening their hands, they should be totally energized, although their wrists remain relaxed. Have them do this for one hundred to two hundred fairly brisk cycles. At this point, have them bring their hands up so that they are almost touching the person next to them. Their palms should be almost touching the palm of the actors on either side of them. Remember, I said *almost* touching. They may be able to feel the heat and the energy coming through the other actor's hands. They should now direct their focus to someone else in the circle. Their aim is to gain the other actor's eye contact. They should stay focused on them, even if they do not receive a reciprocal response. Have them hold this for one minute. After the minute have everyone let their hands down. Have the actors stand there for another thirty seconds in complete silence. Follow up with a group discussion. Find out what was going on for the students during this exercise.

Purpose
To create sensory awareness

The aim of this exercise is to create a sensory awareness of what is happening inside the body. It is also necessary for the actor to address the external aspects of each role. Some actors grow up very aware of their own emotions. As Edward Dwight Easty discusses in his book *On Method Acting,* "Just as the two kinds of relaxation, physical and mental, are so closely related, so it is with concentration and relaxation as a whole. The actor will find that one cannot exist without the aid of the other. An actor needs relaxation to achieve stage concentration and he must certainly concentrate on either mental or physical exercises to promote relaxation."[13]

This exercise also works with chi and taking the body towards homeostasis and balance. In conversation with Alex Mathews, coordinator and instructor for massage at Austin Community College, he told me, "Movement and thought originate from homeostasis. A body that moves away from homeostasis is moving towards disease. Disease is going to affect every aspect of a life. It is going to show in lack of movement, rigidity, and it is also going to exert extra effort and energy in order to function. It becomes a huge effort to move between thoughts or even to develop thoughts. If a muscular skeletal system is in balance then movement and thought become effortless." Great actors make it all seem so effortless.

There are also aspects of creating an ensemble unit here. Part of this exercise is bringing the actors' focus of attention into play and infecting their partner in this manner. So this exercise is one example of hundreds of possibilities. The added advantage to this particular exercise is that it can bring a unity to the cast. In this respect, this exercise is also a great preshow warm-up for the entire cast.

---

13. Edward Dwight Easty, *On Method Acting* (New York: Ballantine Books, 1981), 73.

When the actors go into the play with a feeling of togetherness, this will permeate throughout the performance. The audience will be able to sense that the actors have a common bond.

Variation
In regards to preshow warm-ups, look into an exercise called Go Bananas. I think it originated out of Second City in Chicago.

Industry Connection
With all the stress and constant changes and challenges going on around actors on a set, it is up to the actors to work with their own instruments in releasing any unnecessary tensions. This applies to both internal and external tensions. If you look around a film or TV set on any given day, you will become aware of the fact that most of those involved have nothing to do with acting itself. You have the grips, light, sound, makeup, wardrobe, script advisor, assistant AD, PAs, and so on. Generally speaking, what you don't see are very many actors. It is up to the actors not only to prepare their instrument but to keep it in a constant state of readiness. They will want to strive to get to that unknowing truthful reality of being. There are numerous people running around the set with varying degrees of tension coursing through their bodies. An actor should not be one of these people.

Note
Some actors are unable to make the connections between their training as an actor and the industry they are entering. As the actor starts to join the dots he will find that the connections and the parallels are endless.

41. Blind Leading the Blind
Explain in the following way:
INSTRUCTOR: To start with, I would like everyone to find a partner. With your partner, find a space in the room. Please name yourselves A and B. Start by facing your partner. Both of you should put your hands together so that you are touching with all ten fingertips. The only parts of your bodies that are touching are your finger tips. At this point, As should close their eyes. Now Bs are going to lead As around the room, continuing to keep their fingertips connected at all times. There is one more part to this exercise. Bs cannot move forward, but must lead As by walking backwards. Bs, you still have your eyes open and can see to your sides, but you cannot see what is going on behind you. This is why the exercise is called the Blind Leading the Blind. For safety, everyone should be moving slowly. You also need to be spatially aware of what is going on around you. Remember that you must stay connected at the fingertips the entire time.

After a few minutes you can ask them to reverse their roles. You can also let half your actors watch the rest of the group do the exercise. Then switch the order. A lot of the actors' discoveries will come through their observations. Ask your actors to spend some time watching humanity. The actors will always want to be looking through the keyhole of life.

Purpose

To fall in line with one another

In this exercise, the actors have to fall in sync together. Moving around the room without their vision or limited vision is a challenge in itself. The fact that they also have to stay connected at the fingertips means they really have to be aware of one another. When an actor is playing opposite another actor, he has a choice of working off the other actor's performance or forgetting he is there all together. Some actors simply wait for the other actor to finish so they can say their line. The dynamics are totally missing, and the performance becomes dead in the water. An actor has to listen, feel, sense, and respond to everything that the other actor is giving him. The most gifted actors tend to be the most generous in what they give to their fellow actors. The generous actors also let the audience into a few secrets. In this exercise, the actors with their eyes closed have to put their trust in their partner. In a performance, actors have to be in the moment. They need to find that in-between place that takes away certainty. They will want to bring something raw to the performance. Most actors desire that their work feels organic and not manipulated. They can only achieve this if they put their trust in their instrument. They have to know how to be open to anything that is happening around them. An audience will want to see an actor who is emotionally accessible. Each actor has to find out how to make their instrument available, venerable, and accessible.

Industry Connection

If actors are not careful, they are going to find themselves being led up many blind alleys. One thing that seems common in LA, New York, and London is that many actors part with their money too quickly. There are any number of people who are only too happy to help them do so. They will tell them that they need: headshots, a demo reel, a website, business cards, acting classes, and on and on and on. Actors may need all these things, but not in their first week! Ask your actors to do their homework and research first. Some actors do a tremendous amount of research for every role they play. The more work actors put into their character the more it will show in performance. In film it is often too expensive for the actors to rehearse, so preparation is vital. Let us say they got their headshots done and they looked awful. They decided to go somewhere else and get them done again and they still look awful. They get an agent and she says, "You need to get them done again. They look awful!" They have now cashed out for three sets of headshots, most of which were of no use to them anyway.

Explain to your actors:

INSTRUCTOR: Do your homework and research first! Interview the photographer. Visit their website and see their work. It may take a little longer at the outset. In the end it will save you a lot of time and money. You are not going to build your acting career overnight. Be willing to build a strong foundation from which you can grow. Even actors who make enormous amounts of money can spend it frivolously. A number of actors have commented on how they are always one movie behind their debts.

Note

There is no substitute for research. Ian Fleming, who wrote the twelve *James Bond* novels, was in Naval Intelligence during World War II. This gave him tremendous insight for his writing.

42. Sensory Awareness

Have the actors sit in the audience. Have four actors come forward and explain in the following way:

INSTRUCTOR: Robert, in a moment you are going to be asked to complete a number of tasks. Lisa is going to stand next to you on your left. In a moment she is going to present you with a number of simple arithmetic problems, such as three multiplied by three. Helen, you are going to stand on Robert's right side. You are going to ask Robert a number of basic questions such as, "What did you have for breakfast?" George, you are going to stand in front of Robert so that he is facing you. You are going to begin with slow movements. These are like the ones that we have previously done in the mirror exercise. Robert, you are going to mirror every move that George makes. George, please remember to make your moves slow and fluid so that Robert can follow you. The challenge is that all of these things are happening at the same time. You have to be able to answer the arithmetical problems, the personal questions, and perform the mirroring simultaneously. There should be no let up of questions from you two. If a question is ignored or unanswered, keep repeating it until Robert has answered. Robert, you are not allowed to ignore any one of the questions.

There are no "outs" in this exercise. Have your actors stay in the center until you decide to change them. It is a very beneficial exercise, so you want to enable your actors to experience it for a few minutes. It is OK if they get frustrated with themselves. Be aware that they probably will.

Purpose

To listen and respond with the senses

This exercise integrates the actors' senses of sight and hearing. It is not enough to converse with another actor on-stage. Actors actually have to listen to what they are saying. This exercise asks the actor to listen and respond to two conversations at the same time. We actually do this in our own lives all the time. A character may say to her boyfriend, "I love making dinner for you." The subtext may be, "I wish you would take me out for dinner once in awhile." In other words, the character has spoken dialogue and inner dialogue. Each character often has two conversations at the same time, even though we may only be aware of one. Your actors have to be aware of the internal as well as the external dialogue. They will want to be aware of their character's inner monologue.

Industry Connection

There will be times on-set when actors have to complete a number of tasks at the same time. Hair and makeup are on their left side getting them ready. Behind them is sound putting a mike under their lapel. On their right side is the director giving them a few suggestions of what she is looking for in the next shot. In front of them is the cameraman, asking them to walk through the blocking. A film set is a notoriously distracting place to work. All of these people have questions, and all of them are asking for the actors' attention. Actors will want to develop a questioning mind. They have to develop the tools and the muscles that enable them to cope with the demands made upon them. Every actor has to bring their A-game.

Note

It is not unheard of for a makeup artist to spend four or five hours preparing the character makeup for an actor. This is especially the case in science fiction and fantasy or adventure movies. An actor may be called in to the studio at two or three in the morning to start this preparation. Those who believe the actor's life is one of pure glamour are in for a rude awakening.

43. Shot in the Dark

Have your actors sit in the audience space but towards the back of the room. Choose two actors who have a scene prepared to go up on-stage. Have them perform the scene for the group. Have your audience make mental notes of their observations of the piece. Have the actors perform the scene again, only this time, it is going to be done in darkness. Turn out the lights and darken the space. You may also have the audience and the actors close their eyes during the scene. For the actors, make sure that this can be done in safety. If not, then do not have them close their eyes, but ask them to perform the scene in the darkness of the room, with their eyes open. Once they have finished, follow up with a group discussion. Find out if the audience made any new discoveries the second time. Perhaps the actors also found out new things about their characters or made other discoveries. Actors really have to take responsibility for their character. Feel free to continue this exercise with another scene and different actors.

Purpose

To experience a shift in awareness

Both the actors and the audience experience a sensory change in this exercise. By turning off the lights, the whole room experiences a shift in awareness. Think about what happens when you go to the movies. All the lights are turned off and suddenly our focus and attention goes on the screen. If the same audience saw the same movie in their living room with the lights on, they may come out with a totally different experience. It is important that your actor's are aware of these influences even when they do not control them.

Industry Connection

Raise the following discussion with your actors:

INSTRUCTOR: Sometimes you will be filming a scene in the small hours of the morning. It is dark outside, but through the magic of technology, stage fifteen looks as if it is three in the afternoon. You know it is the middle of the night, because you just went outside for some fresh air. The challenge is that you cannot bring this knowledge into the scene with you. You cannot bring lethargy or dreams of falling into bed into the scene. So, while you know it is night, you are going to have to convince us it is day. You might say, "This is not an industry link!" I would argue that on the contrary it is very much an industry link. There will be numerous occasions when you will be on-set at all kinds of odd hours. Odd hours for you is actually two in the afternoon for your character. We are living in an age of virtual technology. With technology we witnessed the virtual disappearance of black and white movies. This was seen as a real step forward and yet night scenes such as those in Hitchcock or Joan Crawford films are much more powerful in black and white.

44. Mold Me, Please

Have your actors split up into groups of three. Each group needs a guide, a sculptor, and a piece of clay. Have each group find their own space in the room, away from the other groups. Have the sculptor and the piece of clay close their eyes. At this point, give the guide two to three minutes to adjust the piece of clay into any shape he wants. Make sure it is the same amount of time for each group. Next, have the guide take the sculptor over to face the piece of clay. He should be close enough so that if he put his hands out he can touch the piece of clay. Give the sculptor three to five minutes to touch the piece of clay from top to bottom. Have him move slowly and cautiously. As much as possible, you want them to avoid touching their partner's personal parts. They should also move slowly because their aim is to memorize in their minds and bodies the shape of the piece of clay. When the time is up, have the guide move the sculptor so that he is standing side-by-side with the piece of clay. At this point, have the sculpture, who still has his eyes closed, attempt to recreate the shape of the piece of clay with his own body. Give the sculpture two to three minutes to complete this part. While his eyes are still closed, the guide may want to take a picture with his phone so that afterwards he can show the actors how alike they were. Once they have finished, have everyone join together for a group discussion. It is going to be a challenge for the piece of clay to remain still for so long. He may find that his arms begin to ache.

Purpose
To utilize your sense of touch
For this exercise, the sculptors have to utilize their sense of touch. Through touching the piece of clay they have to attempt to recreate what they feel. Actors must develop a deep sensitivity in their sense of touch. They may be in a scene where the director asks them to tenderly stroke their girlfriend's cheek. This is easier said than done. If they simply stroke her cheek, it might look like they are swatting a fly or wiping off some melted ice cream. It is the subtleties in the sense of touch the actor must develop.

Industry Connection
The pieces of clay have to allow themselves to be put in other people's hands. They have to allow both the guide and the sculptor to lay their hands on them. This takes a large degree of trust on their part. While we have often said actors' careers are their responsibility, they are, nevertheless, going to have to put some of that trust in others. An actor is constantly looking for the right vehicle that will launch his career. There are some auditions they cannot get into without a good agent. Finding a good agent and putting their trust in that individual is not always easy, but at some point they will have to. They will also have to put their trust in many other people, such as: photographers, hairstylists, managers, lawyers, makeup artists, and so on. The good thing to remember is that if they abuse that trust, remind your actors that they can always walk away.

Note
I want to remind you of the importance of the industry connection sections. You might be saying things like, "My actors are only twelve, they do not care about the industry," "We live in a small town. This has no relevance to us," or

63

"Most of my students will never be professional anyway." If you think in these terms, then you are doing your students a disservice. Your students want to know how an exercise you are giving them relates to the world around them. If they do not see any relevancy, then at best they will say it is a bit of fun. How do you know what their dreams and aspirations are? How do they know for certain what their dreams and aspirations are? Actors have to fantasize about their future if they expect to have one. They will want to learn to destroy their cynicism. Acting is fantasy fulfillment. Your responsibility is to do everything in your power to ignite the passion of acting within them. It does not matter if a career in acting becomes their final destination or not. Part of that passion will be ignited through the industry connection sections.

45. Squeak, Piggy, Squeak

This activity comes from the well-known children's game. Have all of your actors sit on chairs in a circle. Explain this exercise in the following way:

INSTRUCTOR: Derek, in a moment you are going to be blindfolded. You are going to start out as the farmer. Everyone else who is sitting in the circle, you are going to be the pigs. Derek is going to start by standing in the middle and will be turned around three times. He then has to carefully and cautiously make his way over to the lap of one of the pigs. When he arrives he will sit on the lap of the first pig he comes to and say, "Squeak, piggy, squeak." The chosen player then squeaks and the farmer has up to three guesses to work out who the pig is. If the farmer guesses correctly, the pig becomes the farmer in the next round. If the farmer does not get the correct answer, he will stay the farmer in the following round.

Purpose
To utilize the senses
In this exercise the farmer is able to work with his senses of hearing and touch. While sitting on the pig's lap, the farmer also is given a clue as to who the pig might be. This is more subtle than hearing the voice, because it is not stressed as being an important part of the exercise. It is up to the farmer to take full advantage of his senses. In fact, when he is sitting on the lap of another player, he is close enough that he can also engage his sense of smell, which may give him another clue. Perhaps one of the actresses in the class is wearing a light perfume that is recognizable. By using the sense of hearing the farmer may be able to figure out who the pig is through his breathing. It is not just actors who rely on their senses for information. The difference is that the actors need to develop their senses so that they are fine-tuned. The actors need to develop their senses so that they are at their maximum potential. This can only happen if they are constantly being exercised and taken to the next level.

Industry Connection
Raise the following points with your actors:

INSTRUCTOR: In this exercise, the actors have to find a way to disguise their voice. If the actor is unable to do it, that is a challenge they will have to meet. If they are to transcend themselves into different characters, they must discover how to let go of part of themselves. They must discover the different energy point for each character. The important lesson in a city like Los Angeles is how to remain who you are and not as a carbon copy of everyone else. The challenge is that you have to become the best version of yourself you possibly can. When you go to an audition, you are not there to disguise yourself. However, what you want is for the director to see what you want them to see. This is going to depend on the role you are auditioning for. In regards to auditioning, senior acting coach for one of England's leading drama schools, Amanda Fawsett, told me, "During your audition or interview, don't waste valuable time trying to second-guess what the panel are thinking. You can easily misinterpret their expressions or body language. While you are focusing on them, you are not fully committed to the real purpose of the exercise, which is to prove you are right for the job. You can never over prepare for an audition. Spontaneity takes practice and knowledge. The better you prepare the more power you have to control the audition and be confident.

46. Catch the Prey

This exercise is very similar to the exercise, Detective, in my book *112 Acting Games*. To play this game, you will need a set of keys and two blindfolds. You will also need a newspaper. Have all the students sit in a large circle so that they are at arm's length. This game is not really good with fewer than fifteen people because you need a large circle. Explain the game as follows:

INSTRUCTOR: Today we are going to play a game called Catch the Prey. In a moment, I will choose one of you to be the prey and one to be the hunter. The hunter's job will be to try to catch the prey, and the prey's job will be to try to find the food. We will use a set of keys to signify the food. It sounds simple enough, but there are a few catches. The hunter will have a rolled up newspaper. In order to catch the prey, they have to gently tap them on the head with the newspaper. It is not good enough to bump into them. They have to tap them on the head with the paper and not the shoulder or the arm. Both the hunter and the prey will be blindfolded, and they will not be walking around the circle, but moving on their hands and knees inside the circle, so that they are not heard by the other person. This exercise is not about running around as fast as you can, but about moving like a snail so that it is virtually impossible for the other person to hear you. I recommend you to take off your shoes for this activity. The slower you move, the more interesting this game is to play and watch. Hunter, if you find the keys, try not to make any sound with them. It is not your objective to find the food, so if you come across it, you must leave it and move on.

In a moment, I will ask someone to silently place the keys somewhere in the circle. Two other students will place the hunter and the prey somewhere inside the circle. They will be spun around in both directions so that they lose their bearings. Those of you who are forming the circle are playing a vital role. You must not make any noise whatsoever. Also, you cannot laugh if the players get close to each other. It is quite possible that while looking to tap the prey on the head, the hunter could end up tapping one of you in the circle. Hunter, be aware that the more noise you make with the paper the easier it will be for the prey to stay away from you. You do not want to give them any clues as to where you are. I have you sitting at arm's length apart so that you can cover the entire circle between you. If the two appear to be about to move outside the circle, put out an arm and gently guide them back in. Do not push them back, just guide. Everyone must be concentrating at all times. Remember, safety is of the utmost importance. Hunter and prey, don't worry if someone guides you back in. I will tell you if you have been caught. Remember that you must move as slowly and as quietly as possible.

It is better to roll up part of a newspaper than the whole thing. It is also worth reminding the hunter that they are to *gently* tap the prey on the head and *not use force*. We are not trying to give anyone concussion here.

Purpose

To heighten the senses

Your students are certainly developing their sense of hearing as they lose their sense of sight. The sound of the newspaper suddenly becomes quite heightened. I also find many students comment on the importance of their sense of touch, which is enhanced during this exercise. Teamwork plays a big part, too. If the people in the circle do not work together and stay focused, this exercise will fall flat on its face. This can be quite a challenge if they are hit on the head with the newspaper. The more opportunities you can give the students to take responsibility for each other and work together, the better. You want the students to feel that even when they are just a small part of the game (sitting in the circle), they are still a vital part of its success. At a future date, when they have a tiny part in a play, hopefully they will be able to transpose this information and apply it. There are no small parts!

Industry Connection

One of the interesting aspects of the exercise is that the prey is moving around the circle, at times with the anticipation of pain. Even though the newspaper is light and does not hurt, it is the anticipation of pain that affects them. Nobody likes to be hit on the head. The fact that the prey knows someone is trying to tap him with a newspaper will cause, among other things, involuntary flinching. It is not so much being tapped by the paper, as the anticipation of it happening. Some actors spend their entire careers in self-inflicted pain. By this, I do not necessarily mean physical pain. They say things like, "I will never work again," "I have been hired for a great part, but I will probably lose it," "What if I never get another role?" "Sure, I am famous, but I am so upset I have never won an Oscar," "I can't get an agent! I hate myself," or "I can't pay my bills! I hate acting." Actors who constantly consider that the glass is half empty, rather than half full, will never allow themselves to be happy. They will always find themselves moving away from pleasure and towards pain. Numerous actors have gotten their lucky break because another actor did not show up or because the preferred actor was committed to another project. Actors who embrace their situation have the best opportunity to move away from pain and bring pleasure to their own life and to the lives of others.

47. Love Thy Neighbor

This is a variation of the exercise Kitty Wants a Corner, a well-known children's game. Instruct your actors to stand in a circle and explain in the following way:

INSTRUCTOR: Maggie, I would like you to go into the center of the circle. Everyone else is a neighbor of Maggie's. In a moment, Maggie is going to walk up to one of you and ask for something. If Maggie is baking an apple pie, she might walk over to Cliff and say, "I am baking an apple pie. Can you lend me some apples?" Whatever Maggie asks for, you are unable to provide, but I do not want you to just say "no," I want you to say, "I am afraid I cannot help you, but I think I know someone who can." At this point you have to point to someone else in the circle and Maggie is going to walk over to them. Maggie, when you go to the next person, you are going to ask for something different. What might you ask for?

MAGGIE: Does it still have to be related to the apple pie?

INSTRUCTOR: It can be any topic you like.

MAGGIE: OK. My car has just broken down outside your door. Can you help me fix it?

INSTRUCTOR: Very good! Now there is one more activity in this exercise. While Maggie is busy asking everyone for help, I want the rest of you in the circle to change places with each other. You can only change places in agreement with someone else. In other words, if Mike and Chandra make eye contact and agree to change places, they can. Chandra must go to Mike's place and Mike to Chandra's. If Maggie becomes aware of this, she is going to try to steal a place in the circle. If she is able to do so, there will be a new neighbor in the center.

ANANDI: Can we change places as much as we like?

INSTRUCTOR: That is an important question. If you change places too often, the situation will become chaotic and cause mayhem. I want you to change places only occasionally. There can be pauses in which no one changes place.

Purpose

To keep a sense of alertness

What I like about this exercise is that it asks the actor to keep a sense of alertness in a variety of ways. When the actor is in the middle, he first has to decide who he is going to walk towards. When he arrives at his neighbor's place, he must be ready with a question. He must also pay attention to who his neighbor is going to send him to next. While all this is going on, he must also be alert to what is happening around him. When other actors are changing places, he must remember that his objective is to steal a space. In the same way on-stage, the actor must be alert to everything that is happening around him. This does not necessarily mean in terms of obvious external reactions. Let us say a character is in a scene, sitting in a coffee shop, quietly reading a book. After a few minutes, into the coffee shop come two men who are loud and obnoxious. Our character may not say a word or make a sound. He may simply look up and make a subtle observation and go back to his book. He is alert to what is going on around him.

Industry Connection

To perform this exercise with any justification, the actors must work with two main objectives. They must continue to come up with good questions and also aim to steal a space from a neighbor. Your actors may say their only objective is to steal a space. If this is the case, they are only going to complete half the exercise. Some actors obsess about being a working actor. This is totally understandable, and of course, important. Their error is that they put no focus into becoming a good actor. The actor must never stop asking questions. Other actors are very well-trained, but turn their nose up when it comes to embracing the industry and accepting what they need to do in order to book work. Both of these are important pieces in the actor's puzzle and to negate one will eventually affect the other. Notice I said *eventually,* because an actor can develop a degree of success before the public says, "So and so can't act." Actors can train for years before ever trying to get professional work. If they do not become industry savvy, it is unlikely they will get much paid, on-camera work. Some actors believe that when they reach the top they will be happy and be able to retire. Other actors believe there is no top and they would prefer to go on working indefinitely. In many careers people retire through old age. In acting it is often the industry that prematurely retires the actor.

48. Phone Book Finesse

This exercise comes from my book *Acting Games for Individual Performers* and has been adapted here for group work. Explain in the following way:

INSTRUCTOR: Michelle, come and join me. For this exercise we are going to need a phone book, or another thick book, and a hair. Yes, you heard me correctly. You are going to need a hair. Michelle, it can be your hair or the hair of a dear friend, as long as you have one strand of hair. (MICHELLE hands over one strand of hair.) What I would like you to do is place this hair under the first page of your phone book. Now, with your eyes closed, I want you to run your fingers over the top of the first page and see if you can stop your fingers over the hair. Basically, you are feeling the hair through the page. I would like to make it a little more specific and ask you to use your fingertips as opposed to your whole hand.

MICHELLE: That's really weird. I can feel it.

INSTRUCTOR: Good. Let's try two pages.

MICHELLE: I can still feel it.

INSTRUCTOR: Excellent. Now that everyone gets it, I am going to ask you to find a partner and repeat this exercise. Some of you will be using phone books and some of you have other books. Provided the book has very thin pages, you should be fine. Once you have completed the first page successfully, put the hair beneath two pages, three pages, four pages, and so on. See how many pages you can get through and still feel the hair with your fingers. You can both work on each page before moving on to the next. There is no race to complete this activity. For the purpose of this activity, it is important that you close your eyes so that you can only rely on your sense of touch to guide you. Closing your eyes will heighten your sense of touch to its maximum potential. Once you have finished the activity you may discard the hair, unless you wish to keep it for sentimental reasons.

Purpose

To develop your sense of touch

In this activity, the actors are enabling their sense of touch to become heightened and more sensitive. To feel a strand of hair through the pages of a phone book can take an enormous amount of sensitivity through the fingertips. The more the actors practice this activity, the greater amount of sensitivity to touch they will have. Having a skill such as this can be invaluable to the actor. Let us say an actor is playing a romantic scene in a film, and the director asks him to caress his partner's cheek lightly with the back of his hand. If he does not possess the skills of finesse, his hand may feel abrasive. This may set totally the wrong atmosphere for the scene and cause his partner to become frustrated and even aggravated. The greater degree of understanding actors have of their sense of touch, the more flexibility it will give them in their work.

Industry Connection

If the actors do not focus on the task at hand, they will not succeed in this activity. This may seem like a strange statement because they will still be able to feel the hair through a number of pages. However, they will never be able to reach their true potential. Sometimes, when you watch a movie you will say to yourself, "They did a pretty good job." If you think about this statement for a minute, you will realize that what you are saying is that they could have done better. There are many film and television actors who are considered mediocre. There are few who are considered universally great. Without concentration in acting, whether it is during the performance itself or in the preparation stages, something will always be lacking. By performing an activity such as this over a continual period of time, the actors will have the opportunity to make concentration and focus into an automatic process.

Chapter 7
Voice

49. Ten Steps

Have your actors form a circle and stand shoulder width apart. Now, as they stand, ask them to allow their arms to rest loosely by their sides. Ask the actors to take in two nice deep breaths. Do not tell them how they should do it. Look around the group and you will most likely notice one or two whose shoulders will rise up as they breathe in. You may also see their upper chest expand. Ask if they mind demonstrating the exercise again, only this time have the rest of the actors observe them. When they have finished, ask the group to point out what they saw. You may hear things like, "Shoulders were raised, upper chest moved, the neck tensed up," and so on. Ask the actors if they were aware of these things.

Then explain that you would like them to breathe in from their diaphragm. Ask the actors to put their hand flat with the bottom finger beginning just above their belly button. Explain that as they breath in the aim is to be able to push their hand out and allow their belly to expand. Abdominal breathing, also called diaphragmatic breathing, promotes relaxation in the body and supports the vocal apparatus. When you breathe in, the lungs fill with air, the diaphragm is pushed downward by the lungs, and the stomach expands. As you breathe out, the lungs empty, the diaphragm relaxes back to its dome-like shape, and the stomach contracts. It is also worth noting that correct breathing promotes the expelling of toxins from the body.

Have your actors now take a number of breaths using diaphragmatic breathing. Walk around the room and observe the actors. Remind them that as they breathe in, their belly should be expanding and their hand should be pushed away. Tell them that their shoulders should stay pretty still. Tell them that their neck should feel loose and free. If an actor tells you he is feeling dizzy, tell him to take a break. It is worth explaining that when an actor is breathing more efficiently he will be taking in more oxygen. One side effect of this exercise is that the actor may feel a little dizzy or light-headed at first. You can give the example of the long distance runner who may feel slightly dizzy or light-headed after a race.

At this point, have the actors go back to incorrect breathing for a moment. Have them really exaggerate with shallow breaths, shoulders raised, top of chest expanded. Now have them go back to correct breathing using their diaphragm. You do this so that they get a real physical sense of what is correct and what is incorrect. This is not a vocal workshop and you are not expected to be an expert in voice training. You also are not expected to be a total novice either. Your actors will want to have the potential to be able to express themselves richly and eloquently. This is mentioned so that if your actors want specific vocal training, they will seek out a voice workshop. They may also want to consider hiring a private vocal coach or accent reduction coach when their budget will allow.

At this stage, have half your actors sit somewhere at the sides of the room and the other half line up side by side so that their nose is practically touching the wall. Tell them you are going to ask them to count to one. However, you only want them to use enough projection to hit the wall with their voices. You will want the actors to feel as if their voices are bouncing off the wall. Make sure they are using diaphragmatic breathing for this exercise. Their throats should stay loose and free. Next, have them take one fairly large step back (one to two feet). This time they are going to say, "One, two." Now they are going to need to use a little more projection so that their sound can really bounce off the wall. Make sure their hands and arms stay free and there are no clenched fists. Remember that as they stand shoulder width apart, their arms should be resting loosely at their sides. Have the actors continue with this exercise until finally they are counting all the way up to ten. By this point the actors should be at the back of the room. If your room is thirty feet long, then by the last count, this is where they should be. Tell your actors that you want the first breath to be consistent with the breath they take when they reach the higher numbers. This means that if they are counting from one to five, each number should have the same strength and quality. If you notice their sound is becoming fainter, it is because they are running out of breath. Tell them, "You need to take in enough breath through your lungs and diaphragm to last the whole count. You also need to make sure you control the breath so it lasts for all counts."

Once they have finished, change over the groups so that the observers now become the performers. Once everyone has finished, have one or two actors do the exercise alone, allowing everyone else to observe. It may be useful to stop them in the middle and have the rest of the actors make observations. They might say, "You seem to be forcing the sound from your throat. Your shoulders rose on the last three occasions." When they have finished, you can also mention things they did that were great. At the end, you can follow up with a group discussion.

Purpose

To develop vocal awareness

If an actor is in a professional play, then most likely he will be giving eight performances a week. Each performance has to be as strong as the last. It can be quite challenging and frustrating for an actor to do one performance of one play night after night. With the best intentions in the world, actors can find it quite challenging to keep the performance as fresh as they would like. This is not just in terms of their acting but also in terms of their vocal qualities. Let us say on Monday their voice quality is great and the audience can hear every word clearly. By Saturday they have sore throats, and now the audience has to lean forward to try to catch what they are saying. If their projection is coming from their throat, instead of their diaphragm, this is precisely what is going to happen. Over time, actors can permanently damage their vocal chords and develop nodules. Their instrument is their bread and butter, so once they have damaged it, they are now faulty goods. They are selling themselves, they want to keep themselves in the top possible condition. If the audience cannot hear the actor they will say things like, "Her performance was weak," "She is not a very strong actor," and "She still has a lot to learn." Actors may feel this is unfair because it is based on a technicality. If the audience cannot understand the words coming out of their mouths, why are the actors saying them at all? The words are not the actors' privilege. The actor must find a way to contribute to the text. If someone turns the sound down on the television so that he can barely hear the actors talk, he will soon lose interest in what they are saying. This is precisely what will happen if the audience cannot hear an actor clearly.

71

Industry Connection

For the most part, television and film do not require a great deal of projection. One of the reasons for this is that actors are surrounded by microphones and sound technicians. Another reason is that film is a different medium from theatre with different technical requirements. An actor may therefore presume, "I don't need a trained voice for film." This is naïve at best, and at worst it is a dangerous assumption. A good number of people work an eight-hour day. An actor on a film set could quite easily be working a twelve-, thirteen-, or fourteen-hour day, only to do it all over again the next day. The other challenge is that an actor might start at eleven a.m. and work through until two a.m. By this point, not only is the actor's body tired, but so is the actor's voice. It is at this point he is going to have to rely on technique. He might think that a director and producer will sympathize with him, but for the most part, they won't. Any delay in the schedule converts into more money they have to pay out. Movies often work within a great economy of time. It is all about getting the job done in an economical way. Movie actors really learn to be on their toes in terms of being prepared. A producer's job is to maximize profits by keeping the costs as low as they can. A film crew is similar to an army platoon. If the crew is one hundred strong, then every hour wasted is extra payment for one hundred people, let alone all the additional expenses. The actors' job is to be one hundred percent prepared for anything that might come their way and not seventy-five percent. Some directors hire actors who do the job and they let them get on with it. In terms of rehearsal it is worth noting that some film directors never use this word. They will say some like, "Would you like to practice one before we go for a take?" Some film directors require a rehearsal period prior to making a film. It is important in that it is the only time the actors will get to rehearse in sequence. Actors have to know how to adapt to the medium they are working in. It is also worth pointing out that some actors regard a take as an opportunity to fail. By this they mean it is not necessarily a final performance.

Note

Actors in school or college may be saying that, "Nothing can prepare you for the real thing except the real thing itself!" I would agree with them that this is a very good observation. What they can do is create a foundation from which to build. An actor may feel these are only exercises and thus serve no compelling purpose, but they would be very, very wrong. It is exercises such as these that will give them some of the vital tools and skills they need. In college, actors get to play numerous roles that they will never again get to play in their entire lives. They have to be prepared for opportunity when opportunity comes their way.

50. Energy Up, Energy Down

Have your actors form a circle in which they are touching shoulders with the person on either side. Have everyone start by squatting down, so that their bottom is just off the floor. Have your actors count from one to ten, standing up a little more on each count. As the actors are moving up, have them use jazz hands at the same time. The hand vibrations should start small and crescendo as they continue to go higher. This means that by five the whole group should be half way up, their projection should be half to its potential, and the jazz hands should be at a medium pace. By the time they say "ten," they should be fully up on their toes and their hands and fingers stretched up above their heads towards the stars. They should also project "ten" at their maximum capacity. This is full projection, as opposed to shouting. The actors should open their body up to allow the vibrations to come through. It is important for the actors to work together and observe one another. They should reach each stage together, and reach the crescendo together. Everything should be happening gradually and smoothly, as opposed to staccato. Once the actors have said "ten," have them reverse the entire exercise, all the way back down to one and in a squatting position.

Purpose
To connect the voice and the body

This exercise has your actors move up and down and it also has them engage their hands and arms simultaneously. At the same time, their voice has to be connected and in unison with the rest of their body. It is a paradox for the actors to be disconnected from themselves. Think about the polarization of that. They have to be able to connect their voice and body, rather than separating the two. If actors are in a large theatre, then they have to be able to connect with the audience as much through their physical body as they do through their voice. For financial reasons, many of the plays produced these days only have two or three characters. Many of the audiences are not in the position to see a close-up in the actor's face and the subtleties it may be showing. There was a period when the term "a method actor" got thrown around a lot. There seems to have been a lot of confusion and misunderstanding by the audience and actors alike as to what was meant by "a method actor." Some proponents of the method have observed that the method is finding your own method. One thing that method actors were accused of was giving introvert performances on-stage. In other words, the audience could not always hear what they were saying and the performances were of a lower intensity. The interesting part is that their performances may have been absolutely brilliant, but if they had not adjusted it to fit the space they were working in, nobody would ever know. Your actors have to know how to connect their voice and body to meet the needs of the space they are working and performing in.

Industry Connection

If an actor is a versatile actor, then he is most likely going to work in theatre and film or TV. Perhaps the only real difference between the two is that film and television work, generally speaking, requires a quieter technique. Some actors believe theatre separates the men from the boys because the actor has to perform without a net. If they perform in a theatre, their voice is going to have to reach every corner of the auditorium. They have to know how to connect with the guy sitting in the twenty-third row and eight seats to the right. This will come through the technical aspects of their performance, as well as a certain intensity required to fill a space of this size. If they audition for a commercial, it may well be a different story. The actor walks into a tiny room and it is just him and the camera man or director. The setting is so intimate that it is futile to use the same projection and intensity that he used in the theatre auditorium. When your actors work with the above exercise, their intensity at number one is exactly where it should be. To be that low and that close to the floor means little else is needed but a whisper. Each actor is going to have to judge what is required depending on the medium and the space they are performing in. It is not necessarily lowering the intensity as much as adjusting it to fit the space they are working in. There is an English actress whose theatrical career ended almost as abruptly as it took off. By all accounts she was giving absolutely impeccable performances. The challenge was that she did not have the vocal technique to carry the strenuous vocal demands the role required night after night. As the acting teacher Jean Shelton says, "Take care of your gift."

51. Zoom Zoom

For this exercise have your actors stand in a tight circle. Choose one actor to say the word "zoom" and have the word passed around the circle in a clockwise direction. The word "zoom" represents the sound of a car. At this point, tell the actors that another word is going to be introduced into the circle, which is the word "eek." Whenever an actor says this word it is as if the car has stopped and is now going in the other direction. This means that every time an actor says "eek," the word "zoom" should start to travel in the opposite direction. Any actor can shout "eek" at any time. In order to limit the number of "eek" sounds you will tell each player that they are only allowed one "eek" per game. To increase the difficulty of this exercise, have the players speed up the tempo and keep the "zoom" moving at a rapid pace.

Purpose

To enunciate words clearly

This activity is fast and furious. It is true that actors will need great listening skills for this activity. What is also very important is that they enunciate their words very clearly. If they mumble their words, then they are being unfair to the actor who comes next. On-stage, the actor who speaks clearly is able to communicate the story to the audience in a more direct fashion. It is as if he is a spokesperson for the audience. Speaking clearly does not make a good actor, but it is an important technical skill that every good actor must posses. There are a number of famous actors whose vocal placement are somewhat unusual. What is important to note is that we can still clearly understand every word they utter. Certain times actors will perform a role where they are difficult to follow. There are occasional exceptions in terms of certain character-driven performances.

Industry Connection

It is so disheartening to hear so many aspiring actors in Los Angeles say, "Voice is not important because of microphones." When you think about it, this sounds like a logical argument. When you are on-set, you are going to view scenes where famous actors sound very quiet. This is going to back up the novice actors' theory even more. What they are forgetting is that good actors know how to speak clearly. They know how to enunciate every word so that they are clearly heard. Foreign actors are not necessarily told to lose their accents. What they are expected to do is get accent reduction so that they are clearly understood. They may feel freer acting in their own language, but also enjoy the challenge of performing in English. Western audiences can be somewhat lazy and do not want to strain to hear what is being said. If you think this is not the case, turn your television volume down. Watch your friends strain to hear what is being said. After a minute or two, they will begin to switch off, and eventually they will completely lose interest. If actors cannot speak clearly, they are a risk to a producer, and that is a risk they most likely will not take.

Note

We have used a number of children's activities in these sessions. Some of you may be wondering how they can be of benefit to actors if they are children's activities. Some of the most honest performances are given by children. They have a simplicity and naturalness to their work. It is not necessarily the exercise but what you are able to take from it that matters. Many children's exercises can be of great benefit to the actor when taken to another level. It is important to note that not many child actors are able to make the transition to becoming an adult actor. A football player is never going to be a ballerina, so why are so many of them given ballet lessons? It is because their coaches recognize that a 250-pound man who understands agility can be a greater and more powerful force. Many of the good acting exercises are very simple at their core.

52. Breath Tag

Divide your students into a ratio of five to one. If you have twenty-four students, divide them into one group of four and one group of twenty. If you have a group of eighteen, you would only want three players on the tag team and fifteen on the other. Look for a one-to-five ratio. The smaller group, the tag team, should consist of those who consider themselves fast. The larger group is the running group, trying not to get tagged.

Explain in the following way:

INSTRUCTOR: Will the group of five stand here with me for a moment? Please number yourselves one to five. I would like everyone else to spread out around the room. In a moment, Nick (Person number one) is going to run around the room and tag as many of you as he can. If you are tagged, please move to the side of the room. The challenge for Nick is that he is not allowed an extra breath. He is allowed to take only one breath before he begins and then must tag as many people as possible on that one breath. Once he is out of breath, he will come back to his team. Sarah (Person number two) will then take over and repeat the process. The aim for the tag team is to tag all twenty people before their team literally runs out of breath. If all twenty people are tagged, the taggers win. If one person is still left in, the other team wins.

DANA: How do we know if the tag team is really only using one breath?

INSTRUCTOR: That is an important question, Dana. The truth is we do not know for certain. We have to trust in their truthfulness. The challenge of the exercise is to see how many people they can tag on one breath.

BEN: Does the second tagger start straight away?

INSTRUCTOR: Not straight away, but almost. I will give them a moment to take in a deep breath and prepare.

Purpose

To understand the importance of breath-control and intensity

Not only is the tag team under pressure to tag the other players, but they have to do it in one breath. They will quickly come to terms with the importance of controlling that one breath. As the other players get faster, the tag team will find that their energy quickly abates. The fact that they only have a short period of time adds intensity to the exercise. While vocal training is important, it will sometimes fail the actor. In the middle of a performance an actor may become nervous and find that his chest and vocal muscles tighten up. As a result, he is unable to finish the sentence on one breath. He has to pause and take another breath before he continues. This may come across as nonsensical to the audience. It is not enough for the actors to control their breath. They must learn how to do so in intense situations.

Industry Connection

The four fastest runners are chosen to become the tag team. This is done in part to give them a false sense of security. They may be fast, but if they cannot control their breath they may not last five seconds. What this highlights is that to be strong in certain areas may not make up for weaknesses in other areas. Some well-trained actors arrive in Hollywood and complain that they can't get any work. I am a firm believer in good training for actors, but that alone is not enough. An actor who is not industry savvy is unlikely to be an actor we see consistently working. Actors have to be willing to develop their strengths in all areas. On the other hand, an industry savvy actor who cannot act will also be likely to meet with only partial success. Encourage your actors to become well rounded in all aspects of their acting.

53. Tongue-Tied

You are going to need to come up with a list of tongue twisters for this activity. These are easy to find on the Internet, or there are mini books of tongue twisters, or check out a number of voice books. Make a list of tongue twisters that work with different placements of the voice. For instance, the following well-known tongue twister is a great exercise in terms of lip placement:

> Betty bit a bit of butter
> But it was a bitter bite
> But a bit of better butter
> Betty never bit.

Here is a version I was given by a colleague of another well-known tongue twister. It exercises the tongue blade and the front of the hard palate:

> She sells seashells by the seashore.
> If she sells seashells by the seashore,
> Then I'm sure she sells seashore shells.

Find other tongue twisters that work on these areas:
Tongue-tip and upper-teeth ridge
Back of tongue and soft pallet
Tongue-tip and upper teeth
Lower lip and upper teeth
Open resonator

If you do not want to work with placements, you do not have to. However, working with placements allows you to take the exercise to another level.

Instruct your actors to form a circle. Choose one actor as a volunteer and have him read a tongue twister. If he finds it easy, have him speed up. If he is having trouble, ask him to slow down. This will be a good time to talk about enunciation. Saying a tongue twister is one thing, being understood is another. Have your actors separate into pairs. Give each pair one list of tongue twisters with placement notes included. Tell your students to find a space with their partner where they can work on their tongue twisters. They can alternate tongue twisters or let one read the whole sheet and then change over. Give your students about ten minutes to do this. Let them come back and form a circle. Choose some students to read a tongue twister. You can go around the whole circle or you might hear just a few. A great book of tongue twisters is *Anthology of British Tongue Twisters* by Ken Parkins. It also mentions the placement of each tongue twister.

Purpose
Not only to be heard, but also to be understood
This exercise works on the tongue and all the facial muscles. It also works on the lips and the soft pallet. If done correctly, the actors will probably find their facial muscles aching by the time they have completed the exercise. This is not a bad thing. It means they are working and training their muscles. It is a wake-up call as to which muscles the actors are and are not using on a regular basis. Actors do not always like it when a director says, "I cannot hear what you are saying." The typical reaction from the actor is to be louder. A few minutes later the actor may hear, "I still cannot hear what you are saying!" The actor, getting a little frustrated now, starts to shout and possibly hurts his vocal chords. Over time, he could develop nodules and damage his vocal chords. What if the reason the director could not understand is because the actor was not enunciating his words?

Industry Connection
This exercise is about exercising the mouth and all its components. The actors become tongue-tied. There are many occasions when actors metaphorically become tongue-tied with regard to their career. An actor attends an interview before a group of producers of a show and suddenly finds himself talking gibberish. Call it nerves or whatever you like, but it might cost the actor the job. There is no excuse for actors not to be able to talk and communicate clearly. If they are hired, they are going to have to communicate the story. Why would anyone hire an actor who cannot communicate in an interview situation?

Note

Some directors have three projects lined up, not including the one they are currently working on. They have to be experts at multitasking.

54. Vibrations

This exercise comes from my book, *Acting Games for Individual Performers,* and has been adapted here for group work. Tell all the actors to stand in a circle. As you explain, I want you to demonstrate and participate at the same time:

INSTRUCTOR: I would like you all to hum the letter M. If you are doing this correctly, it should sound like "mmmm." Now, place the back of your hand on your cheek as you are humming. You will want to be able to feel a vibration on your hand. Once you have accomplished this, I want you to place your hand on your forehead and do the same thing. You are probably going to find that you have to hum at a higher pitch in order to get your hand to vibrate. Next, I want you to place your hand on the back of your neck and see if you can get it to vibrate in the same way. When you are working with different parts of your body, I want you to shift your focus to these areas. When you are working with your head, I want you to shift your focus to the head. Perhaps you will have to hum in a "head voice." I also want you to adjust your pitch accordingly, depending on the area of placement on your body. Next, put your hand on your belly and find the vibration. Lastly, put your hand on your lower back and see if you can feel the vibration here. This is going to be quite difficult for many people, so I will ask you to be diligent. You may have to hum in a considerably lower octave to achieve the results for this one. So as a reminder, the five areas to look at are: the cheeks, the forehead, the back of the neck, the belly, and the lower back. At this point, I would like you to find a partner and a space in the room. I would like you to work the exercise as we just did it. One of you is going to make the vibrations while the other one will place the back of their hand on your cheek, back of neck, and so on. You are using the back of the hand because it is less intrusive. Your partner is going to let you know if they can feel the vibrations. If they find there is one area for which they can't find the vibration, stay there and experiment for a while. If your partner still cannot get it, move on and come back to it. Have one partner go through all five placements, then change over.

Bring the entire group back for a discussion. See if someone can demonstrate going through all five placements successfully.

Purpose

To understand voice placement

Each actor is being asked to work with different placements of his voice to create different vibrations in his body. When actors take on different accents or dialects for a role, they have to work with different voice placements. In England, a Cockney from London will most likely have a placement of his voice emanating from the throat. It often sounds quite rough and forced. A person with a more middle class upbringing will have a voice placement emanating from his diaphragm and even in the front of his mouth. A person of royal or upper class background will usually have a nasal placement and a thin sound. Of course, I am generalizing about each of these, but nonetheless, the placement for each dialect has quite a profound affect on the sound that is produced. If actors do not understand the vocal placement for a dialect or accent, they will always have something lacking. This does not only apply to dialect work, it is equally true for any characterization work they have to do. Being in command of their voice is an important part of actors' work. As Cicely Berry explains, "I know a great many people worry deeply about how they speak and how they sound, and that this anxiety often stops them expressing themselves as fully as they would wish."[14] It is vital that your students are able to express themselves fully in their work, but this takes time, patience, and a willingness to train and practice.

Industry Connection

Your actors are being asked to focus their attention in a specific way. If they are going to find a vibration through their forehead, they are going to have to focus their attention there. It is even more difficult to focus their attention in areas such as their lower back and yet they must to achieve the required results. When actors are working on a scene, all their attention must be right there. Perhaps the camera crew is in the background, or the producer, or the gaffer, and yet their attention must stay within their bubble of focus. Some actors will want their partner for the scene to stand behind the camera and feed them their lines for the close-up. If, for example, the actor has to use his imagination to transport himself to the ocean, his circle of attention may need to grow to a wider circumference, which means his level of concentration will need to be even greater.

55. Tongue Tipping

This exercise has been taken from my book, *Acting Games for Individual Performers,* and adapted here for group work. Have your actors stand in a circle and explain in the following way:

INSTRUCTOR: For this activity you are going to need a mouth, preferably your own. What I would like you to do is this: Using the tip of your tongue, count your teeth. You can start in the upper left hand corner of your mouth and when you get all the way to the other side, you can work right to left on the bottom teeth. This is not a race against time. I would like you to make sure you touch every single tooth in your mouth with the tip of your tongue. If you are touching more than one tooth at the same time, you need to make a more definitive point with your tongue. I would like you to repeat this activity five times, without stopping. Alternate by first going in a clockwise direction, then returning counterclockwise.

Purpose

To increase your level of articulation for the tongue

Some actors are unaware of the significance of the tongue with regard to articulation. Growing up in London, I was told I had a lazy tongue, which veered my dialect more towards a London Cockney. I was really proud of this fact, but it did not give me the versatility in my voice that an actor needs. This activity encourages the actors to pursue articulation of their tongue, which greatly affects the sounds coming out of their mouth. Let us say an actor is in a film and he is doing an outstanding job, but one fourth of everything he says is lost because of poor articulation. The audience will become frustrated. Hopefully, there is nothing

---

14. Cicely Berry, *Your Voice and How to Use It Successfully* (London: Harrap Limited, 1990) 7.

written in the dialogue that should not be there. That being said, it is the actor's job to communicate completely with the audience. I am a firm believer in actors using their individuality and using their dialects, but not at the expense of others. An actor can have a New York dialect and still articulate. He can have a French accent and still articulate — it's all a matter of practice. When an audience leaves the theatre, they will want to have been communicated to on a kinesthetic, auditory, and visual level. The audience will want to know who the character behind the actors' mask is. It is the actors' responsibility to make sure that this is the case.

Industry Connection

Raise the following points with your group:

INSTRUCTOR: You might be taking one more step towards speaking more clearly, or simply warming up before a performance. When you are at an audition, you are basically putting yourself on the line. You are telling the director, "This is what I have to offer you." If you give a fine performance, but the director has to struggle to understand you, he is unlikely to call you back. You may feel this is not the case, but remember, it is often the producers of the movie who pull the purse strings and they don't like taking risks. An actor who cannot be understood is a risk, because many of today's public are used to comfort and don't like having to make the extra effort. A good example of this is to turn your television volume down so that you have to lean forward to hear what is being said. That extra effort will usually make you lose interest in the scene and possibly in the whole movie. Continue to work on your articulation so that you continue to expand your marketability.

56. Word Projectile

This activity works best if you have a large space. Request one actor to go to the far end of the room, which we will call the performance space. Let the rest of the group move to the back wall, as far away as possible from the actor on-stage. The actor is now going to declaim a sentence in as clear and projected a voice as he possibly can. The sentence can be from a play, movie, or monologue, or it can be something he has improvised. The rest of the group will then repeat the sentence verbatim. If they cannot understand it, they will say, "We can't understand you." At this point, the actor on-stage is going to have to repeat the sentence. This should continue until the group can clearly follow what is being said. Allow each actor to work for up to five minutes, or make three attempts at repeating the sentence. At this point, you can let other actors take a turn.

Purpose

To be understood

Some of your actors will become frustrated during this activity. The group will keep saying, "We can't understand you." The actor on-stage thinks that these people must be crazy. In his mind, every word he is saying is as clear as daylight. The challenge is that on a stage, the actor has to reach a greater distance and a larger audience. It is not good enough to be talking in a way that only the actor in front of you can understand. Another challenge is that some actors project, but do not speak clearly. Other actors have great diction, but poor projection. The actor has to have both great diction and great projection to be clearly understood by the audience.

Industry Connection

When we are watching television, we can always turn up the volume if it is too low. When we cannot clearly hear what is being said, we often switch off mentally. There are many industry events at which an actor has to be clearly understood. Some examples are: an audition, a network interview, an agent meeting, a networking event, and the filming itself. Some aspiring actors believe they do not have to project because the microphones will do it for them. Just ask the boom operator on a set and he will tell you they need the actors to be clearly understood in order to pick up what they are saying. Actors are more likely to be cast when they speak clearly. Turn on your television and watch ten commercials. How many of the actors could you understand? The chances are you could understand all of them. A producer advertising a product does not want his audience to miss even a single word. Some of your actors may feel commercials have no place in acting. Ask any working actor and many will tell you that commercials are their bread and butter and a financial lifesaver. Commercials can subsidize necessary commodities such as food and rent.

57. Vocal Shades of Grey

For this exercise you are going to need to prepare two sets of cards. On one set of cards you are going to write down locations. On the second set of cards you are going to write down different types of characters. These do not have to correlate with the locations. Some examples of locations are:

A library
A park bench
A nightclub
A movie theatre
An amusement park
A doctor's waiting room

Some examples of characters are:
Police officer
Yoga instructor
Elementary school teacher
Parent
Nurse
Postman

Have your group sit as the audience. Bring two actors up into the performance space. They are going to improvise a short scene. Have one of the actors randomly pick one of the cards from the location cards. Have each actor randomly pick a card from the character pile. These actors will create a scene using the information they have been given. For instance, they may end up with an army sergeant and a librarian sitting on a park bench. There is a slight twist to this exercise. Ask the actors to take into account their location and their character in regards to their vocal levels. By this I mean if they are sitting on a park bench, they are going to be in relatively close proximity to one another. This should affect their vocal levels. Of course it could be a noisy park and this may be taken into account. The librarian may be more softly spoken because librarians are used to working in a place where people are asked to keep their voices low. This does not mean they can only be soft spoken, but the actor should at least take this into account. The actors' vocal levels should not drive the scene but they will want to be a consideration. Switch out the actors and work with other pairs following the same protocol.

Purpose
To create tenderness and volatility when needed

Being able to manipulate vocal levels will allow your actors more versatility in their acting. Perhaps in a particular scene a girl is being flirtatious with a young man whom her character wants as a future boyfriend. She inflects soft undertones in her voice to come across as sexy and alluring. Perhaps in another project an actor is playing a part where danger, stubbornness, and lack of self-control are the order of the day. Manipulation of her voice and projection levels is not a substitution for other aspects of her acting; rather it is another vital piece of the acting equation. Some people also assume that in television and film they will never need to project. This is not the case and sometimes they might have to use their projection for the same scene twenty times in a row. This exercise also allows you to see that by changing your vocal levels you can totally change the meaning of the piece. This is powerful and necessary information for the actor to have.

Industry Connection

Raise the following points with your students:

INSTRUCTOR: Let us assume that you are an actor who was raised in the theatre and have also been to college for your acting training. You know more than anyone how important projection is and how important it is to be heard. You have now switched your interests to film and television. Today you are auditioning for an agent and you are going to do a monologue. You remember that you want every word to be heard and understood and so you use a booming voice that vibrates around the room. The challenge is that you are in a tiny office performing for this one poor individual who is sitting two feet in front of you. If your volume is overbearing, he will not hear your piece, just your incredibly irritating voice. This is a complaint that agents make time and time again. You must understand how to adapt to your environment, whatever that may be. You also might come in for an audition where you were going to start the piece off very strong and the reader is so soft that you decide to adapt to a different interpretation. If you are going to do this, you have to have the vocal technique to understand how to do it. It is imperative that you adjust your volume to your space and your environment. Perhaps you are in a crowd scene where there are supposed to be about one hundred people milling around. You are having a heart to heart with your son, who you are attempting to talk some good into. What you have to say is for his ears and his only. If this scene were for television, you could practically whisper it and the mike would pick everything up. If this were for theatre, you would have to work with a projected form of a whisper that would sound totally different. On the other hand, you might be at a party with a hundred friends giving them a speech that celebrates your son being a decorated athlete. Not only do you need versatility in your projection, you need to understand voice and how and when to use it.

58. Abs-olutely Breathtaking

This is an exercise that is popular with a number of abdominal instructors. It can also be put to good use for the actor. Have each of your students bring his chair into a circle. Have your students sit with their backs against the chair and their feet firmly flat on the ground. Ask your students to take in a nice deep breath. As they breathe in they will want to be filling their tummy area and their diaphragm. As they breathe out, ask them to pull their abdominal muscles in as far as they can. They will still want to be pulling their abdominal muscles in as they continue to slowly breathe out. Have your students take a total of thirty seconds to breathe out the entire breath. You should be calling out so they know how long they have left. The aim is not to breathe out all of their breath and then pull in their abs, but to control the breath and do them simultaneously. Have your students repeat the exercise three to five times. Take a thirty-second gap in between each repetition. They may find they get a little dizzy because they are taking in a great deal more oxygen than they are used to. If this is too much, have them sit out the following round.

Purpose

To develop breath control

In this exercise the actors have to learn to control their breath. Correct breathing is important for actors because it allows them to talk for a longer period of time. In other words, if an actor has a long sentence that would flow much better in one breath, he will need proper breath control to be able to do that. Correct use of voice is a fundamental part of an actor's training. A professional play will most likely run eight times a week. The actors have to put their voices through an enormous amount of work. Not only are they using them constantly, but they also have to project so they can be heard at the back of the auditorium. This exercise is a little contradictory for the actor in that they are asked to tense their abs, which is not necessary for correct breathing. It is, however, one aspect of this exercise. This exercise works the deepest abdominal muscle, which is called the transversus abdominis.

Industry Connection

As mentioned above, this exercise is somewhat of a contradiction. It is a great abdominal exercise and also great for breath control. The challenge is that tightening the abdominals literally causes the individual to tense his muscles, which can be a contradiction for the actor. If this is the case, you may wonder why this exercise has been included in this book. There are many aspects of an actor's career that will appear contradictory. Some actors will build their careers by making unconventional choices. When filming, a director may ask an actor to give everything he has to give. They may challenge an actor to catch every little nuance that builds up to the climatic moment of the scene. In the editing room, the director may cut out all the build up and go straight to the climatic moment. This may seem like a contradiction, but it is keeping the movie under two hours and budget constraints. Actors will want to get used to and embrace the contradictory aspects of their career.

Chapter 8
Concentration and Focus

59. Moment to Moment

Have two actors come up to the front of the room while everyone else becomes the audience. Give the actors the following instructions:

INSTRUCTOR: Sarah is going to talk to us about an interesting experience she has had. It can be from today, last week, or last year. Paul, your job is to repeat Sarah's story at exactly the same time as she tells it, word for word. I would like both of you to stand shoulder to shoulder, straight out towards the audience.

DEREK: Are they allowed to look at each other as they talk?

INSTRUCTOR: Thank you for the question, Derek. Neither of you are to look at each other for this entire time. Sarah, if you find that Paul is not able to keep up with your story, you are going to have to slow down. You may also want to elongate your words so Paul can really say them at the same time as you.

Once you have done this with one pair for a few minutes, you can switch out with another pair. If the actors are finding challenges completing this exercise, stop every now and then and get feed back from the audience. What are they doing that works? What do they need to focus on further, in order to get clearer results? Can both actors be heard clearly? Guide the actors into fine-tuning the exercise so it sounds as if one person is talking.

Purpose
To demand focus and concentration from the actors

This exercise demands focus and concentration from the actor. It demands it in a specific manner. The actor is not just listening for the sounds, but must repeat the exact words almost simultaneously. It is this emphasis on specifics and precision that is so important to the actor's work. An actor playing a role cannot say, "My character is about twenty something." He has to know that the character is twenty-three, if that is how old he is. If actors create generalities about their character that they are not buying into, then neither will their audience. The actor will want to connect the dots within the character. This exercise demands such focus from both actors that it takes them to a deeper level of concentration. The actors are drawing on their subconscious. A performance should be developed in a moment-to-moment reality. The actor will want to aim to reach the dramatic sense of the moment.

Industry Connection

Raise the following points with your actors:

INSTRUCTOR: It is the exactness and preciseness of this exercise that can be so telling in the industry. Let us say you have been cast in a coffee commercial. The director works the scene with you a few times and says, "On the twenty-third second, the coffee cup needs to be at your lips. We only have thirty seconds total, so it cannot be a second earlier or later." This may sound ridiculous to you, and yet it is based on a real experience of an actor in a national commercial. If you look at some of the examples in these workshops and think they are not realistic and will never happen, think again. It is precisely because the most odd, bizarre, strange, and unreasonable demands will be made of actors that they have to be prepared for anything. This is good to know considering theatre people are often considered a little bit strange. There are occasions when actors are accused of not being able to bear too much reality. Show business can be a wonderful escape from reality. The actor should live the life he wants to lead.

60. Limitations

Have two actors come up into the performance space. The rest of the actors will sit as the audience. Tell the two actors you would like them to improvise a scene. Have the audience give them some of the details: who are they, where are they, what are they doing, when the scene takes place, why they are there.

Even though you are working with improvisation, you are still looking for justification and truthfulness in the scene. There is a slight twist to this exercise. Tell the actors there is one word they are not allowed to use at any time during the scene. For one of the actors it might be the word "and." For the other actor it might be the word "but." Make it a fairly general word that they are more likely to use. To keep the scene moving, allow each actor up to three chances. Do not stop the scene each time the actors say the word, stop it if they say the word three times. The reason it is done this way is to keep the scene flowing. If an actor is playing the scene and simply thinking about the words, stop the scene and point this out. You want to see a justified scene. At the same time, the actor has to carry out all his objectives.

To vary this exercise, you can add another actor to the scene. The third actor also has a word he cannot say. Remember that even though there is one actor who cannot use the word "and," the other actors on-stage can use this word in their dialogue. Other examples of words you may want to rule out are: you, I, it, to, the, we.

You do not need to wait for the scene to end to stop it. You can stop it because it is boring. You can stop it because it is going on too long. You can stop it because you want to give other actors a chance to have a go. Use your judgment as to when to let a scene go on and when not to. When the actors are stuck, sometimes that is the best time to let the scene continue to see how they will get out of the situation. See if they can find a rhythm and direction for the scene. You could vary the exercise by having the actors have the same forbidden word. You could also whisper the word to the actors that each one is not allowed to use. This may make it more interesting for the audience to try to work out the word.

Purpose
To learn to move between thoughts at a rapid pace
We cannot think two thoughts at exactly the same time. We can learn to move between thoughts at a very rapid pace. In this exercise, the actors have to move between thoughts at a rapid pace. They have to keep the scene moving and justify the dialogue and their actions. At the same time they have to make sure they do not use their banned word. This takes focus and concentration. It also takes the ability for the actor to move between thoughts. If an actor is in a play, they constantly have to move between thoughts. While performing the action of the play, they have to be aware of their blocking, their vocal projection and

diction, their movements in terms of lighting, and their stage awareness. In addition to this, they have to be aware of all of the ingredients of the play itself. The stronger their technique, the more they can rely on their technique for certain aspects of the performance. However, no matter how strong actors' technique, they will always need the ability to rapidly move between thoughts. They are able to find the organic part of each character they play. An actor's work is about making decisions and choices. Actors have to invest in each performance they give with utter conviction. Great actors have developed the ability to do this in an almost effortless fashion. They cannot always explain to you the zone or state they go into. Eleonora Duse was a world-famous Italian actress born in 1858. She was perhaps the first actress who aimed to internally connect with her characters. In regards to great actors, Giovanni Pontiero says in his book, *Duse on Tour of Elenora Duse,* "Loyal admirers discovered something new with every performance and she herself treated every successive performance in the same role as if it were opening night."[15] Sarah Bernhardt was an equally famous French actress of that period. In those days an actress received her public. In the early nineteenth century, Edmund Kean was considered by many as the greatest English actor alive. Perhaps only David Garrick was able to rival his mastery of so many diverse characters. The phrase, "be all that you can be" is particularly relevant for the actor.

Industry Connection

Let's say the actor's character in a film is smoking a cigarette. The director tells him that when he says, "Margaret," he takes a puff on the cigarette. If he does it three seconds later, or five seconds earlier, he is in trouble. He has to do it the same place each time because of continuity. If he takes the puff in a different place each time, then each take on film will look different. This means that when he moves from the master, to the two shot, to the close-up, he will look out of sync. So the actor will have to know how to rapidly move between the thoughts of what is going on in the scene and when to take a puff on the cigarette. Sometimes an actor in class is unable to see the relevancy between an exercise and its meaning in terms of an actor's career. In the example given here, the actor is expected to be able to apply all aspects of continuity. If he has never exercised these muscles, then how is he going to do this effectively? Actors have to learn to compartmentalize their minds in a variety of ways. If they cannot do it effectively, they are going to cost the production a good deal of time and money. Every actor has to be prepared for opportunity when it comes his way.

61. Absolutely Quackers!

This is a good mental warm-up exercise. For this exercise, have your actors form a circle and explain in the following fashion:

INSTRUCTOR: We are going to start a rhyme going around the circle. Damien, you can start. We will go in a counterclockwise direction. Damien you will say ...

DAMIEN: One duck, two legs, quack.

INSTRUCTOR: The next actor will say ...

15. Giovanni Pontiero, *Duse on Tour: Guido Noccioli's Diaries* (Amherst: The University of Massachusetts Press, 1982) 27.

NEIL: Two ducks, four legs, quack, quack.
INSTRUCTOR: The following actor will say ...
CINDY: Three Ducks, six legs, quack, quack, quack.

If any actor makes a mistake, you have two options. You can start the exercise again from the beginning, with a new actor, or the actor who made the mistake can be eliminated. Actors may also be eliminated if they pause too long or stumble over their words. You can have the actors speed up the exercise to make it more of a challenge.

Purpose

Chunking for memorization

In this exercise, the actors have to be able to assimilate the material. They have to be able to chunk the material given. If the first actor said "one duck" and the second actor said, "two ducks," that would be simple enough. The challenge is that all three sections change every time. The number of ducks, the number of legs, and the number of quacks, all change. The actor has to do a form of mental chunking in order to respond efficiently and rapidly. It can be useful to use a form of chunking to memorize lines for a play. If an actor has the lead and tries to learn hundreds of lines in one go, it may become overwhelming. If he is able to chunk the material into smaller sections, it could be that much easier for them.

Industry Connection

Raise the following points with your actors:

INSTRUCTOR: Just as in the exercise, it may be useful for you to chunk your acting career. Some actors say, "I'm going to get a good agent and join SAG and AFTRA. I'm going to get a commercial, get a day-player role, get a part in a movie, and produce my own film." This sounds very ambitious and some may say very positive in its outlook. The challenge is, that attempting to do all this at once, may be overwhelming for the best of actors. By focusing only a few things at a time, they will be able to compartmentalize and chunk their priorities. They will be able to tick off the boxes to what has been achieved, and move on to the next set of goals. An overwhelming journey will be short-lived. Give yourself the opportunity to enjoy the journey while accomplishing your goals. You're going to walk down the road you create. As the character Peekay says in the book *The Power of One,* "He had given me the power of one: one idea, one heart, one mind, one plan, one determination."[16] An actor will want to have a determination to work.

Note

If an actor finds a good agent, he may want to stick with them. A good agent can be hard to find.

---

16. Bryce Courtenay. *The Power of One* (New York: Ballantine Books, 1989), 103.

62. Start-Stop

Have all your actors start walking around the room. At any given moment, one of the actors should stop walking. When this happens, all the actors need to stop walking as quickly as possible. This must happen without any signaling or verbal communication. Once everyone has stopped walking, they can start up again and continue the cycle. Remind the actors that anyone can stop at any time. When one person stops, everyone else must stop as quickly as possible. Do not allow the actors to start another round until they have made sure everybody has stopped.

Purpose

To become aware of your surroundings

This exercise is not a competition against the other actors, but rather an individual competition against themselves. This exercise allows the actors to see how aware they are of their surroundings. They may not see the original person who stopped, but that does not mean they cannot see one of the actors who has stopped. Stage actors have to have the ability to respond to what is happening around them. Every action causes a potential reaction. If someone knocks at the door in the play, who reacts? It is not only the person with the next line but everyone in the house within earshot of the knocking at the front door.

Industry Connection

Make the following observations with your actors:

INSTRUCTOR: There is no award in this exercise. There is no winner in this exercise, except yourself. Many things you have to do for your acting career bring no immediate reward. You run around town to go to the printers to approve the proof copy. When you see it, there is a tiny smudge and so you have to ask the printer to do it again. He tells you to come back the next day and look again. You can't come back the next day because you have to work, and the day after that they are closed. There are many tasks that have to be completed if you are going to have a shot at an acting career. They are thankless tasks that are self-motivated and only of benefit to you. You have to take charge of your acting career.

63. Cat Nap

You will want to have a whistle or a stereo for this exercise. Start off by asking all the actors to take off their shoes and put them safely out of the way. Split your actors up into two groups. One group represents the cats and the other group is to be the couches. The cats should form the inner circle and the couches should form a larger outer circle. When you start the music or blow the whistle, the cats should start moving in a clockwise direction, while the couches move counterclockwise. Instruct them to move at a brisk pace so that they are moving at a light jog or a fast walk. Both circles must keep their formations. While moving around the circle, neither the cats nor the couches have their arms linked. When the music is stopped or whistle blown, the cats have to sit on a couch and take a nap. This happens when the couches go down on one knee and a cat sits on the end of that knee. The last cat and couch pair to team up is out. Each round, one pair should be knocked out. Notice that a pair can only be formed from a cat and couch combination. Two cats or two couches are not able to form a pair. At the end of the exercise there should be one cat and one couch left in. Make sure that the outer circle is some two feet away from the inner circle to avoid collisions. The faster the actors move the more challenging the exercise. You will want to gauge this on the maturity and coordination level of your students. To save the students from becoming dizzy, switch their direction from time to time. It is important that while one circle is going clockwise the other circle is moving in a counterclockwise direction.

Purpose
To make full use of the senses
The actors have to make full use of their senses. In order to be ready to move once the music stops, they have to be alert and use their sense of hearing. If the room is noisy, their first reaction might be from their sense of sight when they see the other players reacting. As they form a pair, the cat has to quickly sit on the end of a knee using his sense of touch. We often tell actors that they have to have vivid imaginations. In order to use this vivid imagination, the actor has to be in tune with his senses. Acting is a game of make-believe. If a director tells the actors to imagine they are on the beach, they literally have to smell the seaweed, see the ocean, feel the breeze, taste the sea salt, and hear the seagulls. This exercise encourages the actors to sharpen their senses.

Industry Connection
The aim of this exercise is not to come in third or fourth. The aim of this exercise is to win. There is not one actor in your group who does not have the potential or ability to win. When those same actors audition for a part, their aim should always be to get the job. They have to be very competitive and aggressive. If they do not book the job, it is OK, but this should never be their aim. They will never want to say, "I am going for this part, but I absolutely know I won't get it." This would become a self-fulfilling prophecy. The sole reason the actor goes to an audition is to get the job. There are many other benefits to auditioning, but the actor's ultimate aim should always be to get the job. There are many benefits to this exercise and if each actor does his best, every one of them has the potential to win. Advise your actors to focus on what they want and not waste their energy focusing on what they don't want. There is an exercise in *112 Acting Games* called Energy Breathing. It encourages the actor to use his breath to generate energy. Coffee will cause the actor to crash. Green tea will give a little boost without the crash. To work a long day on a set an actor has to develop ways to channel his energy efficiently.

64. Line Up
For this exercise, tell all your students to take their shoes off and put them safely out of the way. On small pieces of paper, you will need to write a number for each of the students in your group. If you have twenty students, you should have written out the numbers one to twenty on the pieces of paper. Explain the following:

INSTRUCTOR: In a moment I am going to ask each of you to find your own space around the room. I am going to bring each of you a piece of paper. A number will be written on that piece of paper. When you see your number please do not reveal it to anyone. At this point, you will be asked to close your eyes. You will then be asked to move slowly around the room and search for the person who is the number above you, or the number below you. So if you have number seven, you are searching for numbers six and eight. The challenge is that this has to be done in absolute silence. There is absolutely no talking whatsoever.

DANA: You said there is no talking, so how do we find each other?

INSTRUCTOR: You can do so by any other means necessary. Use your imagination. One example is to clap out your number. If you are number eight, you would clap your hands eight times. What are some other possibilities?

TRAVIS: You could stamp your feet.

BEN: You could tap the person on the shoulder the number of times that equals your number.

INSTRUCTOR: Both of these are good ideas. Of course, remember that things such as clapping and stamping your feet are going to be quite noisy, so you will really have to use your listening skills. This is not the end of the exercise. Your aim as a group is to end up in one line, in order. Number one should be at the front of the line and number twenty-three should be at the back. If you are number nine, you have to make sure number eight is in front of you and number ten in behind you. You can use the same methods to double-check this. This exercise will only come together if you all work together as a team.

Purpose

To use the circle of concentration in a specific way

It is too simplistic to say that this exercise involves focus and concentration in general. It involves a specific type of focus and concentration. When a student comes across another student, they are going to have to listen to their tapping, clapping, or stamping. By doing this, they will be able to work out if this is the person they are looking for. The challenge is that while there is no talking, there could be a great many other noises and distractions going on around them. Each student is going to have to find a way of blocking out the other noises and distractions. They are going to have to bring their circle of concentration into a specific area. As Dave Allen explains when talking about Stanislavski's work, "This represents a small 'circle of attention.' Kostya's whole attention is absorbed in the objects on the table."[17] This is easier said than done and may be quite a challenge for the actors. It would be great to say that all audiences are attentive, but this is not always the case. Remind your actors that while they are performing on-stage, their audience could be fidgeting or even talking amongst themselves. If the actors are in a pantomime, for example, audience participation is encouraged. While a degree of improvisation is expected in such shows, the actors still have to remember their lines. By being able to hone their levels of concentration and focus, the actors will be able to adjust to any circumstances.

---

17. David Allen, *Stanislavski for Beginners* (London: Writers and Readers Publishing, 1999), 125.

Industry Connection

The industry connection behind this exercise is to encourage the actors to multitask. While the actors are moving around the room with their eyes closed, they have to become spatially aware. They have to use their hands as their sensory tools. They are using their sense of hearing to listen to the clapping or foot stamping coming from other members of the group. They also have to use their focus and concentration to block out other noises from around the room. This exercise embraces the idea of multitasking. Professional actors also have to become professional at multitasking: putting their resumés together, mail-outs to agents, meetings with agents, taking acting classes, going to auditions, going to the gym, taking care of their image, meeting with producers, meeting with their managers, meeting with their publicist, and so on. This is just a small sample of the ways in which actors have to constantly multitask. They are actors their colleagues can always count on.

65. Got Rhythm?

Ask your students to sit in a circle. Pick a leader from the group. Go around the circle, and ask everyone to number off. The leader should be number one. The last person has the same number as you have students. Tell the students that they have to remember their number. The leader starts the rhythm. The rhythm should be taught to the students as follows: "Clap your hands three times. Clap your hands on top of your thighs twice. Pat your hands on your head three times. Snap your fingers once on the left and once on the right." Once you have shown this to everyone three times you may begin. The leader should always begin a new round. He should say his own number on the left snap and say the number of anyone else in the circle on the right snap. The person the leader called out must automatically take over without a pause. He should repeat the same pattern. When he gets to the snapping part he should call out his number, followed by another person's number. The activity should continue in this way until someone misses their number. When a student misses his number, have everyone move down one number. Number eighteen becomes number seventeen. Number seventeen becomes number sixteen, and so on. Number two becomes number one, which means number one moves to number eighteen and there is a new leader. Each time someone misses their number this protocol is repeated and there will be a new leader. The new leader can make up a new rhythm or keep the same one. It is up to you to decide how you want it to be played. If he starts a new rhythm, ask him to take a moment to teach it to the group. A new round is also begun if a player forgets the rhythm in the middle or makes an error. This exercise can be confusing unless you are able to get all your students to remain focused.

Purpose

To stay focused throughout

The purpose of this exercise is for the actors to stay focused at many stages. They have to focus to learn the rhythm. They have to stay focused to make sure they remember their number. They have to stay focused to make sure they do not miss their turn. They have to stay focused when they have a new number or rhythm to learn. It is the constant and ever-changing need to focus that is important. It is a given that the actor on-stage must be focused through the performance, but this is not the only time or place that focus is necessary. As actors arrive at the theatre to get into their costumes and makeup, they are beginning the process of focus and concentration. As they warm up their bodies, their voices, and their imaginations, their focus will come into play. As they are waiting in the wings to go on-stage for their initial entrance, their focus will be at a deep level. There are many occasions when focus becomes a key ingredient for the actor. We all start out from a primordial state, and the actor will want to continue to grow from here.

Industry Connection

The actors have to exercise their rapid memorization skills. They do not have a great deal to learn, but they do have to learn it in a short time. An actor on-set can literally be handed new lines to learn on the spot. Some actors will arrive on-set without a plan. Let us say the actor is given two new lines to memorize for the next scene. It sounds pretty easy if he were at home in his bedroom. The challenge is that he is under pressure to get the new lines right. There is a person whose job it is to follow the script line by line, for accuracy. If actors make mistakes, he is going to let them know. This is because every time they forget or misinterpret their lines, it costs the studio and producer money. Let's put it this way, studios are not known for being overly generous. There are many distractions on-set that could cause the actors to forget their lines. It is not enough that they know them. They have to have a technique that is virtually foolproof. They have to have a technique that takes into account nerves, distraction, and high stakes. They have to learn to breathe through these moments. In our exercises, if an actor makes a mistake, it is the leader who will suffer as he will lose his position as number one. On-set, if an actor continually forgets his lines, it is everyone around him who will pay the price. With regards to technique, the authors of *A Practical Handbook for the Actor* say, "Technique is knowledge of the tools that may be used for a certain craft and an understanding of how to use those tools."[18]

66. Eye to Eye II

Set up two chairs on-stage so that they are facing each other and positioned facing the audience. Explain the game as follows:

INSTRUCTOR: I need two volunteers to help me demonstrate this game. Alana, sit in the chair on the left, and Carrie, you sit in this chair on the right. In a moment I am going to ask you to look down at the floor, and when you look up, I want you to look into each other's eyes. As you are staring, if either one of you blinks, you are out. You must hold eye contact. There is no talking during this exercise. There is no second chance. The person who stares for the longest without blinking is the winner. The winner will stay in the chair to face the next challenger.

DAN: Are you allowed to smile and laugh?

INSTRUCTOR: In the exercise Eye to Eye, you would be out for both of those reasons. In this game, you are only out if you blink.

---

18. Melissa Bruder, Lee Cohn, Madeleine Olnek, Nathaniel Pollack, Scott Zigler, Robert Provito, *A Practical Handbook for the Actor* (New York: Vintage Books, 1986), 8.

Adapt this whichever way you want, depending on the age group. You might decide that if the participants make it to five minutes, they have succeeded. This may mean that you can end up with more than one winner. You will need someone to check to see who is blinking. This can be you, the audience, or you may choose an individual to take on this task.

Purpose

To perform to the best of your ability

The purpose of this exercise is for the actors to do the best they can. Notice I did not say for them to *be* the best. When an actor is in a play, he should not feel he is competing with other members of the cast. He will want to be working together with the rest of the cast. His aim should be to give the best possible performance he can give on that particular evening. An actor should not think about being the best, rather he will want to work towards doing *his* best. Acting is not a competition, it is an art form.

Industry Connection

This game is specific in its benefits for focus. Actors in a play or a film are aware of the audience and the technical crew. However, they must know how to block them out and act as if they were not there. If their attention is drawn towards the audience, or anywhere except where it is supposed to be, the magic is broken. The audience will stop believing in the reality of the performance; they are taken out of the land of make-believe. That is why, in this activity, the partners are able to control their blinking by not succumbing to the distractions around them. Blinking in itself has nothing to do with acting, unless it is a character choice. The challenge for the actor who continually blinks in a close-up on-camera is that it is a distraction for the audience. The actor will want to be connected to the camera. Film actors have to find a way to conquer this technicality so as to enhance their overall performance.

67. Sleeping with the Fishes

Ask your students to sit in a circle. Make the circle as large as possible. Explain in the following way:

INSTRUCTOR: I am going to go around the circle and name each of you as a particular fish: eel, pike, catfish, salmon, or tuna. (Use this sequence when assigning. All the students should now have a fish name.) In a moment, I am going to call out the name of one of these fishes, such as salmon. At this point, everyone who is a salmon has to run once around the circle and return to their original seat. Here is the complication: Each one of you has three lives. The last person to reach their seat in each round loses a life. While you are running around the circle, at any moment I can shout out, "shark attack." When this happens, you have to turn around and run the other way to get back to your seat.

CLAIRE: What happens to the person who was in the lead?

INSTRUCTOR: The person who was in the lead is going to find themselves in last place at this point. They will have to be extra fast if they hope to change this. If I shout out, "whirlpool," everyone in the circle has to run around and go back to their seat.

You can call out "shark attack" and "whirlpool" as often, or as infrequently, as you like. You can play until you have a winner, but this could make the exercise go on forever. There is no need to always end up with a winner or a loser. Make sure the students move around the circle safely and go back to their original seats.

Purpose
Focus and concentration
This exercise could most certainly be talked about with regards to action and reaction. At first glance, it may not be clear why focus and concentration are such a crucial part of this exercise. In order to hear their fish, the actors are going to have to concentrate at all times. This can be quite a challenge on its own. While they are running around the circle, "shark attack" can be called out at any time. While they are sitting in the circle, "whirlpool" can be called out at any time. Without focus and concentration, the actors do not stand a chance. Sometimes, an actor uses a purely intellectual approach to his acting. Let us say he bought an acting book that said, "Focus and concentration are necessary for the actor." The actor feels that once he has read it he has automatically taken the skill onboard. Unfortunately, this is highly unlikely. For actors to have excellent concentration, they have to exercise their concentration muscles on a regular basis. It is not enough for the actor to *discuss,* they must *do.*

Industry Connection
The leader can quickly be pushed to last place when "shark attack" is called out. This may seem unfair, but it is a part of the exercise. Sometimes actors will have a career that catapults very quickly. They appear to be on a path to glory when their career comes to an abrupt halt. If actors get a break early on, that is great. However, if they do not do the work to keep themselves there, their break is likely to be short-lived. I do not just mean in terms of training. An actor who is always partying may constantly arrive on-set late, not be prepared, wasting valuable time for the rest of the cast and crew. You can find numerous examples of this. Studios and producers may give these actors a certain amount of leeway if they are big box office pullers. Even in these cases, the studios and producers will only cut so much slack. There will be a point at which they will say, "We will never work with that actor again." That is usually the time when the public asks, "I wonder whatever happened to so and so?"

68. Lace-Up

This exercise has been adapted for group work from my book *Acting Games for Individual Performers.* Your students will want to sit as the audience. Place one chair in the center of the stage. For this activity you are going to need a student who is wearing a pair of lace-up shoes. Tell him to sit on the chair and explain in the following way:

INSTRUCTOR: What I would like you to do is untie the laces on both your shoes. I know it sounds strange. In a moment, I would like you to retie your shoelaces in the most perfect manner possible. I want you to imagine you are being watched by a casting director and that this is for a big commercial that could make you an obscene amount of money. When you tie up your laces, it is important for you to remember that you are not allowed to make one mistake or fumble and that the appearance of the tied laces has to be perfect. (Once the student has done this, give him the following instructions.) Now that you have completed this task, I would like you to untie your shoelaces again. This time, I would like you to make a mental note of all the things you have to accomplish this week starting with today. I want you to think about those things with absolute precision. What is the first thing you are going to do today? What is the next thing you have to do, at what time and where? The most important part of this activity is to recall the tasks you need to complete and the detail that goes with them. An example would be, "I have to take my car into Ted, the car mechanic, at three this afternoon to get the oil changed." Do not say these things out loud, but in your head. At the same time as you are completing this task, I also want you to tie your shoelaces. I don't want you to pay any special attention to your shoelaces. I just want you to get them tied while you are preparing your list of tasks.

Once the student has finished, give him a moment to let everything he has just done sink in. After a few minutes, invite the audience to make some observations. How do they feel he acted in the first half of this activity when tying his laces was of paramount importance? Compare this to how much attention he paid to tying his shoelaces in the second half of this activity, when that part was of secondary importance. Talk about the differences you noticed in his performance.

You can work the activity again today with other actors or come back to it on another occasion.

Purpose
To understand direction of focus
In the first part of this activity the actor is asked to focus solely on the task of tying his shoelaces. In fact, this activity was made to be of paramount importance, as if nothing else mattered. The challenge is that in the vast majority of situations, the task of tying shoelaces is an automatic process in which little focus or concentration is needed. A number of actors will put a great deal of attention and focus into a simple task on-stage or in a movie because they want to "get it right" and this will often appear forced and unrealistic. A simple task rarely demands our attention, unless there are external circumstances, such as a job interview or going out on a date, that dictate otherwise. Having said this, some characters do appear to be bombastic and over the top. To bring a sense of authenticity to a character can be a challenge. In the second part of this activity the attention of the actor is divided by adding a to-do list, which now takes his mind off the tying of the shoelaces. It forces the actor to make the tying of the shoelaces less of a priority, allowing a simple task, which has been made difficult, to become a less important task once again. This activity will help an actor have a clearer understanding of the focus of attention.

Industry Connection
I am going to go out on a limb now and say that many human beings are somewhat lazy. By that I mean that if there is a shorter way of doing something, or a quicker way, we will generally choose it. An actor who attaches too much importance to a simple task, without justification, will also most likely be exerting

too much energy. In the second part of this activity the actor has too much to do to exert all his energy into the tying of the shoelaces, and therefore has to use the principles of economy of effort and economy of movement. This activity will also help the actor to relate to situations in his everyday life when most of us are constantly looking for ways to save time and work more efficiently. Actors will want to find a way to make life their audience. I remember, years ago, hearing an industry coach talk about the resumé. He said that some actors would waste their time updating their resumé on an almost weekly basis. He said this was redundant and a time waster, but it made them feel as if they were "doing something." Encourage your actors to use their time wisely.

Chapter 9
Imagination

69. Create a Space

Split your actors up into groups of about three to five. I prefer to have no more than six groups, so adjust the group sizes accordingly. The main reason for this is so that you have enough time at the end to watch the performances. Have the groups sit down and explain in the following way:

INSTRUCTOR: In a moment I would like each group to create a scene of three to five minutes in length from a space in time. Whatever time period you choose should be outside of the present, at least twenty years prior. Some examples are:

A family sitting around the radio — 1950s America/England

Children in a workhouse — eighteenth century England

Man hunting the wooly mammoth with spears — prehistoric

First man on the moon — 1960s

American Revolutionary War — 1776

I am going to have half of you come up with your own scenarios. The other half I am going to give a topic. The scenes should be somewhat specific rather than "a group of people walking down the street." The scene can be with or without dialogue. Each group will be allowed twenty to thirty minutes and then we will watch the performances.

Remember that time is limited so you are going to have to work very fast. Within five minutes you should be up and moving.

It is very important that the students get moving on this exercise very quickly. You may need to walk around from group to group and nudge them along if necessary. It is OK to help them with ideas and brainstorming if they need it.

Purpose

To utilize a full imagination

In order to work this exercise to capacity, the actors are going to have to use their vivid imagination. As Michael Checkhov says, "The task for the actor is to become an active participant in the process of the imagination rather than just a passive dreamer, to bring the world of the imagination on to stage and give it life."[19] They are going to have to create a scene and then create a moment in time. If they are really using their imagination to its fullest, they will know that people probably sat differently, walked differently, and talked differently from how we do today. This exercise also calls for adaptation on the part of the actors. How are they going to adapt to a different place in time? Everything was different from today. For instance, if they set their scene in 1970, it would be interesting to know that the first cell phone was invented in 1973. In other words, their scene could not involve walking around with a cell phone in hand. Their scene will either be authentic or they will have us laughing for all the wrong reasons. The fact that the actors have time constraints also adds another challenge for them to deal with. Some actors are professional and yet there are never any surprises in their performance.

---

19. Alison Hodge, *Twentieth Century Actor Training* (New York: Routledge, 2000),87.

We have all heard the saying "think outside the box." Some people attempt to "live outside the box." The actor must learn to go beyond both of these. In the actors' world "there is no box." An actor will want to learn to live on the precipice of life.

Industry Connection

Some groups were asked to create their own scenarios and others were given them. If an actor is on a set, some directors will literally show them exactly what they want and physically map out the actions for them. The majority of directors may set the general blocking, but will be pretty hands-off. This means that the actors will have to come up with a lot of their own actions and movement, and their imagination will have to be at its fullest. They will have to be able to live with a profound sense of wonder and discovery. They will also want to have an insatiable curiosity. There are many movies set in different periods in history. The challenge for the actors is if they have just been to McDonald's and Starbucks, then minutes later they are playing an eighteenth century farmer tilling the soil. Or three minutes before they were on the Internet, and now they are a child in a school room writing with chalk and slate. This is so much easier said than done, so how an actor prepares is going to reflect in the end results. In regards to history and acting, author Jane Goodall explains, "During the Renaissance, the actor was a paradoxical figure in social hierarchy. Someone of low birth might make their name playing monarchs and emperors."[20] Brecht talks about the idea that the actor will want to study the history of the past as well as the history of the present. When actors show an audience something from the past that they can relate to today, that is powerful.

Note

When a director is directing a period piece he is often looking for a degree of historical accuracy. If the movie is set in a period before photography, the director may look for pictures painted by artists of the time for historical accuracy.

70. Build Up

Have all your actors find a space in the room and explain in the following way:
INSTRUCTOR: I would like you to start off by walking around the room without talking. Keep walking around the room in any direction you choose. At some point, I will call one of your names out loud, Denise! At this point, Denise will leap in the air and land with her body, hands, arms, and legs in some unusual or contorted position of sorts. It is up to the rest of you to individually decide what you think she is and then add yourself to the scene in some way to complement Denise's creation. For instance, you might think Denise looks like an oak tree, so you decide to become a branch. The person next to you thinks she looks like a tiger and he decides to become a dead deer she has caught. There is no discussion, so you do not have to agree as a group as to what she is. At any moment I might ask any one of you what your contribution to the scene is. I might ask you, "What do you think the first person has become?" When

---

20. Jane Goodall, *Stage Presence* (New York: Routledge, 2008), 52.

everyone is part of the scene, I will ask you to walk around the room again until I call out another name and the process is repeated.

After the first round you may want to choose one of the actors to call the names instead of you. The more the actors are asked to take responsibility and control for what is happening around them, the better.

Purpose

To develop a loose and fluid imagination

Everyone involved in this exercise needs a vivid and loose imagination. J.R.R. Tolkien, who wrote *The Lord of the Rings,* had a vivid imagination and created characters who already had fully realized worlds. When the actor leaps through the air, he can do one of two things: he can let his imagination go wild and land in a contorted position, or he can hold everything back and land in a rather conservative and dull position. Some actors on-stage choose the latter in terms of their characters' choices. They do everything in a formulaic fashion, waiting for their turn to say the line. The performance becomes safe, wooden, and uninspiring to the audience. The actor with the loose imagination keeps most of the control, but allows his loose imagination to take him that little bit into the unknown in each performance. It is in the unknown when some of the most amazing things can happen.

Industry Connection

In this exercise everybody participates, but everybody has to make their own decision as to how they will fit into the scene. It is the same as an acting career. Actors may be in class with many other actors and there may be camaraderie of sorts. When they walk out of that classroom, it is everyone for themselves. In fact, even in the class some of the actors may be vying for the teacher's attention. Perhaps the teacher knows a particular agent or can introduce them to a casting director or two. You may feel this is a negative view. I would prefer to call it a more realistic and pragmatic view. There will certainly be times when each actor feels like he is part of an ensemble, but as far as his acting career goes, he will have to focus on himself. Two movie stars can be in the same film and not shoot one scene together for the first two months of filming.

Explain the following to your actors:

INSTRUCTOR: Each actor has to build a team around him. He cannot do it all by himself. His team will include people such as his agent, manager, lawyer, makeup artist, hairstylist, publicist, and so on. He may say that this team is part of an ensemble. This is true, except for one small adjustment. This ensemble has one goal in mind and that is you, the actor! This ensemble is designed to get you work, and no one else. It virtually takes a whole village to build an actor's career. The world of acting is a collaborative medium. Ultimately, your acting career has to be about you, or you won't have an acting career.

Note

It takes a village in terms of the crew for certain movies. Certain movies will require an enormous art department to design the set. Some movies require the building of towns. Each director will want to form the team he wants to work with. He will want a team that knows what they want and how to get the job done efficiently and effectively.

71. Slideshow

This is another exercise that is very popular in improvisation workshops. Have your actors sit in the audience and call up five actors to the performance area. Explain this exercise in the following fashion:

INSTRUCTOR: Mark, I want you to imagine that you are showing a slideshow of your vacation last year. Your vacation could have been in England, France, Spain, or perhaps you took a European tour. It is up to you to decide. What you are going to do is talk us through each slide. Instead of the slides coming up on the projector, Elaine, Trista, Daniel, and Marcus are going to act out the slides. Let's say that Mark says, "Here's one of me in a French café." The four of you will quickly have to create a freeze-frame photo of the French café Mark was in. Remember, he said, "Here's one of me," which means Mark has to appear somewhere in that photo. If he says, "Here's one I took," then obviously he is not in that picture. These are not talking pictures but frozen, still photos. Mark, make sure you give enough time in between each slide for the actors to create each scene. As soon as you hear Mark talk about another slide, you four should go about creating it. You may not always have a chance to confer together. The key to this exercise is to work with speed and to take action.

If possible, dim the lights and just light up the stage area. This will give the audience the impression that they are watching a slideshow. The slideshow can also come from audience suggestions and does not have to do with a vacation. The show could be work related, hobby related, or anything else they come up with. You can also vary the number of actors you include in the sideshow.

Purpose

To think fast and react fast

For this exercise the actors have to think fast and react fast. They have to have a vivid imagination. Part of the reason is that there is no time to have a group discussion to work out what they want to do. They just have to put their best foot forward and do it. Unlike in film, there are no second takes in theatre. If something goes wrong, or an actor forgets a line, he cannot ask for a do over. Actors have to be able to think on their feet and respond in the moment. They have to continue as if whatever just happened, or did not happen, was part of the scene. They will want to feel their way through the scene. Tension, fear, and inexperience may stop the actor from being able to do so. After almost forty-five years in the theatre, Laurence Olivier developed stage fright. A talented actor can bring that fear into an energy of creativity. It can be a thrillingly frightening experience. Preparation isn't always for what will happen, but also for what can happen.

Industry Connection

In a way, the actors are working with other actors in this exercise, but in a way each one is working alone. There is not really time for a discussion, so each actor has to adapt very quickly to whomever gets each slide moving first. If an actor moves to an acting hub, he will be surrounded by thousands of other actors. They may take class together, live together, workout together, and socialize with other actors. It may feel like they are really all in this together. This may be true up to a point, but after that point each actor is on his own.

Make the following points to your actors:

INSTRUCTOR: When you go to an audition, it is you they are going to see. When you are cast in a day-player role, it is your head on the chopping board. When you meet with a top agent, it is up to you to sell yourself. Friendships and companionships are important, but they will not get you the part. I am not saying you should not have them. I am saying that for the actor, the buck will always stop with you, and no one else!

Note

I always make time for questions and clarification of an exercise. However, I only ever allow three questions. This is not out of any malice. It is because otherwise you might get stuck with thirty questions. Many of the questions are redundant and can be answered by the actor if he takes a moment to think it through. Also, an exercise is often more valuable when the actors are not one hundred percent familiar with every aspect. If mistakes are made, the actors receive a visceral response from which they can learn. They will learn more from the things that don't work out than the things that do. The other reason is that some actors simply love to hear themselves talk, but they have not learned to ask a proper question. If after working the exercise for a while and further clarification is needed, then this is the point at which further questions can be asked.

72. Stop the Press

Explain in the following manner:

INSTRUCTOR: In a moment, one of you is going to be sent out of the room. While you are outside, I am going to bring up seven reporters to the stage. The audience is going to choose a famous person in history, whom the person leaving the room is going to be. The only challenge is that the person out of the room is the only person who does not know who they are. When the person comes back into the room, they are going to give a press conference. In this exercise the actor who does not know their identity has two objectives: give a convincing press conference and try to figure out who you are. The reporters can help out by asking questions that give subtle hints. For example, if you were Ghandi, a question might be, "What was it like starting out your career as a lawyer?" This is a vague clue and the information may not be known by many people. Later on, the clues can get much bigger. Big clues would be, "What was it like to defeat the British?" "How did you survive your hunger strikes?" Another part of this exercise is to see if the actor can let us know that they know who they are without actually mentioning the historical person's name. For instance, the actor may say, "I was pleased to help India gain its independence from the British." This adds an extra challenge to the exercise. It is also important that the reporters are aggressive, though not violently, in trying to get their questions answered.

Purpose

To look for clues in the script

In this exercise, the clues are in questions asked by the reporters. An actor will want to keep searching and asking bigger questions. In a play or movie script the clues are also in the material. It is up to the actors to be detectives and find as much information as possible that is given to them by the author. The actors will want to investigate their characters. They will want to have a curiosity that is incredible. Sometimes, almost every question they have can be answered. It is in the material in front of them, if they take the time to go through it thoroughly. However, this is not always the case. If they are a day-player on a series, they may only have one line: *VENDOR: How's it going, Jim?* This might be all the information they are given. If this is the case, then it is up to the actor to develop his own character. He can do this by using his vivid imagination. If not, then we will most likely witness a one-dimensional performance. Sue Jennings, PhD., lives in England and is a state-registered drama therapist. She told me the following about an Embodiment-Projection-Role exercise for approaching texts:

> Embodiment-Projection-Role (EPR) is a tool to access developmental stages when approaching texts. Too often the actor plunges "every which way."
>
> Stage 1: Embodiment — <even before reading the text <physicalise> in an exaggerated way your ideas, thoughts, and fantasies about your character and its context; move in a "stream of consciousness" way with no plans and no expectations.> Just *move!* Then read the text and move again to express any impact as a whole.
>
> Stage 2: Projection — with text and marker, read the text through and highlight your own part; make notes in the margins of any ideas that come to you; use another color to mark anything that shows where you influence the situation or another character. Be aware of what is going on in your head as you are doing this. If it feels stuck, return to Stage 1 and free-flow movement of the character
>
> Stage 3: Role — having <physicalised> (E) and analyzed (P) the text and your role within it, walk around the room without the text and improvise your scenes through body and voice. Return to the text and read your lines out loud and play with different vocal textures. Finally, integrate what you have learned through EPR and be ready for rehearsal.

Industry Connection

One important part of this exercise is that the reporters have to make themselves heard. They have to put themselves out there and vie for space to get their questions heard. If an actor is going to have an acting career, then he is going to have to operate in much the same way. He will have to continue to put himself out there and continue to be heard. He may say, "I don't want to be pushy or aggressive." Aggressive does not mean being violent, it means letting people know that you exist. It is reminding casting agents, directors, and producers that you are here for the long haul, and that you are not going anywhere else.

Note

When you are explaining these exercises, don't cut corners. You may have used an exercise a thousand times. There is a tendency to sometimes skip over what you consider to be obvious. It may be obvious to you, but to the actor who has never seen the exercise before it may not. Don't miss any details that are necessary for the exercise to be worked fully. You may choose not to tell the actors everything, and this is fine. This sometimes works well, as it allows the actors to make their own discoveries. Actors will want to develop the serendipitous side of their instrument. Some instructors never tell their actors why they are doing an exercise. Some instructors do not know why they are giving an exercise!

73. Inner Circle

For this exercise have all your actors form a circle. They should stand shoulder to shoulder so that they are very close together. Have one of the actors stay outside the circle. His job is to try to get into the center circle. He can do this in any way possible, except that he cannot use any physical force. Some examples of how he may attempt to get into the center are:

1. He may attempt to talk his way in, by persuading one of the actors to let him in.
2. He might tickle someone under the arm making her laugh. This might momentarily break the circle.
3. He might steal his way in when another actor momentarily lapses in her concentration.

Once the actor has made it to the center, you can have another actor take his place on the outside of the circle. The actor in the middle now becomes part of the circle. A new rule should be added at this point. The new actor cannot use the same method as another actor to get into the center. This means, that if the first actor tickled his way into the center, no other actor can use this approach. If actors are finding it too easy to get into the center, the group will have to problem solve. Finish off with a group discussion.

Purpose

To find what works

Make the following observations with your actors:

INSTRUCTOR: When you are playing a part, you may not find all the answers you are looking for straight away. You may not be able to find the meat and bones of the character. You may become frustrated. You may be angry. But if you persevere, you will be able to come up with some of the answers. You have to be willing to put in the time and effort it takes to make these discoveries. In this exercise you have to keep going until you find what works. When playing a character, you have to approach it in the same way. Unfortunately, some actors settle for mediocrity because they refuse to do the work needed. Good actors are prepared actors.

Industry Connection

The number of working actors in Hollywood is considered to be within a three to five percent range at any given time. If you talk to these actors, they will often tell you that there is almost an inner circle in Hollywood. In this circle are the same actors, directors, casting agents, producers, managers, and so on. These are the people who are getting most of the work in Hollywood. These people are in the inner circle. Actors in this circle know about an audition way before the majority. By the time others hear about an audition, it is likely that the role has already been cast. The casting directors in the inner circle get to know the actors who are in the inner circle. They see them audition again and again, and they become familiar with them. They may start to cast them because over time they have come to know them and their work. In this exercise actors have to find a way into the circle. In Hollywood, they literally have to do the same! Some actors spend all their time dwelling on what they consider to be unfair. Advise your actors not to waste their time dwelling on what they believe is "unfair." It is far better for them to put their energy towards what works for their career rather than what does not.

74. If the Shoe Fits, Wear It!

You are going to need some sort of blindfold for this exercise. Instruct your actors to sit in a circle and explain in the following way:

INSTRUCTOR: I would like everyone to take off their left shoe and put it in the center of the circle. I am going to ask Billie to help me with this exercise. In a moment, I am going to put a blindfold on Billie. I am then going to pick up a shoe from the center of the room. I will hand it to Billie, who is then going to have one minute to describe the person who owns that shoe. In order to do this, she is going to have to feel the shoe for clues. Billie, I am going to ask you not to put your hands inside the shoe, for obvious reasons. She is going to have to feel the size, the contours, and the shape. When the minute is up, Billie is going to be asked to name the person she thinks owns the shoe. What are some assumptions Billie might make based on a shoe?

NICOLE: If it feels like a sports shoe, she might guess that the owner is some type of athlete.

INSTRUCTOR: Very good. What else?

DAVID: If it feels like a small shoe she will probably think it belongs to a girl.

INSTRUCTOR: That is true, although it is not necessarily going to be the correct answer. What else?

PILA: If it is dirty, it is probably someone who is scruffy.

INSTRUCTOR: Yes, it is funny, but it is also a profound statement. If she feels mud, that might be a big clue. What Pila is saying is that the shoe is going to give some hints as to the personality of its owner. That is pretty powerful information to have. Billie, I want you to do your thinking aloud. When you make a discovery based on the shoe, I want you to share it with the group. It will be interesting for the rest of us because by looking at the shoe, we will know who the real owner is. Once Billie has had a go, we will change to another member of the group. I need everyone to focus very hard for this exercise. Please do not talk or react in a way that is going to give Billie any information.

Once a shoe has been taken out of the circle it does not go back in the middle. Once it has been identified, it should go back to its owner. The actors love this exercise, but it only works well when the group allows the shoe holder to really focus. How much the actors can tell just from holding a shoe can turn out to be quite surprising.

Purpose

To heighten the imagination

The purpose of this exercise is for the actors to heighten their vivid imaginations and not to put a fence around it. Actors will want to reserve the right to think for themselves. Even by holding an object such as a shoe, numerous pictures and images begin to flood their minds. Perhaps they do not know who owns the shoe, but this should not stop them from fully exploring their imagination. It is the actors' job to create and tell stories. They have to know how to create something from nothing. How can the actors create without a vivid imagination? The answer is *with great difficulty*. Without a vivid imagination, the best an actor can do is imitate others and use superficial gestures. This exercise constitutes one step towards helping your actors to develop a vivid imagination.

Industry Connection

When the actors attempt to name the shoe's owner, they have to fully commit. They may be wrong, but they have to believe they are right. If they think this exercise is impossible, then they are right. If they fully commit, they have just increased their odds. There is no logical reason that an individual should believe he will have an acting career. I do not mean this to be negative, but to be pragmatic. The statistics tell us that they probably have about a one-in-twenty-five chance of finding some level of success. This is the ratio of those who actually move to an acting hub. If this is the case, then why should they believe it is possible? The question can be reversed if the actor asks himself, "Why shouldn't I be that person who is the 'one-in-twenty-five'?" The answer is that there is no reason why he should not. Every actor is looking for the opportunity to shine his light. If the actor is willing to continue to work hard and press on towards his goals, there is no reason why he cannot achieve them. It is giving up before he has really begun that stops many actors.

75. The Unspoken Word

This exercise works best when you and your students are working on a play. What you are going to do is ask each character in the play to write a letter to another character. If you can, choose your recipient from among those characters who seem to have the biggest impact on each other in the play. It may not be possible for everyone to be partnered in this way. You can let the students choose who they want to write to, or you can divide the group evenly. It is important to make sure that everyone is sending and receiving a letter, including those in the stage crew if you have students in that role. For this exercise, you can either allow them to choose or you can allocate them a character from the play. The letter could be on a topic that relates to the play. It could be a love letter, a letter of complaint, or a thank-you letter. It can be anything that the students feel they can justify in terms of their characters' relationships to the other characters. It does not have to be material that is included in the play. It is great to let the students' imaginations run free. Give the students thirty to forty minutes to write their letters. You might choose to tell them a week before so that they have time to think about their letter. Or you might prefer to have them write it on the spur of the moment.

There are a few options as to what to do when the letters are finished. You can collect them and have the students read them aloud next period. A neat way of doing this is to have the character the letter is written to sit in a chair, on the stage, as the letter is being read. Tell both the reader and the receiver to stay in character throughout. Another option is to have each student address an envelope with the actual address of the person portraying the character it is written about. If you do this, you will have to cover the cost of stamps. You should also obtain the students' permission to distribute their private addresses. It takes the exercise to another level when the students receive the letters in the post. Instruct them to put the character's name on the envelope. Another option is for students to simply hand the letters over to each other, without reading them aloud. Follow up with a class discussion. Allow the students to share their discoveries from the exercise.

Variation

Nowadays, we have the opportunity to take advantage of technology in ways that were not available in the past. A good way to continue this exercise is to have the students email, text, or IM each other back and forth, in character, for a week. If you choose to do this, follow up with a discussion and feedback. In conversation with artistic director Paul Gleason, he told me, "I ran into a colleague the other day whose profession is teaching people how to make movies with their cell phone. With all the advanced technology, the market for film has expanded ten-fold. There are also many more networks and cable channels that have expanded the demand and variety of programs being made. Of course, this has translated into more work for the actor." It is also good news for scriptwriters with so many cable channels needing new material. It is not enough for the actors to be aware of technology, they have to embrace it.

Purpose

To understand relationships between characters

By having the characters write letters they learn something about the other character that perhaps they had not thought of before. What is even more powerful is that they may also learn something about themselves. Actors will want to be able to take their characters places they haven't been yet. The reason you ask the characters to write letters is because sometimes we can say in writing what we would never mention face to face. After this assignment, actors will say things like, "I didn't know that about my character," "I never knew she felt that way," or "Now I understand why my character has always felt so cheated." If you were doing the play *The Crucible,* you could have Abigail Williams and John Proctor write letters to one another. I am sure they would have a lot of questions to ask each other. The impact of this exercise is not always immediate and will sometimes sink in weeks into the rehearsal process.

Industry Connection

This exercise highlights the importance of different forms of communication. The spoken word is powerful, but it is not our only means of communication. Actors seeking a career are going to have to use many forms of communication. They are going to need experience and exposure if they wish to thrive. They will mail their resumé to a potential agent. They will send personal thank-you cards to directors, casting directors, and producers. They will go to networking parties where they can introduce themselves in person. They need to know how to work the system. They will communicate through the power of the Internet. They will use email, Facebook, text messages, personal websites, blogs, and Twitter to name just a few possibilities. Today's actors have to be open to many means of communication if they want a chance to compete at the highest levels.

76. Skills

This exercise is a variation of Alphabet Soup as seen in *112 Acting Games*. This exercise works best with twenty or more students. You also need plenty of space and a piece of paper and a pencil to keep score for this exercise. Have your students take off their shoes and put them out of the way. To start with, have the students separate into teams of four to six. Designate a generous space for each group and ask them to sit down as a team while you explain the rules. To begin with, you will call out a shape and ask the teams to form that shape using their bodies. They must be lying on the floor, and everyone on the team must be used to contribute towards each shape. For example, you may call out, "circle." Each group must form a circle. The first team to complete the shape gets a point. This game is fast-paced, so do not give them too much time between shapes. After a few rounds you are going to want to take it up a notch or two. Instead of calling out shapes you are now going to call out anything you want. Some examples are: chicken, tree, box, chair, car.

A word of warning: It is very hard for you, the judge, to find out who won each point, so you must be assertive and make your decision final. Sometimes you may find there is a tie between three teams. In this case, you can give a point to all three teams. Make sure you stress that this is for fun, because students may get upset if they don't win a round. Be careful what you call out, because you are going to have to judge it. If you call out something that is too subjective, no team will be able to form the shape. Remember, it is the first team to complete their task that gets the point, not the first team to say they have finished!

Purpose

To stretch the senses

The students are required to stretch their senses. The students need to feel where the other students are so as to form the shape correctly so the sense of touch is engaged. They need to see where their teammates are placed and that they are all where they should be. They have to listen to know what to create and to communicate well within the team.

Actors are constantly involved in listening moments. This can happen on- and off-stage. A director might be giving notes after a rehearsal. If some of the actors are not listening properly, they might miss the notes or misinterpret them. Directors hate having to unnecessarily give the same notes twice, so listening skills are imperative. It is only when we delve further we realize that things we take for granted are an absolute necessity for the actor. In the same way that a surgeon has to keep his skills up-to-date, the actor has to continually keep his instrument sharpened.

Industry Connection

At times the groups are going to be asked to form a shape that they think is impossible. Two groups may give up, one group might not quite get there, and the last group might find a way. They found a way because they chose not to give up. An actor may have an audition at midday. His agent may text him at the last minute and say, "You have another audition on the other side of town at two p.m." The actor may choose not to do it, because he thinks it might be impossible to get there. If he had gone to both auditions, the second one may have been the one that actually gave him the job. If he were running late, he could phone or show up and give his apologies. He could say he was at another audition. This is an explanation that everyone in the business understands, even if they don't always like it. The worst thing actors can say is, "No. There isn't enough time." The actor who can perform the impossible is the actor who has potential. The actor who is never searching for anything will never find it.

Note

Sometimes there is an integration between film and theatre directors. It has been observed that some directors are able to create a film sensibility on the stage. This may come in part through the subtly, economy of effort, specific areas of focus and concentration, lighting, and cutting of scenes.

77. Imagination Station

This activity has been adapted from my book, *Acting Games for Individual Performers,* in order to be used for group work. Have the students sit as the audience. Bring two actors into the performance space. Explain in the following way:

INSTRUCTOR: This is a fairly well-known activity that I think you are going to enjoy. I am going to give you a delightful opportunity to discover your imagination. What I would like the two of you to do is stand side by side, but about two feet apart from each other. At this point, I would like you both to close your eyes. I would like you to hold your arms out in front of you and imagine you have an empty bucket in one hand and the other hand is holding one hundred helium-filled balloons. I would like you to imagine that water is beginning to pour into the bucket. Now I would like you to see and hear the water pouring in. Perhaps you feel the water as it splashes gently against your skin. Feel the bucket getting heavier and heavier. You now discover, to your surprise, that you have an ever-increasing number of helium balloons. See them, hear them gently bumping into one another, and feel them as they slowly begin to pull your hand up, up, and up. Now, notice that the bucket is getting fuller and heavier and someone has recently added a heavy weight to your bucket. You realize that your arm is getting heavier and heavier and there is a sensation of pulling on your hand. Now, bring your attention back to the hand with the helium balloons. You realize that it feels lighter and lighter, as the number of helium-filled balloons continues to increase. When you feel ready, keep your arms where they are and open your eyes. Notice how much your arms have moved since the beginning of the exercise. Do you see that the imagination is the language of the subconscious? It is also worth noting that the mind thinks in pictures and images. As an actor, it is important to have some understanding of how your mind works in real terms.

When you have finished, review your findings for this activity. Follow up with a group discussion before calling on other actors to participate. If you like, you can ask four students to come up instead of the original two.

Possible discussion questions could be:

Did you find that your arms had moved?

Were you surprised at the extent that this had happened?

Is it really beneficial for an actor to have an understanding of the language of the subconscious?

Purpose

To experience the imagination's effect on the subconscious

The actors are most likely going to find that one arm has raised higher and the other arm has sunk lower. It is interesting to note that at no time were they asked to raise or lower their arms, and yet this is what has happened. By using their imagination, they have caused a physical response in their body. We could also say that they have influenced their subconscious by exploring their imagination. The subconscious is a powerful part of human nature and has an influence on pretty much everything we do. Imagination is the ally of the actor and can take acting to a whole new realm. In *Giant Steps,* Anthony Robbins quotes Einstein as saying, "Imagination is more powerful than knowledge."[21] I like the fact that actors get to experience the power of their imagination firsthand. Often they will not be on location, but on a studio set, a theatre stage, or in front of a green screen. They are going to need all the imagination they can muster to convince us they are in a castle instead of on stage twenty-two. Later on, computer generated characters may be added to the mix. Good directors are always looking for ways to keep the movie experience alive. They have a vision. They want to pry open Pandora's box. They will want to come into a picture better prepared than anyone else. They create their own method of directing. It is very important that your actors can connect with the bigger picture of both their acting and their career.

Industry Connection

In a way, this exercise is an optical illusion. The actors don't have a bucket. There is nothing heavy or light in their hands and yet there does appear to be something happening. The film industry is a wonder of optical illusions. In the 1970s, Hollywood brought us battles in space with movies like the *Star Wars* series. These movies captured the imaginations of millions all over the world. As we all know, special effects are built mainly on optical illusions that create realities through our imaginations. We are continually breaking into new frontiers in technology. Movies like *Avatar* by James Cameron and *Alice in Wonderland* with Johnny Depp have raised a higher bar in regards to 3D technology and filmmaking. Dbox has also taken a huge leap in the integration of movies and technology by creating motion seats. It is where the computer visuals become integrated with the visuals that are taking place on the screen. This may mean that as a gunshot goes off on the screen or as there is thunder, the seat will shake and move accordingly. It has been integrated into a number of movies including *The Book of Eli* with Denzel Washington, *Terminator: Salvation,* and *Sherlock Holmes* with Jude Law and Robert Downey Jr. I interviewed an usher at a local theatre in regards to motion seating. The usher told me, "Motion seating is really great in a good action flick. I am not sure if it is worthwhile for a slow drama or comedy." Both 3D and Dbox technology are enabling the audience to receive enhanced sensory connections to the movies they are experiencing. An actor who is interested in being in the movies has to believe in optical illusions. It is also worth pointing out that special effects alone are rarely ever enough. Without a good story, good actors, good cinematography, the right casting, a good

---

21. Anthony Robbins, *Giant Steps* (New York: Simon and Schuster, 1994), 96.

director, etc., a blockbuster movie full of special effects will be considered a bit of fun, lame, or entertaining at best.

A-list actors will receive numerous scripts every day and say no to almost all of them. They get to pick and choose what they want to do. Sometimes they will receive a script that they are immediately intrigued by. It is an entirely visceral reaction to the words on the page. When a script comes from a studio they will take it seriously because they know it is going to be distributed. Before taking on a project they will often want to meet with the director first to understand his vision. Some actors will turn nothing down with the premise that an actor has to keep working. They believe they will regret what they say no to and not what they agree to. Some actors are so prolific they go beyond famous. They create empires for themselves and become a global brand. These actors achieve a certain power that very few actors will ever reach. Some of these stars become exploited stars. There are actors and then there are movie stars. Sometimes the two are able to blend together. A number of A-list actors are happy when the bubble finally bursts. They are able to press the reset button on their careers. It means that they have something to climb up to once again.

Note

Actors may make an independent movie that they really believe in. It's hard to get leverage when they are competing against blockbusters with multimillion dollar budgets. The lower budget movies need to create a buzz about them in order to find a place in the cinema and receive wide distribution. They cannot rely on special effects to bring in the audience. They are going to have to be good movies that can stand their ground on their own merits.

Chapter 10
Creative State

78. Random Thoughts

For this exercise bring up one actor from the audience and explain in the following way:

INSTRUCTOR: Cynthia, come and help me with this exercise. What I would like you to do is start listing off random words. The only catch is that they may have nothing to do with each other. If the words form some sort of association, then you are out. So, for example if you said, "grass, cow, milk," you would be out. The object is to keep the words as random as possible. The other rules are that: you cannot pause, you cannot speak at a slow pace, and you cannot say "umm" or "err." Before you begin, take a moment to get focused. You might do this by looking down for a moment or two or closing your eyes. Do whatever is necessary for you to have your concentration primed.

RICK: How does someone become the winner?

INSTRUCTOR: Good question, Rick. It is the student who says the largest number of random thoughts who wins. There is also a maximum time limit of one minute to name as many as you can.

If you have three students who name the same number, then perhaps you can have a knockout round. Do not forget to commend your students for lasting twenty, thirty, or forty seconds. The most important part of this exercise is to see how many random thoughts the actors can come up with and not who is the winner. Choose another actor who is going to count the number of random thoughts. You can probably work through your entire group with this exercise. The actor with the highest number of random thoughts wins. The actors should begin to make the transition of the next thought before they finish the previous one. Finish off with a group discussion.

Purpose
To focus specifically

If the actors do not use a specific form of focus, then they will not last fifteen seconds in this exercise. The specific focus lies in understanding the objective of the exercise. To be able to not start making any associations, they are going to have to start the exercise having programmed themselves for it. In order to be able to do that, they are going to have to go into their own toolbox and pull out the required tools. Novice actors may not have these tools available yet. If they do, it might be part of their natural abilities. Some actors will be stronger in some areas and others somewhere else. To really develop as actors you are going to have to guide your students in developing every part of their instrument. Film and theatre both require a different concentration. One is equally important to the other.

Industry Connection

Have the following or a similar discussion with your actors:

INSTRUCTOR: Sometimes, when you read a script, you may be forgiven for thinking that everything that comes out of your character's mouth is planned and predictable. If it is a poorly written script, then this may well be the case. It is not the fault of the character, it is the fault of the writer. However, it is you the actor who will have to attempt to salvage the situation. People often think in random thoughts, and so do your characters. Some things we say are calculated and planned, but many of the things we say, think, and feel are motivated by the circumstances of that precise moment. This is why actors are always told to "act and react." You might plan what you want to say, but suddenly a new thought, a new image crosses your mind and you totally lose your train of thought. This exercise encourages you to allow your characters to think in a random way and not a predictable and unmotivated one.

Note

Novice actors are sometimes at an advantage in that they can still be quite arrogant in their option of acting. They may so love acting that they are fearless and the fact that acting is difficult does not even cross their thoughts. As they become more seasoned actors they realize that to constantly give fine performances is not easy at all. It requires an actor with a fine-tuned instrument. When an actor arrives on a studio set for the first time he can be forgiven for feeling like he is entering Mr. Willy Wonka's chocolate factory. He is finally being given the key to the gate for the first time. He may discover that he falls totally in love with show business.

79. Catch Me If You Can

Choose two actors who have been working a scene together to come up into the performance space. Explain in the following way:

INSTRUCTOR: What I would like you to do first is to perform your scene for the class. (Actors perform their scene.) I would like you to do the scene again. (This should happen with no side coaching coming from you.) This time, I am going to add an extra element for you to deal with. As you perform your scene, Sarah is going to be moving very fast or running around the room. Neil, you are going to chase her as if you are trying to catch her. Even if you are faster than her I do not want you to actually make physical contact, but you can get very close to her. When I clap my hands, the roles reverse. Neil, you will start moving and running away, and Sarah will become the chaser. Remember that you have to keep going with the dialogue from your scene the entire time. When the scene comes to an end, I would like you to immediately perform your scene one last time for the audience. This time there is no running around the room.

After the third performance, ask the actors if anything felt different between the first and the third performances. Discuss the observations made by the audience. Work with other pairs in a similar way.

Purpose

To change the physical makeup of the scene

By having the actors chase each other around the room, the physical makeup of the scene is changed. The actors will have adrenaline pumping through their bodies like never before. There may even be elements of fear that they have never witnessed in the scene before. When they do their scene for a third time, it may have been changed forever. This is because they now have new reference points from which to begin. The scene may now have changed at a molecular level. It is the actor's responsibility to make sure a scene never becomes stale in performance. This does not mean turning the scene on its head in an unjustified fashion. It means continuing to search for subtle changes that his character can make. This exercise uses extremes to highlight the power of change and adaptability. Acting is a rush that numerous actors become addicted to.

Industry Connection

As the actors are being chased around the room, there may be a sense of fear coursing through their bodies. Actors who are pursuing their acting careers may also have to face their fears. They may have fear of successes or fear of failures and rejection. The amount of rejection they take can be a constant bombardment to their ego. They may fear the struggles that an actor has to go through, both emotionally and financially. As actors, they are going to have to learn to face their fears. If they can face their fears, then they can conquer them. For some, acting becomes their alter ego.

80. Compounding the Stakes

Have your actors form a line across the room. Have the first actor, on the far left, step forward and tell the group what object he is and what function he has. An example would be, "I am a plastic lid that closes lunch boxes."

The next person in line steps forward and comes up with a similar object with a similar function. The difference is that, as each actor comes forward, he continues to raise the stakes.

For example:
ACTOR 1: I am a plastic lid that closes lunch boxes.
ACTOR 2: I am a door that closes ovens.
ACTOR 3: I am a door that shuts off the room.
ACTOR 4: I am the boss who closes the factory.
ACTOR 5: I am the moon that shuts out the sunlight.

You do not necessarily have to go down the whole line, but can stop when you feel it is necessary. The next actor can start a new object and a new function. Remind the actors that the stakes will want to be raised gradually, from one actor to the next. There is no rush to go from one actor to the next. Allow the actors time to think about their connection. It is also important that the actors continue through the line established by the actor who began the round.

Purpose
To be free from constraints

To do well in this exercise, the actors have to be free from constraints. They have to be able to stay open to anything. If an actor is standing in the line, he has no idea what the person next to him is going to say. He has to be able to respond at a moment's notice. He can only do this if he allows himself to be open. In a play, actors already know their character's next line. The challenge is their character does not. They do not know exactly what they are going to say until they say it. If the actor has done enough preparation, something spontaneous might happen. Different colors, nuances, and images have the potential to arrive. It is that openness to spontaneity that will allow their characters to stay fresh and alive.

Industry Connection

In this exercise the actors have to continue to raise the stakes. In a particular scene, the stakes might be so high that a character's life is on the line. There are a number of movies where a character is in a shoot-out with the villain. The challenge is that there is nothing in the actor's face, body language, or actions that register any grain of fear. You may say this is because he is thoroughly into his character. While this is possible, I am referring to the actors who have not bothered to raise the stakes. The reality is that the film is being shot on the studio set with blanks in the guns. There is a minimal chance of any injury. I can think of a very famous movie where a shoot-out scene is almost farcical in its execution. They are choosing to play their own reality, rather than that of the character's.

81. Murder Incorporated

This is an amazing exercise that I have seen played with a number of variations. For this activity, you are going to need a pack of cards. Separate the cards so that you have one ace and one king. You will also want to have enough cards numbered between two and nine to allocate cards for the rest of the class. If you have twenty students you will want to have a total of twenty cards. Tell the students to sit in a circle on the floor. Sometimes students will say they don't want to sit on the floor because it will make their clothes dirty. It is up to you to remind them to wear sensible clothing for the class. I am not talking about medical conditions, which is a different matter.

At this point, go around the circle and hand each student a card with its face down, so that no one is looking at his card. Once everyone has a card, tell them they may now secretly look at it. It is important that no one else sees their card. The student who got the ace is murder incorporated and the person who got the king is the police officer. Everyone who got a card numbered between two and nine is a civilian. The person who is murder incorporated is going to try to murder everyone. For the rest of the group, the aim of the activity is to stop this from happening.

The exercise starts by going around the circle while everyone in turn has to say they are not murder incorporated. At this point, the students will want to pay attention to body language. They will also want to look for clues as to who is lying and who is telling the truth. Some possible clues are twitching, fidgeting, looking up at the ceiling, smiling, and nervous tremors in their voice. At this point, the group is asked to say who they think is murder incorporated. This is done by people putting forward their views before taking a vote. Whichever individual gets the most votes from the group is accused of being the killer. If the group is right, the activity stops here and another round can be played. If this does not happen, the activity continues.

Tell the whole group to close their eyes and tilt their heads toward the floor. Ask the person who is the killer to carefully open his eyes. Without talking, he is to point at a person he wants to terminate. He then closes his eyes and looks back down again. Now the police officer is asked to open his eyes. He is then asked to point at the person he believes is murder incorporated. If he is right, the activity stops there. If he is wrong, you will indicate to him that he is wrong by shaking your head. At no point should the group know who is either the police officer or the killer.

Have everyone open their eyes and tell the person who was killed that he is now out. He is not allowed to speak from this point on. This time, ask the group to repeat the process. They are going to vote on who they think is the killer. Once they are in agreement, the accused is allowed one minute to defend himself. When the minute is up, the group has to decide if they believe the defendant or not. If they do, then this person is given a reprieve. If not, then they are out, and not able to speak from that point on. If they are in fact murder incorporated, the activity is over. If they are the police officer, the activity is also over, and the killer wins. Without the police officer the group is no longer able to defend itself. If the accused is neither the police officer nor the murder incorporated, then the activity continues with the same protocol as before.

If the killer is discovered or killed first, the civilians win. If the police officer is killed first, the killer wins. If the only person left in is the killer, he is obviously the winner. Although this sounds complicated, in practice it is not. Your students will love it and get the hang of it very quickly. It is important that everyone participates in the correct way. If a student tries to cheat by looking up, it will ruin the activity for everyone else. I usually preface this by saying this activity is not for everyone. It is only for mature actors with a professional attitude. If the game is spoiled by a participant once, give him the benefit of the doubt. If it happens twice, terminate the activity and move on. Always hold your students accountable so that they can grow and learn from their mistakes.

Purpose
To pay attention to detail
The purpose of this exercise is to pay attention to every detail. At the beginning, no one knows who the murder incorporated is. Fairly early on in the exercise the killer is allowed to choose someone he wants to kill. This means that those sitting around him have the potential to sense movement. It does not mean they will know who the killer is, but they may now have a clue to the area in which the killer is located. When everyone has their eyes open, they have the opportunity to read body language. The actors should be able to discover a good deal from the nonverbal communication of others. When actors are playing a role, they should be like a detective. They will want to continue to hunt for clues as to why their character may do the things they do. They should look for clues as to what might form or dictate their relationships with others. If they take a general approach, they will perform in a simple way, but their character may be a lot more complex than they initially thought. They will only make these discoveries if they go looking for them.

Industry Connection
The civilians and the police try to work out who the killer is. They start to accuse people of being the killer. The longer the activity continues, the more they start to build a case. They will find that the only way they will find the killer, apart from sheer luck, is to look for clues and build a case. When actors go to an audition, they may rely on blind luck. This will occasionally work, but not consistently. The actors who continually work are the ones who build a case. They are telling the casting director, "I am the most talented one. I am perfect for the role. I bring the most substance to the role. I am a professional. My performance will bring in money at the box office. Look at my resumé and past

successes. I can play the role any way you like. You would be a fool not to hire me." These things are not spoken verbally, but passed on through their thoughts and their nonverbal communication. It does not mean that they will always get the job. It does mean that, by building a case, they are doing everything in their power to get the job.

Note

This activity involves metaphorical killing and murder. It is not promoting killing or murder in any way. Violence is ingrained in western societies. Teaching students right from wrong is going to be of more benefit than discarding an activity such as this.

82. Falling

This is an exercise that I first saw demonstrated by a colleague of mine a number of years ago. It had such a profound effect on the students that I have used it ever since. All the students in that workshop were professional or aspiring adult actors. Ask your students to take off their shoes and put them out of the way, in a corner of the room. Explain in the following way:

INSTRUCTOR: In a moment I am going to ask you to find a space in the room. I am going to ask you to walk around the room and at some point, I am going to shout out, "Fall!" At this point, I literally want you to do exactly that. You are going to fall to the ground. We have a hard surface on this floor, so you cannot fall immediately to the ground. You need to go to your knees and slide out using your arm. (You will want to demonstrate this to your students. If you cannot find a way to fall safely, do not do this exercise with your students! If you have never trained in stage combat or martial arts, this may be an exercise to avoid for now. You can also put gym mats down on the floor, if you have them. The actors are not falling straight down without any control. There has to be a degree of control in the fall for safety reasons. By instructing them to fall and slide out to the side, they can do it quite safely on a hard surface. They will want to use their arm to slide out to the side. Obviously, if you have a soft surface it is even better.) When you fall to the ground I want you to get back up immediately. At some point I will call, "Fall!" and you will repeat the process. Sometimes there will be a large gap in between falls, but sometimes you will have just gotten up when I call, "Fall!" Please do this exercise without talking. Please keep going until the exercise is ended. If you are hurt, then obviously you will stop. No one should get hurt, provided you do not literally fall straight down. Go to your hips and fall out sideways as I demonstrated. You know your own body, so work with it safely and cautiously.

JANE: How many times do we have to fall?

INSTRUCTOR: You will find out at the end of the exercise.

LINDA: What happens if you fall into someone else?

INSTRUCTOR: That is a very good question. It should not happen, provided you are spatially aware of your surroundings. Make sure you know who is beside you and who is behind you so that you can avoid a collision. Please remember to fall with caution and practice safety first.

You will want your actors to fall at least twenty times for this exercise. This is because you want them to be free of holding patterns in their body. It is up to you over what period of time you spread it out. Sometimes there can be gaps while at other times there should be one fall after the other. Remind the actors that between falls they are to walk around the room. Every time they fall, they must immediately get back up. After the exercise, continue with a group discussion. Instruct the actors to stay where they are in the room for the discussion. This is because the exercise will be more immediate and with gut reaction in this way.

Purpose
To connect the mental to the physical
One of the purposes behind this exercise is for the actors to connect the mental with the physical. Actors can give a gesture that is purely superficial with very little else happening. If a person jumps up and down, it is virtually impossible to avoid a physical reaction. In other words, adrenalin will start pumping around their body and endorphins will be released. It is very hard to get into a physically depressed state while jumping up and down and smiling. The same premise can be used here in the falling exercise. When the actors fall, it will have an immediate effect on their system. The effect may be different from one actor to another. By the end of the exercise, many of the actors have made profound connections between their mental and physical states. Actors are always seeking to form the mind and body connection in their work. They are complementary. You cannot have one without the other.

Industry Connection
This exercise is a great metaphor for the actor. Every time the actors fall, they have to get back up. The first few times they fall it feels a little awkward. They feel unsure of themselves as they stand up again. By the time they have fallen ten or fifteen times, getting back up becomes second nature. From this point, they no longer give it a thought. Getting up becomes an automatic process for the actor. It is exactly the same for the actors' career. The first few times the actors face rejection it is heartbreaking for them. Gradually, they get used to it, to the point at which it is just part of their job description. They are able to quickly brush off rejection and move on. They say things like, "I was not right for the part," "They chose someone who was more suited," "I will get my next part," and "What did I learn from this audition?" This applies to the working actors. The actors who give up before they have even begun take a different approach. They take everything personally. They say things like, "They hated me," "I am never going to get the job," "My life is awful," and "I am the worst actor ever!" These actors constantly fall, but never learn to get back up. They are experts on focusing on what they don't want. The successful actor can take a fall because he knows how to get back up!

83. Tree Hugger
You will need a stereo for this activity. Explain in the following way:

INSTRUCTOR: In a moment I am going to ask you to spread out around the room. Linda, please come and join me for a moment. Linda, you are going to be the tree. This is a green and ozone-friendly activity. When I start the music, I want everyone to start dancing around the room in any way they choose. Linda, you will be a dancing tree. When the music stops, I want everyone to find Linda and hug the tree. The first person to hug the tree will then also become a tree. This means that in the second round there will be two trees from which you can choose. The next round, there will be four trees, then eight, and so on. The aim of the activity is not to be the last person left.

JANE: Are we allowed to dance near a tree?

INSTRUCTOR: You shouldn't be following the trees around the room, but you should certainly be aware of where the trees are.

GEORGE: How do we know who is a tree?

INSTRUCTOR: At the end of each round we will have the trees raise their hands to identify themselves.

Purpose

To create a sense of awareness

When the actors are dancing in the room, they have to be aware of where the trees are dancing. If they do not keep a sense of awareness, they are unlikely to be the first one to hug the trees when the music stops. An actor has to develop a keen sense of awareness. We use our awareness all the time, even if we do not take note of it. Let us say a character in a scene walks into a party. As he enters the room, the conversation seems to change abruptly. He can cut the atmosphere with a knife. The character does not say a word and yet he can sense that everyone has just been talking about him. The audience may know what was said because they saw and heard the previous scene. The character may not have heard what was being said, but he can certainly sense it. The character's realization that something is not quite right has to be transferred to the audience.

Industry Connection

In a fun way, this activity highlights the environment. It reminds us that we can aim to live in balance with nature. It reminds the actors that they can embrace their environment and choose to be a role model. World-famous actors and actresses have sometimes chosen to be role models in their lifetimes. Audrey Hepburn and Angelina Jolie have both been ambassadors of UNICEF. Goldie Hawn helps raise awareness about the challenges facing schools with regard to kids' mental health issues. Paul Newman has donated all the money that comes from Newman's Own to charity. Being a role model does not necessarily make an actor into a better actor. It does not necessarily bring an actor more work. So why should an actor strive to be a role model? Any actor who is constantly in the limelight and has a mass following is some sort of role model. It can be in a detrimental sense or it can be in an empowering way, a way that helps others and the world around them. Each actor will want to define his own destiny and be who he desires to be. Some actors are loved and respected by their fellow actors. Raise this topic with your actors. Ask your actors, "What sort of legacy would you like to leave behind you?"

84. Music Night

There used to be a show when I was growing up in England called *Name That Tune,* and this activity is inspired by that show. The activity is going to take preparation. Ask the students who play portable musical instruments to bring them to class. Ask them to each have three or more popular songs that they can play confidently. It can be any instrument from a recorder to an oboe. Let us say ten students come to class with instruments. Divide the students into two teams.

Divide those with instruments equally between the two teams. A musician from team one is going to play the beginning of a song. It can be the first five, ten, fifteen, or twenty seconds of the song. The other team can choose how much of the song they would like to hear. If they choose five seconds and are then able to guess the name of the song correctly, they will get the maximum points. Allow them to hear the same section up to three times. The group will want to confer, but should designate a group leader who will share their guess. The first guess they make is the one that counts.

How the scoring is done:

5 seconds = 5 points
10 seconds = 3 points
15 seconds = 2 points
20 seconds = 1 point

The teams will take it in turns to play the game. Team one will send up a musician and team two will guess, then vice versa. Change the musicians each round. Once each musician has gone, they can start again.

Here are some important points to add: Those playing the instruments have to know how to play them! They also have to know how to play the song they are playing. It is also important to choose songs that are well-known and popular amongst their peers. If a student plays Beethoven's Fifth Symphony, this is an unfair, though admirable, choice. Just to be safe, bring a stereo and CDs or an iPod and speakers so that if there is a major problem, you can play music from the stereo or iPod. The students will love this activity because it engages them on many levels.

Purpose

To raise accountability

In this activity there are many levels and layers. One aspect is for the actors to bring their instruments and prepare their songs ahead of time. This task includes accountability. If the actors do not bring their instruments, the activity is a non-starter. You could still present the activity using a stereo, but that would not be quite the same. A cast might be asked to show up at rehearsal by a certain date, with their lines learned. Let us assume that this is halfway through the rehearsal schedule. Half the actors come with their lines learned and the other half do not. This unwillingness to be held accountable not only affects the actors who did not learn their lines, but the entire cast. It leads to delays and causes the rehearsals to fall behind schedule. This type of attitude can take a potentially great play to a mediocre performance. Encourage your actors to hold themselves accountable on a consistent basis.

Industry Connection

In this activity the actors have an extremely limited amount of time to get it right. If they come close, that is nice, but they won't get the points. Even though they may only listen for five seconds, they can take a few moments before they actually guess. In an audition situation, an actor has to aim to make the right choices in a very short period of time. Perhaps the director throws an idea at him on the spur of the moment. It is not enough to make a decision. The actor has to find a way to make the right decisions. It is easy to talk about these things, but a much greater challenge to follow through in reality. This activity asks the actors to make the right choices in a limited time.

85. Emotional Recall

Have your actors work on this exercise by themselves. Ask each actor to pick an emotion from a list you have prepared, or you can ask them to choose an emotion for themselves. Some examples of emotions are: excited, happy, sad, angry, bored, or scared.

Once they have decided on their emotion, tell them to spend a few minutes working out a gesture to symbolize it. For instance, for the emotion bored, an actor might choose to fold his arms and turn his head to one side and look down. The actors are being asked to work from a physical place. They will want to work alone somewhere in the room. Bring everyone back standing in a circle. Go around the circle and have each person act out his emotion. Let the actors perform their emotions on their own first and allow a couple of actors to guess the emotion. If they cannot guess it, tell the actor to share his emotion with the group. Continue in this way until everyone has had a turn.

Purpose

To understand the importance of external action

There is a danger: You are not asking your actors to reach their emotion organically. An example of this could be that a character drops a valuable vase and gets angry and frustrated with himself for his clumsiness. The actors are asked to go straight for the emotion. Some directors actually work in this way. They will say things like, "Get angrier at this point!" It is bad directing, yet it happens in both film and theatre. One of the values of this exercise is to experience the connection between the physical and the emotional. When your actors fold their arms, they will experience an immediate physical reaction in their body. They are able to achieve this without any thought or justification. This is powerful information and gives us some insight into why an actor can still achieve a good performance through external acting. A good performance is likely to be an illuminating performance. You may say this is not possible, but then you would have to negate actors such as Laurence Olivier.

Industry Connection

"Get madder now," "Be happier at this point," "Be really sad now," "When he hands you the ring, I want you to cry," and "Find his joke really funny and start laughing," are pieces of direction that sound really silly and vague. The sad part is they are examples of directions that an actor may well receive on a set. A director does not necessarily speak the language of the actor. The actor has to learn how to translate the language of the director. The actor has to be able to take directions such as these examples and find justifications and motivations for the actions. I always find it interesting when an actor believes a film actor needs little or no training. I would agree that a bad film actor needs little training or talent. The demands of film mean that a good performance will demand an actor of extraordinary talent, which is due in no small part to his understanding of the craft. It is the interior life that the character has the will to be brought out on the screen. When an audience sees a good performance they take ownership for it in a very personal way.

86. Perfect

This exercise has been adapted for group work from my book *Acting Games for Individual Performers*. Divide your students into no more than six groups. Aim to have four or five students per group. Each group is going to need a piece of poster paper four feet long and a pencil. They will also require a ruler, an eraser, a measuring tape, or possibly a piece of string. Explain in the following way:

INSTRUCTOR: What I would like you to do is both simple and complex. I would like each group to draw a line three feet long. I would like your line to be exactly three feet and absolutely straight all the way across. If it is slightly slanted at one end or at one point, then it is not a perfect line. If there is a slight break in the middle where you moved the ruler, it cannot be a perfect line. If it is only one millimeter off at one point, it is still not a perfect line. Your job is to make a perfectly straight line all the way across. I suggested a piece of string because you might want to hold it across while you draw your line. If you use a pencil you can start again as many times as you need to. Have patience with this activity and do not give up. This exercise is based on a picture at a famous gallery in London. It was of the perfect line and was worth thousands of dollars. You may want to brainstorm with the rest of the group on the best way to accomplish this task.

Give the groups a good amount of time for this exercise. I usually give twenty to thirty minutes. Bring the groups back together and tell them to share their work. Let them discuss the challenges of this exercise.

Purpose

To explore the concept of perfection

The actors are asked to draw the perfect line. While it is simple to draw a line, it is quite another matter to draw a perfect line. This is an excellent metaphor when talking about the field of acting. It is fairly easy for actors to learn lines and sound as if they know what they are doing. Actors can give a mediocre performance and still be somewhat entertaining. But to truly move their audience and to be actors who have a true understanding of the craft of acting and convey a deeper message is a quite complex task. These actors will spend many years learning and growing and making mistakes, and learning and growing and never stop learning. It is too subjective to claim that perfection exists in acting. Yet there are performances that we will never forget. There are performances that stop us in our tracks and leave us speechless. Drawing a perfect line could take years. Becoming an actor of substance could likewise take many years of dedication and hard work.

Industry Connection

When you start this exercise, you may find that your students very quickly become discouraged. This in turn can try their patience and make them want to give up. When they are rehearsing a part, they may find that there are times when nothing is going well. They don't understand the character, they cannot find their motivation for the scene, and their fellow actors never want to rehearse. Perhaps they do not understand their character yet, but as they work through the role they will find that they develop ideas to enhance their understanding. By being patient, it will allow their minds to maintain itself in a more creative state.

121

They will enable themselves to develop their creative process. They will enhance their creative soul. If they are getting angry and frustrated, they will find that their minds become saturated with these distracting thoughts. An acting career develops through patience and persistence. It is the actor who wants something for nothing who usually crashes and burns. It is the actor who arrives in town and runs at everything like a bull at a gate who fails to achieve. He may be very hopeful, but also very green and naïve. He spends all his money, burns out, and leaves. The industry machine does not care, because there are plenty of others who are ready to take his place arriving on the next bus. I have said these things on numerous occasions, so one more time will not hurt. Patience is a virtue, when followed through by persistence and hard work. If an actor is lucky, he will get to work with a number of great people during his career. He has the extraordinary opportunity to meet extraordinary people.

87. Antiques

This exercise is inspired by a British television show. Members of the public take items to appraisers to hear about their origin and value. Pick an actor to be the expert and tell him to sit in a chair. Pick a person from the audience to be a member of the public. This person is given an item such as a pencil. Whatever he presents to the expert is a very rare artifact indeed. The expert is then going to describe in detail where the item came from, its history, and eventually its overall value. The member of the public who brought the item can also ask questions of the expert. An important proviso for the expert is to remain confident and fluid. This means that there is no stuttering, because everything he says is accurate and correct. Bring in new people and a new item each round. In some instances you could have two experts who have a heated intellectual discussion over the origin of an item. You can also let the people bring in imaginary items. For instance, someone may go to an expert and say, "I have a picture of an extinct dodo bird. The picture has been hanging in my grandmother's house for fifty years. Can you tell me anything about it?" Finish up with a group discussion.

Purpose
To stay congruent
One of the actors is chosen to be the expert. If he starts to break character, he may say, "I don't know much about this item. I cannot tell you anything." He may not say this out loud, but it may be what he is thinking. If this is the case, it is going to show in his assessment of the item and no one will believe he is the expert. Actors in a play must stay congruent to the main goals of their character. A character may decide her main goal is to marry the man of her dreams. All her actions, throughout the entire play, may be driven by this single idea. The actress has to recognize this and stay congruent to her character's main objective.

Industry Connection
I have spoken about imagination again and again — without it an actor is lost. We have talked about how imagination is essential for plays, but it is just as important for TV and movies. If you were making a film that is set in the Sahara Desert and you filmed it on location, you might ask, "Why do I need to use my

imagination?" Well, let's say you were supposed to be alone in the desert, but it just so happens there are eighty-five members of the technical crew on the set, including cameramen, producers, light and sound crew, and the director. It takes a great imagination to pretend you are the only person in sight. Just like working out in the gym, all of these skills need to be exercised and developed. You don't just walk into the gym and suddenly find you have a great body. You have to work at it with dedication and commitment. This is doubly true for actors who must constantly be developing their craft.

Chapter 11
Trust

88. Blind Faith

For this exercise, move all objects to the sides of the room. You should now have a large, open space without any clutter. Choose one actor to go into the center of the room. This actor should either be blindfolded or have his eyes closed. The rest of the group should be dispersed to all sides of the room. In a moment, tell the actor in the middle to start walking around the room. It is the job of the actors at the sides to make sure the walking actor does not bump into anything. If the actor walking around the room looks as if he is going to bump into something, such as a wall, the other actors should gently guide him in another direction and prevent him from doing so. They should not push him. They will not want to shove him, but gently guide him back by using a soft touch. All of this should take place in absolute silence. You can make this exercise more challenging by having the actor in the middle increase his walking pace. Having the actor run around the room is not useful because of safety issues. After a few minutes, change the actor in the middle. You can also stop for a short discussion in between each performance. The hard part is for the actors to keep moving even when they are hesitant to do so.

Purpose
To heighten the senses

This exercise is excellent at heightening the senses. As the actor walks around with his eyes closed, all his other senses will become heightened. In other words, as the actor is wandering around the room, his sense of hearing will become stronger. Blind people generally have a stronger sense of hearing because their sense of sight has been taken away. Those around the outside will also be utilizing their senses. To make sure the actor does not hit anything, they will have to utilize their sense of sight. They will also want to use a delicate sense of touch in order to guide the actor away from a wall or any potential obstacles. A stage is not a beach, or a mountain, or a castle. It can be by utilizing their senses and their imaginations. It was using his imagination that enabled A.A. Milne to create *Winnie the Pooh* for a single child, his son Christopher Robin. As Don Richardson says in his book, *Acting Without Agony,* "To be a well-trained actor, you should do sense-memory exercises every day during your studies, as though you were learning to play a musical instrument. It's not enough to understand it intellectually, *you must teach it into your body.*"[22]

Industry Connection

This exercise is based on trusting fellow actors to be there for the actor when he needs them. Actors in a movie have to put their trust in the entire crew and task allocation. They have to trust their fellow actors in their performance. They have to trust the lighting guy to catch them just right. They have to trust the sound guy to pick up each and every word crisp and clear. They have to trust

---

22. Don Richardson, *Acting Without Agony* (Boston, Allyn and Bacon, Inc, 1988), 106.

the director in her vision, the editor in his cuts, the wardrobe department in their choice of outfits, and everyone else involved in the production. They are responsible for giving a good, believable, and convincing performance, and the rest they mostly have to leave to trust.

89. Conga

For this exercise, choose a leader to stand at the front. Then bring each actor up, one at a time, and put him behind the leader so that his arms are on the shoulders of the actor in front of him. Put them in this position with their eyes closed. Eventually, you should have every actor lined up, one behind the other. It should look like a conga line or a twisting snake. The only person who should have his eyes open is the leader. At this point the leader starts guiding the group around the room taking them in different directions. The leader should move slowly and cautiously. The idea is not to trick the other actors into crashing and falling, but to keep them together as one cohesive unit. After a couple of minutes, you can keep the actors in the same order and just switch the leader so that all the actors still have their eyes closed. Or you can break the line up and completely start over. By keeping them in their original positions with their eyes closed it adds an extra dimension to the exercise.

Purpose
To develop a sense of trust
This exercise obviously demands trust between the actors, as well as between the group as a whole and its leader. The actors also have to be spatially aware and sensitive to their environment. In this exercise the actors will become more aware of their senses. As your sense of sight is temporarily taken away, your other senses, such as your hearing and your sense of touch, will become more heightened. The activity will only work if the entire group is onboard. If one actor is messing around, not focused, or totally freaked out by the experience, then it could cause a spiraling effect throughout the entire line. Stanislavski's actors were initially praised for their incredible ability to work as an ensemble. An actor will want to be a generous performer. Encourage your actors to work as a unit instead of the star system.

Industry Connection
This exercise is a risk in that it is possible to bump into each other or to end up with egg on your face. An acting career is a risk in that the actors cannot be certain it will turn out exactly how they envisioned it. Acting is not exactly a secure job. Actors repeatedly put themselves out for a lot of risks. They move out to a big city and leave all their friends and support networks behind. This is a calculated risk that many aspiring actors may never be willing to take. You are nobody if you are not willing to take calculated risks. Every time actors go to an audition they take the risk of being told, "No, thank you." Every time they are on television or in a movie, they take the risk of being criticized for their performance by the audience. A number of actors are self-critical of their own work. Being an actor is full of risks that the actor has to be willing to take! Sometimes an actor will have to be brave in order to be brilliant. There are times when the actor will want to swim in the deep end. It is like walking on a high wire

with no net. Actors have to take risks today, tomorrow, and for the rest of their careers. Actors have to be continually willing to get their feet wet. It takes a brave actor to be able to pull out all of the stops. This exercise enables actors to get adventuresome together and take some chances in a scene. In regards to being an actor, Hollywood actor Dante Basco told me, "Acting is not a job, it is a lifestyle. We have chosen to look at the world through different lenses and even the living of your life is part an extension of your art. If you stay present so many great things can happen."

90. Rounders

For this exercise, have all of your actors line up in a straight line. Have the actors hold hands with the person on either side of them. There should now be one continuous line. Explain in the following way:

INSTRUCTOR: Simone is at the end of the line. In a moment she is going to start moving around the room and take the line in any direction she pleases. She can also choose to go under another part of the line that may cause it to become tied in knots. At no point can the line break. Please make sure to move safely and cautiously for this activity.

This exercise is also good to do with music. After a short while you can change out the leader. If necessary, remind the actors that there is only one leader. The leader will want to move around the room at a safe pace. If the line is broken, the actors have to pause and start again. If this continues to happen, have the actors pause and problem solve together.

Purpose

To increase actor awareness

This exercise starts off easy enough. As the leader loops underneath other parts of the line, it becomes more complicated. The actors have to be aware of what is happening around them. If they do not pay attention, the line may end up being broken. When an actor is backstage in the theatre, it can be pretty dark. The area of space available may be fairly limited. An actor may be fully focused, waiting to go on-stage. The challenge is that before he goes on, scenery has to come off and three other actors have to go on, all using the same entrance. He has to be aware of everything that is happening on- and off-stage. At the same time, he has to focus on the scene. Each character at some stage has to engage his self-awareness.

Industry Connection

Raise the following points with your actors:

INSTRUCTOR: This exercise starts off fairly simple. As the line becomes more tangled, so the exercise becomes more complex. When you first decide you want to be an actor, things may be fairly simple. Perhaps you are taking acting classes in school or college. You live at home and do not have to concern yourself with paying bills. You can focus on your acting, which you love. If you give a poor performance, it will mainly be watched by your family and friends. It is not great, but at least it will not affect your career in the long run. As you move further along in your pursuit of a professional career, there are more facets that develop. You discover it is very hard to be an actor. You realize it means you will probably be unemployed a lot. You may have to ask your family for financial support. You have to pay your bills, continue to work on your instrument, work on self-promotion, network, audition, and build a team around you. If you don't nurture it, it begins to dissipate. The professional actor has to develop a multilayered approach to his career.

91. Pause for Thought

Have your students sit as the audience. Bring up two students into the performance area. Set the details of the scene yourself, or they can be decided on by the audience or the actors. Here is the extra twist to this exercise: During the scene, at any moment, you can clap your hands. When this happens, both characters have to stop talking immediately. This means that if one character is in the middle of a sentence he has to abruptly stop. Not only must the actors stop talking, but they must find a reason to justify their pauses. Perhaps the character is suddenly distracted. Perhaps he is suddenly taken over by some deep thought. Perhaps he became grief-stricken by something that was just said. Perhaps he gets a peanut caught in his throat. In any case, the actors must justify the pauses. They cannot start talking again until you clap your hands again. This should be anywhere between fifteen seconds and a minute. When the scene has run its course, get some audience feedback.

Some questions to discuss:

What worked well in the scene?

What were some of the challenges?

What made the pauses work?

Why did you not believe the actor at that precise moment?

You can change over students and work with another group. You can also tell a student to do the clapping from this point on. If you like, you can have more actors in a scene.

Purpose

To embrace silence on-stage

The actors have to find a way to become comfortable within the silence. A number of novice actors feel uncomfortable when there is silence. They feel as if they are doing something wrong. They begin to gallop and speed through the dialogue because they only feel comfortable when someone is talking. They feel that when someone is talking, something is happening. What they fail to realize is that a great deal can be happening when nothing is said. Let us say a police officer comes to a family's home with their twelve-year-old son. The officer tells the parents that their son was caught shoplifting. At first, the parents are so surprised they are speechless. They stare at their son in disbelief. They are shocked by what they hear. They want to say, "How could you have done this after the way we raised you? After all we taught you about values and honesty?" The challenge is that they are in such shock that no words come out. Encourage your actors not to be afraid of silence and pauses. A great deal can be happening when nothing is being said. To see further examples of this, look at plays by the world-renowned playwright Harold Pinter.

Industry Connection

In an actor's career, a good deal of time is spent conversing with people. This is not always the case, but it certainly is important until an actor has become established. I am not just talking about in the audition room. If an actor is at a party and he meets a producer, the producer may ask the actor about himself. The challenge is that if the actor is nervous, he may babble on incoherently. Nevertheless, he has told the producer virtually nothing and bored him in the process. If the actor had paused for thought first, he could have taken a moment to gather his thoughts. He could make a point or a statement and pause again if need be before continuing. The phrase "less is more" will want to be taken to heart by a number of aspiring actors. It is better to say less with meaning than to talk on and on without purpose.

92. Eye for an Eye

Ask your actors to split up into pairs. One member of each pair will close his eyes. The other partner is going to help him move around the room by calling out signals such as, "Walk forward, turn left, take three steps to your right," and so on. In other words, his partner is going to be his eyes. Give the actors a few minutes to get used to doing this. At this point, you are going to turn this exercise into a game of tag. Choose one actor to be the catcher. The catcher is going to move around the room with his eyes closed, or blindfolded, and try to catch any of the actors who also have their eyes closed. The catcher is at a disadvantage in that he does not have anyone to help navigate him. The other actors are able to receive help from their partner. If the catcher is coming towards them, the partners may shout out an instruction such as, "Take two steps backwards." Make sure the partners are aware of actors moving around the room. It is their responsibility to keep their partners from being caught, but also to prevent them from bumping into other actors. They cannot physically move their partner in any way. There is an added challenge: When a partner is calling out instructions, the catcher can also hear what is being said. It may make it easier for him to catch someone. If a person is caught, he takes over and becomes the new catcher in the next round. The catcher has to catch the member of the pair who has his eyes closed and not the partner. This means they have not completed the exercise until you tell him he has. Ask the catcher to keep his eyes closed until you tell him he has caught a competitor and not a partner. It could be interesting to have the actors switch to a new partner each new round.

Purpose

To put your trust in others

The partners who have their eyes closed have to put all their trust in their partners. They have to trust their partners to keep them out of harm's way and protect them from being caught. They have to give virtually all the ownership over to their partner, which is not always easy. Actors in a play may not want to put their trust in the lighting team. They may not want to rely on the vision of the director for the play. They may have a disagreement with the person in charge of wardrobe. While actors are able to finesse certain situations, for the most part, they are going to have to put their trust in others. I have mentioned the importance of ensemble and teamwork on a number of occasions, but it takes trust to allow a true ensemble to be formed.

Industry Connection

The catchers appear to be at a disadvantage. They cannot see anything and they have no one to help them. They could begin the exercise by insisting, "This is impossible!" If they look at it objectively, they will realize it is not as one-sided as it may first appear. They can hear the instructions being given by the partners and can use this to their advantage. Even if instructions are given, it does not mean that they are clear, or that the partners can follow them. This gives the catchers another opportunity to catch people. If they keep an open attitude, they will find they can be very successful. Some actors believe that everything about the industry is unfair. They say things like, "It is impossible to get an agent!" It is fair to say that getting an agent can be a challenge, but it is not impossible. There are thousands of actors who have agents, so this is obviously an incorrect statement. Some actors say, "There is no work!" There may be a lot of competition, but there is always work. Some actors say, "It's not fair!" There is not much that is fair about having an acting career. Actors cannot always control the outcome, but they can control how they approach each situation. They can choose to create opportunity, or they can choose to push opportunity away.

93. Hand Hypnosis

Instruct your actors to sit as the audience. Bring two actors into the performance space to demonstrate this exercise. One of the pair will want to put his hand about three inches from his partner's face. He will now lead his partner around the room. The trick is that the pair must keep the same distance between hand and face during the entire time. The partner has to follow the hand, and the hand has to be aware that it is being followed. The hand has to move at a smooth and fairly slow pace. The pair doesn't necessarily need to move around the room. Sometimes the hand may just move in circles, and so on. This activity is only successful when the two actors work together. After a short demonstration, tell everyone to find a partner. They should all work the activity simultaneously.

Purpose

To synchronize with one another

It is not enough for the pair to simply be aware of one another. The hand and face have to move as if they are one. They have to find each other's rhythm and fall in line together. Actors in a play have to synchronize with that play. They have to find the rhythm of the play and take it into account. Harold Pinter's plays are often marked with long pauses and silences. The actor has to find this rhythm in order to execute the playwright's vision. When actors in a production do not mesh with one another, we may see moments of cohesiveness rather than a complete picture.

Industry Connection

One actor is leading while the other actor is following. The actor who is following has to blindly trust that the leader knows where he is leading him. Some actors blindly follow anyone who offers an attempt to help them achieve their goals. The people who offer are usually doing so for a financial gain. They say things like, "You must join my class if you want a chance to make it big!" If a coach is a genius, it is probably a good thing to blindly follow him, but this is quite rare. Actors should always be in control of their journey. It is true that actors have to put their faith and trust in others, but this does not mean they have to give it in its entirety. An agent may tell an actor, "Trust me, I will make you a star." If it sounds too good to be true, it probably is. Even if an actor has an amazing agent, a good agent still expects the actor to do a great deal of the work. The actor is paying the agent about ten percent, not ninety percent. The actor therefore will still want to be doing ninety percent of the work.

Chapter 12
Improvisation

94. Continuation Story

Have six students join you in the performance space. Three will be the actors and three will be A, B, and C. Explain in the following way:

INSTRUCTOR: In a moment a story is going to be told. Before we can begin, we need to come up with an outline covered by four criteria. First, we need to come up with a location for our story. Let's name some possible countries or cities where our story can take place.

ACTORS: France, Spain, Jamaica, the Amazon.

INSTRUCTOR: Let's go with the Amazon. That sounds like a good one. Next, give me another location where some type of action is going to take place. This time, make it more specific to our story.

ACTORS: McDonald's, the grocery store, the shopping mall, a Star Trek convention.

INSTRUCTOR: Let's go with the Star Trek convention. Next, we need to come up with a famous person who will appear somewhere in our story.

ACTORS: Miley Cyrus, Martin Luther King, Jr., Elvis, Queen of England, Big Bird.

INSTRUCTOR: Let's go with Big Bird. Finally, we need to come up with some type of treasure for our characters to find.

ACTORS: A diamond. Gold. A vaccine.

INSTRUCTOR: Let's go with the vaccine. So we now know that the outline of our story is as follows: Our story will take place in the Amazon Rain Forest and involve a Star Trek convention, Big Bird, and a quest to find the vaccine. I need one more actor to come into the performance space. Sarah, please come and join us. In a moment, Sarah is going to start to narrate an action-packed story based on our criteria. Our three actors will act out the story as it is being told. So for instance, she might start, "It was a cold, gloomy morning and our three intrepid explorers were trekking through the rain forest when suddenly ... (Pause)" At this point, actors A, B, and C will give a one-sentence statement as to what happens next. Action has stopped at this point.

ACTOR A: A large tree crashes to the ground, narrowly missing our explorers.

ACTOR B: A giant fish jumps out of the pond and eats their lunch.

ACTOR C: They all fall asleep, exhausted from their journey.

INSTRUCTOR: Sarah will now want to choose a member of the audience who picks A, B, or C based on whoever he liked best. The audience member is not able to listen to the sentences again or comment on them, but simply respond with A, B, or C. If B is chosen, then B should repeat his sentence, which is simultaneously acted out by the actors. The story now continues, led by our narrator until the next time she pauses.

Position A, B, and C at the back area of your stage, standing in profile. Have your actors perform in the area in front of them. At no time are they looking at the three commentators. The three actors should perform their scene as if they are the only people there. The narrator does not have to talk continuously, but should introduce pauses to allow the actors to speak their dialogue. It is important for the actors to keep their dialogue in line with the story as it unfolds. The narrator should feel free to call on B first and C second. There is no reason why the narrator should stick to alphabetical order. The narrator has most control over the story. The narrator should not allow it to go for more than four or five minutes. Actors in the scene need to keep the action moving. New characters may appear and disappear at a moment's notice. It is up to the three actors to become these characters, without any form of discussion. It is also important for the narrator to keep the story moving. The narrator will want to stop the action on a dramatic note such as, "when suddenly," "without warning," "amazingly," or something like that.

The first time you use this exercise you might want to demonstrate the role of the narrator. The narrator has an extremely important role as he is the one who creates the structure of the story. The narrator is also the one who keeps pushing the story along. Remind the actors and students A, B, and C to incorporate all four criteria of the story. This sounds like a lot for your actors to take in. In fact, it should only take you about five minutes to explain it. The best way to work an exercise is to get the actors working. If it is going horribly wrong, then you can always stop and clarify any misunderstandings.

Purpose
To create a vivid imagination
This exercise is heavily linked to a vivid imagination. The narrator must use his imagination to create the most marvelous story. If he cannot do this, it will fall flat on its face. The actors have to take what they hear and create the most incredible physical performance. They have to utilize their imagination as if they were in the Amazon. They have to do this as if they were facing deadly crocodiles. The actors who are A, B, and C have no time to think but, using their imagination, they need to respond immediately. If A is never chosen, then the audience is telling him he needs a more keenly developed imagination. Every great acting coach says the same thing, "Imagination, imagination, and more imagination!" The genius actor is able to transcend the human experience.

Industry Connection
Actors have to be able to think on their feet to be a working screen actor. They also have to know how to serve the narrative of the script. Things can change on a dime and they have to be able to absorb anything that comes their way. Film actors very rarely receive the whole script preproduction. Oftentimes the film script is constantly being changed and adapted during filming. In a play, the director may change their blocking, but they may have days or weeks to adjust to it. On a film set, they may have a matter of minutes. Actors have to fit into the structure of the day. Even if the director is weak the actor must still find a way. Not only must they adjust to it, but also make each and every action justifiable. If they cannot do this, or are not willing to learn, then they are in big trouble. When we go to the movies we often complain that many of the performances are mediocre. Actors may be able to give numerous explanations as to why this is so, but no one cares. Actors have to realize that what the audience cares about is the results and not what got them there. They want to be left with a delicious basket of memories. Sometimes actors will say, "I saw this comedian in a movie and he has no acting training." It is worth noting that many

of the tools required of a comedian are also those required of an actor such as: lack of inhibition, a vivid imagination, improvisation, character work, understanding of the physical body, and comedic timing. Some people have the gift to be able to make people laugh. They know how to find that right moment. Comedians can be great actors because they are fearless and will do anything. They are very present in terms of improvisation. They can be laugh-out-loud funny. They can also be insecure, lonely, and tragic figures. They can take things very seriously. Their natural curiosity will take them to a place. Fortunately, there is no formula for comedy. Some people say great actors are fearless in the characters they take on. I also believe that a comedian who wants an acting career will want to train as an actor, but to say they are starting on the same playing field as a civilian with no training is simply not the case.

Note

George Burns and Gracie Allen are remembered as one of the classic comedy double acts of all time. They were a husband and wife team. When they started out together, Gracie was the straight act and George the funny part. This did not go over well with the audience. They switched the roles and the rest, as they say, is history. George Burns became the king of straight men. An artist has to take a pragmatic approach to his work. When something isn't working he has to be willing to change it.

95. A-B-C

Have your actors sit in the performance space. Bring up two actors into the performance area. Get a setting from the audience, along with character descriptions. Tell the actors that in a moment they are going to act out their scene with one added twist. The first sentence must begin with the letter A. The second sentence must begin with the letter B, and so on. The scene should last exactly twenty-six sentences. When one actor has said a sentence, the other actor must say the next sentence. It is important that the actors keep the scene fluid and moving. It is also important that what the actors say is justified and complements the scene. If they say something nonsensical just so they can say the letter of the alphabet, they are missing the point of the exercise. Once they have completed the exercise, follow up with a discussion and work with other groups. You can have a group of four or five, if you choose. Make sure they alternate between actors after every sentence.

Purpose

To know your objective

In this exercise, the actors have to know their objectives. They have to stay true to the scene, and they also have to know that each sentence starts with the next letter of the alphabet. If they ignore either of these objectives, their scene will run into trouble. In a play, it is of the utmost importance for an actor to know his character's objectives. Let us say a character is always teasing a certain young lady. The actions tell us that perhaps he does not like her because he keeps teasing her. Secretly, let us assume he is in love with her. The objective is to get her to notice him and tease her in order to do so. Without understanding the objectives, a character's actions can appear pointless and illogical to the audience.

Industry Connection

In this exercise the actor has to follow the ABCs. The actor's career is also following a series of ABCs. The difference is that these are not spelled out in a straightforward and easy-to-follow pattern. Actors have to put together their own list of what needs to be done and when. Actors without headshots will need to get them. Raise the following points with your actors:

INSTRUCTOR: If they don't know what you look like, not only are they not going to hire you, they are not going to see you. You need a good agent to get in to certain auditions. Without an agent, you are, generally speaking, limited to smaller budget projects. You don't have to take big leaps as long as you are taking compounding steps in the right direction.

96. The Sound That Moved Me

To begin this exercise, have your actors spread out around the room. It is important that they are within visual and auditory distance of the other actors. Explain as follows:

INSTRUCTOR: This exercise is very simple. At all times, someone must be moving and someone must be making a sound. This can happen in a variety of ways. One person can be moving while another person is making the sound. It is also acceptable for one person to be moving and making the sound simultaneously. Without warning, an actor who is making a sound will stop and another actor anywhere else in the room must take over with a new sound. There must be no gap in between so that the sound and movement are continuous. You are going to have to really be aware of what is going on. If three people all of sudden start moving around the room, two of them will immediately have to stop. At all times, there should only be one person moving and one person making a sound. Do not simply walk around the room, but move in a creative fashion. Each actor can change the form of movement. There should be no talking or communicating during this exercise.

You might also challenge the actors by seeing if they can complement the sound to the movement and vice versa.

Purpose

To enhance spontaneity through developing improvisation skills

This is an excellent exercise in improvisation. You cannot plan ahead and you have to react to each and every moment. There is always room for spontaneity. This exercise is more about responding to each moment, rather than trying to plan ahead. To some extent this is true of actors' careers. They can always perfectly plan ahead and will on occasion have to learn to go with the flow. Discuss the following with your actors:

INSTRUCTOR: When you are a in a scene, your character will want to be responding and reacting to what is happening in that moment. If, on your way here this morning, the woman behind you bumps into you with her baby's stroller, you will react. You didn't react half an hour ago because it hadn't happened yet. Just because you have read the play does not mean your character has. Your character does not know the events that will occur before they occur. Your character does not know that his friend is a liar until he is confronted in the instant of the moment.

It is a big challenge for actors not to want to plan their thoughts ahead of time; the character does not have the luxury having the thoughts before they occur.

Industry Connection

When actors forget a line on-stage they will either receive a feeling of terror or see an opportunity. I always cringe when actors downplay the importance of improvisation. Sometimes they will try to belittle it as a bit of fun, and nothing more. What they fail to see is that so many aspects of the actor's work demand good improvisation skills. Some directors will have their actors improvise scenes that are described but not actually in the script. This is so that the actors have something to refer to that has actually taken place. Improvisation is a skill that has to be practiced. In other parts of this book I mention how improvisation has become a common denominator in the audition situation. When actors are on a set, so many things can change in a heartbeat that they have to be able to change and adapt at a moment's notice. No one is going to say, "Can you do it?" They are going to say, "Do it!" They are being hired as professional actors. This means the actors will want to have the tools to adapt to everything that is thrown at them. Hollywood scripts are sometimes in development during the filming process. Scenes are literally being written and rewritten during the shoot. Actors who are weak in improvisation are going to find themselves at a huge disadvantage.

97. Question with a Question

This is a very popular exercise in improvisation circles. For this exercise, have two actors come into the performance space. Ask them to face each other while cheating out towards the audience. They can stand two or three feet apart. In a moment they are going to strike up a conversation with one another. The challenge is they can only talk with questions. An example would be:

ACTOR 1: Where did you buy your shoes?
ACTOR 2: At Wal-Mart. Who does your hair?
ACTOR 1: I did it myself. Aren't you feeling the cold today?
ACTOR 2: No, I feel fine.

In this example Actor 2 would be out, because he did not answer with another question. When an actor is out, ask him to sit down. The winner remains standing and challenges another actor. If a scene runs for three or four minutes, you might stop it and change both actors. To make this exercise more challenging, you might also choose to give each actor a character. The maximum time the actors have to answer a question with a question is two sentences. If they pause or hesitate they are also out.

Purpose

To understand character motivation

In this exercise, both actors continue to look for the upper hand. It is a similar situation in life. Many people look to gain the upper hand or advantage in each conversation. Some people do this consciously, while others do this without even being aware of it. In part, this may be because we want to keep what we have. We are always in fear of losing it. It may seem like we are getting out of our depth here, but it is a necessary point for discussion. Actors have to understand what motivates their character's behavior. They have to know why they do the things they do. Being an actor is like being a detective in that the actor is always looking for different pieces of the puzzle.

Industry Connection

Raise the following points with your actors:

INSTRUCTOR: In this exercise you have to ask questions. In your acting career, you have to learn how to ask a good question. It is no secret that most actors love to hear their own voices. In terms of performance, this is all well and good. In terms of everyday conversation, this could verge on being narcissistic. Let's say you are being interviewed by fifteen members of a television network for a lead role on a show. They ask you if you have any questions. At this point, you begin to waffle and list off fifteen questions. What would be more impressive is if you ask one question at a time. The questions you ask should be clear, concise, and directed at a particular person. Don't waste their time by asking a question to which you already know the answer. Leave them with a strong impression of you rather than one of confusion.

Note

Warn your actors to be careful they do not become a caricature of themselves!

98. Poetry Jam

For this exercise you will need some paper and a pencil. Have your actors sit in a circle. Explain in the following way:

INSTRUCTOR: In a moment I am going to hand this piece of paper and a pencil to Derek. Before I do that, I need some themes. An example would be peace and calm.

ANGELO: Ripples of water in the lake.

INSTRUCTOR: I like it. What else?

ANNE: The excitement of summer is here.

INSTRUCTOR: That's another good one. What I would like the group to do is to write a poem. You are not going to do it by yourselves. Each of you is going to write one line. The theme for our poem is going to be "The Excitement of Summer." Derek is going to write the first line at the top of the page. I don't want you to take too long to think about this. I want you to write anything that comes to mind with regard to our topic. When Derek has finished, he is going to fold the line backwards. Try to just fold that small strip of paper so that it is out of sight. The pencil and paper will be passed in a counterclockwise direction. We will continue in the same way until everyone has written one line. If we run out of paper, I will give the next person another sheet.

MIRANDA: Can we see what other people wrote before we do our line?

INSTRUCTOR: Actually, the whole idea is not to see what other people have written until the end. When we have finished, we are going to read the whole poem aloud. The poem may sound absurd or you may be surprised to find it has a cohesive feel. Either way, allow yourself to enjoy what has just been created.

If you have a small group, you may choose to repeat the exercise. When reading the poem out loud, you might have one person read it or you might ask each person to read one line at a time. If you want the whole group to read it, pass the poem counterclockwise around the circle.

Purpose
To formulate ideas
In this exercise the actors create something out of nothing — sometimes the result is an amazing creation. Sometimes the result is bizarre. Nevertheless, there is value there. A number of your students probably never write any poetry and yet in a collaborative effort they have just written a poem. The actor's character work starts with nothing and builds from there. The actor may have a script in his hand, but unless something is done with it, the character will remain as words on the page. It is up to the actor to bring the character to life. It is up to the actors to find out why their character sniffs their nose or wipes their chin. It is up to the actors to take these words and turn them into a living, breathing, thinking person. When we see a movie on the big screen, it is worth noting that the movie originally started as just an idea. This exercise encourages the actors to create something out of nothing.

Industry Connection
When an actor is given a play, the dialogue is set. The same play can be performed on numerous occasions year after year. When an actor is handed a film script, the film will probably only be performed once. That occasion is when it is actually being filmed. During filming, the director, producer, or writer may find problems with the dialogue. There may also be a problem with the dialogue due to a last minute location change. At this point, the writer may be asked to write some new dialogue or perhaps even a new scene. Industry writers have to get used to creating something out of nothing at a minute's notice. An actor in a television series gets used to being handed revised scripts with last minute changes. An actor will want to be a vessel through which the writer's words can flow. A good comedy writer knows that if it doesn't come out of the character, it probably isn't funny. The writer will want to look for the timing and the mood of the scene. The actor and the audience will know it is a forced line. The actor has to know not to push the audience for a laugh. Until a movie is previewed with an audience, an actor will never really know if it is considered truly funny. With regard to understanding the text, Dr. Minda Lopez, who is a literacy professor, told me that, "When readers approach a text, they rely on their experiences and knowledge of the topic to make meaning (or sense) of what they are reading." The creative actor has to be able to create something where there was virtually nothing only a short while previously.

Note
An actor may be in a television series that is sold for syndication. This means a show is produced and sold in various markets. The producers hope the show will collect a diverse range of fans. They want the fans to become loyal and to make a point of watching the show. This can be powerful leverage for the actor in that a show that is made in the States can end up being sold to British, French, Indian, and Spanish markets. This can make an actor an international household name.

99. Dress Up and Up!

You are going to need a handful of balloons for this activity. You are also going to need numerous sets of extra large or baggy clothing that include: trousers, a shirt, gloves, a hat, and a scarf. Divide your actors into groups of no more than six players. Have the teams sit side by side, from left to right. Tell the team members to sit one behind the other. Explain in the following way:

INSTRUCTOR: Each group has a pile of clothes and a balloon in front of them. When I say "go," the first person in each group is going to get up and start to put on all the items of clothing over his own clothes. This sounds easy enough. There is just one extra challenge: While you are getting dressed, you have to keep your balloon in the air at all times. Once you are completely dressed, you have to get undressed again, keeping the balloon in the air the whole time. As soon as you are undressed again, you have to run to the back of the line, at which point the next player in the line will run up and repeat the process. The first team to complete the task wins.

RACHAEL: What happens if the balloon hits the ground?

INSTRUCTOR: If the balloon hits the ground, that player, not the whole team, has to start again. Every time they drop the balloon, they must get undressed and start again. This will cost his team valuable time and should be avoided as much as possible.

JILL: What happens between players? I mean, does the balloon have to be kept in the air when one player is changing to another player?

INSTRUCTOR: It is a very good question. I will answer you very simply. The balloon has to be kept up in the air at all times. The person who has just finished has to make sure the balloon stays up long enough for the next person to take over. They have not finished until the next person has taken over.

Purpose

To comprehend the role of multitasking

This activity is an excellent example of multitasking. The actors have to juggle getting dressed and keeping the balloon up in the air at all times. This means they have to be able to focus on two tasks at the same time. The less experience an actor has, the better he has to be at multitasking. Novice actors have to focus on projection and diction during a performance. More seasoned and trained actors are able to push this largely over to their automatic functions. The novice actors may also find themselves conscious of their blocking and their line memorization, amongst other things. The seasoned actors are, for the most part, able to push these things over to their automatic processing. This means that there is more likelihood for the novice actors to multitask. The actors discover that multitasking can be incredibly time consuming and draw their focus on a constant basis. Actors will want to work on their body mechanics to counter this. Discuss with your actors the importance of training in allowing them to put their focus where it needs to be instead of constantly having to focus on the technical aspects of their acting.

Industry Connection

During this exercise the actors have to be alert at all times. If they are not alert, even for one moment, the balloon is most likely going to hit the floor. Actors need to be aware of their surroundings at all times. Their alertness may create an opportunity that wasn't there a moment before. A waitress in a restaurant might discover that she is serving an agent. It does not mean that she should drop her resumé in the agent's lap, but by doing a great job she may make an impression. This may open the door for the agent to say, "What do you do?" If he raises the question, she should feel free to share a little. I have known actresses and actors have been offered interviews by agents or managers simply because they were impressed by the individual. It does not mean they were always taken on, but they did create a potential opportunity. Actors who are not alert to their environment are going to miss so much of what is going on around them. Actors cannot afford to miss any opportunities that come their way.

Note

When I say *amateur* I am not talking about the difference between earning money and not being paid. I am talking about the actors' attitude in terms of their profession. Some actors spend their lives being dedicated to their profession and some do not.

100. Organic Orchestra

Ask your students to line up together in three or four rows, as if they are in a choir or an orchestra. What I would like you to do is to group them into five or six different sections. Physically, they are all still together, but each section has its own role to play. One section could be the bass line. Give them some sort of "bom, bom, bom, bom" to sing. Another group could be the tenor or falsetto. Pick a note for them like "laaaah." Another section could be given something obscure to sing such as, "uga chucka, uga chucka, uga chucka." It really does not matter how you break each section up, provided they all differ from one another. You are going to be the conductor. The way the conductor controls the orchestra is by using your hands. If you raise your hands towards one section, their volume should get louder. If you bring them down, their volume should get softer or nonexistent. You might only have one of the six sections singing at some points and bring in all six sections at another point. All sections may have different volume levels, depending on how you set them. You can work out other hand gestures with your orchestra for things such as: increase and decrease tempo, move to a higher or lower key, change vocal placement from diaphragm to nasal, and so on. You can be as creative as you like. Your aim is to create an organic orchestra. You will be surprised how good they can sound. You may also be surprised at how bad they can sound. It is good to first work with each section separately to make sure they all know which voice they are representing and what they are supposed to be singing. It is best that you start off as the conductor. Afterwards you can have a student take over, if you like.

Variable

Make each group a separate section of the orchestra. One section could be the brass section while another is the woodwind section, and so on. Or you could make each section a specific instrument.

139

Purpose

To work organically

You have literally just given the actors their separate rhythms to sing. Within a few moments, you have them sounding like an orchestra. It does not always sound pretty, but they are working organically and continually changing and evolving. An actor's performance in a play will always want to be changing and evolving. If it is exactly the same every night, then the actors may become rusty and uninspired. This may lead to their performance becoming stale and static. When actors step out of their comfort zones, their performances can become more organic. It allows the actors to work in the moment, as opposed to everything being premeditated. To be creative on-stage, actors will want to embrace creative living. This exercise is a good introduction to working organically and in the moment.

Industry Connection

When your actors arrive for class they have no idea what you are going to ask them to do. One minute they are chatting with their friends, and the next you have them becoming this organic orchestra. It may feel pretty surreal, but if they have taken a number of acting classes, they will be used to it. When actors walk into an audition, the casting director could ask them to do anything. A minute before, they were sitting in the waiting area looking over their sides. When they walk into that room, they have no idea what is going to happen. The director might tell them to put their sides down and do something quite different. He may have the actors work with the sides, but give them a random setting for the scene from which to work. There are result-orientated directors who want to see the results immediately. The actors have to be able to put aside a lot of their preconceived ideas, and be able to work organically. If they cannot do this, the director may never get the opportunity to see their true potential.

101. Photo Story

Instruct your actors to sit as the audience. Pick a student who is feeling particularly imaginative to join you in the performance space. Tell him that what you would like him to do is create in his mind a photo that involves five people. It could involve building sandcastles on the beach, having lunch at a fine Italian restaurant, or anything he wants. He has to make sure that the photo is a "doing" photo and not something static like a family standing there smiling. He has to have a definite image of what is happening in the photo. Then ask him to choose one aspect of the photo, put himself in it, and freeze. Gradually, you are going to ask four actors to go up, one at a time, and form the other aspects of the photo. They do not know what the photo looks like, so they are going to have to be guided by what they see the first person do. Leave a small amount of time between each change. This will give the next person a chance to form his contribution, based on what he sees. When all five people are frozen in the photo, ask the audience to share what they think is happening in the picture. You could have someone take a photograph with their camera phone so that afterwards the actors can see what the picture looked like. Then ask the four actors what they thought was happening in the photo. Finally, ask the original person what was supposed to be happening in the photo. It is important that the actors in the photo stay frozen the entire time this is going on.

Purpose

To create the images in our minds

The first actor to go up has a definite image of what the photo looks like. He attempts to pass this image on to the other actors through his action. The other four actors will develop an image of what they think is happening in the photo, based on the images that they have created in their own minds. Members of the audience also create images in their minds based on what they are seeing. When an audience goes to a play, they are constantly being asked to create images in their minds. If you are not going to build a castle on-stage, then you are asking them to imagine the castle in their mind. An actor who cannot create these images cannot expect an audience to take that leap of imagination. The actor has to use definite images to allow the audience to do the same.

Industry Connection

The actors have to create a still photo. The photo is meant to tell a story. A movie is a series of still photos run together at a high speed. Each photo is telling a story. When they are all put together, they are telling the complete story. If one, or ten, or a thousand of the photos don't quite fit into place, we have a story that is disjointed or illogical to the audience. Everything that the actor does must be done with clarity. If an actor cannot do this, the camera will catch it.

102. The Prop Game

This game is very popular in improvisation circles and has been seen on television shows such as *Whose Line Is It, Anyway?* Tell your actors to sit as the audience. Choose two actors to go into the performance space. You are going to need to give the actors a prop of some sort. An example would be a hole puncher. The actors have to use the prop in any way they choose, except for its actual purpose.

Here are some examples:

ACTOR 1: Hey, do you like my new earring?

ACTOR 2: And he hits a homerun and the crowd goes wild! (Used as a baseball bat)

ACTOR 1: If only I could get my bow tie to sit straight!

ACTOR 2: Fire when ready, soldier!

It is important to note that the actors are not playing out one scene together. They have to continue to pass the prop back and forth in every round. The prop exchange should happen at a rapid pace. It is OK if both actors are in the scene, except that only one of them decides what the prop actually represents. The other actor supports him in his choice. After a few minutes, you can work with another pair and a new prop.

Purpose

To develop improvisation skills

In order to adapt the prop from one item into another, the actors are going to have to hone their improvisation skills. Some actors say that improvisation has no place in acting. In theory, they are correct. The challenge is that sometimes things go wrong or someone forgets a line or two. At times like these, improvisation is imperative. Improvisation can teach the actor to develop listening skills. In a scene, actors may hardly be listening to their partner. They are continually looking for opportunities to top their partner in the scene. An improvisation scene that works is one where all the actors are listening to one another. There are also times in the rehearsal process when a director may say, "Let's improvise the scene." This may be because he is not getting the results he is looking for or in order to free the actors from self-imposed restraints. Rob Kozlowski, who wrote the book *The Art of Chicago Improv,* explains that "The Commedia Dell'Arte is the most direct answer to modern improvised comedy. The first records of Commedia Dell'Arte appear to originate from Tuscany, Italy, at around 1550."[23] Improvisation is an extremely valuable and vital skill for the actor. It is also sometimes difficult to differentiate between moments of inspiration and moments of improvisation.

Industry Connection

This exercise involves using a prop, albeit for another purpose. The actors have to get used to handling and passing the prop to one another. During filming, actors may be asked to handle a prop. What seems like a basic task can suddenly become a complex feat. This is because, in filming, actors will be expected to handle the prop correctly on each and every take. Film actors may feel that there is no audience in front of which to feel nervous. This is not quite accurate. There is a cast and crew and a camera before which the actors will be performing. The actors have to be so comfortable holding and handling props that it becomes second nature to them.

Note

Theatre has become so marginalized in today's society it is sad to see. If theatre wants to survive and thrive it is going to have to learn to constantly reinvent itself. The film industry is constantly adapting to what it believes is the pulse of society. Theatre appears to want to live on tradition and the past. Due to the lack of funding and incentives, there are very few playwrights today to compete with Shaw, Chekhov, O'Neill, Strindberg, or Ibsen. It is true there are some fine playwrights such as Athol Fugard, Neil Simon, Tom Stoppard, and David Mamet. These are seasoned playwrights and have been producing great work for decades. The challenge is that, for the most part, their incomes have to be subsidized by their screenplays and novels. Other playwrights turn to becoming Hollywood script doctors to pay the bills. This means they help shape and rewrite other people's scripts.

Audiences have become so conditioned to rapidly moving scenes that to sit through a thirty-minute scene becomes virtually painful for them. The biggest difference between theatre and film is that, generally speaking, in the movies there is a much bigger paycheck at the end of the day. Hopefully theatre will find a way to move forward with the times and reinvent itself. It is far too important a medium for the actor to simply be allowed to slip away.

---

23. Rob Kozlowski, *The Art of Chicago Improv* (New Hampshire: Heinemann, 2002), 9.

Chapter 13
The Physical Actor

103. Status Symbol

For this exercise you are going to need a deck of cards. Take all of the jokers out of the pack. Pick out four actors to come up into the performance space. Once you have your four actors, have them line up shoulder to shoulder. Walk along the line and have each one pick out a card and, without looking at it, hold it up against their forehead. The picture side should now be facing the audience. At this point, have one or two actors from the audience come up and attach the cards to the actors' heads. This can be done with ribbon, a piece of string, or an athletic headband. If you want to, you might have each one wear a cap and hold it that way. No one in the audience should give any indication as to which actor has what card. At this point, have the actors improvise a scene. It is up to you what parameters you want to give the actors. During the scene, the status of each actor should be established. The other three actors in the scene will be the ones to do this. If an actor has an ace of clubs, their status is going to be very low. If an actor is holding a king of hearts, their status is going to be very high. The scene should be driven by the status of the four actors. It is not a literal translation that we are looking for here. In other words, if someone is holding a queen, it does not mean that everyone has to treat her as a queen. Perhaps during the scene it will be established that she is a judge. It is not necessary for the actors to guess their card, though you could add this as another challenge. It is also possible that all four actors will have the same number card and therefore, in theory, the same status.

Variable

Instead of status, the card value could indicate personality traits. The higher the card value, the more pleasing the individual's personality traits are. If an actor is a two of clubs, then the rest of the group can establish him as being the scum of the earth.

Purpose
To highlight the importance of status

Sometimes actors will play a part where the dialogue does not always clearly define the relationships. This is more often the case in a badly written play or film script. There may be hints that can help the actors out in this regard. If the actor playing a son talks to his mother, then his mother may have earned the right to a higher status. By the end of the play, *The Glass Menagerie,* the status roles seem to switch in regards to mother and child. An actor might be in a scene where he walks past a police officer in the street. He automatically lowers his status and raises the officer's because of the power he wields. He also has the ability to change the course of his life forever, if he chooses to. Children may feel their status lower as they walk past a headmaster in the hallway. By understanding status the actors will have a clearer picture of their relationships with other characters.

Industry Connection

Hollywood is full of status and status symbols. It is everywhere you look and you cannot get away from it. A status symbol might be driving a flashy car or living in a big mansion. It might also mean being seen at a certain restaurant or bar. Actors play the status game all the time and may not even know it. When actors meet an agent, they may automatically raise their status. They may put the agent up on a pedestal. Advise your actors to be very careful if they do this. Explain in the following way:

INSTRUCTOR: The agent may be really bad at their job and take advantage of you because of your naïve behavior. Keep them on a level playing field until they have earned the status of a person worthy of your respect. You might meet a celebrity at some event and be in awe of them. It is great that you admire them, but be careful of elevating his status into the stars. If you do this, you will not be able to have a coherent conversation with them and will have learned nothing. They may also regret this, as they might crave intelligent conversation. Help your actors to see the relationship that status plays in our day-to-day lives.

104. Jungle

Ask your actors to come up with any jungle animal. Tell them to do this without discussion with their fellow actors. Then explain the exercise in the following way:

INSTRUCTOR: What I would like you to do now is begin performing as your animal in all its physical being. Move around the room as your animal would move around the jungle. If your animal makes sounds, then feel free to use them. If you pass another animal and want to communicate, then you must do so as your animal. (Allow three to five minutes for this part.) Please stay in character while I explain the next stage.

What I would like you to do now is continue to be in the jungle. I would also like you to establish a pecking order. What I mean by this is if anyone is a lion, they will most likely establish themselves as king of the jungle. If there is more than one lion, then only one of you is king. (This does not involve a physical fight to find out who is king. Perhaps there is some kind of posturing to prove dominance.) As you continue now, I want you, as a group, to establish which animal belongs where. The only way you can communicate with each other is as your individual animals. (Allow seven to ten minutes for this part.)

It is important that you do not mention the hierarchy to the actors until they are already engaged in the exercise. The reason for this is you do not want everyone choosing to be a lion. A twist to this exercise could be if you make one of the actors a human. Follow up with a group discussion.

Purpose

To release inhibitions

If the actors participate fully as their animals, then they will become totally uninhibited as their animals. Actors have to learn antisocial behavior. This does not mean sitting in a corner and hiding. It means they have to engage and embrace behavior that society may frown upon. In most countries, people are raised to believe that burping in public is wrong, although in some places it is considered rude not to burp after a meal. Nevertheless, actors may be playing a character on-stage who likes to burp out loud. If the character burps out loud, then the actor has to burp out loud. If this embarrasses the actor or makes him coy, then he probably won't do justice to the character. It may make it challenging for the actor to play a character who is off the wall. Just like the animal, the actor has to be unfiltered. As Phillip Seymour Hoffman explains, "In front of strangers, you have to bring in vulnerability and privacy that normal people run screaming from."[24]

Industry Connection

In this exercise the animals discover their pecking order in the same way actors quickly discover their pecking order. If actors do background on a movie, they are at the bottom of the barrel. If someone was a PA (personal assistant) on a movie, he is also pretty much at the bottom of the barrel. If an actor were a lead in a student film, he might feel quite important. If he put it on his resumé and took it to a Los Angeles, New York, or London agent, the agent might look down upon it. If an actor plays a lead in a big movie, he will be right at the top of the totem pole. He will know this because everyone on-set will be at his beck and call. The best advice to dealing with the pecking order is to be humble to it, whether you are at the top, the middle, or the bottom.

105. Tag

You are going to have your actors play that well-known children's game, tag. To make it more interesting you can change the rules. Here are some examples:

Everyone has to walk backwards.

Everyone has to keep their eyes closed.

Everyone has to crawl on all fours.

Everyone has to jump around the room.

Everyone has to skip around the room.

Everyone has to sing continuously as they move around the room.

These rules also apply to the tagger. Make sure that these variations are done bearing safety first.

Variations

You could use all these examples in separate rounds. To make it more of a challenge, you could constantly change the rules in the middle of the game. So for instance, you can call out, "Everyone has to crawl on all fours." After a few minutes, you could change it to something else, "Everyone jump around the room." This will really keep the players alert and on their toes.

Purpose

To become sensitive to your surroundings

This exercise encourages the actors to become sensitive to their surroundings. If the tagger is near, they have to plan their escapes without getting blocked in by other actors. Let us assume an actor is in a scene on-stage where his character is being chased by another character. It has to appear to be a chase that takes place over quite some distance. However, because the actor is on a stage, the whole scene takes place in just six or seven steps. In order for the actor

---

24. Rosemarie Tickler and Barry Jay Kaplan, *Actors at Work* (New York: Faber and Faber, 2007), 336.

145

to do this convincingly, not only will the actor need a vivid imagination, but he will need to be sensitive and aware of his surroundings.

Industry Connection

This exercise has one actor do the chasing, while the other actors' aim is not to get caught. Just as on-stage, a chase scene in a movie is done through adaptation. The audience sees a car reverse at high speed and presumes it is going to drive away and give chase. What actually happens on the studio lot is the car reverses and drives about twenty yards around a corner. The challenge is that the actor has to make it look like he is giving chase or being chased. In addition, it is more than likely he is not even driving. It is a stunt double who does this. The actor has an added challenge in that he is not even performing the physical action. Actors are often limited by what they can do physically because of the insurance companies. The complexities of acting call for well-trained actors if we are to see believable performances. There are performances and there are good performances. They are not necessarily the same thing. Sometimes the actor has to get back to the basics.

106. Balancing Ball

All the actors take their shoes off before beginning this exercise, and they should sit in a circle. There should be a small gap between each player. It should be wide enough for a ball to roll through. Their legs should be stretched out in front of them so that everybody's feet meet in the center. The actors' hands must stay either behind their backs or at their sides, towards their backs. The actors must also keep their heels on the floor at all times. Give the actors a soft sponge ball of some type. The ball must be passed around the circle without the use of hands. The players are going to have to mainly use their legs to keep the ball moving from one player to the next. Remind the actors that their heels must stay on the ground at all times. If the ball gets stuck at a player's ankles, the whole group can discuss the issue and see how they can solve the problem together. To make this exercise more challenging, another ball can be added, but this one has to move in the opposite direction.

Purpose
To work with the subtly of touch

This exercise is tactile in nature. It enhances the actors' sense of touch. An actor may be in a play where his character has to put his hand into the icy cold river. In order to do this, he will need a vivid imagination, and he will also need to utilize his sense of touch. His reaction to putting his hand in icy cold water will be totally different from a situation in which he had to put his hand in lukewarm water. In order to keep the ball from falling on the floor, each actor will have to be able to work with the subtly of touch. There may be many occasions in the actors' acting careers when they will have to work with the subtly of touch.

Industry Connection

This exercise is built on the cooperation of each and every player. A movie is not the success of one person. It is the hard work of the actor, director, producer, editor, writers, cameraman, grip, assistant director, makeup artists, music producer, wardrobe, catering, etc. You might laugh to see catering as an important part of making a movie. If the food is not up to par, do you honestly think those involved in the project will be able to work at their optimal capacity? A project is a wheel with many cogs. The actor is one cog, albeit an important one, who collaborates in the turning of the wheel. When you look for success in a project, you look first and foremost at the top. If the producer and director have no vision for the movie, then there will be none.

107. Balls of Fire

You are going to need a few old newspapers and some scissors for this exercise. Take the newspapers and cut each page into four equal pieces. Scrunch each piece into a ball. You can ask the students to help you do this. You are going to need to make one hundred balls. Divide the classroom in half. You can do this with a strip of masking tape. Now divide the class into two teams. Tell one team to go on one side and the other team to go to the other. Put two more pieces of tape (or whatever you have already used to mark the division) two feet on either side of the center line. Each team has fifty balls randomly spread out in their half of the room. When you say "go," each team has three minutes to fire and throw as many of their balls as they possibly can into the other team's half of the room. No one is allowed to step into the four feet of no-man's-land. If a ball drops in there, it stays there and does not count. No student can throw more than one ball at a time. This is very much a rapid-fire race. After the three minutes, stop the throwing and count which team has the most paper balls. The team with the fewest balls in their half of the room is the winner. Three minutes seems very short, but the students will be exhausted. It really gets their adrenaline pumping. You may want to play the best of three rounds or change the teams. Allow the students to run around the room carefully, as long as they stay in their half of the room. It may also appear to be a bit like a snowball fight. Do not forget to recycle the paper. Always look for ways to help the environment by not being wasteful.

Purpose

Less can be more

The purpose is to highlight to the actors that on some occasions less is more. The fewer balls they have on their side, the more chance they have of winning. The less inhibited the actor, the more chance he will have of getting out of his own way. The more armor an actor uses to hide the truth could render him immensely vulnerable. The actor is immensely vulnerable the second he walks onto a stage or set. The actor is walking on a tightrope between the director's vision, the playwright's, and his own. They need to develop a deep sense of humility. The fewer hang-ups actors have, the more opportunity they will have to throw caution to the wind. When opportunity comes the actors' way they have to grab it. The less actors care about what other people think, the more they will be able to focus on what is really important in their acting, instead of just what is superficial. The less time they waste, the more time they have to use for improving their career. In the actors' world, less can sometimes mean more.

Industry Connection

This exercise requires a good deal of stamina and physical energy. During a performance, it is much the same for the actor. During a play, an actor might not leave the stage for two hours or more. It takes an enormous amount of stamina to be able to hold that amount of concentration. An actor on-set may only shoot a scene that lasts one minute in terms of each take. Rehearsals on-set are oftentimes minimal. The stamina comes in when the same scene has to be shot fifteen times. The stamina and physical energy are also applied when the actor arrives on set at five thirty in the morning and does not leave until ten o'clock in the evening. There is very rarely a nine-to-five day on-set. The amount of stamina demanded of the actor is enormous. Actors must also have stamina in terms of their career. Christopher Lee is perhaps best known for his *Dracula* movies. He is currently in his late eighties and still has numerous projects on the boil. His is a fine example of the stamina of the working actor. This exercise represents a small glimpse into the real world of the actor.

108. Duck and Duckling Tag

For this exercise you are going to divide your students into pairs. Have the pairs spread out around the room and tell them to lie down on the floor, side by side. Ask two students to remain standing. Inform one that he is a duck and the other that he is the duckling. The duckling is going to chase the duck around the room. If you want to, you can tell them to quack and move like ducks while they are running around the room. If the duckling can catch the duck, the roles are reversed immediately. The duck's aim is to lie down next to another pair of ducks before being tagged. If he can do it, the person who is now in the middle is safe. The person at the other end now becomes the duckling and tagger and the roles are reversed. The duck can lie on either side of any pair. Every time a duck lies down, the person on the opposite end becomes the new tagger. This exercise can be confusing at times, so you are really going to have to stay on top of it. The fact that the actors are lying down makes it even more challenging.

Purpose
To stay focused at all times
Everyone in the group has to stay focused at all times. At any moment, the duck can lie down beside any pair. If the person on the end does not remain focused, he will not even know he is the duckling and the tagger. The previous duckling may still be in the chasing mode. The actors have to stay focused to adapt to the game. When we tell actors to focus, it sounds like a simple request. The challenge is that our minds are always moving from one thought to the next. People go to meditation to learn to make their minds still and quiet. Actors don't want to make their mind still, as they are always looking to heighten their imaginations. They do, however, want to learn to push aside all distractions. While they are in the middle of a scene, the last thing that should be going through their minds is what topping to have on their pizza tonight. Some actors take on a role and are completely consumed by it from beginning to end. By exercising and strengthening their focus muscles, the actors can learn to focus for long periods of time.

Industry Connection

This exercise entails a degree of confusion. The duck becomes the duckling. A new duckling is suddenly introduced. A new duckling does not realize he is the duckling. No one knows who is the duck or the duckling. As this exercise gets going, these are just a few of the potential areas of confusion. An actor in a major acting hub will hear conflicting and confusing advice. One acting coach will say one thing while another will say something completely different. One agent will say, "I love your headshot!" Another agent will say, "Change it immediately!" Actors love to give advice, whether they have been asked for it or not. It may be well-meaning, but can often be blurry and limited in value. The actor's journey is a very personal one. Tell your actors that while advice is necessary, they should feel free to pick and choose which advice they listen to. One of the reasons it is sometimes confusing is because acting is a subjective art. Two acting coaches can give contrasting advice, though each can be correct in his own way.

109. Slow-Motion Running Race

This exercise is exactly as the title sounds. What I would like you to do is pick four or five students. Tell them to line up for a race. You can say, "On your marks! Get set! Go!" What they are going to do is race from one side of the room to the other. The challenge is that each participant has to run in ultra slow-motion, while nevertheless trying to win. They are not allowed to run at normal speed. Here is a way to increase audience participation. Divide the audience up into supporters for each runner. As the slow-motion race begins, tell the audience to cheer for their slow-motion runner. When the race is finished, let new runners try. Here is a rule you can add to the exercise: The winning time must be more than two minutes. In other words, if the first person finishes in less than two minutes, they are automatically disqualified. Do not tell them how they are doing time-wise. This will motivate the runners to run slowly.

Purpose
To explore the concept of pacing
If the runners run at their normal pace, the race will be over in seconds. The faster runner will win and that will be that. In this race, the runners are going so slowly they become aware of every muscle and what they are doing. They are able to experience what their body is doing in slow motion. By changing the pace at which the body moves, the whole experience is altered for the actor. While the dialogue in a play is set, the pacing is not. Neither is the cadence. By this I mean the pitch and rhythm of a vocal pattern. By changing the pacing of a scene, the actors can actually change the meaning. Let us say a girlfriend asks her boyfriend, "Do you love me?" If he automatically answers, "Of course I do!" It will send his girlfriend a certain signal. If he pauses for three or four seconds before answering it could send his girlfriend a whole slew of different signals. It could send signals of possible doubt or mistrust, among other things. The pacing and tempo of a scene can change the entire dynamics.

Industry Connection

Let us use this exercise as a metaphor. Let us say that "the race is won at the end." The fastest runner may end up coming in last. This is partly because, if they finish in less than two minutes, they will be disqualified. In order to win, they are going to have to move slowly, but still fast enough to win. Oftentimes, actors pursuing their careers try to run the race as fast as they can. They try to skip over many of the steps and reach the finish line before they have even begun. Statistically, it is highly unlikely that they will achieve anything tangible in this way. It must be said that it is still vaguely possible, which is perhaps why so many aspiring actors still use this approach. The actors who pace themselves and work in a methodical fashion are more likely to create longevity in their acting career. The film and television actors who are brought back are usually the ones who can produce the goods on demand. They move forward in a calculated and career driven way. They don't see their acting career as a race, but more as a journey. Some actors see their career as their testament. It is the thing that they preserve throughout their lives. An acting career is not a job, but a way of life.

110. Physical Expressions

This exercise has been adapted from my book, *Acting Games for Individual Performers,* for group work. Explain in the following way:

INSTRUCTOR: For the next thirty minutes I want each of you to take on a physical condition that is different from your own. You are going to have free time to mix and mingle with the rest of the group during this time. For instance, you could have a limp in one leg so that as you put pressure on one foot, it is as if it starts to give way. If you choose this condition, it is going to affect the knee, the ankle, and the hip as you walk. Taking on a limp will also affect the upper body and will be felt in areas such as your shoulder and neck muscles. You might want to take on a lisp with a lazy tongue so that it is lingering a moment longer in between the teeth. You will find that this creates a slight speech impediment that affects your vowels, consonants, and enunciation. You could choose to show a squint in one eye, so that the eye muscles become contracted. This eye should then appear to be partially closed. It may be simpler and less of a strain to simply keep one eye closed. Make sure that whatever you choose it is not putting too much stress on your body. If this is the case, you will want to switch to a different body part or shorten the length of time you perform the task. It is important that if you choose a limp, for instance, you commit to it in its entirety. Open a door with a limp. Go across the room with a limp. Sit at the table aware of your limp. For the next thirty minutes, in all other respects, implement this limp. Do not revert back to your regular physicality. When something challenging arises, see how you can adapt to the situation. Make observations throughout as to how your circumstances have changed because of the new set of physical challenges that you are facing.

During this time, the students can talk amongst their friends, play games, or do whatever they like. Ask them to avoid being sedentary the entire time. Follow up with a group discussion. If you have a longer class period, give the students more time to work on this exercise.

Purpose

To make the connection between the physical and chemical

If you stand up and start to jump around with your arms in the air, you are going to find that your body starts to release adrenaline and possibly endorphins as well. If you sit in a chair, cross your legs, fold your arms, and droop your head towards your legs, you are going to find that your body reacts quite differently, possibly by releasing lactic acids. These chemical responses in one's body can make quite a difference to a person's life. When actors apply physicality to a character and find that this changes the chemical releases throughout their body, they are probably going to find that this in turn affects the personality of their character. Jonnie Patricia Mobley gives a definition of bio-mechanics that fits into this category. "A theory of early twentieth century Russian director Vsevolod Meyerhold was that actors can use certain patterns of muscular activity to elicit a particular emotion; for example to express joy, the actor could turn a somersault."[25]

Industry Connection

Make the following observations with your actors:

INSTRUCTOR: No two people move, look, or sound exactly the same. This holds true for all the characters that you are going to play throughout your life. This activity allows you to become familiar with a new physical environment that deeply contrasts with your own. The reason I have chosen something physically challenging is that the results can be quite profound. As an actor, you want to know where your character's center of gravity lies. Some people move with their chest thrust forward, others with their head and neck jutting out, and some people walk with their shoulders leading. You are going to find that through physical exploration of a character you will make new discoveries about who they really are. There are a number of actors whom you can see on any day who are successful at playing themselves. A studio often brings them on precisely because they want the actor to play himself, hoping that this will translate into a box office success. If this is the type of acting you are searching for, perhaps this exercise is not beneficial for you. If, on the other hand, you are looking to define each and every character fully, journey onward. It is no easy task for an actor to appear consistently the same. To do so without appearing nervous or forced still takes a talented actor even if he is not a versatile one.

---

25. Jonnie Patricia Mobley, *NTC's Dictionary of Theatre and Drama Terms.* (Lincolnwood, Ill: National Textbook Company, 1995), 15.

Chapter 14
Auditioning

111. Cold Reading

Have your students sit as the audience. Remember that a lot of their learning comes from observing the work of others. Bring one actor forward and explain in the following way:

INSTRUCTOR: Estaban, I would like you to come join me over here. I would like you to look over this script. I am going to give you five minutes to do this and then I am going to have you perform the scene. Please look over the lines for the character David. (During this time the audience can talk quietly amongst themselves. If you prefer, you can give the scene out five minutes ahead of time. When an actor reads a script for the first time it is the only time he gets to be an audience member of that material. It is very important that the student only has five minutes to prepare.) Before you actually start, I want you to slate for the camera. What I mean by this is that I want you to say your name facing forward. I then want you to turn to your left profile and hold it for a count of two. I then want you to turn to your right and do exactly the same thing. I then want you to come back around to the front. (Slating for the camera is a fairly common practice in an audition situation. Why it can be useful for you to utilize with your students is because it is also another way of throwing their concentration and focus. The more you give them to cope with the more challenging the exercise becomes.)

ESTABAN: Who is going to read the other lines?

INSTRUCTOR: That is a good question. Ashley, will you come up here and join us? Ashley, I want you to go and sit in the chair in the corner of the room. You are going to be reading the lines for Natalie. I have purposefully not given you any time to prepare because you are not auditioning. You are the reader. I am also going to ask you, Ashley, to give little thought to your line responses. This is because it is quite common at an audition to have a reader who has nothing to do with acting. He can give very little to you in terms of giving you something to bounce off. Estaban, you still have to give everything you've got in this performance. By the way, I don't want you to be looking at Ashley. I want you to direct your lines to where Natalie is supposed to be standing, which in this scene is just to the left of the camera. (Give the actor an imaginary placement for the camera. If you are going to film the scene, then even better.) Don't forget, Estaban, that you do not want to spend your whole time looking down at the script.

It is up to you if you want to get into the frame size with your students here. In other words, you could tell them they are shooting a close-up or a half-body-length shot or a wide lens shot. This is if you want to restrict them in terms of how much movement they can make.

Variation

You can also work this same exercise with a number of actors. If you choose to do this, then it might be good to have a three-person scene. Give two of the students time to prepare while the third student is the off-camera reader.

In a third scenario, you can repeat the above exercises only this time have the actors begin the moment they receive the hard copy.

Purpose
To hone their cold-reading skills
The actors may already be used to cold readings and may have been doing them for numerous years. You are therefore using this exercise as a reminder for them to hone their skills. World-famous dancers often go back to beginning dance classes precisely for this reason. Go through the audience critique, your comments, and those of the actors. Cold reading may be more about technical skill than good acting, yet the actors who master it are increasing their chances of working. Scripts and dialogue can change at any moment, so a performance can sometimes practically feel like a cold read. A director may even ask you to change a word or a sentence in the middle of your speech. Most of us drive on autopilot, reinforcing all our bad habits.

Industry Connection
This exercise gives the actors the chance to work on their cold reading skills and adjust them accordingly. Let us say they are being filmed at an audition and are wondering if they should look towards the camera or towards the reader who is sitting way at the back and all the way to the left. If the actors look at the reader, everything they do will be profiled on camera. If it is supposed to be a close-up, then they want to perform as close to the lens as possible, in other words right around to the lens. They should not worry about where the reader is, unless they have been asked to do so. Tell your actors, "They are not going to show on the film anyway, but you are!" Some of your actors may say, "I don't care about cold readings. I am a good actor." You can tell them that if they want to get cast in parts, they better learn to like cold readings.

112. Book It

For this exercise, invite three colleagues who are in the industry to be on the panel. One may be an acting coach, one may be an agent, and the other may be a director. Each member should be given a list of the actors, plenty of paper, a pencil, and a bottle of water. These are merely suggestions of where you might go with your panel. In a few moments, each actor will come in the room, one at a time, and audition for the panel. The previous week, the actors should have been told to prepare an audition piece one minute long. Tell them it should be a role they would be cast in. They are going to have to direct themselves and select the piece themselves. When the actors arrive, there should already be an order list printed up. There may be some actors who do not show up. In this case, simply cross out their names and the order stays the same. Tell the actors when they come in to give their name, the name of the piece, and begin when they are ready. Have a helper with you so that when one actor is finished, he can tell the next actor when to come in. This will depend on when the panelists are finished writing their notes. The assistant will want to be moving between the audition room and the holding area. Tell the panelists that they can spend up to five minutes with each actor. After the actor has finished his piece, he can follow up in any way he chooses. Some possibilities are:

Have the actor do the piece again with panel-suggested direction.
Do a mini-interview with the actor.
Give the actor some sort of improvisation.
Simply say "thank you" as the actor leaves.

If the piece goes over one minute by five seconds, cut him off. He was told the time length and therefore should not be allowed to go over it. After all actors have performed, have a Q & A session with the panel. The panel may choose to give individual notes or they may give general notes to the entire group. You will want to facilitate, but let the panel run the show.

Purpose
To become the self-taught actor

In this exercise the actors choose their own pieces and most likely direct it themselves. It is not that often in their careers that they will get to select their own projects and get paid for it. A-list actors usually get to do this, but few others. Some of these actors may find being a star eclipses their career. However, for the most part, when actors receive their sides for an audition, they will direct themselves. Some actors will go to their private acting coaches for help. Many actors cannot afford this option. If this is the case, then they are going to have to know how to make good choices. The choices they make have to be interesting to the actor or they will not be of any interest to anyone else. One of the important qualities of a good script analysis class is to show the actors how to break down the material. Stella Adler was one of the greatest in terms of script analysis. A good script will give the actor numerous hints and clues. A good script is about ideas. There is a good deal of discipline involved in screenwriting. In a good script every word was written for a reason. Some screenwriters prefer to start with the character and see where it leads them. The writer gives the actor every clue he could ever desire. Some actors are lucky enough to work with the screenwriter. This allows the actor to delve into the screenwriter's logic and structure. Actors enjoy a script that constantly surprises them. Some screenwriters are engaged in every step of a movie. They are involved in pre-production, casting, and editing. They want to make sure that the actors do justice to their words. Some people have observed that Truman Capote, who wrote *Breakfast at Tiffany's,* worked in this manner. If an actor does not understand the part he is reading for, then he is more likely to make poor and inconsistent choices.

Industry Connection

Raise the following points with your actors:

INSTRUCTOR: The audition process often seems unfair and flawed. It doesn't matter if this is true, because you still have to deal with it on an ongoing basis. This means you have to learn how to audition and audition well. Part of the reason the panel is given different scenarios to play with is to confuse you. One actor might be kept and worked with for five minutes, while the next performs his piece and is asked to leave immediately. Both of these situations may lead you to question your performance. The former may believe that the extra time means the panel found fault with his performance. The latter may believe the panel spent little time with them because the panel had no interest in his performance. In both cases, the actors may be totally wrong. This exercise has the added psychological caveat so that you start to second-guess yourself. It sets a trap for the actors to fall into and they do it all the time. You may have an audition that dramatically changes your life. This can only happen if you are prepared. The only thing actors will want to be concerned with is giving their best performance and presenting themselves professionally.

113. The Golden Handshake

You may want to start this exercise with a demonstration or you can have everybody spread out around the room, working at it simultaneously. I usually start out with a demonstration, working with two students. Have the rest of the group sit as the audience. Explain in the following way:

INSTRUCTOR: Marcus and Anna, I want the two of you to come forward to demonstrate this exercise. Can the two of you start off by facing one another? What I would like you to do is shake hands. (The students shake hands.) Now next time, when you shake hands, I am going to ask Marcus to force his intention onto Anna. That means that when you shake hands you are going to *send your intention* at the same time.

MARCUS: Am I going to do this by talking to her as well?

INSTRUCTOR: Good question, Marcus. In fact, you are going to do this nonverbally. As you shake Anna's hand, I want you to do so as if you are feeling nervous. You are going to send your nervous energy through your handshake. If you are successful, Anna will receive this through your handshake. (The students shake hands.)

ANNA: I felt it a little bit.

INSTRUCTOR: Good. Marcus, I want you to do this again, and imagine that you are very nervous about meeting this person. Perhaps you could imagine that Anna is a person of authority, such as a school principal, a police officer, or perhaps a girl you are interested in. (The students shake hands again.)

ANNA: That time was a lot better. It really gave me the creeps.

INSTRUCTOR: Good job, Marcus! Yes, nervous energy can send extremely mixed signals. Anna, you are going to shake Marcus' hand in a very confident manner. (The students shake hands.)

MARCUS: It was really clear. I felt from her handshake that she was totally in control of the situation.

INSTRUCTOR: Excellent work, Anna! What strategy did you use to help you?

ANNA: I imagined that I was going to an audition and that I really wanted the job.

INSTRUCTOR: So you used your imagination, which actually translated into a physical reaction when you shook hands with Marcus.

At this point, be ready to answer up to three questions from the group. I rarely take more than three questions. First of all, more questions can take too long. Second, if you give the students all the answers, it takes away from the discovery process. Ask the students to find a space in the room and work the exercise with their partners. You might want them to designate the partners in each pair as either A or B. You can have all the As work first and force their intention on the Bs then switch, or you might choose to alternate back and forth.

You can have your students shake hands as if they are:
Angry
Nervous
Fearful or scared
Tired
Excited or joyous
Shy
Tearful
Bored

Come up with more emotions of your own. You can also have the students do this without telling their partner ahead of time. This way their partner has to guess what they are feeling by reading the handshake they have received. Another suggestion is to have the actors shake hands while holding on for too long. This is likely to lead to the actors becoming uncomfortable and wanting to let go. When an actor is out of his comfort zone, this is when he is at his most vulnerable. You can also ask the actors to walk around the room, shaking hands with random people. To finish off, ask both partners to send a positive and confident message through their handshake.

Some discussion questions to consider with this exercise are:

What are some of the discoveries you made during this activity?

When might it be important to send a confident message through your handshake?

Were you aware of the powerful communication that can be sent through a simple handshake?

What assumptions did you find yourself making through your partner's handshake?

Purpose
To channel thoughts
Your actors are probably already aware of the signals that can be sent through nonverbal communication. What this exercise does is take it one step further. By shaking hands with another actor, they discover they can channel their thoughts and feelings through a handshake. If this is the case, they can do the same things through a hug or a pat on the knee. This is powerful information for actors. Let us say they are in a play in which they have a scene with their girlfriend or boyfriend. They have already given a number of performances, so they feel comfortable in the role and a little bored. As they come to do the kissing and hugging scene with their partner, they are really not in the moment. While the scene is supposed to be romantic, the message they are sending to their fellow actor is, "I am bored and would really rather be somewhere else. Your breath smells." Not only does this affect their performance, but also the performance of their partner in the scene. The actor has to be engaged in each and every moment, as if it were for real. They have to be able to tap into their heightened imagination.

Industry Connection
If an actor goes to an audition, it is usually best not to shake hands. This is because the audition panel members are most likely going to see scores, or even hundreds, of actors that day. The last thing they want to do is to shake two

hundred sweaty hands. However, if they offer an actor their hand, the actor will obviously want to take it. The actors have to know what kind of message they are conveying in that handshake. It had better be the one they want to convey. If they move to Hollywood, Bollywood, New York, or London, they will find that a certain amount of time is taken up with networking. They are going to shake hands with agents, directors, producers, managers, and a whole array of others. If the message being sent through the handshake is one of nervous energy, this is not going to work to the actor's advantage.

114. The Audition

For this exercise you will want to do some preparation. Think of a genre for a movie, such as:

A family movie
A comedy movie
A horror movie
A drama
A feel-good movie
A romantic comedy

Choose a genre such as a romantic comedy then create a number of generalized character types such as:

The jock
The nerd
The cheerleader
The mean guy
The Goth girl

Send out all but five of your actors. Tell the actors what role they are trying out for. If you have fifteen actors outside, invite three to try out for each role. Do not give them a choice of which role they are hoping to get. Have the five auditors sit in chairs, as if they are a panel of casting directors, producers, and directors. Give them some information, such as that set out above and inform them that they are going to be casting a movie. Each of them should have a piece of paper and a pencil. Ask them to come up with a joint checklist against which they are going to rate the actors. Give them no more than five minutes to do this. A sample list would be something such as:

Physical appearance/character type
Personality
Ability to follow direction
How prepared they appear
Confidence

When the actor comes into the room, he will tell the auditors his name, what role he is trying out for, and nothing more. Tell the auditors they will have up to two minutes to spend with each actor. They can have them do anything they want, from an improvisation to a dance. Once they have been through all the auditions, they are going to rate the actors and cast their movie. They will bring the actors back in and explain their choices. What they will not have to do is tell the people whom they didn't cast and why they were not chosen. This may sound unfair, but by and large, actors never truly find out why they were not cast.

Purpose

To practice auditioning

In some instances, the actors will find it more challenging to audition in front of their friends than they would auditioning for casting directors and producers. One of the reasons is that they see their friends on a regular basis, but they only see the casting agents sporadically or perhaps only once. For these actors, this adds an extra challenge to overcome with regards to the audition process. A casting agent may have an actor read some commercial copy for a commercial audition. Some actors will say, "I hate auditioning!" They are going to have to learn to overcome their fear and embrace auditioning. Anything the actor has to do on a regular basis, they will want to learn to love. I will ask, "What is the point of spending your life doing something you hate? Don't you think that if you hate auditioning, it will affect your ability to get the part? How can you compete with those who are enthusiastic and passionate about auditioning?" These are obvious points, but unless the actors learn to conquer their fears, they are likely to be constantly caught up in inner struggle. This is not conducive to living in a creative state.

Industry Connection

The actors have to audition before their peers. The actors are not told why they did not get the part. This may seem unjust, yet it is a bitter pill they are going to have to swallow on many occasions. When you conduct the exercise in this way, some of your actors may complain. They may say, "This is class, and we should know what we did wrong as a learning experience." It sounds like a good argument in terms of logic, but it can be a futile path to follow. Let us say that one reason an actor was not chosen for the part was because he, "mumbled his words." This would be useful to know. What if two other strikes against him were, "Too short for the part and didn't not look enough like the girl we were casting as the sister." Both these pieces of information are useless, because they cannot be changed. They are also subjective in that they are limited to a specific audition. Of course, there are times at an audition when the actor in question could have done a better job, but there are also numerous variables that are out of his control. This exercise highlights the point that actors will want to do everything they can to get the part and not become stressed about what they cannot control. It is also important that if the actors truly want the part, they will be willing to campaign for it.

115. The Hot Seat II

Tell your actors to sit in the audience space. Put a chair in the center of the room and invite an actor to come up and sit in it facing the audience. The actor must sit in the chair as his character. He has to answer questions as his character would answer them. The audience is going to spend the next ten to fifteen minutes asking the actor any questions they like, with regard to his character. Let us say the student sat in the hot seat as Romeo, from *Romeo and Juliet*. The following are some sample questions for Romeo:

What was the first thing about Juliet that made you think she was the one?

How did you know for sure that she was dead?

Do you wish that you weren't a Montague?

What was it like to go disguised to the Capulet ball?

Aren't you too young to fall in love?

How do you dare fall in love with the enemy of your family?

Members of the audience can challenge the actor if they notice inconsistencies in his answers. This does not mean they are allowed to accuse him of lying. It means they can ask for more detail or a more specific answer. To be in the hot seat takes guts. This exercise is not for the faint of heart. Acknowledge the fact that the actor who takes the seat is leaving himself open to attack. Each actor will want to be in the hot seat for fifteen minutes. Aim to work with three or four actors in this way. The audience has many questions they wish to ask the actor. In a play or film, the audience will have many questions they want to ask your character. This is an excellent exercise to use in conjunction with a play you are working on.

Variation
See the exercise, The Hot Seat on page 350.

Purpose
To make new discoveries about the character
Actors may feel they have done their homework on their character. They may feel that they have covered all the bases. If this is the case, they will be able to get into the presence of that character. This exercise may show them that there are certain questions they have yet to ask and yet to answer. By facing a mini-interrogation by their fellow actors, the actor may be forced to see his character in a new light. An actor in a play may stop asking questions of his character. This may be the point at which he begins to stagnate in the role. Once we stop asking questions, we cease to grow. The reason actors will never want to stop asking questions is because their character never stops asking questions.

Industry Connection
When the actors sit in the chair, they are not sitting as themselves. When they answer the questions, they are not being asked to answer as themselves. They are being asked to answer as their character. When actors are being interviewed for a part, they may have already completed the audition part. They may let go and relax as if the interview is just a formality. Some people find it stressful to relax. Let us say an actress auditions for the part of a sophisticated woman. She does a good job during the audition, and the panel is impressed. During the interview stage she relaxes completely. She sags in the chair and sits with her legs slightly sprawled and scratches her head. She feels so happy that she is relaxed and free. She feels the panel will see how fine an actress she is by seeing how much she contrasts with the character she just auditioned for. It is true that actors should be themselves in the interview. It is also true that at the same time they will want to bring in the essence of the character. To say that typecasting does not exist would be a gross misunderstanding of the industry. An actor should allow the panel to see the essence of the character in them at all times. Do not force them to stretch their imaginations too far. In other words, do not force them to try to figure you out. The actress auditioning for the refined character should have brought the refined side of herself to the interview. She is still being herself, but the more elegant side of herself. The actress will want to

159

allow the panel to see the essence of the character in her at all times if she wants to get the part.

116. Industry Awareness

For this activity you are going to need to have Internet access for at least one in five students. You may say this is not available. You need to think outside the box. You are more than likely to find that at least half your students have Internet on their phones. This is not a game, but a very useful activity. Split your actors into groups of five or fewer. What you are going to do is give each group a list of five words or terms. Each group is going to be given thirty minutes to go on to the Internet and find a definition for each word. The challenge on your part is that each word or term you give them has to be related to the industry in some way. Here are a few examples:

18 to play younger — an actor or actress who is eighteen or older but can convincingly portray a younger character

Action — a verbal cue that indicates a scene is to begin and the cameras are rolling

Back-to-one — indicates that the actors are to return to the start of the scene

Casting director — Represents the producer in pre-auditioning actors for a production

Cold reading — An unrehearsed or unprepared reading of lines

Some of your words may fall under film and theatre. This is fine, provided they can be applied to the industry. Give each group thirty minutes to research and come up with their definitions. At this point, bring everyone together in a circle and ask them to share their words and definitions. There is no need to make the whole group write down all the definitions. For now, it is good enough that they hear the definitions. If they are proactive, they will take the responsibility of learning the words and definitions in their own time.

Purpose
To learn about the industry

Some actors say there is no need to learn terms related to theatre because they are not going to perform in theatre. Let's accept this statement for now, regardless of whether we agree with it. Some of these actors will also say it is a waste of time learning industry-related terms and that they don't need to know any. It is baffling that an actor who is going to hopefully face casting directors on a constant basis has no desire to understand their function. It is baffling that an actor hoping to join SAG has no desire to learn about the three-voucher system or the Taft-Hartley Act. An actor who does not wish to learn about the industry he is in will be fast-tracking himself to a career of flipping burgers.

Industry Connection

This whole exercise is an industry connection, so let's expand a little further. Actors who blind themselves to learning about the acting industry can end up creating a painfully slow and clumsy path. I remember meeting a young actress the day after she had been offered Taft-Hartley almost out of the blue. This meant that from being non-union, she would be eligible to join the union. This is no small accomplishment and allows the actor to take a fast-track path.

Unfortunately, the actress did not understand what Taft-Hartley meant, and turned the opportunity down. When I met her later and we discussed it, she kicked herself. Some actors never miss an opportunity to miss an opportunity. Make sure that your actors do not fall into this category.

117. Casting Agent

For this exercise ask one of your students to sit on a chair that is stage left. This person is going to be the casting director. Tell five students to go outside the room. They are going to be coming in, as if for an audition. Place another chair stage right, opposite the casting director. Tell the rest of the students you would like them to watch each of the five actors who enter the room. Say that when they have finished, you are going to ask them to make observations about what they saw. Tell the casting director he is going to be given one minute to spend with each actor. He is not asking the actor to perform at this point. He should rather conduct the interview part of the audition. He can ask any questions he likes. Tell the actors to come in one at a time, and leave the room when they have finished.

Here are some of the challenges the audience may notice of the actors:
They came in really slowly and lethargically.
They slumped into the chair.
They kept their head down the whole time.
They mumbled their words.
They came across as forced and uncomfortable.

Here are some pieces of constructive advice about what a casting director may want to see at the audition:
The actor has good posture.
The chair does not mean the actor should sit. The actor will not want to sit unless he is asked to do so, or it is a necessary part of his scene.
The actor should hold his head high when entering the room.
The actor should smile when entering the room.
The actor should make eye contact when entering the room.
The actor should appear confident because he believes the job is his.
The actor hands his headshot and resumé to the casting director.

These are just a few examples of what the actor can consider when attending an audition. Instruct the five actors to repeat the exercise following this discussion. This time, do not send them outside the room, but let them start from inside the room. In this way, they will also be able to observe the other actors. These are not hard and fast rules, but are useful tips.

Variation
See exercise Acting Natural in *112 Acting Games.*

Purpose
To prepare for the audition
Some actors are happy to prepare for a performance, but feel audition preparation is beneath them. They feel that the audition has nothing to do with acting. In a way they are correct. An audition does not mean an individual is a

good actor. It may simply mean he is good at auditioning. The challenge is that it is the measuring stick by which most roles are cast. Every actor will want to strive to become an expert at auditions. The book *Audition* by Michael Shurtleff is one of the best-selling acting books, and with good reason. The actor who has no interest in mastering the audition process is most likely to be uninterested in a professional career.

Industry Connection

Not every actor has to audition. A-list actors are very often sent scripts from which to pick and choose. Some of these actors seek the advice of those such as their agent to see if the script is up to par. In part this is because they are too busy to read all the scripts they are sent. Directors and producers may virtually plead with actors to take a part. They take them out for breakfast, lunch, or dinner in the hope of convincing them they are right for the part. Sometimes an actor will turn down a movie that goes on to become a huge hit. These actors do not need to audition because their work is out there for everyone to see. Every time they make a movie they are, in fact, auditioning for their next role. They also have a box office pull, which means that their name potentially brings in a large amount at the box office. Some actors have a certain drive that is driven by their ambition for success. When a producer can hire an A-list actor, it is as if they feel they have certain guarantees in place. A-list actors are not necessarily the best actors, but they are the most popular with the biggest box office pull. Some A-list actors become producers so they can have more control over their work. Some actors will take a part depending on who else has already been cast.

Note

Lee Strasberg, Harold Clurman, and Stella Adler were the founding members of the Group Theatre. They were also all students of Richard Boleslavski at the American Laboratory Theatre. Boleslavski was a former student of Stanislavski and a member of the Moscow Art Theatre. It is the cyclical nature of acting that brought these great artists together.

118. Taking Center Stage

Have all your actors line up as if in the wings. Call out a character such as a witch. The actors are going to go into the performance space, one after the other, and perform one sentence or phrase in the character of the witch. An example would be, "I'll put a spell on all of you!" It is important that they each perform in the center of the performance space. Each person should begin a new scene. After each person has performed, they must leave the stage in character and go to the back of the line. There should be no gaps, so the next person should follow immediately. You will want to change the character each time everyone has been through. If you prefer, you can change the character in the middle of a round.

A few character suggestions are:

Doctor
Astronaut
Farmer
Nurse
Teacher

Goblin
Scarecrow
Postman
Ballerina

Remind the actors that they must perform their sentence or phrase from center stage. The actors must work at a fairly intense pace. The idea is to keep the activity moving at all times.

Purpose

To take center stage

For some reason, some actors shy away from the center of the stage. They do anything they can to avoid being in the center. It is as if they feel they cannot be seen from the sides of the stage and can hide there. It is a strange paradox, considering that actors spend their whole career trying to be noticed. A director will hopefully have his actors work the whole space when it is called for. It is important that an actor is not afraid to command the space or to take center stage. There may be many things happening that create the mise-en-scéne behind the actor. By taking center stage, it is as if the actors are giving the audience a blue print of where their main focus point should be.

Industry Connection

When actors go to an audition, they literally have to go to center stage. If they are auditioning for theatre, they have to find the light, so as to be seen. If they are auditioning for television or film, they also have to make an impression. When actors walk into the room, they must command the space. If they back away into a corner, all coy and meek, they will very likely be sending the wrong signals. The actor may take center stage then realize there is a better place from which to start the scene. The director may ask him to start on a mark that is stage right. The important point to make is that when the actor enters the room he will want to do so with confidence and clarity.

119. Cold Reading Companion

For this exercise you will need to have at least two contrasting monologues available of approximately one minute in length. You can work with numerous monologues if you have them. You will need to have one per student. Have the students break up into pairs. One of the students in each group should receive a monologue. They are going to be given two minutes to look over the piece. At this point, have the actors perform their monologues for their partners as a cold reading. Their partners are going to be asked to evaluate the performance, making brief notes with regard to what they see and hear. Some examples are:

You spent all your time with your eyes looking at the page.

You mumbled your words.

You fumbled a number of your words such as especially, jumping, and acknowledge.

You were fidgeting and swaying from side to side.

You were reading the piece as opposed to performing it.

At this point the same person should perform his monologue again. Have his partner comment on what he observed and heard this time. Collect the first set of monologues. Hand out new and contrasting monologues to the other individual in each pair. It is very important that they do not receive their monologue until this point. It will not be a cold reading exercise if they receive their piece ahead of time. Repeat the same protocol as before. Once the exercise is complete, bring the entire group back together sitting in a circle. Finish up with a discussion. Ask the auditioners what were the challenges of cold reading their monologues. Have them comment on anything that surprised them with regard to this exercise. Have the observers comment on any profound discoveries they may have had.

Purpose

To learn from each other

In this exercise the actors are asked to learn from each other. The performers have to be alert and almost preempt what is coming. Their eyes have to sporadically read ahead of the line in between looking up. Outside of the technicalities, the actor still has to find the meaning in the piece. The observers have to listen with critical intent. They have to watch the performance objectively for any and all impediments. Some actors on-set will observe other actors at work and learn from them. This exercise allows the actors to learn from each other's mistakes without judging. Both actors know they have an extremely limited amount of time to prepare. The actors also know that at some point they will switch roles. These are also purposeful aspects of the exercise to take the actors out of their comfort zone.

Industry Connection

In this exercise, the actors are given two minutes grace period to look over the piece. You may think this therefore nullifies the exercise from being a cold reading, but in an audition situation the director is most likely to allow the actor to look once over the script before he begins. Cold reading may be more about technical skill than good acting, yet the actors who master it are increasing their chances of working. Scripts and dialogue can change at any moment, so a performance can sometimes practically feel like a cold read. This exercise also puts the actors outside of their comfort zones. Asking a director if they can look once over the script might also take the actors out of their comfort zones. If they do not ask for it they may not get it. Consequently, the part may go to someone else who was better prepared.

Chapter 15
Action and Reaction

120. Out of Sight

Explain in the following way:

INSTRUCTOR: For this exercise I am going to ask Alex to come up and help me. In a moment I am going to put a blindfold on Alex. She is then going to start to walk around the room. She obviously will now have lost her sense of sight. The rest of you are going to spread out all around the room. You are going to be her eyes from this point forward. The challenge here is that Alex does not have one guide. The entire group is going to have to work as a unit to make sure that Alex does not bump into anything or crash into a wall. If Simon is nearest to Alex, then he will momentarily become her guide. If Lucas is suddenly the closest person to Alex, he will take over as the guide. The only person who should be moving around the room is Alex. Are there any questions?

PAULA: What if Alex is close to two people? Who should guide her?

INSTRUCTOR: This is a great question, Paula. There is no right or wrong answer here. Either one of you can guide her, but the decision is going to have to come very quickly. One of you will have to take the lead before Alex ends up bumping into someone or something. Once one person takes the lead the other person should hold off.

DAMIEN: Can two people guide her at the same time?

INSTRUCTOR: There can only be one guide at any given moment.

Use safety first for this exercise. You should also be moving around the room to make sure that the blindfolded student does not bump into a wall or get injured. It is still your responsibility as the instructor to put safety at the top of your agenda. If the actors are having challenges with this exercise, pause for a moment and allow them to brainstorm together.

Purpose
To think on your feet

In this exercise the actors have to be aware of everything that is happening around them. They have to think on their feet. If they are not focused, the actor with the blindfold could very easily bump into a wall. An actor may be on-stage in the middle of a scene when the actor next to him accidentally knocks over a box of pencils. Because the actor is nervous, he chooses to ignore it. The audience immediately becomes aware of the pencils. They start asking each other questions. "Was that supposed to happen?" "What have the pencils got to do with anything?" "I wonder what was the significance of the pencils is?" The whole palaver with the pencils now detracts from the scene and the audience may become unfocused. When this happens it can be hard to draw them back in. It is in moments like these that the actor will need to be able to react quickly. If the actor who knocked over the pencils ignores them, then perhaps it is up to the other actor to solve the issue. He will have to find a justification to pick them up and move on with the scene. An actor has to learn to use an accident and make it work for the scene.

Industry Connection

I am going to use a metaphor here. The actors who are blindfolded are being led blindly around the room. They have to rely on others to transport them safely from place to place. When actors arrives in Hollywood, New York, or London they may also feel somewhat blinded. They may be well-trained actors but not be industry savvy in their chosen city. They now have to rely, to some degree, on others for good advice and guidance. Perhaps they take an acting class because a friend told them it was a great class. Perhaps they get headshots by a photographer they read about online. Maybe they get an agent who does not help them in any way. To some degree they may feel like they are entering a minefield. It is true that to some degree actors will have to rely on others for help and advice. What is not true is that they have to charge at these things like a bull at a gate. Advise your actors not to be too quick to part with their money or be too quick to take advice from others. They should be willing to step back a little and move forward one step at a time. They will want to be patient enough to back their own talent. Slowly over time they may begin to piece together the beginnings of a career. Some actors recommend never taking advice from another actor. If they are looking for longevity in their acting career, then it would be wise to build a strong foundation. I understand that some of your students are still in school, but there is no harm in having them plan ahead for the future. Actress Gay Storm, who has worked in both Hollywood and New York, told me the following in regards to a conversation we were having over longevity and the actor, "Being an actor is like owning an expensive sports car — you need a lot of care and maintenance. I don't act because I do it better than anyone else. I act because it is the thing I do best."

121. On Guard

One student stands in the center of the room and is guarding a rare gold statue. You can use a tennis ball or any item that is soft and not breakable. The students are going to have to use their imaginations here. Put the gold statue on the stool in the center of the room. The rest of the group will start further back and their aim is to steal the statue without getting caught (tagged) first. The aim is not to storm the guard and steal the statue. The aim is to steal the statue without getting caught. If a student is tagged, then he must stay frozen for the rest of the game. This raises the stakes for the students and encourages them in being more cautious when going for the statue. While the group can walk forward and backward, the guard can only pivot off one leg, but in any direction. Whoever gets the statue will be the guard in the next round. Make sure the actors practice safety awareness for this exercise.

Purpose

To be spatially aware of the surroundings

In a scene, actors act and react to what others around them are doing. In this exercise, the actors act by trying to take the statue, and react by moving away from the guard who is trying to tag them. The actors also have to be spatially aware of their surroundings. If they are not looking around them, they can easily crash into other actors and an injury could follow. It may be quite dark backstage, and if actors are not spatially aware, they could collide with scenery or other actors waiting in the wings.

Industry Connection

Make the following observations with your actors:

INSTRUCTOR: Let us say you are the first actor to be tagged and have to freeze for the rest of the exercise. It will not feel like much fun, and you might kick yourself for getting caught. Now imagine you walk into a room for an audition, you say about three words, and before you can say anything else, the director calls out, "Thank you." Not a very nice feeling, and yet one that is commonplace for the actor. Let us say you win the activity and get the statue. You feel good about yourself and proud of your accomplishment. If you get cast in a role or book a job, you will get some kind of adrenaline rush, but more than likely it will be short-lived, as pretty soon you are back on the trail looking for that next job. Actors need to get used to different extremes of emotions and find a way to balance them out in their lives. In a performance they will want to aim to strike just the right emotional chord. They need to be able to hear, see, and feel the reflections of the emotions of life. Some actors develop sadness in their lives when they are not performing. When the spotlight is on they are happy.

122. Hit Man

This exercise will work better with larger groups of actors. Have the entire group spread out around the room. Explain in the following way:

INSTRUCTOR: In a moment, I want you all to pick someone to be your bodyguard and somebody else to be your hit man. There is no need to say their names out loud. The only person who needs to know who they are is you. In this exercise, everyone tries to protect themselves from their hit man by trying to keep their bodyguard between themselves and their hit man.

JANE: Can you hold onto your bodyguard to protect yourself?

INSTRUCTOR: You cannot make physical contact with another player. This means that everyone in the room should have a hit man, and everyone should have a bodyguard. While you are protecting yourself from your hit man I want to give you another task. I want you to see if you can work out if anyone has chosen you as their hit man or their bodyguard.

DANIEL: How do you win?

INSTRUCTOR: There are no winners or losers in this exercise. It is more a few minutes of organized chaos. There is another part to this activity you need to consider: Someone has been hired to kill you. This means that if you are running around the room laughing and giggling, you are missing the point. At the same time, each one of you is also a potential hit man, which adds another layer to this exercise. Make sure you are taking these considerations into account.

Purpose

To act and react

This exercise is about acting and reacting. Every time a player's hit man changes position he has to react by changing his position. Every time his bodyguard changes position he has to react by changing his position. Explain the following to your actors:

INSTRUCTOR: Every time a character speaks to you in a scene, you react. Sometimes you react with a verbal response. Other times your reaction will come through nonverbal communication. Some examples of this are a shrug of the shoulders, or nod or shake of the head. If you are actively listening to your partner, you will react to what is being said, and vice versa. You learn when you listen. When actors respond off one another they are able to drive the scene. The actor will want to let the examination and interest in their partner shine on the screen. When actors are creating their characters they have to be able to hear who they are. In a scene an actor wants a partner who is generous and accessible. This exercise is a constant flow of action and reaction.

Industry Connection

At first this exercise appears like its only real purpose is to have fun. It appears to be a very superficial exercise and yet the more your actors keep digging, the more they will find this exercise has to offer. An actor may get cast in a number of day-player roles in his screen and television career. When an actor has pages of dialogue he can get invested in the character. A day-player role gives the actor literally no time to get comfortable. In these instances he is usually paid to scale. This is the minimum wages that an actor can be paid under union guidelines. This is literally as it sounds, and usually entails one or two days of filming. It is also likely to have a part of five lines or less. The actor may be handed a script that says: *POLICEMAN: Hi, Jim.* That's it! That's the lot! No more lines. No character breakdown to analyze. As a day player, he is going to get paid a tidy sum to say a few words. If an actor wanted to, he could probably just have fun and wing it. After all, he only has one line and was most likely typecast anyway. He knows what the package is and he is buying that specific package. So now it is up to him to decide how badly he wants to be a good actor. To get there he will have to go through many different manifestations. He could take his two words and build a whole scenario around him. He could take his character who only appears for five seconds and make him a living, breathing human being. He could find the disposition of that character. He could pull on all his tools as an actor in order to do this. He may only have a small part, but he should still desire to be part of that experience. It is his choice.

In terms of type, some actors are constantly regenerating and rejuvenating themselves. Some actors see molds and they are terrified of falling into any of them. Other actors simply fit into the mold. In their career, many actors would like to play a whole different variety of roles. They want to take their audiences on a wonderful ride through life. Some actresses feel that women's roles are limited in film. There are not as many great roles for women. Studios have to make a certain amount of money and so women are often cast to type and formula. By the time they reach forty, many female actresses find their career choices dwindling. On the other hand, there are more roles for men that allow them to have a greater complexity.

Raise the following discussion with your students:

INSTRUCTOR: You may spend hours or days preparing for this role and the only one who will know is you and your roommate. The most receptive comment you will get from anyone will probably be, "good job." So it is up to you. You have to decide what your acting means to you. You have to decide what kind of actor you want to be. Does it truly matter if you are a good actor? Can you make a living as an actor and not be particularly good? Tell me what it is you love about your favorite actor or actress.

You may be opening a can of worms with some of these questions. Good! Open away! You want to get your students thinking. You want them to recognize the difference between mediocrity and excellence. There are numerous actors but there are precious few great actors. Great actors are constantly looking and searching, but very rarely satisfied with a performance.

Note
Sometimes the rules of an exercise may not be one hundred percent clear to the actor. If this is the case, tell him to make up his own. One of the keys to the actor's work is adaptation. An actor will want to have a practical form of optimism. When it is necessary, adapt the rules to the specific needs of your actors.

123. Look Out!
This exercise is a nice way to wake everybody up and make them fully alert. Have your actors sit in a circle. Tell them that they are to look directly at the floor. When you blow your whistle, they have to look straight ahead, to the left, or to the right. They must do this immediately, without any pause or time to think about it. If they make eye contact with another actor, they must scream and die a horrible death. If their eyes do not connect with another actor, they live to fight another day. The actors are not allowed to avoid eye contact by closing their eyes or looking up at the ceiling. Remind the actors that their scream should not be one that damages their vocal chords. The idea is to be one of the last two left in.

Purpose
To commit to the moment
This exercise asks the actors to commit to the moment. As soon as they hear the whistle, they have to react. Some actors may wait a moment so that they can avoid making eye contact with another actor. They feel that they can cheat the exercise in order to succeed. It is the same as the actor who spends her time going over her lines in her head, instead of actively listening while the other actor is talking. She thinks she is fooling the audience. The truth of the matter is the audience has already lost interest in her performance. This exercise also demands that the actors use their voices effectively but safely. If they scream and damage their vocal chords, their career will be short-lived. The actors will want to develop the timbre of their voice. As the famed voice dialectician Patsy Rodenburg says in her book, *The Actor Speaks*, "Before doing any serious work on speaking text, you must warm up both voice and the muscles you will be using to speak."[26] How are your actors going to do eight shows a week in the future if they do not look after their instrument and use it effectively? Remind your actors of the difference between projecting their voices and damaging them. Actors have to work awfully hard to protect their voices.

26. Patsy Rodenburg, *The Actor Speaks* (New York: St. Martin's Press, 1997), 166.

Industry Connection

If the actors play this exercise full out and they commit to it, they could still be the first person out. They could also be the last person left in. If this is the case, then we have to accept that the two soul survivors had a degree of luck on their side. Tell your actors if they are going to be a professional working actor who can pay their bills solely from their acting income, they will most likely have a degree of luck on their side somewhere down the road. The question is not, "Will luck come my way?" but rather, "Will I be prepared for Lady Luck when she comes my way?" If an actor is not prepared for opportunity, it will become a missed opportunity.

Note

I want to explore the word *luck* and what I call the *lottery approach*. Some actors believe in the lottery approach to their acting career. They say things like, "I will be discovered," "Within a year I will be a movie star," "There is no point in doing any training," or "No movie stars train anymore." I wish I were making these quotes up, but I am not. They are more common views than one might believe. These aspiring actors believe in the lottery approach to acting. They don't want to do any of the work but they would like all of the rewards. They long to get their names up in lights. They can always give you an example of someone who has achieved fame and fortune this way, and they are right. Some actors have made a steep climb very quickly. One in a million people have become famous actors this way. One in a million people have won big money on the lottery this way. Explain to your actors that if they like the one-in-a-million odds, then this is the correct approach for them. For the actors who are serious about their acting and making a living, there can be no substitute for hard work and persistence! Great movies are still being made, although not enough. The first performance of Anton Chekhov's play, *The Seagull,* was an absolute failure. Two years later it was performed by the Moscow Art Theatre and eventually became one of Checkhov's most famous and successful plays. It is sad to realize that theatre in the United States is subsidized by the government on far too few occasions. This may be because not enough people recognize the value in the arts. Some actors say there should be no competition in acting and that awards are meaningless. I would agree that is dangerous to rank movies in term of first and second place. On the other hand, I am almost certain no actor ever regrets winning an Oscar.

124. Revolver

Have your actors form a circle. Ask them to hold hands and explain in the following way:

INSTRUCTOR: In a moment I would like everyone to start moving the circle in a clockwise direction. At any given moment someone can shout "revolver." When this happens, the entire circle has to start turning in the opposite direction. The challenge is that any time an actor bumps into another actor everyone must stop, release hands, and then start again. The aim is to keep the circle moving for as long as possible. It may end up changing direction fourteen or fifteen times.

If the group is having a lot of problems with this exercise, then pause the exercise and give them the opportunity to problem solve amongst themselves.

They are not allowed to say things like, "Jenny can say revolver first." While this is a creative suggestion, it breaks the rules of the exercise. Remind the actors that every time "revolver" is heard they must change the circle's direction. If two or three actors say, "revolver" at the same time, this is still only one direction change.

Purpose
To listen and respond
This exercise is not only about listening, it is also about responding at that precise moment. If the actors react a few seconds too late, they will probably bump into another actor. Actors may be in a play that they have performed hundreds of times before. They are listening to the actor working against them, but the challenge is they have heard his line too many times to even remember. Their reactions are delayed, or preempted, because they always know what is coming next. It is the illusion that the actor is always trying to get back to of making it up from moment to moment. To keep the material alive and fresh is one of the major challenges facing the stage actor. It is going to take a great deal of discipline and skill for an actor to achieve this on a continual basis. The actor is going to want to find a way to see his character as endlessly fascinating.

Industry Connection
This exercise appears simple, yet it is quite challenging. Many aspiring actors move to Los Angeles and say, "I'm going to pursue the acting thing and have a small part in a movie by next year." It is the most ridiculous thing, yet it's heard all the time. They have no training, no money, no serious work ethic, and yet they believe what they say. They believe in the lottery approach to acting, which is highly unreliable and very rare indeed. As Constantin Stanislavski says in his book, *An Actor Prepares*, "Most actors before each performance put on costumes and makeup so that their external appearance will approximate that of the character they are to play. But they forget the most important part, which is the inner preparation. Why do they devote such particular attention to their external appearance? Why do they not put makeup on the costumes of their souls?"[27] The professional acting career is a challenging one and not for the faint of heart. The rewards can be great but, in part, that is because the sacrifices are even greater. Actors' careers can be full of extraordinary highs and extraordinary lows. Actors will want to have the richest experiences they can have as an actor. The question to ask your actors is the following: The question is not do you want a career of an actor, but do you want the lifestyle of an actor and all that it entails?

125. In and Out
For this activity you will need a rope four or five feet long. If you do not have rope, you can always use masking tape. Stretch the rope on the floor, down the middle of the room. Explain in the following way:

INSTRUCTOR: I hope that everyone is feeling energetic today. Let me have a volunteer for a moment. Carrie, come over here and join me. Please stand at the right hand side of the rope. Carrie is now in the fire. Please jump over to the left hand side of the rope. Carrie is now out of the fire. (Make sure you make clear

27. Constantin Stanislavski. *An Actor Prepares* (New York: Routledge, 1964), 265.

to the students which is the left and which is the right side of the rope. In other words, is it their left or yours?) When I shout out "in the fire," everyone must be on the right hand side of the rope. When I shout out, "out of the fire," everyone must now be on the left hand side of the rope. If you are on the wrong side of the rope, you are out. That's it. That is the entire activity.

CLAY: What if you call "out of the fire" and I am already out of the fire?

INSTRUCTOR: Good question. This is a very important part of the exercise. If you are already on the right hand side, you just stay there. If you are on the wrong side you have to make sure you immediately jump over to the other side. This activity is a bit like Simon Says in that I am going to try to mislead. My aim is to get all of you out as quickly as possible. Once you have jumped to the wrong side you cannot jump back. I am going to try to distract you as much as possible. The aim is to be the last person left in.

You can call out whatever you want. I have heard instructors call out, "into/out of the coffin" and "into/out of the lake." You can make up your own instructions if you want. If you call out at a rapid pace, it will be harder for the students to keep up, and easier for them to be tricked into jumping to the wrong side. You can have a student do the calling out if you prefer. It is important that this activity moves at a fast pace.

Purpose
To respond and react

The purpose of this exercise is for the actors to be able to respond on the spot. Not only must they respond, they must continue to make the best choices. During a performance the actors have to respond in a similar way. When a character speaks to them, they must respond. When people speak to us in everyday life, we normally react to what is being said. We don't usually stop and plan our responses. In fact, it could be better if we did do this in real life. Many of us live in a "reactionary world." Sometimes we may be more controlled in our responses, such as at a job interview. The actors have to reach a point in their acting at which they can put their trust in the character. Any performance that is contrived will come across as forced and unbelievable. An actor who is not able to instantaneously react will only last a short time.

Industry Connection

I am going to use a metaphor to talk about the industry connection here. Some people will say they are an actor. They have no money to support themselves, a resumé with absolutely nothing on it, and no contacts. They have no training and no intention of getting any. They do, however, have a headshot. They plan to be discovered within the year and be in the movies. Let's call these people "out of the fire." They are going to be in the group that moves to a big city for a short while, then leave dismayed, despondent, and absolutely devastated that their "talent" has not been recognized. There is another group of actors who have very little money. They take three jobs to support themselves. They have already had some training. They take every acting class they can find. They audition periodically, because they do not have much time left in the day. They have an agent, but are not able to attend all the auditions because of their other jobs. They work very hard, but get burnt-out on the lifestyle, and after three to five years, they leave. Let us call these actors "into the fire." There is a third group of actors. These actors have developed a means of income. It may be from their acting alone, or from other means. It does not take up a great deal of their time. It may have taken them years to get to this point. They are trained actors who continue to train. They do not take classes all the time, but do their homework for teachers who are able to work with their specific needs. They have built a team around themselves whose mutual aim is to enhance the actor's career. They work very hard on their careers, but also put aside some time for themselves. They are the actors who make money in their careers. They are the actors with five years, ten years, or more in the industry and longevity in their career. They make up between three and five percent of all actors. Let us call this group "walking on the rope." Sometimes they jump into the fire, but know when to get out. It is unlikely that an actor can start here, but they can certainly work towards getting to this point.

126. Under Cover

I have included this exercise simply because it is such fun. I mention that because it is difficult to play fairly. You will need two queen or king sized blankets for this exercise. Make sure that they are thick enough to prevent the students seeing through them. Divide your students into two teams. Give each team a blanket. Separate each team by about six feet. At this point, each team has to cover their entire team with their blanket. It is OK if their feet and legs are showing, but even better if they are not. On your command, each team must send out one person. That person must come out backwards and with their eyes closed. As the teams send out their person, there should be absolute silence. Give the teams about thirty seconds between each round. You may want to blow a whistle to avoid confusion. Only one person from each team should come out from under the blanket. On your command, both players are to turn around as quickly as they can and shout out the name of the person from the other team. The first person to do so will earn one point for their team. Instead of sitting down, these players then go back under the blanket. Each team is not allowed to send out the same person more than twice. The first team to score ten points is the winning team. The students absolutely love this activity. Make sure that they can breathe under their blankets.

Purpose

To have fun

I am going to say that the purpose of this exercise is to have fun. Of course, it has numerous other values that should also be mentioned. As you look at exercises and activities throughout this book, you are going to see fun mentioned a number of times. Some people may believe that this does not need to be mentioned. As someone who takes acting very seriously, I love to mention the word fun. Some famous actors comment on the fabulous fun they had working on certain projects. If your actors do not enjoy what they are doing, why are they going to bother doing it? They will want to find the joy in performing. They may be involved for a short period, but as a teacher or coach, you also want to create potential for longevity. If you can help the actors light the fire of passion about acting, they will do the rest. There are many occasions when acting takes a lot of hard work on the part of the actor. Look for opportunities to allow them to laugh and let their hair down. If you are a classroom teacher using this book, you are well aware that some of your students may have been "forced" into your acting class. In week one, some of these students will say things like, "I hate acting," "I don't want to be in this dumb class," and "Acting sucks!" And those are the nice ones. At first, this may feel like an uphill battle for you. In conversation with acclaimed school principal, Sheila Anderson, she told me, "A well-developed theatre program contributes enormously to the establishment and maintenance of a highly effective school. Opportunity abounds for students to fine-tune knowledge they learn in the core classes, as well as essential practice in the skills of collaboration, presentation, persuasion, and self-confidence. Often, students who otherwise feel left out of the day-to-day demands of content classes, thrive in the differentiated, multi-dimensional, and opportunity-rich theatre class." If you persevere in passing on what you love, then you will find that those same students will be the first ones looking to sign up for the next course. Your actors, with your encouragement, will want to become the most extraordinary optimists in their work.

Industry Connection

If a team wants to come in first, then they have to win. They cannot come in second and win. If a team loses by just one point, they have still lost. They may have played really well, but they still didn't win. This is not being said to disparage those who came in second, but as a simple fact. Sometimes you will hear an acting coach talk about winning the audition. It may sound blunt, but there is clarity to what is being said. Let us assume that an actor gave a fine performance at an audition. The agent contacts him the next day and says, "They loved you! Unfortunately, they gave the part to someone else." The actor may have done all he possibly could. But he is in a business where rejection is part of the course. The main point is that when actors walk into the room, they have to believe the part is already theirs. They have to win the part. If they don't believe they should get the part, then neither will anyone else. Some actors are experts at losing the part. They can tell you every reason under the sun why they are not right for the part. Encourage your actors to see themselves as winners. If there is only one job available, that is the one they should go after.

127. Hand Bites

This is a well-known activity in which I participated when growing up in London. Tell your students to sit in the audience. Bring two students into the performance area to demonstrate. Instruct the two students to face each other so that they are about a foot apart. Ask both of them to put their hands together into the praying position. At this point have them point their hands forward, horizontally. The fingertips of each persons' hands should now be touching the finger tips of the other person. Explain in the following way:

INSTRUCTOR: Gillian, what you are going to do is slap Meagan's hand. Meagan, you are obviously going to try to stop Gillian from doing so. Gillian can slap coming from the left side with her left hand or the right side with her right hand. Gillian, you are not allowed to bluff. This means that if you move a hand, you have to follow through. Meagan, your aim is to move your hands out of the way by pulling them back when Gillian attempts to slap them. The challenge is that you cannot flinch and move them before she actually attempts to hit them. If you preempt and move your hands before Gillian even makes an attempt, you will give Gillian a free slap. Gillian, if you miss Meagan's hands, the roles reverse and Meagan becomes the one to do the slapping. I am going to ask the rest of you to pair off for this activity. You will find your own space in the room and then begin. Any questions before we start?

RICK: How hard can we slap?

INSTRUCTOR: That is a very important question. Growing up, we used to slap as hard as we could. We are not doing that here. I want you to use minimum force in this activity. The aim is not to slap hard, but to actually have faster reflexes than your opponent. If they tell you it is too hard, then it is too hard.

DARREN: Can we switch partners?

INSTRUCTOR: That is a good idea. I will have you play for three minutes with one partner and then ask you to switch partners.

This is one of those exercises in which you are going to have to judge the maturity of your students. If the students simply ignore you and slap hard, it is going to sting and hurt. This is not the aim of the activity for our purposes, so make a judgment on the maturity of your students. If they cannot follow direction, stop the activity and move on to something else. Sometimes it is good for them to feel a real gut response. As the saying goes, actions speak louder than words.

Purpose
Action and reaction

When an actor attempts to slap (action), the other actor will attempt to move his hands out of the way (reaction). If either actor takes too long to think about this, they will give the upper hand to their partner. The actors have to literally act and react in the moment. Let us assume that two characters are in a scene together. The daughter is about to go upstairs to her room. Her mother calls out her name, "Anna!" In most cases this will get some form of reaction from the daughter. She might turn to face her mom. She might stop in her tracks and listen so as to hear what she has to say. She might simply roll her eyes and keep going up the stairs. In any case, there will most likely be some form of reaction. If the daughter is a weak actress, she may not really be listening, and she may not react in any way. She may just go up the stairs and repeat her own line. If she is not actively engaged in the scene, she may say her line, but she will not be reacting to what has just been said.

Industry Connection

Even if the actors slap very gently it could still sting a little, which adds that extra sting to losing a round. Metaphorically speaking, actors may feel a sting every time they lose in an audition situation. The actors have to learn to get used to that sting and embrace it. This is not to be negative. Statistically speaking, most actors are going to be turned down many more times than they are actually cast in a role. This means that actors have to find a way to cope with this reality. If they get miserable every time they fail to get the part, they are going to find that they are miserable every week. If this is the case, they are probably going to have short-lived careers. This does not mean that they are expected to celebrate not getting the parts. It means that they will want to learn, grow, and embrace every audition that they go to. By doing so, they can take away most of the bite and sting that they could potentially receive.

128. Desert Island

You are going to need several mats or you can use newspaper for this activity. In this example, I am going to use newspaper. Explain in the following way:

INSTRUCTOR: As you can see, I have spread out twenty double sheets of newspaper around the room. In this group, there are twenty-one of you. Each newspaper signifies a mini desert island. When I start the music, I want all of you to keep moving around the room. When the music stops, I want you to find your way to a desert island as quickly as you can. Everything around the islands will immediately become submerged in water. Here is the challenge: There can be only one person per island. The first person to land on each island is able to claim it. The person without an island will be out. For each round, I am going to take away one more island. I may choose to take away two islands. The last person left in is the sole survivor. There is one other component of this exercise: I am going to come around to each of you and give you a general character breakdown. Some examples are: an eight-year-old daughter, mother of three, single adult male, grandfather of six, or father. I am giving you the bare minimum. As you are moving around I want you, in your mind, to expand on your character's personality, traits, and so on. Who are you? What do you do for a living? Where do you live? When the music stops, one person will be left without an island. They are not automatically out. They are going to have the opportunity to go up to one person only and they can ask them to change places by giving up their island. An example would be an eight-year-old girl asking an adult male to give up his island to save her life. I will allow a discussion of up to one minute. He does not have to give up his place. Whether he does or does not give up his place, both of them are going to have to justify their responses. It is important to remember that if you give up your space, you are giving up your life. This should not be given away freely or without serious thought.

Variation
See Shipwrecked in *112 Acting Games*.

Purpose
To build a case
The actors are given a character breakdown. While they are moving around the room to the music, they are asked to develop more information with regards to their characters. When they are asked to give up their place on the island, it is not enough just to say no. They are going to have to look at their character and build a case to justify their response. In a play, a character may find himself in many challenging situations. It is up to the actors to build a case for their character. It is up to the actors to understand why their characters do the things they do. Actors will find challenges in playing a part convincingly if they do not know what motivates the character.

Industry Connection

In this activity the actors have to make a choice. They have to choose whether to save their own life or give it up to save someone else's. In reality, there may not be many people who would be willing to give up their own lives. If actors say, "Sure, I don't mind," ask them to explain why they have offered to change places. I am not saying they cannot say this. I am saying they have to understand the gravity of what they are doing. Hopefully, actors in Hollywood are not going to be asked to give up their life. What they will be asked to do is go the extra mile. Some actors, tech crew, etc., have to work fourteen-hour days on movie sets. A famous actor might say, "I refuse to do this!" He may also say, "I see the importance of getting this shot today, and I am willing to do whatever it takes to make it happen." I am not talking about being taken advantage of, which also happens. I am saying that some actors will say, "I will do what it takes to build my acting career!" In reality, they want to do virtually nothing to make their career happen. When push comes to shove, they don't want to put their money where their mouth is. It is not what an actor says they are going to do, but what they actually do that matters!

129. Sound Bounce

This is an excellent warm-up exercise. Tell your actors to stand in a circle. Ask one to come up with a sound and an action. It is good if the sound and action complement each other. An example would be making two fists and spinning them around, one on top of the other, while making a whirring sound. The actor should throw this action to another actor. Have him lunge forward as he does this and really energize his arms and hands as he throws the action and sound. The actor on the receiving end will absorb and repeat exactly what he has just received. He will then create his own sound and action and throw it to another actor. Have your actors use everyone, rather than only involving the same few people. Do not give your actors thinking time. This activity will want to keep moving at a rapid pace. It is important that the person who throws a sound and action does so clearly. If he is vague, the action may appear to be thrown in the direction of any one of a number of people.

Purpose

To act and react

In this activity, the actors receive the sound and action and react by repeating and then creating their own sound and action. This activity requires the actors to respond in the moment. It depends on the actors' reflexes and puts sensations throughout the actors' bodies. When actors are in a play, they have to act and react. It is one thing to read the play in a book and react to it in the intellectual sense. It is quite different to react in a gut way and in an instinctual way. Activities such as this are working the actor's muscles. When actors have a fully-functional instrument, they are able to be creative at their optimal level.

Industry Connection

One thing I like about this activity is that when it reaches its potential, it is extremely fast paced. Until it reaches this point, the activity appears to be clumsy. In other words, it has to be played at a fast pace. New York, Mumbai,

Paris, London, and Los Angeles are all pretty fast paced cities. They all like to call their own shots and make certain demands on the individuals who live there. A person may move from a city with a more relaxed and easygoing atmosphere. These cities are not asking you to adapt, but they are not going to adapt to you. They are saying, "What you see is what you get. If you don't like it, you know what you can do." Some actors attempt to fight the city they are in. If an actor can make it in these cities, he can make it anywhere. The actor has to learn to embrace the city of his choice, fast pace and all.

Chapter 16
Knowing Your Objectives

130. Lost and Found

Ask one of the actors to come forward and tell him that he is going to be asked to search for some keys that are hidden in the room. These keys can be real or they can be imaginary. Give him a scenario as to why he must find the keys. The rest of the actors should sit as the audience. Here is an example: "You have been late for work too many times this year and your boss has said that if you are late once more, he will have to let you go. You're getting behind on your house payments and know that if you lose your job you will certainly lose your house as well. If you can find your keys within the next five minutes you will make it to work on time." This is one example. Use your imagination and create different scenarios. If you use real keys you might choose to put them somewhere while the actor is watching. This means that as the character begins to search for the keys, the actor already knows where they are. Of course he has to play the scene as if he has no idea where the keys are located.

Variation

You can change the length of time the actors have to complete the task. You can have one actor play the scene and tell him he will succeed, and you can have another actor play the scene and tell him he will fail in the task.

Purpose
For the actors to justify their actions

It is a danger for actors to go through the motions without any justification for their actions. As Uta Hagen says in her book, *A Challenge for the Actor*, "If you repeat the actions without sensory cause, or if you become intent on showing an *audience* what missing realities you are providing, no matter how accurately or impressively you execute your task, it will at best become a slick, mechanical illustration."[28] The actor wants to see, know, and feel. This exercise is great in that if the actor is signaling or indicating he is looking for the keys, it will be quite clear. If you tell him where the keys are from the beginning, it will make it even more challenging for him to create the illusion that it is the first time the keys have been mislaid. So while he has to justify looking for the keys, he also has to justify his actions in terms of the stakes given. Let us say he doesn't find the keys and there is now the realization that he will lose his job and ultimately his home. In other words, we should receive the message that once he stops looking for the keys, it does not mean the scene has ended. Rather, it is at this point that the scene really begins. If an actor is in a play, the scene does not end until the curtain closes or the lights fade.

Industry Connection

How many times do you think actors can be asked to do a take? It may be five, ten, or fifteen depending on when the director is satisfied and there are the

---

28. Uta Hagen, *A Challenge for the Actor* (New York: Simon and Schuster, 1991), 188.

issues of time and money. The director also has to deal with the challenge of losing the light at sunset. So let us say that in this scene an actor is searching for his keys. After ten takes the director is happy with the master and now he wants to do the two-shot (eight takes), the close-up (eleven takes), the actor's point of view (five takes), and an overhead shot (two takes). And the challenge for the actor is that every single take is the first time that the character has begun to search for his keys. When actors say that acting is the easiest thing in the world, they are making an incomplete statement. As Peter Brook says in his book, *The Empty Space,* "Incompetence is the vice, the condition, and the tragedy of the world's theatre on any level: for every light comedy or musical or political revue or verse play or classic that we see there are scores of others that most of the time are betrayed by a lack of elementary skills. The techniques of staging, designing, speaking, walking across a stage, sitting — even listening — just aren't sufficiently known."[29] Bad acting is the easiest thing in the world. Good acting will demand everything the actor has got to offer. Having a sense of the overall character is imperative to the actor. The actor has to be very concentrated within his character. In doing so, the actor is able to be engaged and curious. In this exercise the actor knows it is all make-believe, but the character does not.

Note

If acting teachers say, "Don't act," ask, "Can you name me one of the greatest actors you have ever known? What is it he did on-stage or film? What is he called?" He is called an actor, and what he is doing is called acting. How can we desecrate the word acting? Ask these teachers to be accurate in their terms, because if you tell an actor not to act, what is he going to do? It's like telling a violinist not to play the violin. If what they mean is don't have tension while acting, or acting is external, then why not say this? The phrase, "Don't act" is dangerous to the actor because it is an oxymoron. On the one hand we tell actors to "act," and on the other we tell them "not to act." You can tell a student, "That is not good acting," "Your acting is weak," or "Your acting is lacking believability." As a teacher you need to be careful how you use terms, because while you may know what you really mean, the actor may misinterpret your statement.

131. What Time Is It?

Split your students up so that you have no more than six groups. Give the actors a scene, which should be the same for each group. Pick a scene that is about two minutes in length. Not everyone in the scene necessarily has dialogue. The script can be for one, two, three, four, or five people, but each group has exactly the same scene. Go around to each group and give them a time of day or night in which their scene is set. Some examples are: 9 p.m., 7 a.m., 3 p.m., 2 a.m.

Each group should have their scene set at a different time of day or night. The students will now work their scenes for twenty minutes taking into account the time at which their scene is set. The students can have scripts in hand for this exercise. Watch each group perform, one at a time, while the others observe as

---

29. Peter Brook, *The Empty Space,* (New York: Simon and Schuster, 1968), 31.

the audience. Once all of the groups have performed, discuss each group's performance. Discuss how each scene was affected by the time of day or night it was set. You can have each group go up and sit in the performance area one at a time. This helps give the audience a visual reminder when they are making their observations about a particular group. The number of people in a scene will depend on how many students you have in the class. For instance, if you have twenty students, you will probably want four-person scenes. If you have ten students, you may choose to work with two-person scenes.

Variation
The actors can have scripts in hand for this exercise or the scene can be improvised, if you prefer. The scene can be for one person or for four people, but all the scenes start with the same premise, except for the time of day. Remind the actors that everyone starts with the same premise. Because the scene is improvised this time, each group will end up with separate dialogue and blocking.

Purpose
To be aware of the given circumstances
This exercise, amongst other things, asks the actor to pay attention to and take into account the given circumstances. Let us say the scene that is taking place concerns a bill that has not been paid. A husband and wife are in the kitchen discussing the issue. If the time is three in the afternoon, we might assume it is not such a serious issue. If, on the other hand, it is two in the morning, we might be led to believe the problem is of greater concern. We might wonder why there is a need to have this discussion at two in the morning. This exercise leads the actors to consider when it is and when it is not necessary to raise the stakes. It is also worth reminding the actors that a character may be more tired or alert depending on the time of day. This exercise allows the actors to explore the importance of time. The prologue is given at the beginning of The Folger Library version of *Romeo and Juliet* by William Shakespeare. Part of the prologue is as follows, "Two households both alike in dignity. In fair Verona, where we lay our scene."[30] Actors who are not thorough in their preparation for a role may miss out on some vital pieces of information. As Lenka Peterson and Dan O'Connor point out in their book, *Kids Take the Stage*, "Just as an actor endeavors to determine the 'spine' or main theme of the character, this would perhaps reflect the character's overall lifetime intention. The director and actors try to find the theme of the overall show."[31]

Industry Connection
Tell your actors the following:
INSTRUCTOR: Let us say you are in a comedy television series. There is a scene in which you walk out with your wife and sit down in the park. As part of the same scene, there is a famous guest who comes out as a character and does a song and dance while you sit watching him. The director knows that the famous guest does not want to be kept waiting around and for this reason they film his scene first. So, in terms of time, you film the second part of the scene first, and then you film the first fifteen seconds afterwards. It may sound like a

---

30. William Shakespeare, *Romeo and Juliet* (New York: The Folger Library, 1959), 3.
31. Lenka Peterson and Dan O'Connor, *Kids Take the Stage*. (New York: Back Stage Books, 2006), 95.

piece of cake, but if you as an actor are not on top of each and every moment, it is going to show in your work. Sometimes people will say, "I was on-set with so and so and he was very rude. He wanted everything his way! He wasn't satisfied with this, that, or the other, and he kept demanding certain things had to be a certain way!" Humility does not have to mean the actor is giving up his viewpoint. Sometimes stars may be rude or demanding simply because they can, but there is also another possibility. They know that it is their name, their image, and their work that is going to be held up for inspection. They also know that once it airs, it will be most likely be around for eternity. A bad movie does not totally disappear, but lingers around. Great actors know this, and justifiably will not put their name to anything they do not agree with. It is also the case that on their way up, an actor may take on a movie knowing that it is lacking in finesse. They want to work and they want to act and they know it may springboard them to something bigger. An actor is subsidizing himself on a continual basis. Some actors will make a movie that has a poor script simply to pay the bills. Big movies can subsidize an actor who wants to perform in the theatre.

Note
Sometimes a good actor gives credibility to a project even when the performances around them are somewhat lacking.

132. Intention Blocker

Choose two actors to come forward. Tell them they are going to improvise a scene where each of them has an intention. For instance, you may tell one of the actors, "Your intention is to eat a big, greasy dinner because you are starving." You now tell the other actor, "Your objective is to stop your boyfriend from having that dinner because you want him to go on a diet." Another example is, "One of you wants the two of you to go out for the evening. The other one wants the two of you to stay in for the evening." Whatever scenario the actors are given, it is important to remember that this is the subtext of the scene. The scene can be on anything and go in any direction, but his main objective still remains the same. If one character wants to play music, then the other character doesn't want any music. The scene could get into politics, fishing, and doing the laundry. The actors' intentions to play music and not to play music still remain the same. You can choose to tell the students their intentions privately, or you can create them with the help of the audience. It may be worth trying both approaches with different scenes. The actors will find that each scene has its own dynamics.

Variation
Give the actors their opposite intentions, but instead of having them improvise the scene, you can give them the sides of a movie or a scene from a play.

Purpose
To know your objectives
One character's objective may be to have a big fat dinner because he is starving. The other character's objective is to stop him from having that food because he has high blood pressure and the doctor has advised against it. Not only do they have an objective, but they also have a justified reason in following through with their actions. If the director had simply said, "He tries to eat the food

and you stop him," this would most likely create a scene that is very funny to watch, and yet totally unrealistic. Unfortunately, this might be the type of direction actors get on a set. It is up to the actors to create the backstory for their characters that will allow them to justify their actions. If they wait for others to do it for them, they may have a long wait. The important part of this exercise is not only for the actors to know their intentions, but also to know what drives them. Actors will want to stay interested in their work. Having said this, it is virtually impossible for actors to be totally objective in their work.

Industry Connection

In this exercise, one character wants one thing and the other character wants the exact opposite. When this happens, conflict has been created. So we could say this entire exercise is based on a conflict of interest. An audience loves to see a character faced up against insurmountable odds. There will be many times in actors' careers when they will face a conflict of interest. For instance, let us say an actor gets a call from his agent for a big audition that takes place in one hour. It is too late to call anyone to cover his shift at the restaurant. He doesn't want to let his boss down because she is really cool, but this audition could be his big break. Another example is an actor has been with his girlfriend for three years. They want to stay home and watch a movie, and the actor wants to go to his acting class. She says, "You act like your career is more important than me." Now the actor has to decide whether to go to class or stay at home to please his partner. It is interesting to note that the less seriously actors take their careers, the less conflicts they will face. If actors have absolutely no conflicts in their acting careers, then it is more than likely they do not have an acting career! If your students complain about after school rehearsals, remind them that acting takes commitment. As David Ball says in his book, *Backwards & Forwards,* "People who talk about, write about, or do theatre agree on little. But there is one thing: Drama is conflict!"[32]

133. Time Card

For this exercise you will want all of your actors in the performance space. Explain in the following way:

INSTRUCTOR: In a moment, I would like all of you to leave the room. I want all of you to walk out of this room together. The challenge is that you have to have a good reason for doing so. The other challenge is that this has to be done in complete silence. One of you may come up with a good reason, but you are going to have to find a way to communicate it to the entire group. No one can leave the room until the entire group understands why you are leaving.

Some reasons for leaving are:

1. You're outside and it is raining, so you run to get inside from the rain.
2. The movie is finished and you are going home.
3. You have to catch a bus.

If it is not clear to the entire group why they are leaving, then take time out for a group discussion to problem solve. You can do this exercise a number of times with your actors.

---

32. David Ball, *Backwards & Forwards* (Illinois: Southern Illinois University Press, 1983), 25.

Purpose

To use clarity in performance

The only way this exercise works is if the actors can justify their actions. If an actor's reason for leaving is not clear, then the rest of the group will not follow. The students are going to have to absolutely convince their colleagues as to why they are leaving. When actors on-stage are not convicted in their actions, it creates confusion for them and for the other actors around them. Encourage your actors to create clarity in their work.

Industry Connection

Make the following observations with your actors:

INSTRUCTOR: This exercise requires clarity and certainty. If you are going to have an acting career, you are also going to need these qualities. It is not uncommon to hear aspiring actors say, "I thought I would give it a try." This is the language they use in regards to their acting career. Needless to say, it is highly unlikely they will ever have an acting career. The competition of actors who want it more than anything else is too great.

134. Ultimate Tag

Make sure you have a nice, open area for this exercise. Have your students spread out around the room. They want to start by keeping as big a gap between themselves and everyone else as they can. Explain in the following way:

INSTRUCTOR: We are about to play a game of tag. This game of tag has a little bit of a twist. Instead of one person being "it," everyone is "it." When I blow my whistle, everyone tries to tag everyone else. If you are tagged, please go stand against a wall, so that you are out of the playing area. The aim is to be the last person left in. The only way this can happen is that you do not get tagged. Please note that if you are tagged, you cannot tag someone else. You are automatically out from this point.

CELINA: What happens if two people tag at the same time?

INSTRUCTOR: You are going to have to use your discretion. Either both of you are out or the one you think you tagged first is out. You will have to decide very quickly before both of you are tagged by other people. The last person left in is the winner. Please remember to move around the room safely. To tag someone, simply tap them lightly on the shoulder. There is no pushing, slapping, or hair pulling. This is not tagging, but will most likely cause an injury.

This exercise may be over very quickly. You may decide to play two or three rounds. I would suggest that you have the winner step out of the second round. Perhaps he could be the person who blows the whistle to start the second round. However, for health and safety reasons, that will only be possible if you have a spare whistle available. Allow them back in if a third round is played.

Purpose

To understand your objective

One of the purposes of this exercise is for the participants to complete their objective. Their objective is to tag everyone else while avoiding being tagged. They must clearly focus on this objective to stand a chance of winning. With every character an actor plays, he must ask himself, "What is my objective?" A character does not necessarily have just one objective. The lesser objective for each participant is not to get caught. The overarching objective is to be the last person left in. A character may have many minor objectives, but it is also up to the actor to figure out what is his overarching objective, or as Stanislavski calls it, "super objective."

Industry Connection

In this exercise, it is every person for themselves. If they take their guard down for one second, they will most likely be tagged. This is a great metaphor for the actors. Although there is a certain amount of camaraderie in terms of the projects the actor is involved with, what we are talking about is everything else. In terms of the motivation needed, the actors will need to find this from within themselves. With regard to dealing with rejection, it is up to the actors to find a way to accept this as part of their job. If an actor is at the same audition as two of his friends, the friends will be doing everything they can to book the job. This is not to be selfish, but because they also have to pay their bills. They also desire to get that "big break." They will want to be very singularly focused on their career. The actor who is not willing to look out for himself will most likely have a short or non-existent career.

135. Cup Flip

You are going to need about thirty Styrofoam cups for this activity. Before the students arrive, put the cups all over the room, half turned up and the other half turned down. A whistle will also come in handy for this activity. Explain in the following way:

INSTRUCTOR: I am going to split you into teams of four. As we have twenty-four players, that will give us six teams. Three of the teams will be "flip up" teams, and three of the teams will be "flip down." In a moment, one flip up team and one flip down team will spread out around the room. When I blow my whistle, the flip down team is going to aim to flip as many cups as they can so that they are now facing downwards. The flip up team will be moving around the room turning up as many cups as they can. If a cup ends up on its side, no points are scored. If a cup is accidentally broken, ten points are given to the other team. Each team will have two minutes to complete the task.

JANE: Is the team that flips the most cups the winner?

INSTRUCTOR: Not exactly. We have thirty cups. Let's say twenty cups finish facing up and ten cups finish facing down. This means twenty points will go to the up side and ten to the down side. The up side is now in the lead. In the next round, two more teams will play. At this point, the leads may be reversed.

SAM: Why do you give away so many points for a broken cup?

INSTRUCTOR: To not break the cups is part of the rules. It makes the teams' objectives more difficult to achieve.

DAN: How do we know who the winner is?

INSTRUCTOR: After the three rounds have been played, the team with the most points is the winner. Although we have six small teams, we actually only have one flip up and one flip down team at a time. This is what counts in terms of scoring points. Essentially, there are only two teams. If there is a tie in points, each team can select their top four players for one final round.

Another way to do this is to let the players make their own teams. If you have twenty students, divide them into teams of ten. Tell them now to create two teams of three and one team of four. If they put all their most athletic people on one team, they will probably lose overall. It is a good way for the students to develop tactics. I normally play this as a competition, but you can adapt the rules in any way you prefer.

Purpose
To look at the bigger picture
The purpose of this exercise is for the actors to look at the bigger picture. As has been mentioned, if you let the actors put their own teams together, they will want to evenly balance their teams. If they win one round and lose the other two, it is most likely that their team will lose overall. The actors have to encourage and support each and every member of their team. In other parts of this book I have mentioned that the actors will want to look at their characters' overarching objectives. What they also need to consider is the overarching message of the play. What is the overarching message the writer is trying to get across, and what does it mean to their character? *Romeo and Juliet* is about much more than the death of two young lovers. If the actors stop here, they will be missing out on so much of what the author is trying to get across. Always encourage your actors to look at the complete picture rather than just what is immediately in front of them.

Industry Connection
There is a certain futility to this exercise. Every time a player flips a cup, another player flips it the other way. Each side has to keep going for two minutes. An actor's career often has a degree of futility to it. Actors spend a great deal of time being told, "No!" This is certainly true in terms of auditioning, but it goes beyond that. They are also told "no" by agents, managers, bank managers, and also when looking for the other job. An actor in Hollywood, looking for a job as a waiter, is likely to face many "no's" before they get a "yes." This is in part because every other aspiring actor had the same idea. Every now and then, between the numerous "no," will be the occasional "yes." With any luck, over time, the positive responses will increase. Just like flipping the cup, the number of rejections will make the actors, at times, feel that it is all pointless. It is their strength, vision, and determination that will see them through these times. They will have to be persistent and insistent if they are to have an acting career. It is their willingness to be proactive and resourceful. Actors will want to have confidence that they hold on to very tightly. At some point in their journey, aspiring actors will have to ask themselves how badly they want to be an actor. Confidence can be taken away from every actor who is not willing to constantly rekindle it. How much are they willing to persevere in the face of great adversity? Are they willing to do all that it takes to see that dream through to fruition? Remind your actors that it is not what they say that counts, but rather what they actually do that matters.

Note
A studio might buy the rights to a book for a whole variety of reasons. Once a studio buys it they own it. It means that the author has sold the rights to it. A studio may option a book and never end up doing anything with it. In many

cases they don't create an accurate rendition of the original material. This is one of the reasons why some authors have clauses in their contracts that allow them to write the film script.

136. Location, Location, Location

Split your students up into four or five groups. If you have only ten students, ask them to pair off. If you have thirty students, you may want them to split into six groups of five. I will occasionally make groups with six members, but I do not like anything larger than this. I have found some students become distracted when the groups are too big.

What I would like you to do is give each group two scenes. Each scene should be one or two minutes long. The scenes can be from plays or old movies. Make sure they are not easily recognizable by the students. You also need to make sure that no locations are mentioned or listed. Give your students about fifteen minutes to read the scenes with their group. They need to set and justify a location for each scene. Tell them to write their reasons down or type them on their laptops. Bring the groups back together, allocate roles, and request them to read their scenes aloud. Ask the rest of the class to make suggestions of possible location settings that come to mind. Once this has happened, instruct the groups to explain why they chose their specific locations. Continue with a class discussion.

Purpose

To be aware of the importance of the given circumstances

Let's say two actors were working on an improvisation. When asked where their scene is set they respond, "It doesn't really matter," and continue with their scene. The fact is that where the scene is set matters a great deal. The same dialogue will have different connotations depending on the location. Let us take, for instance, the following two lines:

ACTOR 1: I'm starving!

ACTOR 2: Me, too. I feel like I haven't eaten in days!

Imagine the difference in meaning if this scene was set in a prison as opposed to a restaurant. The actors will want to be aware of specifics that apply to each and every scene. In some cases, it is the directors who need to be more specific rather than the actors.

Industry Connection

A film production will often shoot on location. The average movie takes about three months to shoot but can go much longer than that. Shooting on location can be fun for the actor, but it can also add complications. For instance, on location in a small town, there may be no public restrooms in the immediate vicinity. The production may provide two porta-potties that are to be used by the entire cast and crew. Between scenes, actors may like to go off on their own and work on their next scene in private. On location, this may not be an option if they are filming in a busy high street. Filming on location can be a good deal for the background actors. On a set, the studio does not have to provide food for them. On location, the studio has to provide a catered meal. Filming on location can add many variables to a project.

Note

The whole process of line learning and developing the character's thought process requires an innermost privacy for actors. They need to work in a creative state. The paradox is that actors require privacy and transparency. Actors need people as much as they need to be away from them. It is through the observation of others that the actors can build a foundation of resources.

137. Compounding Action

This exercise is not easy to do well. I usually use it with more advanced students. Instruct your students to sit as the audience. Choose one of your more confident actors to begin. Tell him to move into the performance space. Ask him to mime a simple gesture such as opening a door. He is not to open the door as himself, but as a specific character. For example, he could be a teenage son who is opening his bedroom door to go and brush his teeth. This is a very low-stakes scenario. Now you are going to ask him to open the door four more times. Each time he opens the door, the stakes have to rise higher. This is not one scene where the door opens a total of five times. This is five separate scenes by the same actor. The only action the actor can portray in this instance is to open the door. In the second scene, the character might be a father holding his baby and opens the door to come in from the freezing cold weather. You can see how the action has just compounded slightly. In each of the five scenes the actor can play a totally different character. Actors often look forward to the adventures that a different role might bring. The fifth might be an old man opening his door to escape from his house, which is on fire. You can see how the stakes have been taken to a very high level here. The actors do not have to explain what is happening in each scene as they perform it. At the end, they can tell the group or the group can guess. Follow up with a group discussion. Have other actors work with this exercise.

Some other possible actions are:

Sitting in a chair

Looking through the window

Buttoning up a shirt

Eating a sandwich

You will want to give your actors a very simple action from which to work. It is important in order to create a compounding effect for the actors to begin with a very low-stakes scene.

Purpose

To understand the circumstances of the scene

Sometimes a director will ask an actor, "Where are you going?" The actor will respond, "I am going to exit stage right." Of course the actor is making a literal response. The director, I am sure, was asking for information from the point of view of the actor's performance. An action is not simply an action. Let us say a young woman is driving her car home from a lovely afternoon at the coffee shop where she was reading her book. She drives slowly and is relaxed, cautiously checking her rearview mirror for other traffic. Let us say that the following week she does the same thing, but this time as she is driving home she suddenly remembers she left her wallet behind with all her cards and a good deal of money in it. She suddenly swerves her car around and starts driving like a bat out of hell. She swerves in and out of lanes, honks at other drivers to get out of her way, and does not look in her mirror once. As circumstances change, so do behavior and actions. A safe driver can become a lunatic driver under certain circumstances.

Industry Connection

An actor phones his agent one day and after a while the conversation feels pumped up and invigorated. A few weeks later, the actor phones the agent again, but this time the agent is short-tempered and abrasive. The actor feels that perhaps he has made an error about his agent. Perhaps the agent is an idiot, after all. This could be the case, but there may be more to it than that. The actor may have called his agent after he had received twenty-three other phone calls that day. The last four phone calls were from disgruntled actors who were complaining and chewing his ear off. The agent was in no mood to have another one of these conversations, and thus became short-tempered and abrasive. It does not excuse his behavior. However, unless the actor is aware of the circumstances behind the action, he may not always have the complete picture. A director on-set has so much stress to deal with that he does not always come across as the friendliest person. If you had met him for coffee on another occasion, he might have been the nicest person in the world. It is important to advise your actors to have a better understanding of the situation before they are quick to judge.

138. Elastic Faces

This activity is similar to Action Whisper and Chinese Whispers in *112 Acting Games*. Tell the whole group to line up, one behind the other. The first person in the line should be facing the front wall, while everyone else will face the back wall. Have the person in front make a face of some sort. At this point, he is going to turn around and pat the person behind him on the shoulder. That player will now turn around so that both players are facing each other. The first player will now make the face once. The first player will then turn back to face the front. The second player can now practice, but just once. He is then going to turn around and tap the third player on the shoulder and the process is repeated. When the last person has made the face, bring the last person and first person into the center of the room, so everyone can see. Let the last person make the face first and then first person second. The first person is going to have to remember the original face he made. See how similar or different the two faces have now become. Follow up with a group discussion. If need be, ask the question, "What do you need to do as a group to keep the continuity?" Change the front person so that a new person starts the next round.

Purpose

To be specific

The actor who begins this exercise has to be specific. Let us say he made a face that is not memorable to himself. When he makes the face again at the end, he may not have a clear image in his mind of what he originally did. An actor in a play may choose to make general statements about his character. Let's imagine an actor says, with regard to his character, "He is tired." At first glance this may sound specific, but it is actually a pretty general statement. The actor needs to ask, "Why is he tired?" One reason could be because he went out partying all night. Another possibility could be that he had to get up three times during the night to check on the baby who kept crying because she is sick. The actor must be specific in understanding why his character is tired and how that might affect the rest of the scene.

Industry Connection

In this activity, the actors are aiming to keep the facial expression congruent. The challenge is that if it starts changing in a small way, it often ends by having changed in a big way. During filming, the director is going to be looking for continuity. For instance, let us say he filmed the character crossing the street to go to the bank. He films the same shot as a close-up, a two-shot, the actor's point of view, and the wide lens shot. There may be subtle differences in the actor's movement, but the action is still the same. The actor has to take into account that this is exactly the same moment in the story that is being filmed from different angles. If the actor keeps on changing the scene, the continuity will be lost.

Chapter 17
Life Experience

139. Master Class

The information below should have been given to the actors at the end of the previous week's session as a homework assignment. Some of them will already own an acting book, but if not, they should continue in the following way:

INSTRUCTOR: For this exercise you are going to want to go to a bookstore or you can go to your local library. What I would like you to do is go to the acting section and look at the different books on acting. I want you to pick a book that looks of value to you and read it. Some possible authors and innovators are Constantin Stanislavski, Uta Hagen, Lee Strasberg, Maria Ouspenskaya, Yevgeni Vakhtangov, Joan Littlewood, Jacques Copeau, Stella Adler, Robert Lewis, Peter Brook, Eugenio Barba, Michael Chekhov, Sanford Meisner, Richard Boleslavsky, Antonin Artaud, and Jerzy Grotowski. I do not want to limit you to these. I am giving you some names to get you started.

Often, these books will have practical exercises for you to do, so follow through with them. Make notes that are of value to you from each book. If you have bought the book, then you can highlight the important points. I would always suggest browsing through a book before you purchase it, so that you can see if it holds any interest for you. I would also suggest that you speak with your fellow actors to get their advice on some acting books they believe are valuable. Some of your best friends should be acting books. If you trust their judgment, then this might be a good place to start. If you are a more seasoned actor and think you have read everything of value to do with acting, think again. There are a number of books out there that, although they are not directly linked to acting, do have relevance to the work of the actor. To find these, you are going to have to talk to a friend or instructor who has a good deal of informed knowledge. *The Artist's Way,* by Julia Cameron, is one example of a book that would fit into this category. When you arrive in class next week, you are going to be asked to defend the book you have chosen. If you do not find it of any value, then go ahead and bring an acting book that you do value. This does not mean you have to love the whole book. It means that you have to find at least one aspect of it of great personal benefit to you. Please bring the book with you so that you can refer to what you are talking about. Other actors will then be able to comment on what you say. It does not matter if all actors bring the same book because you all may have different opinions. In comparison, when an actor is playing a character, he needs to bring his own point of view. It is also important to recognize that every acting book is flawed. There is no substitution for being in the room with a teacher who can diagnose and prescribe for you, personally. A good teacher does not create a rubber stamp for his actors, but allows them to use who he is. He encourages his actors to excel. He is able to distill it all down to something quite simple. He teaches acting as a craft and encourages his actors to make it something real.

You may only hear the opinions of three or four actors depending on how long you spend on this exercise. You are not there to say who is right or wrong, although you can certainly provoke questions. It may also be interesting to work through one or two exercises from these books. This exercise is not about declaring the best acting teacher of all time. It is about finding what works in each approach. It is about finding out where they all meet in the middle.

Variation

In this exercise your actors have been asked to read a book. In their own time, ask them not to just read an acting book, but actually to do it. A number of acting books have many exercises and are "doing" books. Encourage your actors to use their acting book fully to see what it really has to offer.

Purpose

To utilize the readily available resources

The more your actors learn about acting, the less they will know. I know that this sounds like a contradiction. I mean that as one's knowledge grows, he will have more questions instead of fewer. He will be able to articulate questions that other actors cannot even comprehend. I do not necessarily mean in a redundant, intellectual sense, but rather in a very hands-on and practical sense. It is a sad fact that some actors know nothing about their craft and have read nothing about their craft. I do not know any other field in which this takes place. The argument that I will receive back is that it does not necessarily get you more work, and this is valid. Nevertheless, I believe that actors want to be informed of their craft and of its roots so that they are better versed and become well-rounded actors. As William Esper says in his book, *The Actor's Art and Craft,* "I believe that, in the best of hands, acting becomes a creative art, and that the excellence in its practice can only be attained by total mastery of technical craft."[33] Today's actors have more resources at their fingertips than ever before. For instance, they can turn on their television and see some of the most incredible actors on *Inside the Actor's Studio.* This is one of numerous resources readily available. There are no excuses for the actor not to learn his craft.

Industry Connection

Raise the following topics in a discussion with your actors:

INSTRUCTOR: Move out to Los Angeles, Paris, New York, London, or any acting hub and you will find coaches who will teach you acting that is passed down from all of acting's greatest teachers. So how do you know which one to pick? Some of them will tell you, "This is the only way." You may want to run a mile if you hear that, unless you believe they have the right to say it. One thing you can do is go and audit almost everybody in town for free. Decide whose class you like the look of and the sound of. You wouldn't buy a car unless you took it for a test drive first, so why act differently in terms of your career? This exercise also highlights the possibility that perhaps there is not only one answer. Perhaps you will study with five teachers and pull something away from each one. If a teacher tells you, "I am the only person you should study acting with," you may want to listen, if they are a confirmed genius in the field. If they are not, then you may want to question their motivations. Some teachers may say, "I studied with Meisner for twenty years." This may be true, but it does not mean they share the insights of their mentor. This does not mean they are not a good teacher, but it

---

33. William Esper, *The Actor's Art and Craft* (New York: Anchor Books, 2008), 27.

does mean that they are not Meisner! If you are seeking a mentor, then it may not happen immediately. Linda Weitzler, who is the Mentor Program Coordinator for Women In Film, told me, "Finding a good mentor is not necessarily the most famous name, but someone who is responsive, who will answer questions, and someone who is accessible. Many people will say yes when they are asked and then you will never hear from them again. Even a bad mentor who doesn't return your e-mails is good because it is a learning experience. This is a tough business and many people mean well but do not follow through." When you move out to an acting hub, you may feel that all of your support system has disappeared. Look for those who can be great mentors to you.

140. Seven Steps to Heaven

You will need to have created a long list of questions for this exercise. You can create questions on general knowledge or specialize on the field of acting, if you prefer. Ask one actor, who is the quizmaster, to stand at one end of the room. Have all the other actors stand in a line, shoulder to shoulder, at the other end of the room. Mark off seven levels that lead up to the quizmaster. To do this you can use chairs, beanbags, or what ever you like. Explain in the following way:

INSTRUCTOR: For this exercise, I would like everyone to line up against the back wall. The room has been split into seven different levels. You are all starting at level zero. In a moment, Gillian, who is the quizmaster, is going to call out a question. If you think you know the answer, you are going to make a buzz sound. The first person to buzz will get to answer the question. If you get the question right, you move forward to level one. The first person to get to level seven will become the new quizmaster. Some of the more challenging questions are worth two or even three levels. If you get a question wrong, then you have to move back one, two, or three levels. There is another challenge to this exercise. Five people may buzz at the same time. The quizmaster may not know who buzzed first. In this case, the quizmaster will choose the buzzer who catches his attention first. You are not allowed to catch his attention by talking. What you are able to do is buzz as creatively as you possibly can in order to draw attention to yourself. You can also draw attention to yourself through your physicality. As a reminder, the only verbal sounds you can utter are your buzzer sounds. You will also be answering the question verbally. When a new quizmaster takes over, everyone else starts again. The winner of each round becomes the new quizmaster.

Variations

Here is an extra item you may want to add to this exercise. The actor who comes last is given a forfeit that is decided by the group. The forfeit has to be related to acting in some way. If three people are last, then all three have to do the forfeit. An example of a forfeit could be, "Recite a few lines from a Shakespeare play."

Purpose

To have good general knowledge

Raise the following points with your actors:

INSTRUCTOR: In order to do well in this exercise, the actors have to have good general knowledge. Actors who work on a number of different plays should also become somewhat worldly. Let us say you were playing a sixteenth century upper class English gentleman. The script told you that you have a handkerchief, which you wave across your face. You go home and work on this and practice it, and that is where it ends. Another actor playing the same part, on a different occasion, does his research. He discovers that in those days, people did not brush their teeth and thus had foul breath. He also discovers that the handkerchiefs are full of perfume. They are fanned across one's face in order to fight off the stench of foul breath. What is obvious about a character is interesting, but what is not obvious is far more interesting to an audience. With this knowledge, they are able to look at that moment with a totally different perspective.

Industry Connection

In this exercise the actors have to draw attention to themselves to have a chance of succeeding. Let us say an actor goes to a cattle call audition where twenty of them are brought into the room at the same time. The actor may stand there all polite and hidden in the corner. This is totally the actor's prerogative to do so. Another actor refuses to stand in line with the rest. He insists on standing half a foot in front. The casting director might think he is rude, obnoxious, and cannot follow directions. On the other hand, he might be the one who sticks out in the casting director's mind and is brought in for the callback. Every situation has to be weighed by the moment. Tell your actors not to allow themselves to fade away into the background. It is not enough to want the job. They have to fight for the role. They have to campaign for the job!

Note

When actors are researching their characters, they will want to be unprejudiced about it. They will not want to be prejudiced or biased in any way. Even if they have some knowledge on the topic they do not want to make general assumptions about their character. They will want to start off with a clean slate.

141. Spelling Bee Twister

For this exercise, split your actors into two teams. Have a number of note cards. Each note card should have a word and beneath it there should be the definition of the word. In a spelling bee, the actors are asked to spell the words. In this exercise, each team takes turns sending an actor into the performance area. The first actor is told a word for which he has to give a definition. If his definition is correct, his team gets three points. If he doesn't know the word, team number two gets to confer for fifteen seconds. If the other team knows the word, they will get one point. The exercise then continues with team two sending up an actor, and so on. Both teams will want to work out an order so that everyone gets to go up. The teams cannot just send their best person up each round. There is no spelling involved in this exercise. The words obviously have to be prepared in advance. The words should come from all areas of life.

Here are some examples:

Frugal: economical in expenditure; a person who requires few resources
Lament: to express grief; to regret something deeply
Obtuse: (a person who is) not quick, sharp, or alert in perception
Avant-garde: the advanced group in any field, often related to the arts; usually use unorthodox methods to get there
Narcissism: excessive love or admiration of self

These are merely examples of how you can organize your words and definitions. You can use a dictionary, an encyclopedia, or a thesaurus. You can also find all of these definitions online. You will want to have a degree of leeway with regard to the definitions. As long as the actor gets pretty close, that should be sufficient. Depending on the maturity of your actors, you can make the words easier or more complex.

Purpose
To develop a wide vocabulary

This exercise encourages the actors to have a wide range and understanding of vocabulary. The characters they play will each have their own understanding of vocabulary. This means they have to understand all the vocabulary of every single character they play. If an actor is in a classical play, this is going to be a tall order. The word *erinaceous* relates to the hedgehog family. An actor may never have heard of it but his character may still use it. If he plays a character who has an accent, or who speaks in a dialect, this may also be quite a challenge. An individual's dialect may affect his jaw movement. Think about all the slang words that people use. As George Bernard Shaw once said, "England and America are two countries separated by a common language." When talking about dialects Ginny Kopf, author of *The Dialect Handbook*, says, "Actors approach dialects with both delight and terror. The bottom line is you want to be believable."[34] The actor has to move from mimicking to inhabiting a dialect to truly embracing it. This exercise highlights the importance of vocabulary for the actor. In the Folger Library version of *Julius Caesar* by William Shakespeare, in one speech after the death of Caesar, Marcus Antonius says, "You all do know this mantle. I remember the first time ever Caesar put it on."[35] If the actor does not know what a *mantle* is, how can he talk about it with any justification? The actors must have adequate vocabulary to meet the demands of the role they are playing. One way your actors can increase their vocabulary is by playing Scrabble. It may not be considered a trendy game, but it does wonders for developing the actors' vocabularies.

Industry Connection

Raise the following points with your actors:

INSTRUCTOR: When you walk into an audition, you may be asked a question by the casting director. You need the vocabulary so that you can articulate what you want to say. As Margie Haberr says in her book, *How to Get the Part without Falling Apart,* "'Can you tell me about yourself?' Does that mean you should give the interviewer the order in which you ate breakfast, lunch, and dinner, or should it be an almanac of your family or a recitation of boring facts (like how old you

---

34. Ginny Kopf, *The Dialect Handbook* (Orlando: Voiceprint Publishing, 2003), 11.
35. William Shakespeare, *Julius Caesar* (New York: Pocket Books Publishing, 1959), 59.

are or where you were born). Your response should be a story, a memorable experience that means something to you."[36] You will need to be able to do this clearly and concisely. The wider your vocabulary, the more you can answer in an individualistic fashion. Anything you can use that makes them remember you is to your advantage. It is as if the actor is presenting his trump card. If you want them to be interested in what you are saying, then you better be interested and passionate about it yourself! The casting director wants to be able to define the actor and put him in a box. The actor gets known for his work that most people go and see. It may mean that an actor is known as the action guy for a number of years. He may end up getting pinned down to a certain type of role. An actor may spend many years working very hard to get out of the typecast box he has been put in. To do this he will have to be convincing in everything he plays. Being an actor means trying to play every part you possibly can. It does not mean limiting yourself to the safe roles.

142. Board Game Bonanza

This is an activity I am borrowing from my parents. When my sister and I were growing up, my parents would have these board game parties. They would invite over a group of friends. They would set up board games all over the house. The guests would then walk around the house and decide which game they wanted to play. At this point, they would look for one person, or more, who might also be interested in playing the same game. There would be ten games being played all over the house at the same time. As a kid, I was fascinated to watch the adults playing board games. I would walk from room to room to see who was playing what. You are going to do precisely the same activity with your students. Ask your students to bring in their favorite board game. With today's technology they may say that they do not have any. However, if they dig into the back of the closet, they will find a board game. You can also buy some for next to nothing from a local thrift store. Have them put their name on their game and bring them in ahead of time. Set them up all over the room so that when the students arrive, the games are already set up. Allow them to play the board games for the rest of the period or session. You may want to bring in a number of board games yourself, just to be safe. A few examples are: Chess, Poker, Scrabble, Draughts, Monopoly, Connect Four, Chutes and Ladders, and Twister. While Twister is not a board game, it is a lot of fun. The only rule for this activity is that at any given moment, every student is engaged in a game or choosing a game to play.

Purpose
To develop a multifaceted approach to acting
The purpose behind this activity is to encourage the students to take a multifaceted approach to their acting. Let us say two students decide to play a game of Chess. In order to play a good game, both students are going to need to use higher order thinking skills. They cannot just think about their next move, but need to also be thinking three moves ahead. Students playing Twister have to engage their physical abilities and agility. Students playing Scrabble have to

36. Margie Haberr, *How to Get the Part ... Without Falling Apart* (Los Angeles: Long Eagle Publishing Company, 1999), 36.

show their command of language. Students playing Connect Four have to be able to consider the best tactics and strategies. Students playing Monopoly have to be willing to build their portfolio of properties throughout the game. Think about how everything that has just been mentioned can be applied to the actors' work.

Industry Connection

As the students decide what games they want to play, they have many choices. Some may rush to the first game they see, while others may take their time. Some students may start a game, decide they don't like it, and move on to something else. There is a parallel here in terms of the actor's career. One actor may jump to the first agent who offers to sign him up. He may find after awhile that this agent is not a good fit. He drops the agent and starts to look for a new one. He has lost some time, but perhaps he has learned some valuable lessons along the way. Perhaps he learned what to avoid in an agent. The next time he might decide to shop around a bit more first. It may take him longer to get the agent he wants, but in the end, it may be well worth it. This isn't to say that every actor doesn't have to start from somewhere. It is just reminding your actors that they are choosing the agent, and not the other way around. At the end of the day, the agent does not pay your bills, your commission pays his! Remind your actors not to be afraid to make mistakes and not to be afraid to be selective in finding exactly what they are looking for.

143. The Aviator

For this exercise you are going to need forty sheets of paper and colored felt-tip pens. Explain in the following way:

INSTRUCTOR: In a moment I am going to divide you into two teams. I will give each team twenty pieces of paper. (To conserve paper, you can cut your paper in half.) You will each have fifteen minutes to make twenty airplanes per group. You will receive coloring utensils so you can design and color your planes as you wish. You can fold your paper any way you want to in order to make sure it flies. When the fifteen minutes are up, I am going to ask you to line all your planes up so that I can make sure each group has twenty planes. I am going to come along and check that each group is ready. (What you are going to do here is play a little trick on the students. Walk along and observe each group's planes. Look at the design and the way they have colored them. Decide which group has made a better set of planes overall. This should also be based on how much time the students actually worked on their planes. During the fifteen minutes, you will want to observe which students worked hard and who just took it easy. Give minus twenty-five points to the team that has the most attractively designed planes. I will give more explanation later. Here is the most important part of this: Do not tell the students they have just been judged. Do not tell anything to the team that has just lost twenty-five points. Allow them to believe you were just counting the planes and having a quick look.) I am then going to divide the room in half. One group will be on one side of the room with their twenty planes and the other group on the other side of the room. You will then have three minutes to fly as many planes as you can over to the enemy's side. You can only fly one plane at a time. You can only hold one plane per player at any time. Anyone who throws or holds two planes at once will automatically award ten points to the other team. At the end of the three minutes I will count the number of planes on each side. Each plane is worth two points.

WENDY: Is the aim of the game to score the fewest points?

INSTRUCTOR: Exactly. If team one ends with twenty-five planes, that equals fifty points. This means team two will only have fifteen planes and thirty points. Team two will therefore be the winner. (The two teams take the fifteen minutes to make their planes. They then work the activity for the next three minutes.) Team one has eighteen planes on their side and scores thirty-six points. Team two has twenty-two planes on their side and scores nineteen points. Team two is the winner!

LORAINE: That doesn't make any sense. They ended up with twenty-two planes. They should have forty-four points. We are the winners.

INSTRUCTOR: Loraine, technically speaking, you are correct. The challenge is that I told a white lie. When you designed and decorated your planes, I judged them. The team whose members showed the best overall work ethic and design was given minus twenty-five points. That is how team two went from forty-four points to nineteen points.

YVETTE: That is not fair. Why did you not tell us about the design points? If we would have known, we would have tried a lot harder.

Purpose:
To be prepared
INSTRUCTOR: That is precisely why I didn't tell you. I know it seems unfair, but I want you to think about something for a minute. If you are in a play, you might do just enough to get by. You are very busy and feel you can only put in a limited amount of time. You will learn your lines, your blocking, your cues, and so forth. You basically show up and are able to give an adequate performance, but not much more. In order to give potentially meaningful performances, the actors have to put in the work, whether they have the time or not. They have to find a way to commit to the role and give it everything they have. Here is the key point: Even if no one tells the actor to put in the time and effort, he is still required to do so. It is up to the actor to be self-motivated. I know I was unfair, but it was to give you a gut response that you would remember. The more prepared you are as an actor, the more potential you will have for growth in your work. Actors who come prepared will give their director a sense of security.

Not all the students left happy after this exercise. Not all of them will see the point today. It will sometimes take weeks, months, or even years to sink in. Sometimes the lesson of today will reap the results of tomorrow. It is not just the student who needs to consider the bigger picture, sometimes it is the teacher as well.

Please make sure you recycle the paper that is used.

Industry Connection
In this activity the actors are given incomplete information. They often think this is being unfair, yet it is a reality they are going to face more than they would like. When they eventually start booking roles on television and film, it is more than likely that these are going to be day-player roles. Statistically speaking, this will be more than likely for a number of years. Ask any day player how many lines he got and you can count them on one hand. A day player traditionally gets

five lines or fewer. It may even be one or two words. Now ask the day player to tell you all about the character breakdown they have been given and they will probably laugh. There may be one or two words of character description. There may even be one or two lines, but more than likely it is the actor's imagination that is going to create the character. The work is going to be left to the actor, and he is going to have to do it in his own time. He is not going to complain that this is unfair. He is going to get on with it and do the work. He will be very happy to have the work and an influx of cash. A day-player role may lead to more work in the future. Discuss with your actors why it is necessary for them to be pragmatists. Discuss with them the reason why it is necessary for them to be able to adapt to any situation. If an actor expects everything to be fair, he is going to be in for a rude awakening. If actors are able to flow with the tide, their journey is likely to be that much smoother.

Note

One day I was talking with a well-known television personality. I couldn't help but notice that her ability to take direction was outstanding. Instead of being asked to grasp something, she automatically went about doing it. I watched her memorize things in an automatic way when no one had asked her to do so. She was the consummate professional who had technique ingrained into her subconscious. This is the type of working professional that the aspiring actors are hoping to compete against. In order to do so, they are going to have to work towards never ending improvement. Some movie actors watch their past work and feel that if they did it again they could do it better. They become their own harshest critics. They watch themselves to study their past mistakes. Overachievers will often have this line of thinking. The actor has to know how to be relaxed and open to anything that is thrown at him.

144. Pass the Parcel

This is an old party game that I used to play growing up in England. We are going to add a few adaptations here. Take an item such as an apple, a mini Snickers bar, or anything you like. If it is a fruit, put it in a protective wrapper and then wrap it up in newspaper. You are going to want to have it wrapped in separate layers, anywhere between ten and twenty times. You are also going to want to have some music for this activity. Explain in the following way:

INSTRUCTOR: Everyone, come and sit in a circle. In a moment, I am going to give this parcel to Emily. When the music starts, Emily is going to pass the parcel in a clockwise direction. You have to keep passing the parcel at a regular pace. You cannot just hold on to the parcel. When the music stops, the person who has the parcel must keep hold of it. At that point, either I or someone from the circle will initiate an acting dare to the parcel holder. Some examples are: recite four lines from any Shakespeare character, name three of the latest Oscar winners, tell Derek you are breaking up with him as if he is really your boyfriend. (You may want to prepare a list of these dares ahead of time.) If the majority of the group agrees that you have completed the dare sufficiently well, you get to remove a wrapper from the parcel. If not, then you don't. Please be reminded that the dare must be related to the field of acting in some way. At this point, the music starts again and the process is repeated. The person who takes off the last wrapper, and reveals the item, is the winner.

MICK: What happens to the item?

INSTRUCTOR: The winner gets to keep it.

GALE: How many wrappers are covering the item?

INSTRUCTOR: That is a pretty direct and assertive question. I like it. Unfortunately, I don't remember how many layers I put in. If I did, I would not tell you, because it adds a little more suspense.

In terms of music, it is always a good idea to have something upbeat. You can also have the students bring in their own music. It is much more likely they can relate to their own music than yours.

Purpose

To build a foundation

The purpose of this activity is for the actors to discover their basic foundation of acting knowledge. The actors will want to pay attention not only to their own dare, but also to the dares asked of others. They may find that they can meet all their challenges, or on the other hand, that their knowledge of acting is limited. This activity will help to highlight this point. Many professionals such as doctors, lawyers, teachers, musicians, artists, and engineers are all willing to study their fields in the broadest sense. It appears that sometimes there is apathy on the part of an actor. Some teachers talk about "natural" talent. The way some aspiring actors like to interpret this is that they don't have to study anything. They do not have to know or learn anything about acting. Even if there were such a thing as natural talent, it is a danger for the actor to follow that concept in practice. In his book *History of the Theatre,* Oscar G. Brockett explains, "The actor had given way to the director as the dominant artist in the theatre. Saxe-Meiningen's example influenced such men as Antoine and Stanislavsky, who were to figure significantly in the formation of modern theatre."[37] Do your actors know that it was D.W. Griffith who invented the on-camera close-up? Understanding the history of acting will not necessarily create a better actor. It will not necessarily help your students to get work. But it will allow them to create a stronger base and foundation from which their acting can grow. In a conversation I had with theatre professor Dr. David Deacon, he made the following observation, "Acting can be instrumental in bringing about public change of opinion, hopefully for the better. For example, Harriet Beecher Stowe wrote *Uncle Tom's Cabin.* This book about slavery was turned into a play. When you see a slave owner take a bullwhip to a young slave girl, you cannot help but be greatly moved and affected by what you see." All good actors have something to say. Actors should not only be aware of the history of acting. They will also want to be aware of the profound influence they can have on history through the way they tell the story.

Industry Connection

It is fair to say that a large part of who wins the wrapped item is luck. One actor may find he ends up completing five dares correctly and taking off five wrappers. Another actor may find that the parcel stops with him on two occasions. The first time he cannot complete the dare. The second time the parcel lands with him he does complete the dare and takes off the last wrapper. For him to win obviously means there is a degree of luck involved. After all, the

---

37. Oscar G. Brockett, *History of the Theatre* (Austin, Texas: A Viacom Company, 1999), 425.

person who got five dares correct won nothing. He may think it was all a waste of time. Some actors may feel this about their careers. They go up for a part and give a fine performance. They are sure they will get the part. Later, they discover that the part went to someone who could hardly act, but looked perfect for the role. They cannot believe the lucky break the other actor got. What they have not taken into account is to look at the long-term picture. Perhaps the other actor got lucky on this one occasion. If that actor is no good, then it may be the last lucky break he ever gets. If an actor is a strong professional and if he persists, he will eventually start to make inroads. This does not mean he will become a movie star, but it increases his odds of becoming a working actor. It is true there is always a bit of luck involved. It is also true that you make your own luck. The actor who opened the parcel last got a lucky break. The actor who got five dares right created five possible opportunities for himself to win. That is five more chances than he would have had if he had not been prepared. His foundation knowledge and practical acting skills increased his odds. The actor will always want to be looking to stack the odds in his own favor, because no one else will. Movie stars will stamp themselves into every role, but a great actor is a true chameleon.

Note

An actor may decide he wants to be a movie star. In the end it is the public and the people who buy tickets who will decide if this is the case. This can be a delicate and sensitive topic. An actor's career is full of triumphs and disappointments. If an actor focuses solely on being a star and not on his acting, he may destroy all his dreams.

145. Zombie

Instruct your actors to stand in a circle. Choose one of the actors to be the zombie. The zombie will start off in the middle of the circle. He is going to close his eyes or be blindfolded, if you prefer. He is to put his arms out in front of him and move across the circle in a slow and zombie-like fashion. Whoever he first makes contact with is automatically out. He will then turn and move in another direction, and the next person he makes contact with is also out. Once a student is out, he should move out of the circle. At this point, the circle will want to close in a little and become smaller. Here is a twist to the exercise: The students cannot avoid being caught. If the zombie is moving towards them, they just have to take it. The last person left in is the winner. In other words, the last person left in will win by pure luck. If an actor tries to duck or move out of the way, he is automatically out. No one is allowed to move out of the way of the zombie.

Purpose

To experience destiny

If an actor is out immediately, then it was his destiny to be out. This may sound flippant, but it is the case. It is important for the actor to feel comfortable with terms like *destiny* and *fate*. When actors read a play, they already know the destiny of their character. They already know the destiny and fate of every other character involved in the play. The actors have to accept the destiny that has been predetermined for them. Here is the important part of that equation: The character has to accept his fate, but the actor does not. The character has no idea what will happen to him or how things will truly play out. The actor has to ignore the destiny that awaits his character and begin to look at the situation from his character's perspective, not his own. There is the actor's view of destiny and then there is the character's worldview.

Industry Connection

I use this activity for a number of different reasons. One of the most important is to give the actors a taste of something that is out of their control. The winner of this activity has no more skill than anyone else. The only reason he won was because of pure luck. When someone is out immediately, a look of frustration usually appears on his face. It is almost pained, as if to say, "Why me?" For all the skill, hard work, determination, and everything else that goes into an actor's career, no one doubts that there is also a degree of luck involved. There is, however, still a major difference between luck in this activity and luck in an actor's career. Let us say an actor, by sheer luck, lands a major role in a movie. If he does an awful job, it might just be the last role he ever gets. Having luck is not enough for the actor. This is why preparation is so vitally important. An actor will also need tenacity, resilience, and inner strength. With regard to preparation and auditioning, Stephen Book says, "Going in and winging an audition, or telling the casting directors that you have just received the sides, and haven't had time to prepare, will guarantee that you are not called back."[38] The actor has to be prepared for luck when it comes his way.

Note

Some Hollywood actors have been written off time and time again and yet they are still acting. It is most likely tenacity, technique, and persistence more than anything else that keeps them working.

146. Background

Ask two of your actors to come into the performance space. The rest of the students will take the part of the audience. Tell the two actors to perform a scene that they already know. If they are not familiar with one, you can give them a script to work with. The scene should be up to two minutes long. Once the scene has been performed, bring up half the audience and explain in the following way:

INSTRUCTOR: (Let us assume that the scene was set on a bench in the park.) In a moment we are going to watch the scene again. Daniel and Claire, you are going to do your scene exactly the same way on the park bench. This time, I want to integrate some background. All of you are just walking around the park. Simon, you are a man in a rush. Helen, you are carrying your shopping bags. Steven, you're waiting for your friend, and she is running late. I want the rest of you to decide who you are and what you are doing here.

BILLY: I don't even know who I am supposed to be, or what I am doing here.

INSTRUCTOR: That is up to you to decide.

DARREN: Can we talk to one another?

INSTRUCTOR: That is a great question. You can talk to each other in mime,

---

38. Stephen Book, *The Actor Takes a Meeting* (Los Angeles: Silman-James Press, 2006), 256.

but you cannot actually say anything. As you know, in this scene, you have no lines in the script.

You should still have half your class as the audience. Follow up with a group discussion.

Purpose

To utilize your imagination

You are asked to give basic actions and basic character breakdowns to some of your actors. In other cases, you don't tell the actors anything and leave them to their own imaginations. Some people will kick up a fuss and say that this is unfair. Unfortunately, this may be the reality they face on-set. The people who are setting the background are the PAs (personal asssistants). A number of them have no training whatsoever in acting. It is their job to place the background, but they will expect the actors to do the rest. The actors' play voucher will have a general description of who they are. For instance, a voucher may say, "pedestrian." That is all the PA has to go on, and it is all the actor has to go on. The PA may tell the actor, "Go!" This does not sound like great direction. It is then up to the actor to work out his own motivation and justify his actions. Because background actors are usually given so little direction, they have the opportunity to create their own. Background work can be invaluable for actors when they recognize the opportunities. The background is also very important to the audience visually, and helps create the *mise-en-scéne* — the visual elements of a theatrical production. Stanislavski would sometimes spend months, or even years, working with the ensemble on a production.

Industry Connection

The actors get a small taste of what it is like to be a background actor on a set. Some of your actors may say, "I am never going to do background work!" This may well be the case. There are a number of instructors who speak against it. It is also worth noting that there are numerous aspiring and working actors who have worked background at sometime or other. They still have to pay their bills and background work can help. They also see everything that is happening on a movie set, which can be an invaluable experience. Most instructors do not want their actors to have a prolonged career in background. This is an important observation. But for a limited period of time, it can be a useful experience for an actor who has newly arrived in Los Angeles. It is up to the individual actor to decide what works best for his career. Sometimes in a movie, a lead actor will be in a scene with a background actor. You will see him talk to the background actor, put his arm around him, and interact in many ways. You sit there, wondering why the other actor does not verbally respond. In some ways, it makes the scene look a little surreal. The director may want the background actor to say something, but does not tell him to do so. The reason for all of this is money. If the background actor says one word, the production company will have to pay him ten-fold.

147. Osmosis

This is a very well-known activity that can be more challenging than it first appears. Ask the students to stand in a circle. Tell them to give you some suggestions for a category. Some examples are: music, fruit, countries, cars, animals. For this example, I am going to use animals. Explain in the following way:

INSTRUCTOR: Paul, I would like you to start this exercise for me. I would like you to name an animal that begins with the letter A.

PAUL: Armadillo.

INSTRUCTOR: Very good. Rick, you are now going to name an animal that begins with B.

RICK: A bear.

INSTRUCTOR: Good. That is how this exercise works. We keep going around the circle until someone gets stuck or cannot name an animal. That person is then out for the rest of the round. Once we get to Z, we go back to A and start again, until eventually we have a winner.

SARAH: Can we change the category?

INSTRUCTOR: We can play a few different rounds and we can change the category each time. Every time we start a new round everyone is back in.

If you want to make it more challenging, you can be even more specific. An example is to name different breeds of dog, different towns in London, and so on.

Purpose

To possess general knowledge

Actors have to have very good general knowledge. They discover this very quickly, whether they appear to have general knowledge or not. Actors may know a good deal about acting, but they also need to know about the world around them. An actor is going to play characters from all walks of life. Perhaps an actor is playing a student who used a chalkboard and chalk before the invention of the pencil. Maybe an actor is working on a play set in Alabama during the time of the Great Depression. If the actor has no general knowledge of the Great Depression, he is going to be missing a massive influence of the time period in which the play is set. This means that many things his character does are influenced by the Depression, even if only subconsciously. Advise your actors to further their knowledge of the arts and sciences and of the world around them, including current affairs. Actors need a strong foundation from which to work.

Industry Connection

The actors are required to have good knowledge of a broad array of subjects. Working actors spend a good deal of the time conversing with others. Many of the people they will come across are articulate, intelligent, street-smart, and worldly. The question each actor has to ask himself is: What do I really have to say to these people? The actor will also need to know if he is going to be able to banter back and forth in a decent conversation. You may think this sounds a bit far-fetched and verging on the ridiculous, but think again. You always hear actors talking about the famous line, "It's who you know." Everyone accepts that there is a degree of truth in this. If this is the case, people are not going to want to know you if you cannot participate in a decent conversation. Encourage your actors to develop a keen mind and a broad knowledge base.

148. Three, Four, Five

Tell your actors to sit in a circle. Teach them a basic rhythm such as: "pat, pat, snap." This means they pat their legs twice then snap their fingers. Now, choose a category such as animals. In the first round, you are going to go around the circle with everyone performing the rhythm. The first person is going to have to call out an animal that is spelled with three letters. This means that the rhythm would be "pat, pat, cat." The second person could say, "pat, pat, dog." He could snap his fingers as he calls out his animal. The participants must choose three-lettered animals for the first round. If someone cannot name a three-lettered animal when it is his turn, he is out or loses a point. For the second round, the students have to use four-lettered words. Change the category each round. Perhaps the second round could be different types of fruit. An example would be, "pat, pat, plum!" Continue adding a letter and a new category for each round. Remind the whole group that they will want to keep the rhythm going at all times.

Purpose

To have a good foundation of knowledge

There are many professions where individuals have specialized training to hone their skills. In a sense, acting is an oxymoron in this regard. The actor needs both a specific and a general type of training. The specifics come with regard to the actor working on his instrument. The general part comes in how the actor observes and digests the world around him. An actor is not playing one character. During his lifetime, he will play many characters with varied backgrounds. He has to be familiar with his character's words, language, and culture if he wants to have a chance of doing justice to the part. The seventeenth century French playwright Molière was specific with his characters' language. In his play *The Miser*, Harpagon says, "Out of my house. Get out of my house this instant — and don't come back! Go on, get out, you lying, thieving, sniveling little toad."[39] An actor must speak and understand the character's language.

Industry Connection

This exercise integrates a variety of words and a constant rhythm at which they should be spoken. One of the exciting things about acting hubs like New York, Los Angeles, and London are that people got to these places from all over the world. This means that directors in Los Angeles are from all over the globe. Producers in London are not all from England. Actors in New York come from virtually every country you can think of. These people bring with them a wealth of words, iambic pentameters, and cultures that can be vastly different from one's own. The more worldly your actors, the more they will be able to communicate at a deeper level. Ignorance may be bliss, but it has no place in the working actor's life.

---

39. Moliére, *The Miser* (London: Methuen Drama, 1991), 7.

Chapter 18
Ensemble

149. Grab a Seat

Explain this exercise in the following way:

INSTRUCTOR: I would like everyone to stand in a circle, really close to each other, facing inwards. You should be so close that you are almost touching. I want everyone to make a slight turn outwards. You should now be even closer to each other. You should now be virtually touching one another. In a moment, I am going to ask you all to slowly sit down. If you are all really close, you will end up sitting on the lap of the person immediately behind you. The whole construction will support itself. If one of you is not close enough, the whole thing will topple over. You can all move slowly, but you must all move together. If one person is too slow, it will create a domino effect.

There is a degree of physical contact during this exercise. It is interesting to note that you will usually have more challenges with adult actors than youth. Young actors are quite often less inhibited and more open to physical contact than their adult counterparts. As Maria C. Novelly says in her book, *Theatre Games for Young Performers,* "Adolescent actors are full of energy, emotion, and curiosity about the theatre."[40]

Variation

If it is not successful, have the actors problem solve and work the exercise again. They can discuss between themselves how to solve any challenges that arise. It will be interesting to observe which students take the leadership roles and which choose to take a backseat.

If it is very easy then you can literally add an extra step. After the actors are seated have them try to start moving around the circle in their seated position. They can achieve this if everyone starts on the right foot and proceeds from there.

Purpose

To bring the actors together as a cohesive unit

This exercise can only succeed if everyone works together. If one actor only half participates, the whole group will fall over like a row of dominoes. In a play, an actor has freedom within certain boundaries. Without the boundaries he might fall off the stage. A play cannot succeed unless every member of the cast does their part. Sometimes an actor forgets that without the lighting team, his performance will not be illuminated. It was not until the nineteenth century that theatres began using gas lighting. Oil lamps and candles were previously used in the theatre for illumination. Without the production team, no tickets will be sold. Without the director, there will not be cohesiveness or vision for the project. For the good of the play, every member of the cast must do their share. It is still possible for an individual performance to stand out, even if the show itself fails, but this should never be the actor's ultimate goal. Under the star system of acting in the nineteenth and eighteenth century and earlier, an actor working solely for

---

40. Maria C. Novelly, *Theatre Games for Young Performers* (Colorado Springs, Colorado: Meriwether Publishing Ltd., 1985), Introduction.

his own glory was almost a given. The modern theatre director really did not emerge until the later part of the nineteenth and early twentieth century, possibly originating from those such as the Duke of Saxe-Meiningen.

Encourage your actors to work as part of ensemble unit. By doing so they will gain the sense of a dynamic relationship. Functioning actors learn to become a little bit director-proof when they learn to become their own director. To get a great performance, the director has to create an atmosphere that his actors can create in. He allows for the statement and development of the theme to be expressed. It takes courage to be a good director. Some people say directing is an extrovert's game. A good director aims to understand the actor's process. Some directors like to use a dictatorial approach to their work. It takes courage to ultimately be an actor's director. A good director allows his actors to do their work and support their quest. They are generous and freeing for the actor. They are managerial in being time and task orientated. At times he inspires creative freedom in his actors. Directors are encouraging of spontaneity. They can be an antagonistic ally. They know how to let their actors play. They are able to build trust and rapport with their actors. They find a place where they and the actor can meet. They give the actor the best they have to offer. For some directors the camera is like having another actor on the set. They direct their actors without making them feel like puppets. Directors discover the images they are looking for through trial and error. They know where the beginning, middle, and end are, but they allow the actor the freedom to choose how to get there. They are really prepared for anything that can happen. They seem to be able to say the right thing at the right moment. They give their actors a net. They allow the actor to do his best work. They understand the importance of the relationship in the work. Everything focuses towards the work. It is quite possible that the actors do not even feel like they are being directed. It is also worth noting that behind every good film director is a good cinematographer. These observations are very important if we accept the premise that filmmaking is a director's medium.

Industry Connection

This exercise forces actors to wipe away any sense of personal barriers they may have. They have to get up real close and personal to the actor immediately in front and behind them. There may be numerous occasions throughout an actor's career when this will be the case. Actors in a play have a couple of weeks to get used to another actor and encroach on that space gradually. If they are a day player on a TV show, they have half an hour or no time at all. One minute they are shaking an actor's hand, and the next minute they are falling into each other's arms. If this repulses you, if this offends you, if this insults you, then you better consider your options. Good actors are constantly engaged in antisocial behavior. They are constantly stretching their limits and boundaries.

Note

Give your actors the following information in your own words:

INSTRUCTOR: Antisocial behavior does not mean you should go out and rob a bank. It does not mean you should break the law. It means that you have to learn to break a lot of self-imposed rules that society has given you. One example is that society often tells us to talk quietly and not be too loud. An actor has to learn to work the full range of his voice on a constant basis. This in itself is a form of antisocial behavior.

You may be opening up a can of worms if you like a quiet classroom. Your actors have to learn to strip away many of the inhibitions that society places upon them.

150. Symbiotic Scene

Bring up three to five actors into the performance area. Have the rest of the group sit as the audience. Have the audience give the performing actors each a character and set the scene for them. It is good to create a mini-set for this exercise. For instance, you could set up a living room by putting out some chairs and a table. You are going to have the actors improvise their scene with a slight twist. During the scene, whatever one character does, the others must also do. Let us say that the mother goes and sits on the couch because she is exhausted. The son and the father must also find a reason to go and sit on the couch. Let us say the son decides he is going to have a drink because he is thirsty, then Mom and Dad must also find a reason to have a drink. Not only must the characters copy each others' actions, but they must do so in a justified manner. If the characters get a drink, they must find a reason for doing so. It is probably not possible for the actors to do every single action the same, but they should do as much as possible while keeping their actions justified. It is also important to note that there is no leader for this exercise. The characters must follow whoever takes the lead at that particular moment. Allow the scene to run for a few minutes and switch to another group. If a scene is static, have the actors pause for a moment. Have the audience make suggestions as to why the scene is not working and give the actors some things to think about.

Variation

Have only one leader. Everyone has to find a reason to follow and copy this one individual's actions. You could also give the audience permission to pause the scene and comment if they feel an action has no justification behind it. They could make a suggestion and the scene can continue.

Purpose

To justify your actions

In this exercise it is easy to copy another character. It is easy to walk around the room and do exactly what he does. The challenge is that if there is no justification behind the action, it will appear superficial and meaningless. The actors have to find a way to justify their actions. Sometimes we go to a play and feel that the actors are just saying their lines. The challenge is that this is exactly what is happening. There is no point or purpose to anything they are doing. We will sometimes find this quite amusing because bad acting can be a lot of fun to observe. However, this is not what your actors want to be aspiring towards. If something appears unjustified, pause the scene for a moment. Ask the actors, "Why did you do that? What was your justification and motivation?" If they say they do not have one, then help them discover one. It is important that your actors grasp that if they do not know why they are doing something, then neither will their audience. When two actors work in a symbiotic fashion they become aware moment to moment.

Industry Connection

In this exercise the actor's have to find a way to mirror each other's actions. Actors pursuing the industry will have to do a lot of networking. They will have to be comfortable meeting any number of different people and leaving an impression. They will meet agents, managers, directors, casting directors, producers, and scriptwriters to name but a few. Some scriptwriters are told, "That's a great writing sample. What else do you have?" What they do is unbelievably difficult. They have to persist. It is not enough to just meet these people. It is also important that the actor finds a way to leave a good impression. People like people who are in some way similar to themselves. When you mirror the behavior of another person they will generally like you. They see a little bit of themselves in you. They do not necessarily know this but it is OK that the actor does. (See Building Rapport Exercise on page 307) By learning to mirror other people's behaviors your actors can learn to build rapport with the people that are most important to their acting career.

Note

On numerous occasions right up to the moment of filming some actors text their friends. They are still doing this after the take has just been slated. The mind boggles that this is not acceptable behavior for a professional actor and yet it happens all the time. The directors often say nothing to contradict the actor for various reasons. Bad acting is amazingly easy. Mediocre acting takes some work. Good acting is only mastered by a select few. This exercise is very easy to do badly and very difficult to do with a believable performance.

151. Toboggan

Have your actors split up into teams of five or six. If you have twenty actors, then four teams of five will suffice. Everyone will want to take off their shoes and put them out of the way. Have all your actors move to one end of the room. Explain in the following way:

INSTRUCTOR: For this exercise everyone is going to sit on the floor. As a team you need to sit one behind the other. You need to wrap your legs around the individual who is sitting in front of you. I want you to imagine that you and your team are a snow sled. The only way you can move is by using your hands to slide across the room. If your sled breaks apart, you must go back to the beginning and start again. Each team must start from behind the same line, which is marked by this chair. The finish line is twenty feet away and marked by another chair. Please remember to use safety first. In order to win, you are going to have to work as a team. Be careful not to overextend your wrist as you move forward. Please be careful not to kick the person immediately in front of you.

This can be quite a physically demanding exercise. If the teams seem drained, play it only once. If everyone seems full of energy, the winning team is the first one to win two races.

Purpose

Being a willing part of an ensemble

For a team to do well, they will have to work together in this exercise. Good actors know they are part of an ensemble. A very famous actor in a play in London was given his own dressing room away from the other actors. He moved his dressing room in with the other actors. Not only was he a team member, but he chose to be a willing team member. He knew that being and working with the other actors was the key to his own success.

Industry Connection

This exercise is quite physically demanding. An acting career is also quite physically demanding. Actors may have to run to one audition and sit through an hour of traffic and then run to another audition and sit through another hour of traffic. That same day, they might have their acting class followed up by their job at the restaurant. The physical demands of an acting career can be quite draining and demanding. Russell Grandstaff is able to put a metaphor into action when he explains, "To be a good actor you almost must have the stamina of a mountain climber, the endurance of a marathon runner, the patience of a turtle, the strength of a weightlifter, the courage of a lion trainer, the memory of a computer, the agility of a gymnast, the imagination of a child, and the confidence of the devil."[41] An actor promoting a movie may have to give dozens of individual press interviews in one day. These demands may be made of the actor on an ongoing basis.

152. Jump Rope

For this exercise you are going to need a large jump rope. Explain in the following way:

INSTRUCTOR: I hope everyone is full of energy. Let me have Sarah and David start, one on each end of the rope. I would like everyone else to line up, one behind the other, ready to jump. Please make sure that you are close by, but at a safe distance. The first player in line should jump the rope once. At this point he should run to take one end of the rope. The player they take it from should run to the back of the line. The next player in line has to jump twice. The third player has to jump three times, the fourth player four times, and so on. Each round, a new player has to take one end of the rope. If a player fails to jump the rope, the players have to begin from one again for the next round. Continue to alternate by switching out the rope holders at either end.

Purpose

To create an ensemble unit through teamwork

The apparent simplicity of this exercise is actually quite deceiving. To get up to the higher number is going to take a lot of focus, concentration, teamwork, and agility by the entire group. When seeing a performance by a great actor people often comment, "Look how easy that was." It is this deception that makes anyone believe they can act without the slightest bit of training. David Garrick was considered by many as one of the greatest and most innovative British actors of the eighteenth century. Garrick believed that actors should develop through observations of real life. He is said to have promoted a realistic form of acting. In this aspect he was well ahead of his time. The deep complexities of great acting are what allow it to appear effortless and seamless. It is true, creative art. When talking about acting, Peter Barlow, Chair of Conference of Drama

41. Russell Grandstaff, *Acting and Directing* (Lincolnwood, Ill.: National Textbook Company Publishing Group, 1975), 1.

210

Schools throughout England, told me, "Everyone in the world thinks acting is easy, as long as you can learn lines and say them with confidence, then you can join any amateur company in the world. Some people think you don't need to train to be a professional actor. Occasionally you can be lucky and be on TV or film without having any training, you may have good instincts and sometimes this can be enough to get you through one job. Imagine you want to be a dancer and you have good movement instincts, you could be in an experimental dance group and perhaps successfully produce some movement which an audience thinks is interesting, but you would never be invited to join a ballet company or even a contemporary dance company unless you had trained and practiced to achieve a very high level of competence and skill. I think acting should be treated in the same way; an untrained actor may be able to get by in an undemanding television role but would never survive in, say, the Royal Shakespeare Company."

Industry Connection

This exercise uses the premise of creating a compounding effect. Each person has to jump one more time than the previous person. Actors can also view their acting careers as a compounding experience. In their first six months, their aim may be to get their headshots done. By the end of their first year, they might aim to get their first commercial agent. By the end of the second year they may aim to have joined the union and have a theatrical agent. Each step is like building a strong foundation and moving them in the direction they want to go. Many actors move to LA, London, New York, and Bollywood and crash and burn. The reason is that they try to go from nowhere to fame and fortune, overnight. They throw everything into this philosophy and when it doesn't happen after eighteen months, they leave broke and shell-shocked. An actor must be willing to have patience, an enormous amount of patience. Build a strong foundation and you will have a better chance of building longevity in your career.

Note

Some actors believe that only America and England have potential work and produce actors. This is a very limited worldview. Bollywood superstar Shah Rukh Khan is idolized in India. He has acted in over seventy movies in a career that spans more than twenty years. France has produced a number of fine actors such as Audrey Tautou, Romain Duris, Jean Reno (Moroccan descent), Marion Cotillard, and Maurice Chevalier. Spain has brought us directors such as Guillermo del Toro and Pedro Almodovar. Germany has given us plays such as *Mother Courage* and *The Threepenny Opera* by Bertolt Brecht. Japan has given us the theatre writings of Tadashi Suzuki through his book, *The Way of Acting.* Japan has also given us the Noh Theatre. Norway has given us Henrik Johan Ibsen, a world-famous playwright. Russia gave us Constantin Stanislavski, Vsevolod Meyerhold, and the Moscow Art Theatre. The list goes on and on. The contributors to the field of acting are truly global.

211

153. Fugitive

You will need a fairly large space for this exercise with good places to hide. Explain in the following way:

INSTRUCTOR: To start off with, I am going to divide the group into police and fugitives. I am going to pick five police officers. In a moment, I am going to ask the police to go next door. First of all, we are going to pick a fugitive. The fugitive the police are looking for is going to be Kara. The fugitive will be given five minutes to hide. This sounds like a lot of time, but there is a reason for it. During this time she is able to change clothes, jackets, hats — whatever she chooses. She can do this from the shoes up. She can do anything she'd like to disguise herself. At this point, the police are brought back into the room. Remember, I said you are looking for the fugitive, Kara. Kara is now hidden amongst the other fugitives. The fugitives are hiding Kara because she is their leader. If she is caught, they are all caught. It is their job to protect her. This exercise is similar to hide and seek, but with a twist. Even if the police find someone, they do not necessarily want to arrest them. If they cannot see their face, they may not know who it is. They cannot make any physical contact without an immediate arrest. The reason for this is that you only have three chances. Any time you find someone, unless you think it is Kara, you will want to ignore them and move on. If you tap someone on the shoulder, or go up to them in any way within two feet, that counts as an arrest. You can only afford to make two wrong arrests. Once a fugitive has been discovered, he cannot run away. If the fugitives have done a good job, it is going to be hard for you to tell where Kara is. If they have done a poor job, it will be a breeze. Remember that the other challenge is that they are also in hiding. You will be given a total of five minutes to complete the task.

NICKI: What happens when we accuse someone of being the fugitive?

INSTRUCTOR: At this point he will stand up. If you are wrong, he will simply sit the rest of the exercise out. If you are right, the exercise is over.

PAUL: In what way can we disguise ourselves?

INSTRUCTOR: Use your imagination here. When the police are looking for Kara, they are looking for a female subject. If Kara is disguised as a male, this may make it more challenging for them. You can change clothing to really confuse the police.

Purpose

To know your objective

In this activity it is not enough to have an objective. The participants also have to know their main objective. Kara's objective is not to get caught. If she is seen, it does not mean she is necessarily caught. The police's objective is to find the correct fugitive. Finding the wrong fugitive is of no use to them. If they make the wrong assumption it could cost them dearly. The fugitives may believe their objective is to look out for themselves. This is partially true, but their main objective is to look out for their leader, Kara. If she is caught, it's all over. They have to be aware of their main objective. In a play, a teenager may shout and be rude to his parents. The actor playing the part may decide it is because the teenager is rude and obnoxious. If he had delved further into the character and the plot, he may have discovered something quite different. Let's suggest that if the actor had delved further, this is what he would have discovered: The parents are always busy and have no time for their son. The son loves his parents very much, but is hurt that they have no time for him. He is crying out because he is longing for their attention and assurances. He acts up because it is the only way they notice that he exists. His objective is to get his parents to love him. Of course, this may not be clear by the character's dialogue and actions. It is up to the actor to discover what lies hidden beneath the words.

Industry Connection

If any of the three groups don't work as a team, they will most likely be the group that fails. If one of the police officers thinks he knows best and accuses the first three people he sees, the police lose. It is possible he may be immediately right, but he will want to confer with the other officers. If the fugitives don't help disguise and hide their leader, they will be discovered very quickly by the police. If the fugitive leader tries to work alone, he won't stand a chance. Imagine actors in London, Paris, New York, or LA who decide to go it alone. They decide to take their own headshot because they don't want to pay a photographer. They do their own resumé without asking for any help or advice, even though they are not really sure what should go on it, and despite the fact that their punctuation is poor. They don't bother trying to get an agent, even though they personally don't have any of the contacts that the agent took years to build up. They have never trained with an acting coach, but once glanced through an acting book. On-set, they get a small role and tell the makeup lady they will do their own makeup even though they have never done it before. I am obviously exaggerating to a certain extent here. The point is that working actors need a successful and supportive team behind them. Remind your actors to be team players, so that others will desire to be a part of their team.

154. Seven-Eleven

This is a simple yet complex exercise. Divide the group into two teams. Give each team some paper and a pencil. Each group needs to select a leader. The leader should be the person who believes he is the fastest writer in the group. Give the teams a topic, such as fruit. At this point, both teams have eleven seconds to write down seven different types of fruit. Some examples are: apple, orange, pear. Anyone in the group can call out the answers. If they do it too loudly, the other group might steal their suggestions, so they will also want to discuss tactics. After eleven seconds the leader of each team has to put his pencil down. If both teams have seven fruits, they get two points each. If only one team gets all seven, they get three points. If a person continues to write after eleven seconds, he is disqualified from the round and a point is given to the other side. If neither team gets all seven fruits, no points are given. If a team wants to change their leader, they may do so after five rounds. If they choose to do that, the opposing side will receive two bonus points. You will want to make sure that you come up with a whole array of topics. If you cannot read their writing, they won't get the points. This exercise is high pressure, hilarious, and quite intense, all at the same time.

Variation

If the students find it too difficult to write the answers, they can say them aloud. If you choose this approach, let one team go each round. Give the second team a new topic.

Purpose
To work under pressure
The purpose is to produce the goods under intense pressure. Eleven seconds is a very short period of time. The actors have to think, process the answers, and get them all written out within eleven seconds. On top of that, they have to write the answers legibly. Actors can feel under a great deal of pressure while preparing for each performance. Every night, their audience is expecting to see a fine performance. They have not paid good money to see something average. Good actors know this. They have to produce the goods every night, even if they have had a bad day. With all the pressures that an actor faces, it is quite incredible that they can give a fine performance, let alone repeat that achievement night after night. Great actors know how to do this. They know how to produce the goods under any circumstances. They know how to tap into other peoples' lives and magnify it.

Industry Connection
An important aspect of this exercise is accountability. When the groups choose their leader, they hope they have made the right choice. If they haven't, there are consequences that may end up costing them the game. The only person who is going to hold aspiring actors accountable is themselves. There are many actors who, after a number of years, find that they have attained very few of their goals. I do not mean becoming a movie star, I mean sub-goals, such as: work ethic, persistence, and ability to stay on task. The challenge with living in a city like Los Angeles is that the actor can drift along while very little gets done. No one else is going to hold them accountable. Some people feel the need to hold other people accountable. Actors are very rarely given this luxury in terms of furthering their craft and their career. Remind your actors that the buck stops with them. As I once heard a director say, "A movie star is like a horse, and all the money is riding on them!" The movie stars of the golden age had size and charisma. There are some actors who, during a close-up, the audience cannot take their eyes off. There is a twinkle in their eye that the audience cannot resist. It is the actors who can hold the screen who will hold their audience. Some actors say that after many years of hard work they eventually became an overnight success.

155. Balloon or Bust

You will need a pack of regular balloons for this exercise. You will also need a stopwatch. You will also want a pencil and piece of paper. Divide your students into teams of three to six players. This exercise works best with three to five teams. Adjust your team sizes accordingly. Explain in the following way:

INSTRUCTOR: I have divided you up into four teams. In a moment, I am going to give each team five balloons. I want you to divide up your balloons amongst your team members. As we have six players per team, it means all but one of your players will have a balloon. When I tell you to begin, you will have one minute for one of your players to blow up his balloon. In that minute he has to make the balloon as big as possible, without actually bursting it. The whole group should be involved in helping the player decide when to keep going and when to stop. It is very important that you listen to the next part carefully. When your minute is up, I will ask you to stop blowing. You may have stopped before that time if your group agreed. At this point, I want the player who blew up the balloon to hold onto it. Do not, under any circumstances, tie a knot in the balloon. We are then going to watch each team, one at a time, release their balloon. Please do not release your balloon until I ask you to do so. I will then use my stopwatch to time how long it takes each balloon to release all its air and fall to the ground. The team whose balloon lasts the longest will receive five points. The team in second place gets three points, the team in third place receives two points, and the team in fourth place will receive one point.

BEN: So all four teams let go of their balloons at the same time?

INSTRUCTOR: I am glad you asked for clarification here. The teams will not release their balloons at the same time. We are going to watch each team release its balloon individually, so that we can get an accurate reading.

MELANIE: What happens if we accidentally let go of our balloons, or they burst when we are blowing them up?

INSTRUCTOR: Those are two excellent questions. (It is important to praise your students' questions from time to time. For the sake of space, I only give brief words of praise in this edited version. You need to be more specific as to what you like about their answers. An example would be to tell a student that you like the fact that their question was so relevant to the topic.) If you let go of your balloon by mistake, it is going to lose all its air. In that particular round, your team will finish in last place. If, while you are holding the balloon, you accidentally let go of some of the air, you are not able to add more to make up for it. If you blow up your balloon and it bursts, all the other teams will automatically receive ten points. Remember, you have to find the balance between expanding your balloon to its maximum potential and blowing up a balloon that bursts. These rules may seem unfair, but they are there to make the exercise more challenging for you. There are five rounds, so each team is going to want to discuss their tactics.

This is an exercise that may require a few minutes for going over the rules. I normally only allow three questions per exercise, but sometimes more clarification is needed. Adjust your group sizes to meet your particular needs. You can also adjust the points awarded as you see fit.

Purpose

To work as a team

The purpose behind this exercise is for the teams to work together. Let's say a group tells a player to stop blowing his balloon. The player decides that he knows better than everyone else and keeps blowing. The balloon bursts and now he has given ten points to every other team. This lack of cooperation could cost his team the whole activity. If we go back to the nineteenth century and before, the star system was very much a part of the theatrical world. It was as it sounds. The star was the important person, and little or nothing else mattered. Even today, to some extent, we can see this in productions. It is certainly possible to focus solely on one person, but it will usually come at the cost of the overall production value. It was the likes of Stanislavski who first introduced ensemble acting to the western shores. In 1923, the Moscow Art Theatre arrived in New York for the first time. As David Allen points out, "The tour was a sensational success and left a lasting influence on American acting."[42] When actors are willing and able to work as an ensemble, the overall quality of the production becomes that much stronger. It is almost as if an ideal community has developed into a Utopia. Go on any movie set and see what happens when the cast and crew do not work well together. The production will suffer in the long run. Remind your actors that being a team player is a requirement, and not an option.

Industry Connection

The actors are encouraged to take calculated risks. If they blow their balloons too much, they will burst. They will therefore be giving a large number of points to the other teams. On the other hand, they want to blow them as big as possible in order to win the round. The groups are going to have to take calculated risks. In his career, an actor is going to have to think in much the same way. Let us say a twenty-year-old actress is offered the role of a high school freshman in a television series. This might sound like a no-brainer, but perhaps it is not so black and white. If a production company can cast an eighteen-year-old who looks as if she is fourteen, they don't have to deal with all of the welfare rules. Her agent tells her it is a golden opportunity, and she should grab it while she can. A casting agent friend of hers tells her the role will result in her playing teenagers for years to come. If the actress takes the role, she might be stereotyped as her casting agent friend predicts. If she turns the role down, perhaps nothing else will be on the horizon for some time to come. The actor is constantly put in the position of having to take calculated risks. Good actors are willing to take chances in a performance. Even when a series is doing well people will tell the actor, "It will never last." The actor's life is not black and white, but full of shades of grey.

Note

Once you have made your rules, stick to them. If you bend your rules, you are going to weaken the overall benefit and value of an exercise. You are doing your students no favors by being lenient to them. You want them to have an authentic and gut response from these activities and exercises. If you water them down, you water down the overall results. Actors who are in a successful television series can potentially become a celebrity. They can also make a good deal of money. The challenge is that to have longevity in their career the actors are going to want to play different roles. In the long run, playing one part may turn out to be a disadvantage for the actors' overall career. This may be one of the reasons popular television stars sometimes ask for more money and a percentage in regards to syndication.

156. Last Man Standing

For this exercise, give each student a chair. Tell them to take their chairs to some place in the room, as far away from other people as they can. At this point, ask them to sit in their chairs. However, one person needs to do things differently. Once that person has placed his chair, instruct him to move to the furthest point away from it. Tell him that his objective is to get back to an empty chair and sit on it. The objective for the rest of the group is to stop him from doing so. This

---

42. David Allen, 104.

particular student is given one more challenge: He is to carry a piece of paper between his knees as he moves around the room. If the piece of paper falls, he must go back to the furthest corner of the room and begin again. As he moves towards his chair, another student is going to move to sit on it and cover it. The challenge is that as he does so, another chair becomes vacant. The person looking for a chair keeps moving around the room until eventually he finds an empty chair. At this point, the person who moved from that chair becomes the "sitter." You will want him to start in a corner and receive the piece of paper from the previous person. The people trying to stop him from sitting cannot do so by using any kind of physical contact. He can only do it by sitting in the empty chair that becomes available.

Purpose
To work as a unit
The person looking for a chair only needs to find one empty chair. When moving towards a chair, three people may decide to stop him. At that moment, three other chairs will become available and it will be virtually impossible to stop the person from sitting in one. The way the group can beat the "sitter" is to work together and to communicate. In the first few rounds pandemonium results, but gradually the group will understand that only by working as a unit can they participate in the exercise effectively. Actors who work entirely alone can give very strong performances. People can leave the theatre and say, "Her performance really stood out. It is a shame that the rest of the play was so awful!" I highlight this point because it is important for the cast and crew to work together. It is important that there is an overarching vision for the play and a commonality in what they want it to achieve. It may be the director's job to communicate this, but it is the cast's and crew's responsibility to make that vision a reality. When this does not happen, we are left grasping at individual performances instead of looking at the production as a whole unit.

Industry Connection
When the "sitter" begins this exercise, achieving his objective may seem virtually impossible to him. Not only does he have to make it to an empty chair, but he has to do so with a piece of paper between his knees. When a chair does eventually open up, he comments that, after all, it wasn't as difficult as he expected. Actors may struggle for months to get their first voucher to join the union. They may say that it is virtually impossible to get vouchers and that they are thinking of giving up. Eventually, they somehow manage to get the other two. Once they join the union, they quickly forget about all the struggles it took to get them there in the first place. Talk to your actors about the idea that anything worth having is worth working towards. Most things we truly want in life do not come easily. We have to be willing to work and build towards them.

217

157. Clap Around

This is a very simple exercise that has been around forever. Tell your actors to sit in a circle. The aim is to have the group create a continuous clap. Choose one person to begin. He will clap once, and the person sitting on his right will clap immediately after him. That person will also clap once. The aim is to have everyone clap once, one after the other, so that it sounds like continuous applause. Here is the caveat to this exercise: It is easy to do badly and challenging to do well. Let's say the actors find that someone misses a turn, or claps out of rhythm, and things are just not working out. Allow them to brainstorm together to see how they can solve the challenges they face. It is OK if they have to try three or four times. This is a very simple activity, but it can be quite a complex activity to perform well.

Purpose

To create preemptive reactions

It is not enough for the actors to simply react to one another here. By the time they react, they will have delayed their clap and be slightly behind the pace. The actor almost has to preempt his reaction in order to stay on top of his clap. This may sound far-fetched, but we use preemptive actions all the time. Let us say you are talking to a friend. It is a friend who is telling you a story about another mutual friend. She says to you, "So Sarah spilled her coffee all over the carpet. You know how clumsy that girl can be." You have started nodding and reacting way before you have heard all the facts. You have known Sarah for a while, so you assume you know where your friend is taking the story, long before she has finished telling it. Invite your actors to consider opportunities in a play in which their character may preemptively act. It is very important that they do not confuse this with bad acting. A bad actor can react before he even knows what the other person is going to say. This is because he is reacting as the actor, and not as the character. As Jack Lemmon once said, "An awful lot of actors really don't act with you, they act at you."

Industry Connection

The actors almost have to be one step ahead of the game. The world-famous ice hockey star Wayne Gretzky allegedly said something along the lines that he didn't go where the puck was, but where he thought it was going next. It is this same approach that the working actors take with their career. They are always looking down the road and preparing for what is coming next. This does not mean they are not living in the present. A well-crafted actor's career is built on a strong foundation, ready for any eventuality. In this way the actors are preparing to create longevity in their careers.

158. Yeah!

For this activity ask your students to stand in a circle. Tell them that in a moment, one of them is going to jump in the air, clap his hands, and shout out, "Yeah!" All these things have to happen at the same time. The challenge is that you are not going to tell them who will begin. The aim is to get ten people in a row to do this exercise, one after the other. They cannot discuss it or come up with an order. They are also not allowed to simply go around the circle, in either direction. If more than one person jumps up at any time, the group has to start again. I always tell the students there is no rush. They need to focus and aim to sense when they can go and when they should wait. Remember that their aim is to have ten people do this in a row, with only one person participating at a time.

Variation
See Count Off in *112 Acting Games.*

Purpose
To sense the energy of the group
The actors have to sense everything around them. It is almost as if they have to sense when another actor is about to go. They have to be focused, but that is taking it one step further. The actors have to be able to feel the energy of the group. In a scene, a character may walk in on a conversation that abruptly stops as he arrives. He has heard nothing, but can immediately sense that something was being said that was not for his ears.

Industry Connection
I always ask the actors at the start of this exercise not to rush into it. I recommend they sense the energy of the group before anyone starts. Everyone always nods in agreement and understanding. As soon as they are able to start, three people jump up immediately, and they have to start the whole process again. It is as if some of the actors chose to ignore what had just been said. Sometimes, an actor seems to miss every word that his director has said to him. It may be because he is thinking of other things, or it may be because he chose not to hear what was being said. In any case, the director will translate it to mean that the actor cannot take direction. He will also make a mental note never to work with that actor again.

Chapter 19
Listening

159. Critic

Have your actors sit as an audience. Call up eight actors to the performance area. One actor is the host, one is the interviewer, one is the movie critic, and the other five are the actors. Have chairs downstage left for the interviewer and the critic and explain the exercise in the following way:

INSTRUCTOR: Anita, you are conducting the interview, and Paul, you are the movie critic. Anita, you can ask any questions you want about a fabricated movie of your choice. Please give me an example now.

ANITA: What was the climax of the movie?

PAUL: It was when Sergio ate the chocolate éclair while his wife massaged his left foot.

At this point, the host can choose to let the interview continue, or he can choose to have the actors act out the scene. The host can point to any of the five actors he chooses to be involved in the scene, which must be acted exactly as it was described by the movie critic. The above scene would obviously require the two characters mentioned. The host may choose to include other characters outside of those mentioned in the interview. The scenes need to move very quickly with a minimum of discussion. The more efficiently the host keeps this exercise moving the better. Allow the interview and scenes to continue for five or ten minutes and then switch out with another group of actors.

Purpose
To actively listen

This exercise is about actively listening. The five actors must be listening with their full attention, so that when the host calls on them, they are able to act out the scene as described. If they are only half paying attention, their scene will probably be lacking in accuracy. So much of the actors' work is about listening. This applies to listening to the other actors on-stage, listening to the director, and listening to their character's own inner dialogue. Actors who refuse to listen will find their careers cut abruptly short. This exercise also demands that the actor be in the moment. Preparation is futile, because you never know which scene the host is going to choose and which actors he will pick to perform it.

Industry Connection

In this exercise, every actor who is participating has to be able to think on his feet. The actor's career will have to be approached in much the same way. If a person works in a bank, he will work nine to five, with holidays and vacation time. As an actor, he might be in a production that shoots on New Year's Day and has fourteen-hour days. Actors have to be prepared for any occasion. If your actors can think on their feet, not only will they be prepared, but they will be able to embrace whatever comes their way. Instead of getting stressed, they will know that all of the curve balls that are thrown at them are part of an acting career — the career that they have chosen — and that no one is forcing them to follow.

Remind your actors of this any time they complain to you that your rehearsals are too long.

160. Food for Thought

Start off by having all your actors sit as the audience. Bring two actors into the performance space and explain in the following way:

INSTRUCTOR: I am going to have the two of you work a scene from the play *Children of a Lesser God*. Tim, you are going to play James, and Melanie, you are going to play Sarah. As you work through the scene, I am going to give you one rule. After each person has spoken, you must wait at least ten seconds for your character to respond. Use this time to allow your character to digest what has just been said. The audience does not just want to see you counting to ten and then saying your next line. We want to know what is happening in those pauses. Perhaps your character is about to say something but then thinks better of it. It is the unspoken dialogue that grabs our attention. Let the information sink in before they choose to respond to it.

Give the actors a few minutes to look over the scene. You can work with any scene you like. While this is happening, you might choose to hand out another scene for two other actors to look over. What you want to avoid is having all the actors looking at their own scenes, rather than watching what is happening on-stage. The scenes can come from a play, a movie script, or, if you prefer, the actors can improvise the scene. You can also choose to have the actors do the scene sitting, facing one another, so as to take away the blocking. These are just suggestions to get you moving in the right direction.

Purpose

To develop the ability to listen

This exercise encourages the actors to listen to one another. By pausing in between every sentence, the actors really have time to digest what has just been said. Let us say an actor is in a play where his girlfriend says she has been cheating. The audience doesn't just want to hear the actor respond with dialogue. They want to know what is going on beneath the dialogue. They want to see the actor thinking and processing what has just been said. Perhaps it takes a few seconds to really let what has just been said sink in. Encourage your actors to not be in such a rush to play he said, she said. A moment of silence can speak a thousand words.

Industry Connection

Raise the following points with your actors:

INSTRUCTOR: Sometimes you go to an audition and you are full of excitement, and the adrenaline is pumping around your body. So much so that you hardly hear what the director is saying to you. If the director becomes aware of this, it will not go in your favor. If the director says, "You may begin," pause for a moment and gain your composure. Allow your scene to begin from a clean slate. If a producer says to you, "Why do you think we should give you the part?" pause for a moment before responding. By pausing you are telling them, "I have heard your question. I am digesting your question so that I can let it sink in and give you a heartfelt response."

221

161. Standing Ovation

Have your actors sit in the audience. Have two actors come into the performance space. Explain in the following way:

INSTRUCTOR: Tom and Vicky, I would like you to stand so that you are looking at each other face-to-face. You can stand about two feet apart. Tom, you are going to clap your hands together one time. After a short pause, Vicky, you will clap your hands together one time. This sequence will continue with an even space in between each clap. As you keep going, the claps will want to get a little faster and the space in between becomes shorter. It is very important that the space in between each one is still even. Eventually you will reach a pace to where you are clapping. Remember that you have to keep the same form so that every time Tom claps it is Vicky's turn to follow. There should never be a time when Tom claps twice in a row.

TOM: What happens if I do clap twice?

INSTUCTOR: Then you have to start from the beginning again. This means that the gap in between each clap will be fairly large again. Make sure you allow yourselves to gradually build up to a clapping pace rather than skipping all the other stages.

VICKY: Can we talk to each other during the exercise?

INSTRUCTOR: That is a very good question. You can talk to each other before or after the exercise, but not during. I want you to stay as focused as possible during the exercise and utilize your sense of hearing. You may want to discuss before or after in case you need to problem solve what isn't working.

Once you have watched two actors work, have the group split up into pairs. Have the actors spread out around the room and work the exercise with their partners. It is very important that they do not try to build up too quickly. This is a good opportunity for you to walk around the room and observe. After a few minutes bring everyone back together for a group discussion.

Purpose

To work in symmetry

In this exercise each actor has to sense what the other actor is about to do. They cannot plan it, but they have to feel it. In other words, they have to fall in line with their rhythm. If the two actors work alone, they will never be able to get up to a clapping pace. When an actor is in a scene with a fellow actor, it is much the same way. He has to listen and respond to what is being said. He has to feel and react to his partner. Actors will want to have an instrument that is fully available. They have to respond without actually planning their response. If they already know exactly the way they are going to say the line, their performance will come across as contrived and meaningless. We sometimes call this a *polished performance*. They have to work in symmetry with their partner rather than working against them.

Industry Connection

Raise the following points with your actors:

INSTRUCTOR: Some people move to a Los Angeles and they fight against it. They say, "I hate this city! I hate the traffic! I hate the noise! I hate the rude people! I hate the dirt in the streets! I hate the shallow people!" By focusing on everything they dislike about the city it stands to reason that their time there will be short-lived. It also makes their time spent there miserable. It is often said that what we focus on is what we get. If you are moving to London, New York, Paris, or Los Angeles to pursue your acting career, this is a big step. Instead of fighting against it, the actors now want to embrace it by finding things they love about London. Find what it is that makes New York unique. To give themselves the best shot of having an acting career, they are going to have to find symmetry with the city where they live. Los Angeles has great weather, beautiful nature, and the most influential film industry in the world. They should focus on what they want, and not on what they don't want! As Tom Logan explains it, "We need to bear in mind that old Hollywood saying: *Be nice to people on your way up because you are going to see them again on your way down.*"[43]

162. Slow Dance

Have your actors start off by sitting in the audience space. Bring two actors into the performance area, one male and one female. Have a scene and character breakdown come from the audience. At this point, ask the actors to start dancing together. They should be dancing a slow dance. At some point their heads should be resting on each other's shoulders. They should now have absolutely no eye contact with each other. It is at this point that the scene should begin. Even if the scene dictates that an actor is supposed to walk over and fetch something, this will now only happen in the actor's imagination. The actors should stay with their head on their partner's shoulder throughout the scene. They do not have to have full body contact, but they have to be pretty darn close. You can work with a number of different pairs in this way. The actors have to play the scene full out while dancing and resting their head on their partner's shoulder.

Purpose
To listen to your partner
In this exercise the actors have to be listening to their partner at all times. They cannot see their partner, so their listening becomes more heightened. Good actors are always listening to their partners on-stage, and bad actors, generally speaking, do not. When one actor is listening to another actor, it registers on his face and in his body. The audience is aware of this and it intrigues them. They say, "I wonder what he is thinking right at this moment." An actor who is simply waiting for his next line registers absolutely nothing. The audience knows this and wonders if they can get their money back.

Industry Connection
Raise the following points with your actors:
INSTRUCTOR: To put your head on another actor's shoulder and keep it there means you are going to be dancing quite intimately. This means that you are immediately forced to break down barriers. I have mentioned this on many occasions, because on a movie set this may be invaluable information. You are playing a day-player role in which you have to run up to your father and literally leap into his arms. The only time you have met is in the last five minutes, when he shook your hand. You have to make this hug look very intimate and

---

43. Tom Logan, *How to Act and Eat at the Same Time* (New York: Limelight Editions, 2004), 65.

connected and yet you hardly know this man. The inhibited actor could not achieve this with any conviction in a million years. You have to know how to brush aside any personal barriers or hang-ups immediately. If it takes you twenty takes to find it, you will not be asked back. You will become an out-of-work actor. You are being paid to be a professional.

163. Syll-A-Ble

To begin the exercise, have all of the actors sit in a circle. Select one of the actors to wait outside the room. At this point have the group quietly come up with a word of three or more syllables. Some examples are: aluminum, detention, conspicuous, celebration, meditation.

Count off by syllables so that each player is given a syllable. Let's say you use the word "meditation," which has four syllables. If you have twelve players, then three players will have "me," three will have "di," three will have "ta," and three will have "tion." At this point choose a simple tune such as "Happy Birthday." Now, each player sings his syllable to the tune of, "Happy Birthday." So, for example, the first group should be singing "me" to "Happy Birthday." They should all be singing their own syllable at precisely the same time. The person outside should now come in and listen to the singing. His job is to work out what word is being sung. This may sound easy, but with everyone singing their own syllable, it can be quite confusing. Allow the person to have up to three guesses. The actors should keep repeating the song without stopping during this process. Remind the actor that no one should be singing the actual words of the song. "Happy Birthday" is just one example of a well-known song you can choose. You can change the song to anything you like, provided everyone knows the tune — they do not have to know the words. Give the guesser up to three minutes to get the correct answer.

Purpose
To develop a sense of timing
In this exercise the actors have to keep their timing so as not to fall behind or surge ahead of the other actors' singing. This can be pretty challenging, as everyone is singing their own syllable. In order to do this, the actors really have to focus. If an actor is in a play that is a comedy, timing will be of the essence. Great comedians edit and change their thoughts in nanoseconds. There is a great deal of effort that goes into making comedy look effortless. Comedy is all about timing and tempo, so the more the actors understand it, the more they can appreciate it and manipulate it. Perhaps they are strong dramatic actors, but have not been able to stretch to comedy yet. Actors may find a mix of humor and nostalgia in the same scene. There is a big temptation in a funny scene to try to play the comedy. The more versatile the actors are the more opportunity they will have of being a working actor. Patrick O'Sullivan, producer of the show *All About Walken*, told me in regards to comedy, "Acting in comedy is so specific. You can't fool an audience in comedy. The results are out loud. I find that most good comedic actors are also good dramatic actors, but it doesn't necessarily work the other way."

Industry Connection

The actor who has come in from the other room will have to listen very carefully to hear the word that is being sung. He probably will not get it all in one go, but will get it piecemeal. When an actor sings there is a lot of make-believe going on. If actors move to London, New York, Paris, Barcelona, Los Angeles, or Bollywood they will not make all the necessary discoveries overnight. They will not make all the necessary adjustments overnight. Even if they took an industry crash course, they would still not learn everything overnight. The reason for this is that many of their discoveries are going to come through their own experiences. Their experiences will come from their hard and focused efforts. An actor will want to be comfortable with a lot of hard work and the value of it. Just like this exercise, their acting careers will happen piecemeal. It will move forward one step at a time.

164. Name It

This activity is based on a famous game show I used to watch growing up. Have your students bring in some of their favorite CDs. Make sure that there is no cursing in the songs. Each student needs to label his CD. You can also work with iPods if you have speakers for them. Divide your students into two teams and explain in the following way:

INSTRUCTOR: In a moment, I am going to ask each team to choose a captain. Shortly after that, I am going to play a small part of a song. I may choose to start from any point in the song. Your team is going to have to vote on how quickly you can name that song. You can choose anywhere from twenty to two seconds. This means that if your team says five seconds, I will play the song for five seconds only. You have to decide together and pass on your choice through your captain. Whichever team says they can name the song in the fastest time will go first. Each team is able to outbid the other team until we come up with the team that thinks they can do it in the shortest time. There is a challenge here though: If your team goes first and names the tune correctly, it will receive three points. If your team gets it wrong, the other team will be given the three points. They will then be given the opportunity to guess the name of the tune. If they get it right, they will receive an additional two points. If no one has got it right, I will play the song again in the rapid-fire round. This time I will continue to play the song for up to one minute before someone buzzes in. The team that guesses correctly will receive two points. If no team knows, we will move on to the next round. I may choose to give you some clues, or I may not. A possible clue is the type of music. I may say that the song is rap, rock, hip hop, R & B, etc. Another clue might be, "The singer in this song is a teenager." Remember that I may not give any clues at all.

JANE: Can anyone buzz in during the rapid-fire round?

INSTRUCTOR: Good question. You can only buzz in through your captain, at which point he must give the answer immediately. If he pauses, the other team will be given the opportunity to answer.

PAUL: How do we know when there is a winner?

CHANDRA: When one team makes their bid, isn't the next team going to automatically make a lower bid?

INSTRUCTOR: They would not necessarily be wise to do so every time. Remember that if they get the answer wrong, three points will automatically be given to the other team. We are going to play for the next thirty minutes. At the end of that time, the team with the most points wins. I am going to be choosing songs randomly from my hidden pile of music. I will choose any song from any CD and begin from anywhere I choose.

You can set a time limit, or you can choose a certain number of points. For example, the first team to reach thirty points is the winner.

Purpose
To build a complete picture
Listening is obviously an important part of this exercise. What is also important is for the actors to attempt to create a complete picture. They may only hear five seconds of the song. From this, they have to build the rest of the song in their mind. If they can complete the picture, they will do very well. Actors may only be given a very short character breakdown. In some cases they will be given hardly anything to work with. It will be up to them to complete the picture. They may choose to create their character's family. Perhaps they decide they are divorced with two children. Perhaps they decide their character was an orphan who never met his parents. Maybe no age is given for the character. Not only do they decide an age, but they also decide to come up with his birthday. Anything the actor can do to make the character more real is going to be of great benefit in terms of their performance. If the actors do not know who their character is, neither will the audience.

Industry Connection
In this activity, the actors are given very little information to work with. It is up to them to decide if they want more time or less. If they choose more time, they may be knocked out by the other team. If they choose less time, they may end up losing points to the other team. Aspiring actors in Los Angeles or New York are sometimes in a hurry to "be discovered." They choose to race through everything, often missing important advice and experiences along the way. In the end, they spend more time and money finding out the hard way that some good advice is better than none at all. Some actors become lifetime students. They spend all their time and money in class. At first this sounds commendable. After all, they are learning their craft. The challenge is that all of their time is taken up by class. They feel it is a safe and protective environment and so they choose to stay there. Ten years later, they still have not started their acting career because they have not taken that leap of faith. The actor has to find a way to balance their time to further themselves and their career as an actor.

165. A Picture Is Worth a Thousand Words
You will need a pencil and some paper for this exercise. You will also need a hard surface, such as a book, to write on. Instruct your students to sit in a circle and explain in the following way:

INSTRUCTOR: I am going to give this pencil and paper to Seth. In a minute, Devon is going to whisper the name of an object or item into Seth's ear. A possibility is a cat. Devon will only whisper it once. At this point, Seth is going to draw one piece of the object or item he heard Devon say. If Seth heard "cat," he might choose to draw one half of a pair of whiskers. Seth will now whisper what he heard Devon say to the next person, who happens to be Sarah. He will now pass the paper and pencil to Sarah. If Sarah heard Seth say "cat," she might choose to draw a tail. If, however, she thought Seth had said "'bat," she might choose to draw an ear. The exercise continues in this way until everyone has drawn on the piece of paper. When the picture eventually makes its way back to Devon, he is going to add his one additional part of the object or item to the picture. At this point, he will show the picture to the entire group and share what the original word was.

NEIL: Should we hide the picture from each other?

INSTRUCTOR: That is good question. I think it is a good idea to hide the picture from everyone, except the person you are passing it to. This way, it is more challenging and more fun at the end when we are all allowed to see the picture. In the case of the cat example, anything could happen. We could have ended up with a cat, or we could end up with a three-headed monster!

Remind the students that they can only whisper the word once. If the other person did not hear them properly, they have to draw what they think they heard. It is important that they whisper the word clearly and audibly. Each person can only add one small piece to the picture.

Purpose
To listen and respond

The purpose behind this exercise is to get the actors to listen and respond. They have to be listening carefully in order to hear what the other actor is saying. By this I mean that their mind has to be clear of other distractions. Even if the actor appears to be listening, but is thinking of what he is going to have for dinner, he may be caught off guard by a momentary lapse in concentration. The actors are then asked to respond in two ways. They are asked to respond verbally and kinesthetically. The verbal response involves passing on the word to the next person. The kinesthetic reaction is in terms of their sense of touch. In drawing, they are engaging their sense of touch, plus the use of motor skills. We have mentioned before that actors need to listen more, but this does not only depend on appearances. Remind your actors that sometimes characters may pretend to be listening when actually they are not. Many of us become distracted by other thoughts. The important part is that it is the character's choice not to listen, and not the actor's choice. A character does not always respond verbally. A character may also choose not to say anything and respond in a nonverbal way. Guide your actors in exploring these ideas.

Industry Connection

The actors have to keep going, no matter what. They may not be sure what they heard the other person say, but they still have to draw something. If they choose to give up, the whole chain is broken, and the exercise ends there. Actors in a play face challenges on a grander scale. In the middle of a play, they might suddenly forget their lines and blank. They can choose to break character and say to the audience, "I'm really sorry I just forgot my lines!" Or they can choose to find a way out of the situation. If they use their imagination and improvisation skills, they will hopefully get back on track. Another actor on-stage may, by this time, realize what has happened and help the actor come through the predicament. You may laugh at my suggestion of breaking character.

Unfortunately, it happens to varying degrees more than one might think. You may feel that this is not an issue on-camera. It is true that if you break character, the director can always shout "Cut!" The challenge is that he may not want to shout "Cut!" If you stay in character, you might still come up with some great material. Anything that didn't work can be taken out in the editing room. The actor has to keep going until the director says "Cut!" and not because the actor wants to stop.

166. The Storyteller Whisperer

Tell your actors to sit as the audience. Instructing your actors to sit and listen means you can explain the exercise in a controlled and orderly manner. Explain in the following way:

INSTRUCTOR: In a moment I would like you to find a partner with whom you have not worked before. You are going to find a space in the room. What I would like you to do is tell stories to each other.

JILL: Do they have to be true stories?

INSTRUCTOR: They can be true, or they can be the product of your imagination. There is a twist to these stories: I want you to tell them to each other in a whisper. The aim is so that only the person you are telling the story to can hear it.

ADAM: Does it matter if another person can hear the story?

INSTRUCTOR: It does not matter too much. However, that would probably mean you are talking too loudly. Each of you will be given five minutes to tell your story, at which point I will say "switch." If you have not finished your story, you are still expected to switch storytellers. That is it. That is the entire exercise.

Purpose
To enhance listening skills
Actors have to be able to listen to one another. The actors have been asked to whisper. If they are not truly listening to each other, there is no way they will be able to hear what is being said. The whisper may be so soft that the other actor may actually have to close his eyes to hear what is being said. Listening sounds obvious, but it can be taken for granted by actors. Numerous established actors say that listening is everything and the point at which you learn everything. The challenge in a play is that one actor already knows what his fellow actor is going to say. He has been to the rehearsals. He has heard his fellow actor recite his lines on numerous occasions. The temptation then is to mimic listening while actually thinking about what he is going to have for dinner tonight. He is rarely able to pull the wool over the eyes of the audience. The audience will recognize bad acting and they will not appreciate it. If one actor is not truly listening to the other, he cannot react to what is being said at that moment. The actor can still make an intellectual response, but not a visceral one. This exercise encourages your actors to become good listeners.

Industry Connection
The actors are asked to manipulate their level of projection. They are being asked to speak in a whisper, which is specific direction. I have talked about this before, and would like to refer to it again. When actors walk into an audition room or a large auditorium, they have to be able to command the space. The challenge

is that they also have to adapt to the space. If they are having an intimate audition in a room that is only one hundred and fifty feet square there is no need to project for all they are worth. If the director is sitting two feet away, then a softer vocal quality will be more appropriate. If actors are performing in a large auditorium, they will also have to be able to adapt to that space. Their projection and gestures will have to be able to reach the very back of the auditorium. The actors must adapt to the space and environment in which they are working.

167. Center of Attention

Instruct your actors to sit on chairs in a circle. There should be enough chairs for one per student, minus one. Ask the remaining student to stand in the center of the circle. He is going to become the center of everyone's attention. Ask that student to look around the circle and find someone who has something that is visually in common with him. An example could be that he is wearing a black T-shirt and five other people are also wearing the color black. The student then shouts out, "Everyone wearing the color black!" At this point, everyone who is wearing the color black must change to another seat. The person in the center is also going to attempt to find an empty seat. If he manages it, the person left without a seat will go into the center. The only people who change seats are those who fit the category called out. Another example is, "Everyone with blonde hair!" Anything that the student in the center can visually see is fair game. Obviously, we are not looking to make it personal. Don't identify, "Everyone who has acne!" This is not what we are looking for. A word of caution: Some students may move extra slowly pretending to look for a chair. This sometimes happens because they want to go into the center. That is not the point of the exercise, so find a tactful way of handling the situation. It is, however, another way the actors are practicing their acting skills.

Variation

Look at the game Everyone Touch Someone Who ... in *112 Acting Games*. This is a similar activity, with some variations. You can also change this exercise from visual to other topics. An example would be, "Everyone who went on vacation this year." The only challenge here is that there may be some rounds where no one changes places. If you operate the activity this way, ensure that the students make broader and more generalized statements.

Purpose

To listen with intent

In order to participate, the actors have to focus their attention on the person in the middle. They also have to be listening to him, but there is more to it than that. It is possible to be listening to someone but not really hear what he is saying. The actors have to be listening with intent. In a play, one character may be telling another about some hidden treasure. Let's assume that the actor being informed has his mind on other things. He is going on vacation next week and planning his trip in his mind. He is fake listening and believes he is so good that the audience won't notice. Unfortunately, the audience does notice, and they are left believing that the character has no real desire to discover the treasure. His performance also weakens the overall performance of the actor he is playing against in terms of reciprocation. If an actor isn't listening with intent, how can he respond with intent?

Industry Connection

Some actors may end up getting out of their chair to find a new seat every round. They may be running around and sweating profusely. Other actors may not even get out of their chairs once. They are considered to be lucky by the other actors. Their friends say, "You got a lucky break." But did they really? Did it really do them a lot of good only having to partially participate? Some actors involved in the industry appear to get lucky breaks. Perhaps a parent is a famous actor or director and can get their son an introduction. Perhaps he is cast in a cameo role simply because his parent is famous. If this is the case, then he may have achieved the role despite having little or no talent. If this is true, his acting career will probably be short-lived. If he is given a lucky break and then he works hard, more power to him. Everyone gets a bit of luck now and then. It is not the bit of luck that counts. It is what you do with it that matters. An actor may have had contacts to get into an audition, but unless he develops his auditioning skills, it may not do him much good in the long term.

168. See-Hear

Ask your students to sit as the audience. Choose four actors to join you on the stage. Instruct two of the actors to stand in the middle of the stage. They are going to be the performers. Let the audience set the actors a scene, with character breakdowns. An example could be a customer paying at the checkout. In a moment, you are going to ask them to improvise a short scene based on the following information. Let the other two actors sit at the side of the stage, each wearing a blindfold. They are going to be able to hear the scene taking place, but they will not be able to see what is happening. Once the scene is over, they are going to perform the scene as best they can, to emulate what has just taken place. Remember that they heard the whole scene, but they could not see anything. Their aim is to get as close to the original scene as possible. Follow up with a group discussion. Work different scenarios with four new actors.

Purpose

To visualize the scene

The two actors sitting down have to visualize the scene that is taking place. In a play, actors may have to do much the same thing. Their characters may talk about something that we have never seen, which has taken place previously. Let us say a character talks about when his house caught fire last year. We may not see the house on fire, but in his mind the actor is going to have to. It is an experience that the character has lived through on a cellular level. If the character can visualize what has taken place, then so can the audience.

Industry Connection

When actors give a stage performance, it ends the same night. The next night they will give a new performance. Each actor has to learn to own and claim each performance. When an actor films a show or movie, in theory it will last forever, even though it may evolve. The very same performance can be seen again and again for eternity, all over the world. This should raise the stakes in the eyes of the film actor and stimulate him to give his best possible performance. Every take has to be the actor's greatest because he does not have a say in what is left in and out of the movie. The actor's best work may be left on the cutting room floor by the director.

Chapter 20
The Coordinated Actor

169. Head Spinner

For this exercise you will want to prepare ahead of time. Take out some thick, soft gym mats and spread them out across the floor. If you do not have mats, make sure you cover the floor with some type of soft, sturdy material. You will also need a soft, padded stick about one foot long. If you do not have this, you can use the end of a broom handle. Failing that, you can even use an umbrella. Tell your students to take their shoes off and put them safely in the corner of the room. *Before starting this exercise, ask if there are any students whose health situation means that they should not spin around for any length of time, so that you can avoid choosing them.* Introduce the exercise in the following way:

INSTRUCTOR: I am going to split you up into two teams. I will come around and number you "one" or "two." Team number one should sit on my left, at the edge of the mat, and team number two on my right at that edge of the mat. Please make sure you are sitting at the edge, but not on the mat. I would like to call for a volunteer who feels adventurous. Ingrid. Thank you for volunteering. Ingrid, please come and stand in the center of the mats. Here is a small padded stick that I would like you to hold onto. In a moment, I would like you to hold the stick above your head. I would like you to look at the top of the stick and spin yourself around, as fast as you can, for thirty seconds. I then want you to throw the stick a little in front of you, at which point you must immediately jump or step over the stick. This is easier said than done. You only have one attempt to do this. (INGRID spins around for thirty seconds and attempts to jump over the stick. She falls down landing nowhere near the stick. The whole class falls about with laughter.) I told you it was easier said than done. Every member of your team will take one turn. For every member who steps or jumps over the stick successfully, your team will receive one point. The team with the most points at the end wins. Are there any questions before we begin?

MICHAEL: What if a person is spinning really slowly?

INSTRUCTOR: That is a very good point. If a person is judged to be spinning too slowly, they will be asked to speed up. If they still go very slowly, their round will be disqualified. (Give some leeway here. You will be able to tell if someone is purposely going slowly. Some students are not as capable athletically as others. Use your judgment.)

AMANDA: What if it is a tie?

INSTRUCTOR: If there is a tie, each team can choose a person to do a face-off round. We will keep going in this way until we have a winning team. Please remember that safety is the most important aspect of this exercise. The only person who should be on the mats is the spinner.

There are two teams, so if you have enough room, one player from each team can spin at the same time. If the space is confined, then only one player at a time should spin. In this situation you are going to have to set aside a lot more time for the exercise. When the students fall, they really do fall. This is why it is imperative that you use a protective surface such as gym mats. A hard concrete classroom floor is unsuitable for this activity. By the way, once your students get a taste for this activity, they are going to want to play it again and again.

Purpose
To increase coordination and agility
The purpose behind this exercise is to increase the actors' level of coordination. As the actors spin, they lose all sense of coordination and become disorientated. Suddenly they find actions such as walking and jumping have become challenging. Actors have to develop a fully-coordinated body. They may be playing the part of a Duke or Duchess. This requires not so much walking across the room as gliding across. They have to know how to stand and sit like a person of royalty. If an actor is playing the role of the Hunchback of Notre Dame, he will need to have just as much coordination in his body. A hunchback may move in an unusual way, which will put extra demands on the actor's abilities. The coordinated actor is able to undertake the challenges of a character's physical makeup. He is interested in human behavior and what makes people do what they do.

Industry Connection
The actors will usually become dizzy and disorientated. At the height of this disorientation, they still have to perform a task by trying to jump or walk over the stick. On-set, there will be stunt doubles to do the most intricate stunts. This is not the actors' responsibility. However, the actors are still required to work in unusual and varied situations. They may be filmed in a forest, up a tree, or with a big spider on the next branch. They may be filmed jumping off a diving board. They may be filmed ice-skating. There are numerous possibilities of situations in which the actor can and will be filmed. The challenge is that throughout them all, they still have to stay in character and give a believable performance. If what they are thinking about is being scared or nervous, or feeling sick, this is what is going to come across in the scene. This exercise is about being able to cope with a physically unpredictable situation. By the way, you are probably going to find that most of your students are unable to jump over the stick. The actors will want to continue to condition and sharpen their instruments.

170. Mummified Frenzy
For this game you are going to need two sheets from single beds. Divide the actors into team "one" and "two." If you have an odd number of actors, ask one member of the smaller team to go twice. Explain in the following way:

INSTRUCTOR: In a moment I am going to ask you to line up one behind the other and sit on the floor. Half of each team will be at one end of the room and the other half will be at the other end. Team one will be on the left hand side and team two will be on the right hand side. Each team will be given a sheet. Simon, please come over here and help me. (A sheet is laid out on the floor.) Simon, what I would like you to do is roll yourself up in this sheet. You have to make sure that your arms and hands are completely covered. The only part of your body that can be visible is your face and neck. Simon, I would now like you to stand up. (SIMON has some difficulty doing so, but eventually manages it.) I am now going to make sure Simon's sheet is tucked in and secure. At this point, Simon, I would like you to make your way to the other end of the room as quickly as possible. When Simon gets to the other end, he must lie on the floor, where he is unraveled by up to two of his teammates. Please do this safely and cautiously. Each team is allowed up to two helpers on either side. The object of the game is

232

to be the first team in which everyone has become a mummy. The helpers also have to change over, because every team member has to take a turn to be a mummy. The winning team is the one that is able to move their entire team from one end of the room to the other.

SOPHIE: You mean everyone who is sitting on this side of the room should end up on the other side?

INSTRUCTOR: Exactly. There are a few extra rules to make it more challenging. Your arms and hands must stay inside your sheet. If they come out of the sheet the whole team starts again.

SOPHIE: From the very beginning?

INSTRUCTOR: Exactly. If your sheet falls down, or you attempt to hold it up, the whole team starts again. Remember, it is up to your teammates to make sure it is safe and secure. The winning team will also want to be sitting down, one behind the other. There is no winner until this happens.

Purpose
To connect the mind to the body
The purpose of this exercise is for the actors to connect the mind to the body. There are many physical aspects to this activity, such as rolling around on the floor and getting across to the other side of the room. There are also a number of mind related aspects that the actors have to utilize. They have to make sure their arms and hands are tucked into the sheet. They have to make sure that at the end of the exercise, the entire team is sitting in a straight line. They have to help each other wrap up correctly and securely in the sheets. Only through connecting the mind and body will the actors succeed. Some actors are thought to prefer an external approach to acting — the physical approach. Some actors are said to utilize a more internal approach to their acting — the mental approach. Both schools of thought have produced fine actors. Laurence Olivier is said to have come from the external school. Marlon Brando, on the other hand, is considered one of the finest examples of method acting. What is important to note is that both these actors used mind and body, even if their preference leans more to one side than the other. In *112 Acting Games* there is an exercise I used called Roller Coaster. The actor is told to jump up and down while being depressed. It is virtually impossible for anyone to jump up and down continuously and feel depressed at that precise moment. The mind and body are not separate entities, but are entwined with each other. It is important that your actors learn to utilize both mind and body to their full capacity.

Industry Connection
At times, this exercise is going to feel unfair. One team is about to win when the sheet falls to the floor. The whole team must now start again from scratch. Some of the actors may begin to be annoyed and frustrated with each other, yet this will not change the actual circumstances. Actors may be cast in a role, only to find at the last minute that the funding has fallen through and they have lost the part. They may go to an audition, only to find out at a later date that the role they were up for was precast. They may be in a non-union commercial and earn one tenth as much as a friend who was in a union commercial. Remind your actors that they cannot necessarily change the circumstances, but they can control how they themselves respond. An actor's career will have many challenges along the way to success, and he will have to learn to overcome them.

171. It's the Pits!

For this exercise you are going to need two softballs, or you can use tennis balls or hacky sacks if you like. Divide your actors into two teams and explain in the following way:

INSTRUCTOR: I hope everyone is feeling limber today. In a moment I am going to give each team a ball. Each team will then form a circle whose members stand shoulder to shoulder. The first person will start with the ball under his left armpit. Your mission is to pass the ball to the next person in line, only through the use of your armpits. You cannot use your hands in any way. The ball should be moving in a clockwise direction. If the ball hits the floor, the team has to start again. This is a race, and the first team to get the ball all the way around the circle and back to the original person wins.

MINDA: What happens if the ball slides to someone's arms?

INSTRUCTOR: As long as they move it back up to their armpit before passing it along they are OK. The ball can only be passed from armpit to armpit. If a person uses their hands in any way, the whole team has to start again.

STELLA: Who gets to start?

INSTRUCTOR: Each team can decide that for itself.

Purpose

To develop coordination

We have talked about this in other places in the book, so let's talk about it again. The purpose behind this exercise is coordination. You want to encourage your actors to become more coordinated. Actors have to be incredibly well coordinated to portray the vast array of characters they are going to play. If you walk down the street and watch ten people, you will find they all move in different ways. Their gait or their stride differs. One person may hunch forward, while another person may lean back with his chest protruding. (See Center of Gravity exercise in *112 Acting Games* for more on this subject.) Actors have to move with the coordination patterns of every character they play. Only the well-coordinated actor will have the potential to do this.

Industry Connection

I want to stay on the coordination track with regard to movies. In one movie, an actress may be playing an upper class woman of royal blood — a debutante. As the character, the actress has to spend her whole time wearing high heels with her posture held high. The next year she is cast as an army cadet. Now she has to wear these big, bulky army boots. Soldiers in the army also have to have excellent posture, but it does not look the same as that of the debutante. The way they carry their weight is quite different. Think about the enormous challenges for an actress wearing high heels. She is also going to have to negotiate her way around a set that is full of big wires and electric cables. She may use the opportunity to take her shoes off between shots, but it may still be a fourteen-hour day. The army cadet may face different challenges. Her boots may clunk and make loud noises. The director may tell the actress, "Very good, but move lighter on your feet. You are making too much noise." The actress is wearing heavy army boots, and he wants her to make less noise! Well, yes, for technical considerations this is a possibility. Only the well-coordinated actor is

ELENA: Can someone else grab the sock for Dana?

INSTRUCTOR: That is a fair question, and the answer is no. The head will, however, need the support of the rest of the body as she moves around the room chasing the tail. At no point can any of the body of the snake separate.

SIMONE: Can the tail get away?

INSTRUCTOR: The main job of the tail is to stay away from the head. The challenge is that they cannot separate from the rest of the body. The tail can move as best it can, but it is not allowed to use any physical force in stopping the head from taking the sock.

I use a sock for this exercise, but you can use a face cloth, or anything else reasonably small that comes to mind. Set a time limit of your choice. I usually give the head up to three minutes to complete the task. At this point, you can change over the head and the tail and have another go. You can change around the whole group if you like. Make sure that this exercise is conducted in a safe manner.

Purpose

To move with your core

The purpose of this activity is for the actors to move with their core. The person who is the head has to get everyone working as a team. It is up to him to have the body move as one unit. In order to do this he is going to have to move from his core. He is going to have to send his messages and signals so strongly that the rest of the actors are willing and able to fall in line. If he is unclear and hesitant in his movement, it will create confusion among the group. Every actor has to find the core, or the center of gravity, for each character he plays. (See Center of Gravity exercise in *112 Acting Games.*) Not only does the actor have to know how his character moves, but he also has to know from where he moves. Some people literally walk with their shoulders rounding forward. This means that gravity is pulling them down as they walk. Other people lead with their chest pushed out. This makes us think of an individual who is proud and maybe arrogant. The actors have to be congruent in understanding the ways in which their character moves. They have to be congruent in understanding how their character holds themselves and their posture. Sometimes you will hear an audience member say, "That actor literally became the part." This is because the actor was willing to explore all aspects of his character.

Industry Connection

It is very important that the actor who is the head in this activity does not give up. If something does not work, he has to keep going and keep looking for new ways of finding a solution. Sometimes it will appear as if the actor has given up before he has even begun. The same could be said for some actors pursuing an acting career. They say they want an acting career, but when push comes to shove, they are not willing to do what it takes. If a door closes, they let it stay closed. Working actors will always find a way to open the door. This is not necessarily because they are a better or stronger actor. It is because they do not accept "no" lightly. They find a way to move through it, over it, and around it. In this activity, the actor who is determined to catch the tail will eventually do so. The actor who does not believe he can catch the tail is absolutely correct. Instead of finding a hundred reasons why he cannot succeed, the actor will want to find one reason as to why he can. An actor will want to have the audacity to succeed.

174. Wheelbarrow Race

The following exercise is the time-tested wheelbarrow race. Divide your students into two groups. Have each group divide itself into two lines, standing side by side. One person is the wheelbarrow and the other person is going to be pushing the wheelbarrow. Have the first pair from each team get into position. The wheelbarrows should move with their hands. Their legs should be raised by the wheelbarrow pushers, who will also help guide their movement. Instruct the students to race to the other end of the room and back again. The pushers have to sense the best speed for their partner. If they go too fast, their partner will fall over. If they go too slowly, their team will lose. As soon as the first pair returns the next two players from each team sets off. The two players who have just had their turn should sit at the back of their respective lines. It is first and foremost a race. The first team to get all their players back and sitting straight in their lines are the winners. If you have an odd number, have one player go twice. I have tried this exercise by having the wheelbarrows maneuver around an obstacle course. While this is more challenging and visually interesting to watch, I prefer not to use it. The reason is it can cause the students to twist their wrists and is more likely to cause an injury. For safety reasons, this activity is better on a padded floor. You can always put down mats or blankets of some sort. Make sure the two teams are set far enough apart so that they do not collide.

Purpose

To encourage agility in the actors

A fast runner may be poor in a wheelbarrow race. Speed is not the only ingredient in this activity. The actors have to be agile and have understanding and control over their movements. The pushers also have to be agile in sensing their partners' strengths and limitations in terms of their movements. It is not the fastest team, but the most coordinated team that usually ends up winning this activity. An actor who wishes to play any character that differs from himself needs to be an agile actor. When Helen Mirren took on the role of Queen Elizabeth, she did so knowing she would have to find the grace and etiquette that comes with the role of royalty. She had to use her agility to create the role in a physical sense. In the 1939 movie *The Hunchback of Notre Dame*, Charles Laughton played the hunchback. While the character may appear clumsy, be aware that the actor had to use all his agility to create the role. Discuss with your group the importance of being a well-coordinated actor.

Industry Connection

At its core, this activity is a race. At the end, one team will be the winner and the other will be the loser. Even if the race is won by only a hair's breadth, the end result is still the same. You may feel I am being unfair in my assessment. "It is the taking part and participation that counts," I hear you say. This is true in a protective environment, but the industry does not always see it that way. For instance, an actress friend of mine made it to the final two when up for a television pilot. The other actress got the role and a large financial package. The second choice actress got a pat on the back. It was a great achievement to be second choice over hundreds of actresses, but at the end of the day, only one actress could get the role. My colleague Paul Gleason likes to say, "If there is just one role, then that is the one I want!" It is not always as cut and dried as it sounds. An actor who is third choice is still seen and may be remembered for future projects. It is up to the actor to take away everything of value from every experience. The industry may be cut and dried, but the actor's worldview does not have to be.

175. Air Ball

You are going to need two volleyball-sized sponge balls for this exercise. Explain in the following way:

INSTRUCTOR: I am going to divide you into two teams. To make things simpler, I am going to call you teams A and B. In a moment, I am going to ask the members of team A to lie down on the left hand side of the room, side-by-side, in a straight line. You should be lying so that your arms are parallel with those of the next person. Team B will do the same on the right hand side of the room. I am then going to ask you to close your eyes. At this point, I am going to give a ball to the first person in each line. They are then going to pass the ball along the line using their feet. That means you will pass the ball to the next person by using your feet only.

GERRY: What happens if we drop the ball?

INSTRUCTOR: If the ball is dropped, it goes back to the beginning of the line. The reason we use sponge balls is because they could hit you in the face and a hard ball would be quite painful.

AMANDA: If our eyes are closed, how do we know where the ball is along the line?

INSTRUCTOR: That is a very good question. For the most part, you will not know where the ball is. I do not mind the person who has the ball calling the name of the person next to them to let then know they have the ball. There are two potential ways of winning this activity. Each team is going to have a time limit of six minutes. This means that the first team to get the ball to the end of their line wins, or the team that gets the ball furthest along their line wins. The fastest team will not necessarily be the winning team. Please remember that you have to keep your eyes closed at all times.

Purpose

To develop physical mastery

In order to control the ball, the actors have to be in command of their own bodies. To pass it along successfully to another actor is an even greater challenge. The fact that they do not have their sense of sight adds to the complexity of this exercise. If actors on-stage are swinging their left leg from side to side, the audience wants to know why. It may be because the actors are nervous and unaware of what they are doing. The challenge is that the audience is aware of the leg swaying, and begins to analyze its meaning in relation to the scene. Anything that is happening on-stage must be happening for a reason. I mean physical mastery because the actors have to be master of their own body and not the other way around.

Industry Connection

If a team rushes through this exercise, they may finish as the winners in grand style. On the other hand, at the end of the six minutes, they may end up with the ball back to the first person for the fifth time. Some actors try to rush through everything and skip all the steps. They are in a rush to be discovered and feel that they are using the best approach. Occasionally, this approach works and spurs on many thousands of other aspiring movie stars to try the same approach. They often crash and burn, and leave heartbroken and disappointed. There are other actors who work at a slower and steadier pace. Their journey is not necessarily a glamorous one, but it is more methodical and meticulous. They are able to see the reality of the profession. They research their photographers, acting coaches, and agents. They don't sign with any such person before they know his background. They don't necessarily get a lead role in their first year, but by their third or fourth year, perhaps they start booking small roles on television. Some working actors look to be cast in small roles with good directors. They enjoy working with directors who are sensitive to the actor's work. While many of their fellow actors have come and gone, they are finding that more and more of their income is beginning to come from the field of acting. This approach reminds me of the tortoise and hare race — and we all know who won that race.

176. Beat the Beat

For this exercise, tell your actors to sit in a tight circle, so that their knees are touching. Explain in the following way:

INSTRUCTOR: In a moment, I would like one of you to start a beat. An example could be snapping your fingers to a continuous rhythm. Once you start your beat, you cannot stop or change it in anyway. At some point, I would like another person to join in with a new beat. His beat will want to complement the beat that is already playing. There is no rush to join in. Find the right moment to add your beat. We will continue until everyone in the circle has added their beat. Remember that the key is to make your beat complementary to the beats that are already playing. It is easy to make it simply sound like a lot of noise. The challenge is to make it sound like beats that complement one another.

JAN: What happens if someone's beat is totally off rhythm?

INSTRUCTOR: Once someone had added their beat it cannot be changed. The next person will have to find a way to complement it and help it to fit into the overall picture.

HAILY: How do we know when it is our turn?

INSTRUCTOR: There is no order. You can add your beat whenever you find the right opportunity. Do not join in until you really feel you have a complementary beat. As the overall sound changes, you will have to adapt and come up with a new beat before joining in.

Purpose
To develop coordination skills

It is easy for the actors to add a beat. It is not so easy for them to add a beat that complements the other beats. In order to do this, each actor is going to need to be well coordinated. He is going to have to synchronize with his fellow actors. When characters walk across a stage, it is for a specific reason. Perhaps they are going to the kitchen for a glass of milk. The audience does not need to pay particular attention to their walking, as this is an automatic process. The challenge is that for the uncoordinated actor, it becomes anything but automatic. Their muscles tense up, and suddenly something as natural as walking seems like rocket science. As they begin to move across the room, all aspects of coordination seem to have failed them. Tension and nerves can cause the actor to forget how to perform the most basic tasks. The actor will want to be able to delve into every corner of his character. The actor who is highly coordinated can counter these measures.

Industry Connection

When twenty people are beating their beat, it can sound like absolute chaotic noise, or it can also sound like beautiful music. When the actors and crew on a set work together, they can come up with an amazing production. Even though everyone is running around doing their specific job, it is like a well-oiled machine. Everyone knows what they should be doing and when they need to do it. When this is happening, the potential for making a good production goes up. Some sets, on the other hand, look absolutely chaotic. They appear as if no one knows what they are doing. Everything that is happening appears fragmented, as if there is no clear vision. These projects often fall by the wayside, or into the garbage can of history. It is only when a cast and crew work in symmetry that a good production, a great production, has the potential to evolve.

Chapter 21
Characterization

177. Radio

Give each student the same paragraph to read. It can come from a play, film script, or whatever you choose. The only stipulation is that it is one character talking (monologue) and that the gender is not revealed or implied in the dialogue. Give each actor a character breakdown with five or six traits. For instance:

Age: 40
Sex: Male
Occupation: Lawyer
Personality type: Cocky and self-assured
Physicality: Big, strong, and muscular
Facial features: Eyes cold as steel
Hobbies: Swimming, rock climbing, gambling

Each actor receives the same dialogue, but a totally different character breakdown. Give each actor about five minutes, and then ask him to read the paragraph, one at a time, taking into consideration his character breakdown. They should not be discussing their character breakdowns with each other. As each actor reads, have the other actors close their eyes and listen. Once they have finished, the actor should also share his character breakdown. Then discuss with the group their assumptions in terms of age, personality, physicality, and so on. In other words, discuss each actor's choices one at a time, rather than going through the whole group.

Purpose
To utilize the actor's instrument
It is possible for the actors to fall into patterns such as using their external bodies to show who their characters are. The actor playing a bouncer may choose to puff out his chest. While this is a possibility, it is not necessarily characteristic to all bouncers, so the actor wants to be careful about falling into stereotypes. The actors should definitely utilize their posture and so forth when developing their character, but be careful not to make it their sole form of preparation. The actors will want to discover the spirit of their character. As Russell Grandstaff points out in his book, *Acting & Directing,* "Have you ever seen an actor, playing an old, old man, suddenly assume the old man's position just as he enters? Fine way to blow a scene!"[44] The actors have to make sure they are serving the character's needs and not their own. By taking away all visual apparatus in this exercise, the actors are going to have to draw on a whole range of apparatus to get their message across to the audience.

Industry Connection
The information given here for the character breakdown may seem to be virtually nonexistent, and yet at many auditions the actor goes for, they will

---

44. Russell Grandstaff, *Acting & Directing* (Illinois: NTC Publishing Group, 1999), 22.

receive even less. The casting director knows what he wants, or thinks he knows what he wants, and when an actor walks into the room, the character he is playing has to jump out at the casting director. Some casting directors will say, "Let me cast a girl who is as close to this as is humanly possible." If he needs to figure out who you are, it is already too late. If he is looking for Johnny, then you had better be Johnny the second you walk through that door. Actors want to prepare their character in as much detail as possible from the clues they have been given, even if they are relatively few. They should not just do this externally, because if their performance comes across as too superficial, they will be called bad actors and the casting director will say, "Next!" The actor must have professional ears. As Michael Redgrave explains, "It would not be unfair to say that there are, roughly speaking, two kinds of actors: those who, whether by instinct or method, see the cause before making their effect."[45] Be prepared to adapt to any situation in any given moment.

Note

Make the following observations with your actors:

INSTRUCTOR: A small note of caution here is necessary. If you do not get a part, take a deep breath, let it out, and move on. If you want to spend a little time analyzing your past audition, then that is fine. In fact, it could be of great value to you. However, do not dwell in the past. Learn to move forward and live in the present. Learn to focus your energy where it needs to be focused. A part is often not handed to an actor on a plate. If they want it bad enough they will go after it.

178. Body Alignment Investigation

Trained massage therapists are able to look at their client's body and tell them where their alignment is off-balance. They may say things like, "Your left shoulder is higher than your right." They may then explain that this is because the client favors mostly one arm in their day-to-day life. They may then ask the client to engage both arms on a more frequent basis and give them exercises to create bilateral function. They mention a pelvic rotation as another possible cause. For the purpose of this exercise we are not going to be diagnosing. We are going to utilize the first part for this exercise. Before you begin, have your actors strip to a T-shirt and shorts. If they do not have shorts, have them roll up their pants. Also, each actor needs to be equipped with a pencil and paper. You should not be giving them these things, because they should automatically be bringing them to class! Explain the following:

INSTRUCTOR: I would like everybody to find a partner and then find a space in the room. For simplicity, just label yourselves A and B. What I would like you to do in a moment is have the As stand in a comfortable position with their arms by their sides. Bs are going to observe them now and look at their bodies. Their job is to notice any alignment that is off center. In other words, anywhere their body is not in symmetry. B may notice that one foot points forward, but the other one turns out. One arm appears to be slightly longer than the other. One kneecap goes straight forward but the other one turns out. As they make these observations, they should silently write them down on a piece of paper. There

---

45. Michael Redgrave, *The Actor's Ways and Means* (New York: Theatre Arts Books, 1952), 13.

should be no discussion between the partners at this point. (You will want to allow four or five minutes to do this.)

Once the Bs have finished, you will want to share your findings with your partner. You are not diagnosing your partner. You are an actor and not a doctor. This means there is no need for the As to be concerned or offended by the findings. What I would like the two of you to do at this point is to look at the findings, pick out a few, and explore them in detail. For instance, let's say your partner wrote, "Your left shoulder is higher than your right." What I would like the two of you to do is spend a minute or two walking around the room with your left shoulder higher than your right. Do this is an exaggerated way so that you can really experience the physical effects. So, in this instance you should both raise your left shoulder higher than was originally observed. After you have done this, decide together what type of person might move in this fashion. You might say, "A person who is tense and angry, or a person who is frightened." You might also decide on a character who may move this way. A possible example is the hunchback of Notre Dame. Obviously, he would walk in a more exaggerated way. When you have finished, switch roles and A will now become the observer. (See the Center of Gravity exercise in *112 Acting Games*.)

Give the actors about five minutes each for the observations, and about ten minutes to explore them together. This means that each half should last about fifteen minutes. Once they have finished, bring everyone back together to observe some of the findings.

Purpose
To explore the mind/body connection
This exercise connects the body and the mind and vice versa. Actors will discover that by changing the way they stand or walk, it can actually change the way they feel. So an actor whose muscles are always tight might be a more stressed individual. This is powerful information, not only for the actor's health, but also in terms of his character work. Actors can manipulate their bodies until they find their character. They won't just move like their character, they will actually feel like their character. Most people do not move exactly the same way, and so actors will want to find what sets each character apart as well as what brings them together. It may be quite subtle. Perhaps they discover there are no major differences in the way they move, except that their character walks a lot faster than they do. Some actors wrap up their characters and take them home and some do not. Some of the great innovators in terms of the body, posture, and alignment are Moshe Feldenkrais and F. Matthias Alexander.

Industry Connection
Quite often on a set the main actor will wear slippers or sandals when he is being filmed above the waist. He does this purely for comfort. The challenge is whether this changes the physiology in his body. You could argue that most of his body is not seen, so why would it matter? A woman who wears heels may have more strain in her neck muscles than a woman who wears sandals. These are not absolute statements being made here, but simply observations. Actors often have stand-ins for lighting and camera blocking. This is for stuff that won't eventually be on-camera. However, they also have photo doubles for things like a hand close-up or a shot of the actor's back. There is nothing wrong with this, but it does

beg a few questions: Is his back as interesting as yours? When his hand picks up the glove of your murdered daughter, does it do so with the compassion and grief that yours would? Perhaps it does, perhaps he even does it better than you. It is certainly worth contemplating. The body gives many signals and many messages that have nothing whatsoever to do with seeing your face.

Note

Let's say at an audition an actor is asked to fill out some paperwork. He doesn't have a pen and neither does the secretary. Instead of focusing on the audition, he spends the next few minutes wasting his time, thinking about the form and where he can get a pen. It is important to remove any obstacles that get in the way of focusing on the task at hand. In this case it is to get the job!

179. Reflection of Self

Explain in the following way:

INSTRUCTOR: Please find a space in the room. In a moment I would like you to imagine you are standing on a mirror that covers the entire surface area of this room. When you look down, your reflection is going to be looking back up at you. I would like you to perform a series of actions that you do on a daily basis. Some examples are: brushing your teeth, combing your hair, tying your shoelaces. As you do these things, look down every so often so that you can see the reflection of your own actions. I am going to give you five minutes to do this. Please do this exercise in absolute silence. (Five minutes pass.) I'd like you to pause where you are. In a moment, you are going to do this exercise again, only this time not as yourself. This time, I would like you to do the same exercise as a character you have played, or a character you are going to play. You may find that you come up with a whole different set of actions, or you may find that some of them are the same. Let us say your character is tying his shoelace just like you did a few minutes ago. How does he tie his shoelace differently from you? Perhaps he makes double knots? Perhaps he ties in a more erratic fashion? Perhaps he is more meticulous and undoes the lace three times until he is satisfied. As you work through this exercise, remember to look at your reflection looking back at you.

Once the exercise is complete, follow up with a group discussion.

Purpose

To fire off mirror neurons

In this exercise the character sees what the actor is doing and mirrors it right back. This fires off mirror neurons in the actors' brains. In other words, by their character copying them and the actors copying back, they start to absorb each other's traits. Firing mirror neurons actually has a chemical and physiological effect on the actors. In part, they become the essence of their character, and in part their character becomes them. Do you know that one of the main reasons people like to go to the theatre, movies, sports, or circuses is because of mirror neurons? Simply put, when you watch somebody do something, say something, or wear something, if you copy his action the same neurons in your body fire as in his body, and make you able to perform that action. When we act on-stage or on-screen, because of mirror neurons in the brain, if the audience is empathetic, the same neurons are fired in them. They become interested in the character's humanity. It is as if the audience is going through the process with you. The actors have to ask themselves if they are looking to affect their audience. We join actors in murdering people, in stealing, in falling in love, and we do these things. This exercise helps the actors gain a better understanding of their characters, not simply on an intellectual level but on visceral and kinesthetic level — in other words, right down to their very bones. The actors will want to be very present in each and every moment.

Industry Connection

When actors go to an audition, they don't necessarily need those casting them to fall in love with them. They do, however, need them to fall in line. There has to be something about the actor that sets them apart from the rest. There has to be something about the actor that simply will not allow the casting director to hire anyone else. We can use our mirror neurons to some degree when we build rapport with others. We often do this subconsciously, but we can also choose to do this consciously. If the actor mirrors some of the actions of the person auditioning them in a subtle way, they will begin to build some of that rapport. If they sit down and cross their legs, the actors may also choose to cross their legs when they sit down. If they speak in a clipped tone, the actors may also choose to speed up their own pace of talking to some extent. Tell your actors to experiment with friends before doing this in an audition situation. The reason it works so well is because people like people who remind them of themselves. This is true more on a subconscious level rather than on a conscious level. It does not mean they should mirror the casting director throughout the entire audition process. Building rapport with others is of great benefit to the actor in audition situations and when working with other actors.

Note

You may choose to limit the number of questions to three. This may sound petty, but otherwise you may find you have twenty minutes of questioning. After three questions, you may have enough to get started. If, during the activity, more clarification is needed, you can always stop for a moment. If questions are unlimited, you may get all kinds of irrelevant points raised. If the group is only allowed three questions, they are learning to ask better questions.

180. Transcending the Character

There is an out-of-class portion to this exercise. Ask your actors to pick two remarkably contrasting roles by the same actor. This should be an actor whose work they greatly admire. Have them watch the two movies. When they come to class, they should be willing to explain:

1. What makes these roles so contrasting?
2. What was so great about the actor's performance?
3. How, in each case, did the actor manage to transcend the role?

As they put their views across, other actors can ask questions and voice their opinions. This is subjective opinion and will have room for discussion and disagreement. Remind the actors that it is key that the roles are extremely contrasting, and in the actors' opinion, excellent performances.

Some possible examples are:
Kathy Bates: *Fried Green Tomatoes* and *Misery*
Dustin Hoffman: *Tootsie* and *Rain Man*
Daniel Day Lewis: *My Left Foot* and *There Will Be Blood*
Meryl Streep: *Out of Africa* and *The Devil Wears Prada*
Sean Penn: *Fast Times at Ridgemont High* and *Milk*

Purpose

To discuss great acting

This exercise attempts to discuss the concept of great acting and great performances. It is these types of performances that leave an audience mesmerized. What makes a great actor? What makes a great performance? What does it take for an actor to truly transcend the role? If your actors are interested in the craft of acting, then this exercise will be of interest to them. When they watch great actors, they will want to be asking, "How did he do that? His performance moved me in ways that I never knew were possible!" I hope that it is their desire to become this type of actor, but that is not necessarily the case. Before we can ask a question we have to be willing to define our terms. Raise the following question with your actors: The question is what type of actor do you want to be?

Industry Connection

Cover some of the following points with your actors. Feel free to add your own.

INSTRUCTOR: There are a number of professional actors who make money who are not very good. Turn on your television, or go to the movies, and you can see this for yourself on a daily basis. No one has to convince you of this. There are ample examples out there for you to choose from. This is said not to be negative, but to let you know that you don't have to be a great actor or even a good actor to be a working actor. Maybe you do for longevity, but certainly not for short-term gains. Not all actors want to be good actors. Some are doing it only for the money. Some are doing it only for the love. Some are doing it more for the fame. Fame is usually the sign of an acting career that is doing well. The actors will want to discover if they have the spirit for fame and fortune. There is a heavy weight attached to fame and legendhood. These actors still have to struggle to do their best. Hollywood is an extremely powerful illusion. Hopefully, on top of everything else, you want to be a good actor. Some famous actors gave up trying to become famous and decided to become good actors instead. I say this because saying you want to be a good actor and working to become a good actor are two vastly different things.

In the forward to his book, *The Dramatic Imagination*, Robert Edmond Jones says, "The reflections and speculations which I have set down here are the fruit of twenty-five years of almost continuous work in American theatre, during which time I have had the good fortune to be associated with the foremost artists of my time."[46] To be a good actor you have to walk your talk on a daily basis. You have to continue to want to grow and create a more functional instrument at every opportunity. You have to be able to paint with a vast pallet of human emotions.

---

46. Robert Edmond Jones, *The Dramatic Imagination* (New York: Theatre Arts Book, 1969), Forward.

You will not want to limit yourself by the size of the part or the size of the budget. Great actors are not born, they become. Famous actors sometimes have to compete just like everyone else. They meet with the director but then so do numerous other actors. They are going to have to convince the director through their persistence and passion that they are the right person for the job. I have heard of a famous actress sending the director a couple of letters after an audition explaining why she felt so strongly about the project. She campaigned for the job and she got it.

Note

We have all been asked at some stage, "Who is your favorite actor?" It may be better in the future to answer this by mentioning your favorite performances. There are great actors who have given weak performances. There are mediocre actors who have occasionally given great performances. I prefer to talk about great performances, because actors are judged on each and every performance they give.

181. Eye to Eye

Split the actors up evenly into As and Bs. Have them all spread out around the room. Explain in the following way:

INSTRUCTOR: In a moment I am going to ask all of you to start walking around the room. As you are doing this, I am going to ask you to make eye contact with the other people you come across. If you are an A, you are going to hold the other person's eye for as long as possible. If you are a B, you will glance at each person you come across, and quickly look away. So As hold eye contact for as long as possible, and Bs only hold eye contact for a moment. Please remember that you should be continually moving around the room the whole time. There are no opportunities for you to stand still. The activity takes place without any verbal communication.

Different scenarios will create different responses:
A and B — A holds eye contact while B quickly looks away
B and B — both persons quickly look away after initial contact
A and A — both persons hold eye contact for as long as possible
Finish up with a group discussion.

Purpose

To understand the influence of status

This exercise explores the issue of status. The actor who holds the eye contact will most likely feel empowered and more in control. The actor who looks away will probably feel weaker and lacking in confidence. Holding eye contact in a performance is not always necessary, and does not need to be planned in each moment. It is, however, important to realize that if a character never looks another character in the eye, he will most likely be perceived as the weaker of the two. On the other hand, avoiding eye contact can sometimes be seen as a position of strength. Everything that is happening on-stage should be because it is a choice. Nothing should be happening that distracts or detracts from the play itself. Understanding the status of their characters, in terms of their relationships to those around them, is of absolute importance to the actors.

Industry Connection

Raise the following discussion points with your actors:

INSTRUCTOR: Let us say you are having a meeting with an agent and you feel very nervous. As they are talking to you, spend most of your time looking away and only make occasional eye contact. They will get this message, and it will empower them. If they are looking at representing you, this may turn them off. It may tell them that they like your acting, but that perhaps you are too weak for this business. It may also tell them that you have no interest in what they are saying. If they have already decided to take you on, then the lack of eye contact may allow them to command the whole situation. Perhaps they are an agent without scruples, and because they can sense your fear, they take advantage of this situation via your contract. In regards to finding a good agent, Romie Szal, owner of the K-Hall Agency, said to me only partly in jest, "You never want an agent who has a clean desk or is caught up on *all* their email by Sunday ... " Remember, in regards to getting an agent, you are interviewing the agent and not the other way around. An agent is going to want to know what is intriguing about an actor in order to piqué his interest.

182. Base Stealers

For this activity you are going to need the same number of chairs as you have students. Set the chairs in a circle. Leave a small gap between the chairs. Explain in the following way:

INSTRUCTOR: I hope everyone is feeling alert and energetic today. Rachel, would you go and stand in the center of the circle. I would like everyone else to find a seat. Please do not move the chairs off their marks. (The students go sit in the chairs.) As you can see, we have one empty chair. Rachel, your aim is to sit in that empty chair. When we start, Rachel is going to dash to the empty chair. It is everyone else's job to stop her. To do this, you must move one chair to your left or right and sit in the chair she is running toward.

DEBBY: Can we move along by more than one chair?

INSTRUCTOR: Good question. You can only move one chair to your left or right. You cannot skip over another person. Remember that when you move to a seat, your previous seat is momentarily open and Rachel may try to steal it. Provided she finds an empty seat, she wins. Remember that as you change seats, the empty chair is always changing. If Rachel finds a chair then she has succeeded. At this point everyone will most likely be sitting in a chair and a different person should be chosen to go into the center of the circle to start a new round. At this point the whole activity is repeated.

VIRGINIA: Does Rachel have to go back to the center of the circle each time?

INSTRUCTOR: Excellent question. Once she has made the move for the first chair, it becomes open season. She does not have to go back to the center of the circle, but will now just keep going for the empty chair, wherever it may be.

The reason you leave a gap between each chair is to make this exercise more of a challenge.

Purpose

To understand tempo and rhythm

The purpose of this exercise is to find the exact tempo and rhythm required. At first, an actor may have to dash to cover an empty chair. Simply dashing from one chair to the other is not the answer. The person in the middle may suddenly find the next chair empty and simply sit in it. The actors have to move from one chair to the next with the exact tempo and rhythm required. If they can do this, they can keep the person in the middle from getting to an empty seat. It is important to recognize and observe how human beings communicate. One moment a couple may be arguing back and forth (fast tempo), and the next minute they may be hugging and apologizing to one another (slower rhythm). This tells us that not everything we say or do is on one rhythmic level. The actor has to find how the tempo and rhythm changes for his character throughout. It may turn on a dime at a moment's notice, yet the actor must find this. A person may be laughing one minute and bursting into tears the next. The actor needs to find the exact tempo and rhythm required at any given moment.

Industry Connection

One of the purposes behind this exercise is for the actors to never let their guard down. The moment someone lets his guard down, or loses his concentration, the person in the middle will sit in the empty chair. In the industry, actors can never let their guard down. This is not in terms of their performance, but in terms of the business side of their acting career. Unfortunately, the more money actors make, the more someone else is going to try to get their hands on that money. If you want proof of this, just look at what happens to the money of many up-and-coming music bands. They will often say they never got to see a dime of it. Actors need to keep their guard up at all times. This is with regard to contracts, agents, studios, managers, book deals, and anything else you can think of. There are some great people out there, and there are some not-so-great people. In a city like Los Angeles, a number of agreements are made verbally. This may sound odd, but it happens all the time. It is up to the actors to guard their own interests and make sure they are well looked after. They need to make sure they have everything in writing. Remind your actors that they are going to have to work tremendously hard to make money as an actor. If this is the case, then the last thing they should do is simply naively give it away. As former president of The Associated Actors and Artists of America, Merill Joels, once said, "There is a general belief that actors as 'artists' have little or no business sense. Unfortunately, this often seems to be true. Most people who aspire, who attempt to enter this field lack the understanding that it is a business as well as an art."[47] Actors who are willing to learn the business side of their craft will be able to develop a strategy.

---

47. Merill E. Joels, *How to Get into Show Business* (New York: Hastings House Publishers, 1955), 11.

183. Bus Stop

Bus Stop is a well-known exercise that has been used by acting instructors all over the world. It can be utilized in a variety of ways. Instruct your actors to sit as the audience. Set out three chairs in a row, side by side. Ask one actor to come up and sit on the chair that is stage right. Tell them that he is to play the scene as if he is sitting at the bus stop waiting for the bus. Allow this to go on for a minute or two. At this point, send up a second actor who is going to sit on the middle chair next to the first actor. At this point they must change the scene. An example would be that they play the scene as if they are in the doctor's waiting room. The first actor must go along with whatever the second actor has decided, and the scene continues. These scenes are not mimed and can have as much dialogue as is required. After another minute or so, send in a third actor who is going to change the scene again. Perhaps this time they are sitting on a park bench feeding the birds. The important thing to remember is that the actor coming in must utilize the chairs in the scene. Every time a scene is changed, the actors have to become new characters. It is not good to be playing a game of football sitting in the chairs. The scene does not end with the three actors. At some point during the third scene, the first actor who entered has to find a reason to leave. At this point, the other two actors must find a reason to move along on the seats, and a new actor enters with a new scene or setting. In theory, this exercise is like a revolving door that can go on forever.

Purpose
To suspend disbelief
When the first actor sits on the bench waiting for the bus, he has to use his imagination. The reason for this, among other things, is to create a reality for himself and for the audience. When the second actor enters the stage, he is going to create a new scene and a new setting. It is quite difficult for the first actor to suspend disbelief. It has just taken all his imagination to create the bus stop. He is now being asked to create a new scene, such as a doctor's office. A good actor will be able to do this with conviction, but a weak actor will not stand a chance. During a play, an actor has to suspend disbelief time and again. An actress knows that her husband in the play is not really her husband. The husband knows that the daughter in the play is not related to him in any way. The husband and wife are aware that they are not really in a house, but on a set on a stage. The actor must suspend disbelief and embrace belief in every aspect of the play.

Industry Connection
Every minute or so, a new scene and a new location are formed. A play can take place in the same scene for thirty minutes or more, but this is very rare in movies. A movie is constantly moving from one scene to the next. This exercise asks the actors to get used to working in a number of different scenes in rapid succession. Another important aspect of this exercise is that one scene may be followed by a random new scene. On a movie set, actors are often asked to film scenes out of sequence. They have to find a way to adapt to this challenge. I say challenge because at one minute they may have to film a kissing scene. In the very next shot they film the location at which the actor first meets the person he had just been kissing. In real time, this is illogical. In the producer's eyes it may be totally logical. In terms of budget and logistics, it may make total sense for

the scenes to be shot in that order. It is the actor's responsibility to make this seem perfectly natural. The actor also has to be able to factor in when his character changes and grows. Some actors claim that TV and film acting is so easy. I disagree with this statement. Turn on your television set or go to the cinema and you will find you are privileged to see good acting. It is harder to come by than some would like to believe.

184. Definition of Self

This is a good exercise to use when you are working on a play. Tell your students to sit as the audience. Put one chair in the center of the performance space. Ask a student to take the seat as his character. The rest of the class members are then going to ask questions of the character. The challenge is that they are going to repeatedly ask one question. "Who are you?" Let us say the actor in the chair is playing Atticus Finch from the play *To Kill a Mockingbird*. The conversation may go something like this:

STUDENT 1: Who are you?
ATTICUS: I'm a father.
STUDENT 2: Who are you?
ATTICUS: I am a lawyer.
STUDENT 3: Who are you?
ATTICUS: A believer in justice.
STUDENT 4: Who are you?
ATTICUS: A good shot with a rifle.
STUDENT 5: Who are you?
ATTICUS: A clever, yet simple man.

You can set a limit to the number of questions you want each character to answer. Perhaps each character can answer ten or fifteen questions. The audience is only allowed to repeat the same question.

Variation

The actors can answer questions about a character they are playing. Another way is to ask the person in the chair to create a character in his mind. The audience could have no idea who he is and only make discoveries through their questioning.

Purpose

To delve into your character

At first, some actors appear frustrated with this exercise. Being asked the same question repeatedly can seem redundant and annoying. Some actors in the chair become visibly frustrated. After awhile, something interesting happens. As they repeatedly have to answer the question "Who are you?" a light may appear to go on in the head of some of the actors. At that moment, they have made a new discovery about their character. This is possibly because they have had to answer the question, "Who are you?" more times than ever before. How can actors play the same part for an entire year and not allow it to become stale? They can do this by going on autopilot and giving adequate performances. They can also do this by continuing to ask questions of their character. In doing so, they can make new discoveries, even after a year, thus keeping their performance fresh and alive. Actors will want to be more revealing each time.

They are not only asking, "Who are you?" but also other questions that come to mind.

Industry Connection

The actors on the set are asked the same question repeatedly. Actors pursuing their career in the big acting hubs often ask themselves questions. Some of the questions they ask are:

Why am I here?

How can I pay my bills?

How can I get my SAG vouchers?

How can I get an agent?

How can I get my big break?

These types of questions are not asked once only, but over and over again. If they ask themselves these questions frequently, over time they are able to turn some of their answers into reality. It is well known that what we focus on in life is what we get. In this regard, actors have to learn to ask themselves good questions. "Why do I always fail?" is a poor question because the mind will come up with numerous reasons as to why the actor always fails. A better question would be, "What do I need to do to improve my success rate in audition situations?" An actor has to really want to get the part.

185. Journal

Your students are going to need a pen or pencil and notebook or paper for this exercise. They can also use laptops if you have enough of them. What they are going to do is spend a good thirty-five minutes writing about their previous week. They will spend about five minutes on each of the last seven days. Have them write about their physical behavior such as, "I had cornflakes with soy milk for breakfast." You also want them to write about specific events and their reflections. "I got into an argument with my parents over what my first car should be. When will they learn to let me grow up?" Because they are only spending five minutes on each entry, they are not going to record everything. What we are looking for is a sense of each day. Instruct them to make entries for each day, from Monday to Sunday. When the time is up, bring everyone together to sit in a circle. At this point, give your students the opportunity to read a journal entry to the group. This should not be required, but optional. A journal entry is very personal, so it is up to the students if they want to share a particular experience or not. You are looking to ignite your students' passion in writing a journal.

Variation

When I was a classroom teacher, I used to tell my students to spend five minutes every day writing in their journal. I would then choose three or four people to read their journals aloud to the group. Everyone knew they would have to read their journal aloud at some point, and adjusted the content accordingly.

Another way I used to do the journals was in audio form. Each student would have a daily partner. He would turn to his partner and share experiences about the previous day. I would then call on the friend to recall the events his partner had just shared with him. In other words, they would verbally share each other's journal.

Purpose

To do character analysis research

Someone once said, "If a life is worth living, it is worth recording." I would probably say for the actor, "If a life is worth living, it is worth observing." As Stella Adler says in her book, *The Art of Acting,* "The world is in front of you. You have to take that in. You have to see things that you never saw before. Then you have to give it back to the world."[48] If actors observe their own life in detail, they may come up with a valuable number of resources from which to work. There are experiences in our lives that if we had not actually experienced them, we would not believe were possible. This is important information, because sometimes it can be a challenge to justify the behavior and actions that a character portrays. A journal helps the actors to remember things that otherwise might be forgotten. The journal helps the actors to become specific about their own lives, rather than simply seeing them as a general blur.

Industry Connection

Part of the idea behind a journal is to be organized and to commit to something over a lengthy period of time. Anyone can write one journal entry, but to still be writing journal entries a year later is another matter. It takes a disciplined actor to stay the course. It takes guts for actors to pack their bags, leave their friends, and move to a big city like London, Madrid, New York, or Los Angeles. It takes even more guts for the actors to stay the course once they arrive. Some actors will quickly find out they have no interest in the industry, and this is fine. Those who are interested in their acting career will have to be extremely disciplined on a daily basis and commit to their own journey. If they want an acting career they cannot simply wing it. They are going to have to remain committed and focused throughout.

186. This Is Your Character's Life

This exercise is based on a famous television show called, *This Is Your Life.* On this show, a well-known personality is surprised and the host proceeds to share the person's life with the audience. Friends and relatives are invited to appear on the show to help share the story. The friends and relatives are usually brought up in chronological order in terms of at what point in their lives they met the individual. You are going to do the same thing, but using a character from a play or movie. This is an excellent exercise to use when you are working on a play. Let us assume you are doing the musical *The Wizard of Oz.* You could have the wizard sit on the chair while the other cast members come up and share fond stories and facts about him. Give your students time to invent some interesting things they can say with regard to the wizard. I tend not to use this exercise as an improvisation. Another interesting variation is to have real and created characters involved. An example would be the mother of the wizard. While she does not appear in the musical, it would be interesting to meet her here and have her talk about the wizard as a boy. Not every character has to make purely positive remarks. For instance, the lion might say, "When I first met the Wizard, I feared him and did not find him very friendly." What each character says should

---

48. Stella Adler, *The Art of Acting,* (New York: Applause, 2000), 27.

be based on facts, and observations will want to be based on the given circumstances. Do not rush through this exercise, but allow it to take as long as is necessary.

Purpose

Character development

The characters sitting in the chair are often able to make new discoveries about themselves. The characters who talk about them are able to solidify their relationship with the individual. They may find out pieces of information that they had not considered before. Good actors are always seeking to make new discoveries with regard to their characters. By doing so, they avoid stagnating in the roles and becoming stuck within them.

Industry Connection

As mentioned above, the show this exercise is based on is called *This Is Your Life*. This is a title that says a great deal. When actors consider their career, they also have to consider what legacy they intend to create. If a person is a successful accountant, he can develop his career in virtual anonymity. A highly successful politician or athlete is likely to be in the public eye. They are constantly under the intensity of the media spotlight. This is also an accepted part of the actor's world. The actors have to find a way to make the private part of their work public. Some actors seldom choose to raise the curtain on their private life. They can be intensely shy people. They may be out for a private dinner with friends and be in a quiet mood. The public may be disappointed to have their illusions broken. They do not give much of themselves publicly beyond the films they are making. The reputation that goes ahead of the actor can sometimes be hard to live up to. High profile actors will often have their life shared with the whole world. They have a very public private life. It is worth remembering that *fan* is short for *fanatic*. Some actors put on a private veil when in the public eye. A number of actors have virtually spent their entire lives under public scrutiny. In return, these actors may get fortunes, fame, and privileges. They may love their work but not always the reality of being famous. This means that their life is no longer only about their acting. They will be judged on how they conduct themselves and how they treat others. This is not suggesting what makes a better actor, but is raising the point that the actors' off-stage life can be followed as much as their on-stage life.

Note

If you research the highest paid actors, you may be in for a surprise. The highest paid actors are not necessarily the ones you might consider to be the greatest actors. Sometimes, this is because the actors chose to receive a percentage of the movie's gross sales as their payment. It pays to be a business-savvy actor. It pays to be an industry-connected actor.

Chapter 22
Spatial Awareness

187. Moments in Space

Have two actors sit in chairs opposite each other and work a dialogue. The rest of the group is to sit as the audience. Explain the following:

INSTRUCTOR: I am going to need two volunteers for this exercise. Let me have Maya and Neil. I want you to sit in the two chairs that are facing each other. As the rest of you can see, the two chairs are almost touching, so the actors in this exercise are sitting very close together. In a moment I am going to ask the two of you to perform this scene together. I am going to give you two or three minutes only to look over the scene. (Three minutes pass. If two actors already have a rehearsed scene, that will work just as well.) You are now going to perform the scene for us as a virtual cold reading. (The actors perform the scene still seated in the chairs.) What I would like you to do now is move your chairs to the opposite ends of the room. They are going to be as far away from each other as they can possibly be. Maya and Neil, I still want you to make sure your chairs are facing each other. Please sit in your chairs. I would now like you to perform the scene again in its entirety. (All this is done without any comment from the actors or the audience.)

Once they have finished, you can hold a discussion with the actors and the rest of the class. If you want to vary this exercise, have the actors stand for the entire exercise instead of using chairs.

Purpose
To understand the relevancy of spacing

The intimacy or lack of intimacy in terms of spacing not only changes the perception of the actors, but also that of the audience. You have not changed the dialogue or the blocking, and yet you will most likely find the scene has turned itself on its head. The actors will learn about intensity in a physical and mental sense. There are also times when the intimacy between the actors and the audience may influence the performance. Think about the difference between inviting an audience into your classroom to watch your students perform and performing on the main stage. The classroom may not look like much of a performance space and yet its intimate setting may make for a very powerful performance.

Industry Connection

What if an actor performs a scene in an agent's office one day and then performs the same scene in a theatre the next? Is he going to use the same technical skills for each performance? I hope not, because each setting will require a totally different vocal and physical approach. What should remain constant is the truth of the piece, the subtext, and the essence of the character. The actors will want to search within their character to find their root. A film actor is not only doing subtle facial work. If you think this is not the case, go to the movies and you will find yourself contradicted on many occasions. What the actor learns to do is adapt to the size of the frame. He will need to be much more subtle for a close-up than he would for a wide shot.

188. Zones of Influence

Have all of your actors sit in the audience. Bring up two actors to demonstrate this exercise. Explain in the following way:

INSTRUCTOR: John, I would like you to go stand at the other end of the room. Sarah, you are going to stay at this end of the room. I want you to turn, so that you are facing each other. John, you are now going to slowly start walking towards Sarah. What I would like you to do is walk as close to her as you can, without breaching your comfort zone.

JOHN: What do you mean by comfort zone?

INSTRUCTOR: In other words, go as close as you can without breaking your personal barrier. You will know where this is, because you will feel it in your gut. (John walks forward and stops at his comfort zone. He moves forward a little and backs up a little to find exactly where it is.) Before Sarah has a turn I want you to see, John, if you can adjust yourself to where you think Sarah's comfort zone ends.

SARAH: Should I help him here?

INSTRUCTOR: Actually, you are helping John just by being there. You will be signaling your comfort zone through your energy and your body language. John should also be able to sense this. (John adjusts his position and ends up taking two steps back. After he has finished the exercise it is repeated with Sarah.)

What I would like you to do now is to find a partner and spread out around the room. Decide who is going to go first and then begin. Do not rush the process. As you are walking toward your partner, you may find you have to move forward and back a few times until you reach the exact edge of your comfort zone. Make sure you start far enough apart (about twenty-five feet) so that you are nowhere near invading your personal space.

Once the actors have worked this exercise, get back together as a group. Watch some of the pairs and discuss the findings.

Purpose

To understand comfort zones and personal space barriers

This exercise explores your students' comfort zone. Your students will also want to explore this in regards to any character they play. Personal space can also be affected by culture. Many of my friends from India will stand very close when having a discussion. There is nothing insulting in this, as it is perfectly acceptable in their culture. In England, we tend to greet people at arm's length and keep this distance during the conversation. Zones of influence can change a great deal, depending on the given circumstances. If a character is drunk, he may break all of his own rules and be practically on top of whomever he is talking to. A bouncer might break a customer's comfort zone in order to intimidate. A bully will break his victims' comfort zones for much the same reasons. It is important not only to understand this on an intellectual level, but on a very real and visceral level. It is important that the students' characters explore this too. If an actress is in a scene on a park bench with her boyfriend, the personal space barrier between is likely to be virtually nonexistent. Of course, this does depend on the given circumstances as they relate to the scene. The actors will want to know how to present the simple ideas if they are going to be able to discover the big idea. Your students must understand the dynamics of zones of influence as they relate to their characters.

Industry Connection

Discuss the following with your actors in your own words:

INSTRUCTOR: If you go to an audition for a network, there might be fifteen people in the room watching you. Let's say you decide to be assertive. You walk right up to the table, thrust your hand forward, and force all fifteen of them to shake your hand. You have just smashed right through the personal space barriers of fifteen people. You have done so in total disregard to their body language. Your audition is over before it's even begun. You haven't even started and you have left a bitter taste in their mouths. They will say things like, "Great actress, but I don't think she's right for the part. She's not what we're looking for. There was something about her that didn't sit well with me. She seemed nervous and anxious." These observations could be for a thousand and one reasons, or they could be because you missed all the nonverbal cues they gave you and you invaded their personal space. They are not necessarily going to know why they don't like you, but the fact that they don't is enough. Don't give them any more ammunition than is necessary. Don't fuel the fire. Find out where their personal space is. I want to encourage you not to shake a casting agent's, director's, producer's hand unless they offer you theirs first.

189. Musical Chairs Nightmare

This exercise is very similar to musical chairs, with a small twist. Put out a number of chairs in a circle. There should be one less chair than there are actors. Play some music and have the actors move clockwise around the chairs. When you stop the music, the actors have to sit on a chair. Of course, there is one fewer chair than there are actors. You are not out if you don't have your own chair. You are out if you don't have your feet off the ground. Actors might sit on the laps of other actors. They may choose to stand on a desk. Provided the actors' feet are off the ground when the music stops, they are still in. Do not help them out here. Let them figure this out for themselves. This is not a teamwork exercise. Every actor is out for himself. Before every round you should continue to take one more chair away. This may mean five people end up sitting on the lap of one person. Remember it is not your job to help the actors out. You want to see how well they are able to problem solve on their own. While actors can learn acting technique, in the end, each actor is working toward developing his own technique. Actors make their own method and find their own way to get their character's center. They have to find their own method that works for them. As Jerome Rockwood explains in his book, *The Craftsmen of Dionysus*, "Let the techniques here described be but a start, a point of reference. If they work for you, use them; if not, toss them out. With experience you will come to know what your artist-self needs, what stimuli are most effective, what kind of expression is your forte."[49] If you have five people sitting on one chair, make sure it is being done safely.

---

49. Jerome Rockwood, *The Craftsmen of Dionysus* (Illinois: Scott, Foresmen and Company, 1966), 208.

Purpose
To be prepared
In this exercise, the actors have to react as soon as the music stops. If they are too slow, they will be out. In a scene, when one of the actors does not know his lines thoroughly, the scene does not flow. Instead of responding or reacting to what is being said, the actor begins searching for his next line. This creates delayed reactions and pauses where perhaps they don't exist. There are times when a character will pause for thought, and there are also times when a character will react to what has just been said, without really thinking things through. Actors who do not know their lines will not be able to react in this way. They wouldn't trust themselves to be able to do so.

Industry Connection
To do well in this exercise, the actors have to be able to problem solve. If there is no chair available, then the actor has to quickly find a way to get his feet off the ground. As is stated in the exercise description, this is not a teamwork exercise. It is every actor out for himself. At times, an actor may feel that there are other actors, directors, and casting agents in the industry who are willing to help him. There are many examples to prove that this is true. The challenge is that each actor has to understand to what degree it is true. There are those who will help, but ultimately the actor is on his own. When push comes to shove, each actor is on his own. When the network show he is on starts to drop in the ratings and no one wants to hire him, he is on his own. This is being said not to create an air of pessimism. It is being said so that your actors become independent thinkers. Actors are working in a business that is based solely on themselves and the advancement of their career. The more they are able to take charge of and responsibility for their own career, the better.

Note
You can repeat these exercises two or three times in a row if you see it of benefit to your group of actors.

190. Ball
I have called this exercise Ball because this is the basic name it was given when I was a kid. You will need a soft foam ball for this exercise. Growing up, we used a tennis ball, but you will not be using one here. Explain as follows:

INSTRUCTOR: What I would like you to do is all line up with your backs against the wall. All of you are now standing in an enclosed space and virtually shoulder to shoulder. This is purposefully done. Devon, you are going to be the thrower. I want you to stand fifteen to twenty feet away. You are going to throw the ball at the players lined up against the wall. If he hits any part of your body, then you will become the thrower and Devon will go against the wall. You don't have space to really move out of the way so you have to duck, turn, or move a limb out of the way as best you can. Please be spatially aware of those around you. You are going to have to use your quick wits and your agility for this exercise. Devon, please avoid throwing at the neck and above. If you hit these areas you will still be the thrower.

The actors are working in close quarters, and through the excitement, an injury can occur. Remind the actors that they need to be consciously aware of those around them at all times.

Purpose

To increase the actors' agility

Because of the tight spacing, in order not to be out, the actors have to use their agility. They have to be able to move and bend their bodies at will. They have to swerve, dodge, and duck to avoid getting hit. Stage actors also have to be agile in the use of their body. An actress who never wears heels in real life may be playing a character who wears heels on a daily basis. If she does not practice, the actress may look clumsy and out of place. By practicing her agility, the actress will look poised and move in an effortless and easy fashion. It is not easy to have command of one's body. For the actor, it is something that has to be worked at until it becomes second nature.

Industry Connection

In this exercise the actors are boxed in, whether they like it or not. They have to find a way to adapt to their surroundings. Actors may also feel boxed in by their chosen industry. They may have an agent telling them to do one thing, a manager telling them to do another, and a casting director yet another. The actors may begin to feel claustrophobic, as if they are about to explode. They are going to have to find a way to create space and distance between themselves and those around them. I am not talking about a big gaping hole. I am talking about enough to give them some privacy and allowing them to keep some perspective.

191. Vacuum

This activity works best with a minimum of twelve players. You can explain in the following way:

INSTRUCTOR: Ladies and gentlemen, I am going to split you up into As and Bs. I would like the As to line up on the left hand side of the room and the Bs to line up on the right, so that the lines are facing each other. There should be a space of six to eight feet between the two sides. You are now, in effect, two walls. The space between the walls represents a vacuum. (Spread your students out so that the walls are fifteen to twenty feet in length.) Tamara and Roman should join me. Tamara, you are the hunter and Roman, you are the prey. In a moment, I am going to ask you to go to opposite ends of the vacuum. Roman, your aim is to get to the other side of the vacuum without being caught. Tamara, your aim is to catch the prey before it can complete its objective. The way you will do this is by tapping or touching the prey before it can complete its journey. For this exercise, neither the hunter nor the prey can move on two legs. This means that you will have to crawl, slide, or move in whatever other way is most efficient for you. This exercise works best in silence. The last thing the prey wants to do is let the hunter know where he is. I would like Tamara and Roman to take their shoes off. Those of you who are part of the wall will also need to observe this silence. You will also want to move your arms out to the side, if need be. This is to make sure that the hunter and the prey do not wander out of the vacuum. This means that the gaps between you and the people on your left and right should be no wider than it would take for your hands to connect as a wall. It also means you have to stay alert at all times. At that point, I am going to put blindfolds on Roman and Tamara. (You can let your students do this. You can also allow them to spin the hunter and prey around three times, to help disorientate them. If you do this, have the students help lower them to the ground safely and carefully. If you prefer, you can have them close their eyes instead of being blindfolded.)

If you want to take a few questions first, feel free to do so. Sometimes, it is better to play a few rounds first before taking questions. This allows the actors to make discoveries and learn what works and what does not work for them.

Purpose
To heighten the senses
Your students are certainly developing their sense of hearing as they lose their sense of sight. I also find that many students comment on the importance of their sense of touch, which is enhanced during this exercise. In other words, their senses become heightened. Teamwork plays a big part, too. If the people in the vacuum do not work together and stay focused, this exercise will be of little benefit. The more opportunities you can give the students to take responsibility for each other, and work together, the better. Actors always have to take responsibility for their work. You want the students to feel that even when they are just a small part of the exercise — being part of the wall — they are still a vital part of its success. At a future date, when they have a tiny part in a play, hopefully they will be able to apply this information. A play only succeeds as a result of the efforts of all the individual members of the ensemble.

Industry Connection
There is the hunter and there is the prey. The prey has to make it from one end of the vacuum to the other, without being caught. When your actors eventually arrive at one of the big acting hubs, they need to be careful that they do not become the prey. There will be many people who will be only too happy to help them part with their money. The hunter will come in many forms and guises. They will be the photographer, the agent, the acting coach, the director, the producer, and so on. Of course, there are many excellent and noble people in all these fields, and then again, there are some who are not. There are people who are looking to prey on the actors' desperation. It is important to encourage your actors to stay grounded and focused so that they do not become the prey. For this exercise to work, everyone has to stay focused and disciplined, which is the same approach your actors are going to need for their careers.

192. Fetch!
Split your students into two groups. Have the groups sit in two rows, side by side. The rows will want to face each other, with a gap of about four feet down the middle. If the teams have twelve players in each team, number them one to twelve. Number the teams in opposite directions. If the first person is number one on team one, make the facing person on team two number twelve. Make sure the players are sitting exactly opposite a player from the other team. At this point, take a bone and put it somewhere down the line. You can use a real bone or a toy of some sort, if you prefer. Tell the players that they are all dogs. Explain that in a moment, you are going to call out two numbers. Let us say you call out "three and six." It is very important you establish which team's number you are

calling first. Players numbered three and six — one from each team — have to run and try to pick up the bone. The first player to do so, and get back to his seat with the bone, will get one point for his team. There is another challenge to this exercise: If, when he is running back to his seat, the other player tags him before he is able to sit down, the point will go to the opposing team. You can change the team you call first as often as you like. To be fair, you need to call out the numbers at virtually the same time. If the wrong person goes to get the bone, the points are automatically given to the other side. To make this exercise even more challenging, you can have the students change seats with their teammates every now and then. This will keep them on their toes in terms of memorizing their number.

Purpose

To connect the mental to the physical

A fast runner is not necessarily going to do well in this activity. A quick thinker is not necessarily going to do any better. It is the actor who is able to connect the mental to the physical who will do well in this activity. An actor may hear his number, but in order to beat his opponent, he has to get up and run quickly. If his reaction is delayed, it will be too late. Actors may intellectually know their cues. In their mind, they may have thought through what they are going to do at each moment. If they do not react physically, they are always going to appear to be one step behind the action. Everything they do will appear safe and calculated and not impulsive in any way. One of the beauties and challenges of human nature is that it can be so unpredictable.

Industry Connection

I am particularly fond of this exercise because there is a twist. An actor may pick up the bone and still lose the point. Sometimes, two actors will reach the bone at the same time. They both have to use their wits to get the bone and get back to their seat in order to win the point. In other words, it is not over until it is over. An actor may go to an audition and say, "I failed! It is over!" Failing to get a part does not mean the end of his career. It just means there was another part someone else was more suited for. Actors can choose to look at their career as a glass that's half full or a glass that is half empty. Everyone knows that an actor's career is not an easy one. It is only those who take it one step at a time who have a chance of truly having the career they desire. It is up to the actor not to be a victim in this business.

Chapter 23
Making Specific Choices

193. Sugarcoated

This exercise will cost you a little bit of money, but not too much. Have your actors sit in a circle. Put ten pieces of candy or chocolate in front of each actor. These are small pieces of candy such as M&Ms or Skittles. You can mix up the candy however you like. Tell each actor he can take as many pieces of candy as he wants without eating them. Some actors may have picked two, and others may have picked all ten. Go around the room and take away the extra pieces of candy. Ask each actor to count how many pieces of candy he has kept and hold up on his fingers that number. Tell the actors that they are now going to have to share information related to acting. If they have taken seven pieces of candy, they will have to give the group seven pieces of useful information. Go around the group and have each one share information on acting in this way. An actor cannot give the same information as another actor. An actor cannot pass, but must give information based on the number of pieces of candy he took. Do not move on to the next actor until this has been achieved. We are looking for insightful information on acting.

Some topic examples are:
1. Historical facts on acting
2. Information related to technique
3. Industry related information
4. Famous actor, director, producer, agent information
5. Personal challenges and achievements related to acting

Once everyone has completed the exercise the actors can eat their candy. Follow up with a group discussion.

Purpose
To expand knowledge on acting

Raise the following discussion with your students:

INSTRUCTOR: What do you know about acting? What do you really understand about your craft and your industry? A doctor knows about the anatomy and physiology of the human body. A lawyer is trained in the rules of law. A gardener is familiar with soils and climate. It is your responsibility to know about acting. Acting will want to be the template with which you look at everything. This should only apply to those of you who want to be a professional or good actor. Sometimes a person will say, "They used a person who had never done any acting before, and he gave a great performance!" This is certainly possible under the guidance of a fine director. A fine director will have a great respect for actors. Here is the challenge: Take that same untrained individual and put him with a bad director and the results will be drastically different. Take that same individual and give him ten different roles to play, each with contrasting characters, and he will most likely be totally lost in where to begin. We are not talking about one performance. We are interested in the longevity and the lifetime career of actors. Over their careers they will hopefully play a broad spectrum of characters. There are actors who are constantly reinventing themselves. These actors are trained actors and committed professional actors.

Industry Connection

Some actors will take every piece of candy in front of them. They will then have to give the maximum pieces of information related to acting. This exercise is fun, but it is also a powerful metaphor for their acting career. Some actors want everything immediately. They ignore the small steps of progress and want to be famous overnight. For one actor in a million, this may work out. The challenge is that instead of getting what they want, many of these actors crash and burn. They try to do everything at once, and everything collapses around them. We could say that they were too greedy and did not want to work toward their success. The greedy actors who want to cut all the corners may pay a high price. That price may be their career. To want to succeed is commendable, and to believe in yourself is admirable. However, each actor has to be willing to put in the time and effort it takes to reach these goals. Remind your students to not be too greedy, but be patient and willing to take it one step at a time. Actors also have to believe they have the potential to be as great as they think they can be.

194. A Story for Every Occasion

To begin this exercise, send half of the players out of the room. Make sure they are somewhere they cannot hear the conversation. Tell the rest of the group that is left:

INSTRUCTOR: You are going to pretend to have created an amazing story. In truth, there is absolutely no story whatsoever. When the group comes back in, they will only be able to ask you yes or no questions. So, as in twenty questions, you can only answer, "yes" or "no." You are going to answer "no" to every question that starts with a vowel and "yes" to every question that starts with a consonant. The only other rule is that any time you have said "yes" twice, the next time you will always answer "no." In other words, there should never be more than two "yes" answers in a row. Remember that you have to listen to their questions with absolute interest and enthusiasm. You have to do so with a curiosity and enthusiasm. You have to make them believe that they are getting closer to discovering the story. Remember that you are going to be giving them clues with your nonverbal communication skills. You don't want to let on that this is all one big scam.

At this point, you can bring the other actors back into the room and begin. A way to set this exercise is to have the actors who are guessing the story sit on the floor. Have the actors who are answering sit on chairs in a line. This way, the questions can go up and down the line. It will also give the actors who are in the chairs a superiority feel, as the other actors will have to look up to them. It makes it appear as if they are in control of the story and are more authoritative. This may also make for some interesting twists in the story. At the end of the exercise you can tell the actors who are guessing how the exercise works. Do not simply leave it at that. If they do not understand why they participated in the exercise, nothing will have been learned. Follow up with a group discussion.

Purpose

To commit to the moment

In this exercise, the actors who are making up the story have to choose to commit to the exercise. They know from the very start that there is no story. It is up to them to hold the interest of the group who are entering the room. If they do not commit, then it will be obvious to the actors coming in that something is not quite right. While they may not know the specifics, they will be looking to find out how they are being tricked. As Sanford Meisner says in his book, *On Acting,* "If you do something, you really do it! Did you walk up the steps to the classroom this morning? You didn't jump up? You didn't skip up, right? You didn't do a ballet pirouette? You really walked up those steps."[50] An actor who is playing a part has to choose to commit to that part. Actors may be in a play where they know that their character is going to be murdered on page forty-eight. The challenge for the actor is that his character does not know this on page forty-seven! If he plays this intent from the beginning, the audience will know that something is not quite right from the start. In other words, the actors have to commit to the scene in that moment because they cannot commit to the next moment until they get there. They may take the attitude that they are going to play the part very apathetically, because they are only going to die anyway. The point to remember is that in the character's eyes, he has everything to live for, and everything to fight for.

Industry Connection

At the end of this exercise the actors who came back in the room are told how the exercise works. They may be offended. They may look at you as if you have just wasted their time. After all, there really was no story to begin with. It is up to the actors to realize that they may just have created an amazingly original story. They did this using their vivid imaginations. In the Folger's Library version of *Twelfth Night* by William Shakespeare, Viola asks, "What country, friends, is this?"[51] What is the actress looking at in reality when she says this line? She is either looking at some part of the stage or she is looking through the fourth wall and into the audience. It is only in her mind and through her imagination that she is able to create the vision of the country of Illyria. If she sees a bare stage, then this is what the audience sees. Bertolt Brecht was a world-famous German playwright, poet, and theatre director and the co-creator of the epic theatre. He believed that the audience had to be reminded that a play is merely a representation of reality rather than actually being reality. You need structure in playwriting. There are certain rules that the writer has to follow. They cannot break the rules if they do not know what they are.

When actors go to an audition, they may not get the part. They may feel that for this reason they just wasted their time. They need to ask themselves, "What did I learn from going to that audition? What did I gain? How will it make me stronger for the next audition? What did I learn?" They may even go to an audition and find out later that the part was already cast. This sometimes happens due to the complexity of union rules. The actors may now feel that they totally wasted their time, but they should not be so sure. They have now been

50. Sanford Meisner, *On Acting* (New York: Vintage Books, 1987), 17.
51. William Shakespeare, *Twelfth Night* (New York: The Folger Library, 1960), 3.

introduced to the casting director. If they made a good impression, the casting director may remember their faces. They may not be hired for this project, but it doesn't mean they won't be used for future work. It is not always the end result that we will want to be looking for, but where it might lead. There is always a positive to a negative if we choose to see it. An actors will not want to be a negative person who never tries to live their dreams.

Note
It is important to be aware that copyright laws exist and you need to respect these at all times.

195. Raising the Stakes

Start this exercise by having all your players stand in a circle. Choose one player to perform an action, but without sound. An example could be to mime brushing his teeth. The next player takes over the action and makes it a little more exaggerated. The key is that he still has to keep it justified and believable. He can do this by raising the stakes. An example is he is brushing his teeth frantically because he is late for work. The third person could be brushing his teeth and finds a chunk of food. Keep going around the circle until the last play takes the action as far as it can possibly go, while keeping it truthful and justified. Each player continues to raise the stakes. It is important that players continue to work with the original gesture. If someone takes it down a different road, call him on it and have him do it again. This fits under the category of "following direction." Once you have worked this exercise silently, you can have the actors add sound with their gestures. An example would be driving a car. This is quite a challenging exercise for the actors to do in a justified fashion. As the stakes keep rising, so it becomes more challenging for the actors to come up with justified actions. It is important to start out with a good original gesture. It is also important that the actors raise the stakes in small increments. Finish up with observations and a group discussion.

Purpose
To raise the stakes in a justified manner
This exercise demands that the actor raise the stakes in a justified manner. An actor may be in a play where his character kills someone because he didn't give him the correct change. This sounds like a very unlikely event, but, in fact, is based on a true story. Of course, the man wasn't really shot for not giving the correct change. It was the straw that broke the camel's back. He was shot because everything had built up so much in this other man's life. Everything in his life had built up to this point. The stakes had become so high that the next tiny thing or event in his life pushed him over the edge and made him snap. Discuss the following with your actors:

INSTRUCTOR: When your characters are working with extreme behavior or extreme actions, you are going to have to find out where it is coming from. If it is coming from nowhere, though your actions may look good, we just won't believe there is any justified point to what you are doing.

Industry Connection

One of the biggest challenges of this exercise is to stay on task. Most likely, it will start out that way and then some actors will begin to stray. Brushing hair gradually becomes picking a nose. Unfortunately, this was not the assignment they were given, no matter how well they can do it. When actors go for an audition, they may have been given the script a week before. Being a professional they have spent the week pouring through it and putting hour upon hour of rehearsal into getting it right. They have to know how to utilize the rehearsal process. As they walk into the audition room the director says, "I want you to play the character this way. At this point, I would like you to do this." The actors are not really listening too much, because they want to show the director what they can do. They want him to see all the amazing things they have done with the scene. When they are finished, they leave full of confidence. The director turns to his colleagues and says, "He was a really good actor. I just wish he could follow direction!" If actors cannot follow direction, it may cost production an extra five or six takes. That translates into cold, hard cash, and no producer is going to stand for it. The stronger an actor is in his craft the more directors and producers will want to work with him. An actor has to learn how to think left brain/right brain because the people who call the shots are often not thinking from a creative viewpoint. A producer wants to know how he can make money off what the actor can do.

Note

Raise the following discussion with your actors:

INSTRUCTOR: There are times when you might work with a television director who you think is a really nice guy. The question you will want to be asking yourself is, "Is he a good director?" Everyone on the crew might like him because he doesn't do very many takes. He might have the technical vocabulary to talk to his crew. The actors might love him because he leaves them alone and hardly ever comments on their acting. The makeup artists like him because he tells a good joke. However, the question you should be asking yourself is, "Is he a good director?" If the answer is yes, then you have hit the jackpot. If the answer is no, then you better be a really good actor. You had better know how to cover for his directorial mistakes. You had better know how to justify his weak directorial choices. I have heard actors say, "It does not matter what we do, it all happens in the editing room." I would agree with this to a certain extent. However, if everything happens in the editing room, why is it there is so much garbage on television? A good editor can still only work with the material he has been handed. You may have a director who is difficult, edgy, angry, and a taskmaster. If he knows how to pull the best results out of you, then it is worth it. Some directors know everything about human behavior but nothing about the camera. Some directors know everything there is to know about camera angles and lens sizes, but nothing about the human instrument. A nice director who isn't any good will not be the one to look ridiculous. It is your face in front of the camera. The buck stops with you. If your work is laughable, it is your head that will be on the chopping board. The next time you are working with a director or a cast who constantly joke around, ask yourself, "Are we getting the best results?" If the answer is no, then you had better figure out how you can! This only applies to actors who want longevity in their career.

196. Stronger and Stronger

Each actor will need a pencil and piece of paper for this exercise. The whole group can sit together on chairs or on the floor. Explain in the following way:

INSTRUCTOR: For this activity I would like you to put your thinking cap on. I would like you to come up with a weak statement — a generalized statement. An example would be, "I want something to drink." I would like you to take this statement and make it into a stronger and clearer statement. An example would be, "I want a cup of coffee, please." This is much more specific and tells us exactly what you want. Another example would be, "I will try to meet you there sometime later." A stronger and clearer statement would be, "I will meet you at Bingos restaurant at four p.m. on Thursday." I would like each of you to come up with your own list of five weak statements and turn each of them into clear and specific statements. (Give the actors about five minutes in which to do this.) As a reminder, a weak statement is more general, with no clear direction. A stronger statement will be more specific, with clear objectives. It might be easier to fold your paper down the middle. Then write your list of weak statements out on one side and the stronger statements on the opposite side.

Go around the circle and have the actors share their weak and strong statements. Discuss their statements and changes as you go around the group. It is not necessary to hear all five statements but you may, if you prefer.

Purpose

To get specific

Here are some ideas you may choose to share with your actors:

INSTRUCTOR: I have asked you to accept the idea for the purpose of this activity that a vague statement is a weak one. I want you to think about when you are given a script. Let's say you have a script for a short or a student film. You will quite often find the character breakdown says something like this: "John in his twenties, white, gets angry a lot." (Please do not hunt me down if you are a scriptwriter of student films.) I am obviously generalizing, but I have seen many scripts with breakdowns such as this. If this is all you are given, then it is up to you as an actor to create a background. Let us say you accepted the idea that your character is twenty-something. This is a very weak statement. Have you ever met anyone in your life who is twenty-something? Even though it is true, this is sometimes how people describe themselves. You can now create your own clearer and stronger statement such as, "I am twenty-four-years-old and my birthday is on November fourth." By doing this, the character will start to become more real to you. What if the script tells you that your name is Tom? This again is a vague statement and you would do well to create a last name for your character such as Tom Edwards. Be aware that some directors might take offense to your background work, so there is no need to share it with them if you do not feel it is necessary. The idea of creating a clear and concise character background is to help you as an actor. Constantin Stanislavski says, "Any role that does not include a real characterization will be poor, not lifelike, and the actor who cannot convey the character of the roles he plays is a poor and monotonous actor."[52] Every role is different and it is up to you to find out why.

---

52. Constantin Stanislavski, *An Actor's Handbook*, (New York: Theatre Art Books, 1994), 33.

Industry Connection

In this exercise the actors are asked to make very strong, clear, and specific choices. By the end of their sentences, we will want to know exactly what they mean and exactly what they want. When actors go for a professional audition, there is no time to be wishy-washy. No one is trying to strike up an in-depth conversation with them. They just want to get to the facts. If they are asked, "Where are you from?" then they are expected to give a straightforward answer, "I'm from Denver, Colorado." The actors do not need to give their whole life history at this point. Some actors believe the more they talk the better chance they will have. However, quite the opposite is true. Can you imagine a day in which the casting director has to audition one hundred and fifty people? Do you really think he has time for small talk and vague answers? It is up to the actors to sell themselves at the audition and be professional in every sense of the word. If they don't like the sound of being professional, then they can go get another profession, because they won't last five minutes in this one. Raise the following point with your actors:

INSTRUCTOR: If you audition for someone who is really chatty and wants you to delve deeper, then go ahead and do so. This is where the actor's ability to read each situation as a separate entity is very useful.

Note

You do not have to repeat my words verbatim. You may totally disagree on something I have said or feel it is not something that needs to be shared with your students. This is absolutely fine. I have never met your students. You are the one who knows exactly what they need at this precise moment. A good acting teacher or coach is able to diagnose and prescribe specifically for his students in the moment.

197. From Start to Finish

Have two actors come up into the performance area and perform a short improvisation. When they are finished, ask the audience if they would like to see more. If they say yes, ask them if they want to see what happened just before the scene began or what happened just after the scene ended. Have the actors follow through with the audience request. The audience is also able to say they do not want to see any more of the scene. If this is the case, they have to justify their decision. At least half the group has to also say they do or do not want to see anymore of the scene for it to be abandoned. This may happen if those acting in the scene are not compelling to the audience. Have other pairs or groups come up and perform scenes in the same way.

Purpose

To know what comes before

In this exercise the actors have to know what comes before. In a play, an actor may come on-stage from stage left. A novice actor may use this as his motivation for an entrance. It is the actors' responsibility to know where their character has just come from. Perhaps she has just come from telling the children a bedtime story. Perhaps the verbally abusive husband just came from the pub where he got drunk. When the actor leaves the stage, he also has to know where he is going. If the actor simply walks off into the wings, then this is exactly what the audience will read.

Industry Connection

Some actors believe the audition starts the moment they begin the scene. In fact, the audition starts the moment they enter the room. In fact, the scene starts before they enter the room. What is your character doing before he enters? Where is he coming from? A colleague of mine tells a story that goes one better. He said that a director happened to be looking out his window when he observed the actor getting out of a car. He cast the actor in his mind before he had even got in the room. The audition was over the moment he got out of the car!

198. Musical Chair Twister

Put out a circle of chairs just as you would for musical chairs. You will also need a stereo or an iPod hooked up to speakers. There should be one chair less than the number of students. Explain in the following way:

INSTRUCTOR: In a moment I would like you to start moving around the chairs, just like in musical chairs. I would like everyone to move in a clockwise direction. When the music stops, instead of sitting in the chairs, there is a twist to this game. What I would like you to do when the music stops is touch the chair with a body part. For instance, when the music stops I might say, "Your right hand." This means everyone must touch the chair with their right hand. The last person to do so is out. If you touch with a body part before one is even called out, you are also out.

DELILAH: What happens if two people are touching the same chair?

INSTRUCTOR: The rule is only one person per chair. The second person will have to find another chair, or they will be out. Each round, another chair will be removed. The body parts will also become more difficult. Later on I may say things like, "Put your bare left foot on the chair." I may say something like, "Take someone else's left thumb and place it on the chair." In this case, you would have to find someone who is already willing to help. If someone comes to you and you are already out, please participate willingly without resisting. Please do not bring someone over by their thumb as this could injure them. Put their thumb on the chair when you have brought them all the way over.

Purpose

To be able to react instantly

In order to remain in the game, the actors are going to have to be able to react on the spur of the moment. If they hear, "Put your left elbow on the chair" and they delay their reaction, by the time they go to put their elbow on a chair it will most likely be too late. When the audience goes to a play, they want to see the actors react to one another. They want to believe that there is an emotional attachment between the characters. By doing so, it appears to the audience that it is the first time the characters have said, heard, or thought the words that are spoken. This can only happen when the actors are able to trust in their own work. Often in a performance, audiences witness delayed reaction. The actors are not necessarily listening to each other, but going over their next lines. Another challenge may be that they have rehearsed the lines so many times their reaction comes out as stale and predictable. A preconditioned response does not always work, but neither is it always ineffective. In order for your actors to react in the moment, they are going to have to become functional actors. Your work with them should be leading them in this direction. In the movie *From Mao to Mozart,* Isaac Stern and his pianist chose not to use the piano that has been provided for them. This is not because they were trying to be difficult or rude, but because they wanted the audience to hear their music under the best possible conditions. An actor will want an audience to see his performance with the best possible instrument he can provide. He will want to recreate the textures of life. Some actors want everything for nothing, but they usually end up with nothing.

Industry Connection

In this game, so much is going on that it is easy to get lost. If twenty-five people are moving around the chairs, the situation is a form of organized chaos. When the body part is called out, semi-pandemonium follows. It is the actor who is able to keep a cool head who does well in this game. Living in the hustle of a big city, the actor is also living in a volatile environment. In New York, London, or LA, people are always rushing and running somewhere. While many actors do not have a set schedule, they are still running around getting tasks done. Some examples are: meeting with agents, picking up prints, going to the gym, taking acting class, going to an audition, going to their other jobs so that they can pay bills, going to the hairdresser, going clothes shopping, and so on. You may think some of the things such as shopping and getting hair done are not related to an actor's career. Remember that in a place such as Los Angeles, perceived image plays a part in whether an actor gets the role or not. With everyone rushing around, actors have to find a way to keep a cool head. By doing so, they will get more done and their journey will be a more beneficial one.

Note

Actors never know when something they do will lead somewhere else. It is Linda Gray's leg that was used in the original poster for the movie *The Graduate.* It was a modeling job. She actually went on to play the role of Mrs. Robinson a few years later. She also went on to play one of the leading roles in the TV series *Dallas. Dallas* is one of the most successful TV series of all time and was on our screens for thirteen years.

199. Moon Walk

Have your actors sit as the audience. Bring four actors into the performance area. Tell them that in a minute you would like them to improvise a scene. You can take some suggestions from the audience. The only catch is that any scene must involve a lot of potential movement. Let us use the example of visiting the zoo. Two of the actors can be the children and the other two can be the parents. The challenge for the actors is that this zoo is on the moon. They can talk at regular speed, but all their movements should be made as if gravity does not exist. This means their moves should be slower and larger as if they are virtually floating in air. Work this exercise with different groups of actors. We are not looking for a group of actors to come on-stage and pretend to be walking on the moon. Give them an everyday event or task to do, but it just happens to be taking place on the moon. Some other examples are: shopping at the mall, going to the local swimming pool, or taking a yoga class. If you want to give your actors something more static, such as having dinner at the table, this is OK, provided that the actors can integrate a good deal of movement. The connecting factor is that all the events are taking place on the moon. It is also important that the characters do not comment on the fact that they are on the moon. They live on the moon so this would be a redundant observation.

Purpose
To connect physically to the given circumstances
The characters may be visiting the park. We have all been to the park on many occasions. However, none of us has ever been to a park on the moon. The actors have to adapt their physicality to counter this. They have to take into account the lack of gravity in every action they make. They are going to need a good deal of understanding and control of their body. An actor may be in a scene in which his character is waking up from a deep sleep. The actor may choose to just jump straight out of bed, awake and alert. This is certainly a possibility and may be given to the actor as a directorial choice. The challenge is that often, when we wake up, we do so with a degree of disorientation. We are quite often slightly groggy and take a moment to get our bearings. Even if we jump out of bed, we tend to take a moment to gather our thoughts. What I mean by this is that there are physical reactions to just waking up that the actor has to be aware of and account for. If the actors ignore the fact that they are on the moon, the fact of being in the park will be inconsequential.

Industry Connection
I am going to talk about the bluntest and least tactful of potential industry connections for this activity — learning to follow direction! It sounds obvious, but so many actors struggle with this concept. They constantly want to show the director what they can do, instead of doing what the director is asking them to do. Great actors may listen to a director and find that the director's justification for doing a scene a certain way is illogical. They may nod as if in agreement, then carry on and create their own motivation, without ever discussing it with the director. Everybody ends up getting what they want. This is different from the actor who refuses to listen to what he is being asked to do. Another seasoned actor may also be asked to do something by a director that he feels is illogical. He may choose to take a moment with the director and make a suggestion as if it is the director's own suggestion. These actors listened intently to what their directors wanted and then found a way to do what was best for the scene. You are going to find that, on occasion, some of your actors will forget that they are on the moon and move around as if they are still on the Earth. Do not let this slide! You must draw this to their attention, highlighting the point for them. A number of potentially good actors will never actually become good actors, because they cannot, or will not, take direction.

200. Prop Explosion

You are going to need a wide variety of props for this exercise. Before the actors arrive, create a small scene such as a living room. You can do this with a few chairs and a table or two. Spread the props around the living room. I like to start this exercise by having only two actors who come into the performance space. Invite the audience to set the scene and the given circumstances: who, what, when, where. Instruct the actors to begin to improvise their scene. Tell them that there is one proviso. Explain the following:

INSTRUCTOR: Whenever you hear me call out "touch," both actors have to pick up a prop and use it in a justifiable fashion. Let us say you pick up a stapler from the table. You cannot just hold it. You have to do something with it. Perhaps you could then walk over to the table and staple some papers. Each of you has to pick up a prop as soon as you hear "touch." The other challenge is that you must find a way to integrate the prop into the scene. If you are in the middle of hugging your wife and you grab the stapler out of nowhere, how are you going to justify that?

BILLIE: How long do we have to hold on to the prop?

INSTRUCTOR: Good question. It can be five seconds or thirty seconds. Provided you do so convincingly, it doesn't matter. The only challenge is that as soon as you hear "touch," you are going to have to get rid of the prop convincingly and move onto another one.

If you find it works well with two actors, you can try the exercise with groups of three or four. Make sure you have enough props set out to cover this. Do not allow the actors to comment on their props. A crude example of this is if an actor says, "I am now going to brush my hair." You do not need the actors to state that fact. You want her to justify it through her actions. If we see an actor brushing her hair, the point has been made. It is for the actors to also know why they are brushing their hair at that precise moment.

Purpose
To work comfortably with props

Actors cannot necessarily work with props on-stage as they would in life. Let us say an actor has to take a box of matches out of his pocket and light a candle. In real life, he may fiddle about to find the matches and fluff around a bit to get a match. He may fail to light the match two or three times before eventually lighting the candle. You may say, "This is all great stuff! It would appear very real on-stage!" You are correct on both accounts. The challenge is that, unless the lighting of the candle is a significant act, it could detract from the important aspects of the scene. Perhaps the actor could have the matches planted within easy reach. Perhaps one match is already sticking out to save time. Stage reality is often not the same as actual reality — it doesn't need to be. If an actor is putting on a sock and the scene is not about the sock, then the actor will not want to make the scene about the sock. Encourage your actors to be comfortable working with props.

Industry Connection

Sometimes props are used in a television series, and sometimes they are avoided like the plague. This is because, unless the director feels that the actor can work well with props, they would rather avoid the headaches. For continuity purposes, the actor has to know on what line to pick up the prop and so on. The use of props goes much further than that. What if an actor has to pour a glass of water? What if he keeps spilling it, or clinking the glass against the jug, or dropping the water altogether? You may think that my suggestions are a tad silly. You may be right. On the other hand, under extreme pressure, to "get things right" the novice actor is more likely to get things wrong. When an actor makes a large number of mistakes, someone has to foot the bill. That person is not going to want to hire a clumsy actor again. Encourage your actors to become comfortable working with props.

201. Out There

For this activity, bring four actors into the performance space. Tell one of the actors to go outside the room. Follow him outside. Tell him that in a moment you would like him to start knocking at the door. Give him a specific scenario for why he is knocking at the door. Some possibilities are: someone in the house has won a great deal of money and you have come to give him the news, the family is behind on their bills and the bank is going to foreclose and repossess the house, you left your iPod in your friend's bedroom and you urgently want it back. The rest of the group is not informed of the scenario. Explain to the person outside that, even if no one answers the door, he is going to have to keep knocking. Go back inside and explain to the actors that someone is going to be knocking at the door. Tell them that they are not allowed to use any dialogue, yet they must react to the knocking. They must interpret what they believe the knocking means and follow through accordingly. The other challenge is that they are not able to actually open the door. They have to find a reason to justify this as well. Each actor will want to come up with his own interpretation of what the knock at the door actually means. He is going to have to persuade the rest of the group through his acting and convictions as to what is really going on behind the door. The fact that they are not opening the door does not mean it is an ominous situation. Perhaps one of the girls in the house decides she is a bridesmaid. The cake has just arrived and she is so excited that she cannot bring herself to immediately open the door. While the audience is also going to want to know the significance of the knock outside the door, this is not a guessing game. All the actors are asked to act out the scenario in a credible way. At the end of the exercise, you can have the person outside share why he was knocking and the actors inside can share who they thought was outside the door. I usually allow two or three minutes for this exercise. If the acting is compelling, I allow it to go on until it plays itself out.

Variation

In this scenario, tell the actors inside the room that at some point they are able to open the door, if they so choose, and the individual can come inside. The challenge is that if the person is a murderer or a debt collector, this would have been a bad choice.

Purpose

To apply the "as if" question

The purpose of this exercise falls under the guidance of some of Stanislavski's teachings. Dave Allen quotes Stanislavski in saying, "As if, acts as a lever, lifting us from the plane of reality into the world where it is possible to create."[53] The actors inside the room have no sure knowledge of who is knocking at the door. To make their decision, they are going to have to use their imaginations, based on the tone, urgency, and pace of the knock. When they believe they know who is knocking, they will react as if that individual is outside the door. Intellectually, an actor in a play knows that the king is really his friend and colleague. The character has to act "as if" this is the most revered and powerful person in the kingdom.

Industry Connection

If actors can use "as if" in terms of their characters, why can't they use the system in their own lives? I think it is possible for the actors to use "as if" to their advantage in terms of their career. Before going to an audition, an actor can use his imagination and visualization skills as if the part is already his. He can do the same things when looking for an agent, a manager, or attending a meeting with a studio. We tend to be experts at focusing on what we don't want, but mere novices when it comes to focusing on what we do want from any situation. Encourage your actors to put the majority of their focus into the solutions, and not the problems.

202. What's in the Bag?

You are going to need to do some preparation for this. You will need a large sack of some sort. Fill it with twenty or thirty objects. Some of the objects can be quite small and simple, like an elastic hair band. Other objects can be more complex, such as a pump-action soap dispenser. It is important that the objects do not spill over the top of the sack, nor should they be seen through the sack. Divide your actors into two teams. Have the teams decide the order in which they are to take turns at the exercise. Team one will send up a person who is going to put his hand in the sack. He is allowed up to five seconds to feel around, during which time he must pull an object out of the sack. His eyes must be closed the entire time. With his eyes still closed, he is given up to thirty seconds to guess the name of the object he is holding. He can guess as many times as he likes, within the thirty seconds. If he identifies the object, his team is given two points. There is to be no prompting or guidance from teammates. See if you have enough time for everyone to have a go. The team with the most points at the end is the winner.

Purpose

To utilize the senses

The actors are going to have to rely on their sense of touch. They have to feel the contours and shape of the object they are holding. They have to feel the weight and get a sense of the material it is made of. All these pieces of

---

53. David Allen, 122.

information are clues for the actor. An actor in a play may be using a plastic gun as a prop. A real gun is considerably heavier. The actor is going to have to portray this in the way he handles his fake gun. Another character may be holding a hot cup of coffee. In reality it may be freezing cold, but the senses of the actor must make it appear to be warm and comforting. Sometimes on television you will see an actor pretending to drink his coffee from a to-go cup. The challenge is that in reality the cup is empty. Watching the actor drink the coffee can be laughable if he is unable to engage his senses and employ vivid imagination.

Industry Connection

This exercise is about searching into the unknown. When actors put their hand into the sack, they have no idea what they will find. They may feel around for a few moments and then they must take the plunge. The actor's career is also about taking this leap of faith. Even the most confident of actors is never certain of what lies around the corner with regard to their career. They have to constantly put themselves out there and hope that their hard work will pay off. Actors can have a very good idea what an object is, but never be absolutely certain until they open their eyes. Because of the nature of the actors' work, they can never be quite certain where their next job is coming from. They have to trust that if they are doing all the right things the job is just around the corner.

Chapter 24
Releasing Inhibitions

203. Rapid Response

For this exercise you are going to need access to a stereo or iPod with a speaker hookup. This exercise is a great one to use on the students' first day of meeting each other. Have your actors spread out all over the room. When the music starts, have the players walk around at a brisk pace in different directions. As they do this they are to avoid making eye contact with anyone else. When the music stops, each player shakes hands with the nearest person. Give the actors twenty to thirty seconds to discover as much personal information about each other as possible. The process is then repeated. Each time the player must greet a new person. The exercise should continue until every person has met everyone else. If you have fifteen players, you will need to have fourteen rounds.

Variation

If the students already know each other quite well, then ask them to share something more specific. Perhaps they could share about a specific event or experience.

To take this exercise one step further, each time the actors stop, have them share a made-up story with their partner. They will be able to do this by utilizing their imaginations. They are developing an unlimited well of creativity. The actor must live in a vivid and imaginary world. Each time he comes across a new person he must share a new made-up story.

Purpose

To break down inhibitions

At this stage, many of the actors have never met before. By asking them to shake hands and talk to one another, the actors are breaking through personal barriers from the beginning. When they come to class next, they will have already spoken to, and made physical contact with, every member of the group. Actors do not have time to follow social etiquette and graces. Next week, you might be in a scene where you are playing husband and wife with a fellow actor. Actors have to learn how to get really comfortable with each other from the beginning. It has to reach a point where it is second nature for them as opposed to something they force themselves to do. Unnecessary tensions will come through in their performances.

Industry Connection

In this exercise the actors get to learn personal pieces of information about the other actors. Let's say an actor is writing a cover letter to an agent. Many actors write a letter that is standard, and not personal in any way. Let us say he decided to do a little bit of research. He jumped on the Internet and in minutes discovered that the agent he is writing to went to college in Seattle. The actor spent a month in Seattle and now uses this as a through line, "It is interesting to note that we have both spent some time in Seattle." Notice I didn't say "great city" because for all you know he may have disliked it. Nevertheless, if the actor is able to get a little personal, he is showing an agent that he is taking the time to get to know him. He has also shown that he is willing to go the extra mile. This in turn may be translated by the agent to mean he has a good work ethic. Actress Gay Storm gave me this advice to the actor, "Take your agent to lunch from time to time — that always helps." An actor has to be fantastic about research. An actor wants to do everything to stack the odds in his favor and set himself apart from the rest.

Note
Many sets have a wonderful craft service and buffet for their actors and crew. So at lunchtime the actors are taken completely out of any imaginary circumstances they have created and are brought back down to reality. They sit with the crew. They eat hamburgers, hot dogs, and cheesecake. They talk about politics, music, and traffic, and then they go back to filming a movie set in the eighteenth century. I hear it said time and again that with increased technology the actors' work is easier than ever — I beg to differ. With today's realities the actor has to be better trained, higher functioning, and more capable and able than ever before. I am talking about good acting, strong acting, and great acting. If you are thinking of something different, then we are not on the same page.

204. Location Change

Have one of your actors come forward and hand him a shirt and pants, or a skirt and blouse for a girl, and tell him that in a moment he is going to change into these items of clothing. Before he begins, set the location for him, in other words, where he is changing. For example: his bedroom, the changing room at a clothes store with a curtain, a public changing area in the gym, in the back of his car, in the park, the alley near a crowded street, a busy parking lot. You can discuss the location with the rest of the class. You can have the same actor, or you can change the actor for each of the scenarios. These locations are merely suggestions, so feel free to create your own, or have the actors create locations. Remind the actors that depending on their location, the way they may go about changing may be totally different. Changing in public places will be a totally different experience from changing in the privacy of their bedroom. The students are not being asked to get naked, but they are being asked to strip to their underwear in order to change clothing. This exercise is not going to be permissible in this form in all classrooms, so adapt the exercise. A junior high teacher is going to have to work differently from a high school teacher or a university teacher. Perhaps you could have the students strip to shorts and a T-shirt. No parents would object as this is what their children have to wear for any sports activity. In a performance actors have to, metaphorically speaking, learn to take their skin off.

Purpose
To release inhibition
In this exercise the actors are going to have to be specific. It is not enough to say, "I am changing at the gym." Is the gym busy? Do you have room to change? Is the person next to you naked and invading your personal space? Does the gym smell like stale feet? Do you have a personal locker? As the actor starts to raise these questions, the situation will begin to come alive for him and

for the audience. Actors have to be willing to live in front of their audience night after night. This exercise is also about throwing away inhibitions. The actors are asked to change clothes in the presence of their fellow actors. This is purposely done to see if there are actors who will refuse to do so. This is not being done for gratuitous reasons. Remember, the scene demands that the actor change his clothes. An actor should not wear clothes that do not serve the part. An actor has to be able to take his "emotional clothes" off in order to play a part. It is only then that he will be able to make the innermost discoveries in his work. Small children have no inhibitions and the actor must get back to this point.

Industry Connection

Let us say the scene is set in the bedroom, which just happens to be on the back lot of some studio. In the scene, the actor is changing in a personal and familiar space, but in reality there are seventy-five crew members and extras hovering around. It is his responsibility as an actor to create that intimacy and privacy for us. The actor has to know how to get into that place that is intimate so quickly. The actor may choose to take in everything from the cameras to the crew and then he can forget it. Set design and special effects can make the bedroom look nice, but only the actor can create the actual feeling of being in the bedroom. The audience will not say, "Of course he looked nervous, there were seventy-five crew members present!" They will most likely say, "I don't know what it is about that actor, but I didn't like his performance." They may not articulate it in actor terminology, but their gut tells them the same thing. If an actor is unwilling to undress to his underwear in front of his classmates at this stage, then perhaps he needs to consider whether he is looking for a professional or an amateur career. (It is understood that this exercise will be adapted accordingly for junior high students or younger.) There are some auditions given where actors may be asked to strip and they refuse to do so. If they can see no justification, if the production feels a little shady, then tell your students to go with their gut instinct. If, on the other hand, a famous director asks them to strip for a specific scene, it is most likely they have a valid reason for doing so. For most of your actors, this will be something that they will face down the road. This exercise gives them the opportunity to prepare for such a situation.

205. Therein Lies the Rub

Start by having your actors take off any extra layers of clothing, such as a jacket or pullover. They should now be wearing a single layer such as a T-shirt. Have your actors stand and form a tight circle so that they are able to comfortably put their hands on the shoulders of the person in front of them. If a very short person is standing behind a very tall person, you will want to adjust this. Have the actors gently massage the neck and shoulders of the person in front of them for about three minutes and then turn around and massage the person behind them. This should be done gently so as not to cause an injury to another student. The actors should still be in a tight circle except that now they are facing the other way. Now have the actors move around the room and as they do so, hug each person they come into contact with. As they are hugging, each actor must pay a genuine compliment to the other actor. An example is, "I like your radiant smile." Only when both actors have made their observations should they release each other from the embrace. If the second student takes a minute to respond, then the hug should last an entire minute. Allow this part to go on for a good five to seven minutes. Follow up with a group discussion.

Purpose
To break down inhibitions

This exercise fits under the concept of intimacy and confrontation. The actors have to be willing to touch and be touched. This might be uncomfortable for some of the actors, yet it needs to be second nature for them. Even standing very close in a circle might be invading their personal space and crossing boundaries, but again, this is something that as actors they are going to want to embrace. When they are hugging another actor, they are asked to hold the hug until both actors have paid each other a genuine compliment. This may be for a brief moment or, if one actor is taking time to come up with something really heartfelt, that hug may last a minute or so. The actors are being challenged to cross boundaries that many of us do not cross on a regular basis. A lot of the actor's training is considered antisocial behavior by the general population, yet for the actor, it is of great importance. Let us imagine you are putting on a play. In the play, two of the actors have to hug in a tender fashion. If they cannot get comfortable doing this in the exercise, how do they expect to do so with scores of eyes watching them on the stage? Some of your actors may be embarrassed or shy. They may prefer to hide in their own shell. They may only pretend to hug. You are doing them no favors by letting them do half an exercise. Half the exercise will only bring half the potential results.

Note

Not every exercise is necessarily appropriate for every group of students. It is up to you to know the potential benefits of each exercise with each group of students. Sometimes you may come across an exercise that you choose to skip over or work with down the road. You know your students better than anyone. It is up to you to decide what is of the most benefit to them. It is better to skip an exercise than to only half do it. On the other hand, there is nothing wrong with adapting an exercise to meet the needs of your students. If you were working with very young children, you might choose to have them shake hands rather than hug.

Industry Connection

Here are some lines of thought you may want to share with your actors:

INSTRUCTOR: A word you will hear a lot in the industry is *fake*. Everyone seems to say that everyone else is fake. I guess this does not apply to them personally. It is certainly worth being aware of the superficial stuff that goes around. This exercise asks you to pay a genuine compliment to a fellow actor. This is not always an easy thing to do, especially if you do not like them very much. Quite often, when an actor is newly arrived to Los Angeles, New York, or London, people say, "How refreshing. How nice. They're like a breath of fresh air." What they are saying is that these individuals have not yet been made bitter, or twisted, or angry, or jaded by the industry. They still have lightness to their being. They are open to the world around them and let opportunity come in. They are also saying they are green and innocent, and that they will have to adapt or be chewed up and spat back out. But if they are able to stay genuine and heartfelt one year, five years, or ten years after they arrive, then they will have something that many actors do not. Do this and casting agents and directors will still be saying, "I don't know what it is, but she is like a breath of fresh air." They are going to have to find their own way within the industry.

Your actors may not be going to London or New York for another five or ten years. It is worth reminding them that what is being commented on here will be as true in twenty years time as it is today.

206. Hands Down

Have your actors form a circle so that they are almost shoulder to shoulder. They should put their hands out in front of them, palms up, with all eight fingers and two thumbs showing. Go around the circle and have each member make a true statement. Have each statement begin with the phrase, "I have ... " Examples would be: I have two sisters, I have a bird, I have never lied before, I have stolen before, I have debt, I have become a vegetarian. Any time anyone in the group cannot identify with one of the statements, they have to drop a finger or thumb. The winner will be the last person to have a finger or thumb still up. No one should be out until he has answered "no" ten times. It is important to remind the actors to be truthful in their statements and their actions. The actors are not being asked to vocalize their answers. They simply respond by dropping their finger or not, depending on their response. I would suggest that when the statement is made, the whole group acts together, rather than going around and asking each person individually. Follow up with a discussion.

Prep your students as best you can before starting the exercise. There are certain topics that you are not going to want to raise in the classroom. For instance, if you are a junior high teacher, you do not want one of your students saying, "I have had sex before." This is an exercise that may not be suited to all your students. You are going to have to decide which groups can approach it in a mature fashion.

Purpose
To release inhibitions in the actor
This exercise is not for the fainthearted, because you do not know what statement each actor is going to make. Even though the actors are only revealing through a yes or no response, they are still revealing some information about themselves. This exercise forces the actor to face any inhibitions he may have. The inhibited actor will be very limited in the roles he can and cannot play. An actor must be uninhibited and not self-conscious. An actor's characters do not necessarily share his morals or his worldview. His classmates also probably have different morals and a different worldview as well. There are a number of occasions when actors will find themselves in unnatural scenarios. Actors have to learn to paint with a thicker brush and not see the world with a narrow view.

Industry Connection
If actors become successful, then it is most likely that they will be in the public eye. Reporters will ask them every possible question they can think of. They will dig up every piece of personal information they can find. The fans will demand to know everything from what cereal they eat for breakfast to what color of socks they wear. There are many actors who are very warm with their fans. They have

a personal magnetism that keeps their fans loyal and coming back for more. There are also many actors who guard their personal lives as much as possible. They shun publicity. This does not stop personal questions being asked of them. An actor has to be prepared for this reality, whether he likes it or not. In a sense the actor is public property. This is an important topic to raise in a class discussion. Successful actors never let anything get the best of them. They don't put up walls, but have learned how to take them down.

Note
This exercise can be like opening a can of worms. Before using it, look at the group of actors you are working with. Decide if you think it would be of benefit for them or not. Remember that there are many exercises to tackle inhibitions. If you do not use one, you can always use another.

207. Animal Magic
Have your actors take a seat in the audience. Have three actors come forward into the performance space. Two of the actors are going to be animals. The audience can choose the animals, but both actors should be the same animal. The other actor is going to be the host of this animal documentary. They are going to narrate everything that is happening. The narrator dictates the scene, rather than the animals. So if the narrator says, "Just look at the way one gorilla is cleaning the other one," then this is what we should see the actors doing. Other examples for a gorilla are: I love the way they enjoy jumping all over the place, look at the way that one puts its leg behind its neck with such ease, they really are rather messy eaters, the way they bang on their chest is quite amazing. The actors can be any animal chosen by the audience. Once the scene has run its course, change the narrator and the actors. There is obviously no talking for the animals, except animal talk. It is also important that the two actors do not look directly at the narrator. They should be actively listening, but the scene should never stop moving. There are no freeze frames in this scene. The narrator should also keep his distance so that the animals do not get frightened and run away. Finish up with a group discussion.

Purpose
To free the actor of inhibitions
Animals work so well because they allow the actors to free themselves of all inhibitions. If they do something a little wacky or crazy, they can blame it on the animal. Some characters' actions appear a little crazy, but for them the logic in their actions is absolutely cast-iron. Actors may be inhibited, but the characters they are playing may not be. In order to find the character, they have to be able to let go of preconceived ideas and anything that holds them back from making discoveries. This exercise will be fun and it will make the audience laugh. This is important, but what is more important is that the actors never fail to find the deeper meaning to the work. Every single acting exercise they do should have a purpose. It is up to you as the instructor to share it. It is then up to the actor to digest it.

Industry Connection

On-stage, the actor is left alone with his fellow actors. In film this is not necessarily the case. Once a scene begins, within about one minute the director will usually say "cut." At this point the actor will be surrounded with makeup, hair, wardrobe, and whoever else wants to join the party. Good actors have to actively listen to those around them while also actively blocking them out. There may be some work they need to do on the scene before the next take. With all the commotion and noise going on around them, they still have to find a way to work on the scene and move it forward. They have to actively listen to the inner voice of their character. In film, the audience is able to see behavior magnified. Some individuals say that, "Screen acting is such an easy medium." I would wager that these individuals have never been on a professional set.

Note

To be a grip on a set in Hollywood, London, Barcelona, Berlin, or New York, you have to be good at what you do. You have to be very good. Who you know might sometimes get you the job, but it won't keep you in the job. The pressures are so intense that you have to be at the top of your game. The same is true of makeup, hair, wardrobe, sound, camera operators, and everyone else involved. Think how many thousands of people are vying over so few jobs. If you are not the best at what you do, then why would they hire you? For some reason, a number of actors think differently. They feel this rule does not apply to them. Everyone around them is professional and yet they do not have to be. These are the actors who have short-lived careers — or none at all. Advise your actors to put all their effort into being the best that they can possibly be. Allow those around them to see them and know them as being a professional.

208. Musical Chairs Pandemonium

In a circle, set out enough chairs to allow one per student. Start the music. When the music stops, the actors have to find a chair just like in the normal version of musical chairs. Here is where this activity differs from the regular version: Play the music again and this time when the music stops, pull out one chair. The person who is left without a chair is not out. What they have to do is go and sit on someone's lap. No one is ever out! As you continue to take away chairs it is going to become very interesting. For instance, if you have twenty-five students with five chairs, there will be an average of five people per chair. If you like, you can keep going until there is only one chair left. At this point there will be true pandemonium. If you want to make it a little more challenging, you can tell the students that if someone falls off a chair everyone has to start again. I wouldn't suggest playing it this way at first. Please make sure this exercise is practiced with safety and caution. The aim is not to have your actors pass out!

Purpose

To have fun

The purpose of this exercise is to have fun. Again, there are many other benefits to this exercise, but it is important to highlight the aspect of fun. If an actor is not enjoying acting, why is he doing it? It is unlikely that he will be acting for very long if he gains no pleasure from it. This does not mean that he should take his role any less seriously. This does not mean that he should play around in the rehearsal process. It means that time should be set aside for the actors to laugh and let their hair down. I have a number of friends who have been involved in the field of acting between fifty and eighty-five years. They couldn't do this if they didn't love what they were doing. Actors will want to find a way to keep themselves excited throughout the process. As an instructor, part of your responsibility to your actors is to light the flame of passion for acting. The other part of this responsibility is theirs. As Marsh Cassady says, "At least one of the reasons people like the theatre is that it is enjoyable. Theatre is a way of pretending, and thus escaping from the everyday routine of chores and homework."[54]

Industry Connection

When you have three, four, five, or six people sitting on one chair, it is going to become uncomfortable, yet the actors have to find a way to do it anyway. Actors are often put into surroundings that are not so physically comfortable. Your actors may question whether this is true for the stars. Not as likely, but certainly when they are on location, it is highly possible. Even the stars have to rough it a little. A producer or director cannot always control the environment. Actors have to learn to adapt to environments that are not always comfortable. This is not talking about being in dangerous situations. No actor should be asked, or agree, to do that. If any of your actors ever work as background on a movie, even if it is just for one week, they will probably get a taste of being uncomfortable. They may have to meet in a holding area outside, in the freezing cold, at four in the morning. This is by no means uncommon. There is money, timelines, and the pressure to get it done. There are actors who are prima donnas, but unless they bring in an enormous amount at the box office, there are few who have longevity in their careers.

209. Roll Over

For this exercise, have your actors lie on the floor so that they are shoulder to shoulder and hip to hip. Have them put their arms straight back, past their ears and settling on the floor. The actors now should be close together like a tin of sardines. No actor should be wearing shoes or sharp objects such as rings, belts, jewelry, or earrings for this exercise. Obviously, no one should have gum or candy in their mouth, which should be the same rule for all workshops — except sometimes for character work. In a moment, the actor to the far left is going to roll over the other actors and end up to the far right at the end of the line. He needs to do this slowly and carefully. Make sure you have enough space for this exercise. If need be, split your actors into two or three groups and watch one group work at a time. It is a good idea to have one or two actors stand up and be helpers, just in case someone veers totally off course or gets himself in a bit of a pickle. If actors are extremely overweight or just too muscular, you may have them sit out of this exercise. Perhaps they can be the helpers. This is not to be prejudiced, but for safety precautions, which should always be at the top of your agenda. When you are finished, have the group discuss its discoveries from the exercise. You may want to play more than one round.

---

54. Marsh Cassady, *The Theatre and You* (Colorado Springs, Colorado: Meriwether Publishing Ltd., 1992), 7.

Purpose

To break down inhibitions

This exercise is another great one for immediately breaking down boundaries and inhibitions. It also forces the actors to confront personal space issues they might have. The actors have no choice but to adapt, because they are lying side by side touching the actors to their left and right, whether they like it or not. When they roll over their fellow actors, they are now going to have to deal with more boundary issues they may have. A man rolling over another man or a woman rolling over a man may feel a little uncomfortable. This is not for sexual pleasure, so the actors must focus within the context of the exercise itself. There are also safety issues in that even though it is a challenge, each actor must still be spatially aware of his immediate surroundings. An actor will never want to get too comfortable in a performance.

As has been mentioned many times in this book, actors have to be able to break down personal boundaries very quickly.

Industry Connection

Being put in compromising situations is a given for just about all actors. It is their career, so they have to decide what they will and won't do. If it is a low-budget film, then an actress might choose not to take her top off. If it is a multi-million-dollar movie with top actors and an Oscar-winning director, and she has a sizable role, she might think differently. If there is no justification for it she still may refuse to do it. There is no right or wrong answer here, because each specific scenario will call for a different response. It is the actors' responsibility to decide what is wrong and right, acceptable and not, justifiable and not, for their career. The challenge comes when even though they know something is the right choice and yet they are too inhibited to act it with any believability. Actors have to be able to let themselves go. Through exercises such as this, the actors are going to find ways to break down barriers and inhibitions. By doing so, they will be more able to freely reveal themselves to the audience. In a performance there should be something happening that the audience is aware of. It is more important than what is being said and creates the conflict and the drama. In this respect, some characters are formidable advisories. The actor is able to give the audience a glimpse into the actor's imaginary world. The audience would love to tell the actor, "Surprise me, impress me, move me."

Chapter 25
Mime

210. Mirror Ensemble

Start by having your actors line up in two rows, A and B. The rows should be facing one another and the actors in each row should be standing opposite another actor. Both rows need to have an even number of actors. Explain the following:

INSTRUCTOR: What I would like you to do is join hands with the actors on your left and right. This means all actors in row A should be holding hands and all actors in row B should also be holding hands. What is going to happen now is row B is going to start some very slow movements from the waste up and row A is going to mirror them. There is no leader. This should be done in a slow, smooth, and continuous fashion. The actors in row A must mirror exactly what the actor opposite them in row B is doing. I mention this because not everyone in row B will be doing exactly the same thing. This is going to add to the challenge of mirroring your partner. Each of you must stay connected and keep hand contact with your neighbors at all times.

After a few minutes, switch out and let row A become the leaders. At this point, tell them they can engage the whole body, but that they are not able to move around the room. For this exercise to work, actors have to move slowly, without sudden, impulsive moves.

Purpose
To work as a unit
This exercise helps the actors stay connected to the group. Actors might want to move in one direction, but they will also have to take into account what the actor on their left and right wants to do. Actors may only be responsible for their own performance, but they can affect and influence the performance of others. There is a famous saying in acting that says "infect your partner." The strength of an actor's performance can literally infect other actors to raise theirs. It can cause them to have a visceral reaction. By being sensitive and aware of what is happening around them, actors will be able to adjust their performance accordingly. To move people and make them feel something is an intimate dance the actor must have with the audience. Each actor should ask himself, "Who did I touch in that scene?" It is also worth noting that no two audiences are exactly alike. In a good performance the sensitivity is so strong. This exercise demands sensitivity and total awareness.

Industry Connection
Have a discussion along the following lines with your actors:
INSTRUCTOR: In this exercise, you may want to go in one direction, but the actor next to you wants to move in another. It becomes an exercise in give-and-take. Your acting career is also one of give-and-take. You may want to move forward in one direction, but your agent or manager want to take you in another. You want to work on one scene, but your acting coach would prefer you to work on another. You audition for one part, but the casting director asks you to read

for another. You never know how this is all going to unfold. There will be a number of times in your acting career when you are moving in one direction, only to find you have to start moving in another. It is not necessarily a bad thing or a contradiction. Rather, it is the nature of the beast. It is the choices good actors make that sets them apart from the rest. As Michael Shurtleff says in his book, *Audition*, "You don't have to fit the actions to the words in the audition situation the way you do in performing. Like an improvisation, impulses may occur that conflict with the words at hand. Go ahead, do the action, trust your impulse. Don't wait for the right moment. He who waits never gets there. Do it now, when you feel it."[55]

211. Morphing Ball

For this exercise, have your actors stand in a circle. An imaginary ball is passed around the circle. As the ball is passed from one actor to the other, it gets heavier and heavier. The actors can show this through the way they bend their knees, how the weight pulls them down, and so on. If an actor is not convincing, have him do it again. You are working with aspiring or professional actors, so you are doing them no favors if you let bad or unconvincing acting go unnoticed. Once the ball has gone once around the circle have it morph in different ways. Examples are the ball gets: lighter, smaller, bigger, stickier, hotter, smellier.

Purpose

To utilize the imagination

The actors have to utilize their imaginations for this exercise. To start with, the ball does not really exist. Only their imaginations can bring it to life, much like when actors are in a play in which their character has a sword. The sword came from the toy store and is made of plastic. It is only through the actors' imagination and the way that they are able to endow it that it becomes a lethal weapon. If the actors cannot create in their imagination, then the audience cannot create in theirs. It is like a dance going back and forth between the actor and the audience. If actors do not invite the audience to the dance, they will not come. It is said that a ballerina's work is never done, and is much the same way an actor's work is never done. I am talking about good actors, fine actors, and great actors.

Industry Connection

The ball does not go from light to heavy in one fell swoop. It has to go all the way around the circle in order to get heavier and heavier. Just like the ball, an acting career is highly unlikely to explode overnight. In all likelihood it will grow in small stages. Sometimes it will feel like taking one step backwards in order to take two steps forward. If actors always stay on task, stay goal-driven, enjoy the journey, and continue to work hard, then they will continue to take steps in the right direction. Make the following observations with your actors:

INSTRUCTOR: Just as in this exercise, look for the small increments that take you toward the end goal. The funny thing about end goals is once we reach one, another one always pops up in its place.

---

55. Michael Shurtleff, *Audition* (New York: Bantam Book, 1978), 181.

212. The Sounds of Music

For this exercise, bring in a selection of different styles of music. You might bring in some classical music and some might be heavy rock. It is preferable that there are no words in any of the music. Select between two and four actors to come into the performance space and explain in the following way:

INSTRUCTOR: In a moment I would like you to improvise a scene together. You are going to have to mime this scene. I am not going to give you a setting or tell you who your characters are. We are going to let the music decide. What I would like you to do is act according to the music. If the music is light and wistful, then perhaps this is a soft and tender moment in your scene. If the music is loud and abrasive, then perhaps there is some sort of argument taking place. Do not stop and start the scene. You need to keep it moving as one continuous scene while adapting to whatever is happening in the music. Characters are not discussed at the beginning. That means that during the scene you are also going to have to adapt to whom you think each actor is portraying. You should have a good indication of this through their actions and behaviors. You are not supposed to be up there playing yourself, but you need to have a definite character in mind.

Another way to do this exercise is to set the scene and give each actor his characters. Work this exercise both ways for full effect. Finish up with a group discussion. Group discussions do not have to come at the end of an exercise, but can happen at any stage where you feel it is necessary.

Purpose

To work with mime skills

In this exercise, the actors have to mime the entire scene. This means they can only communicate via nonverbal communication. They are going to have to express themselves through the action of the scene rather than the words. In a play, they might pick up a pot of tea and mime pouring it into a cup. The pot is empty and yet they have to make it appear that it is full of tea. There are a number of considerations that the actor has to make here. For instance, if the pot is full of tea, then the weight of the pot will be different from one that is empty. If the tea is hot, then the actor will have to poor it cautiously into the cup, so as not to get burned. Through their imaginations and sensory awareness, the actors can make the audience believe they are pouring a cup of tea. Have your actors ignite their imaginations so that the audience can ignite theirs.

Industry Connection

In this exercise, the actors do not know what is going to happen in the music. They have to constantly adapt their actions and the scene to apply to the music. Actors also have to constantly adapt their acting career. With all the best intentions and planning in the world, an acting career could turn on a dime overnight. The actor who is most likely to succeed is not necessarily the actor who has planned the most. It is the actor who is able to adapt to any situation as it arises. If a crisis arises, this actor will calmly adapt to the situation, deal with it, and move on. Another will virtually have a nervous breakdown and waste all of his energy in a direction that is of no use to him. Success is not a one-way street. It is an ever-flowing and continuous journey. Part of your actors' success comes from their ability to adapt in any given moment.

Note

There are hundreds of exercises and activities included in this material. You might say, "The actor does not need hundreds of exercises to be a good actor." To this, I would say you are correct. The actor does not need hundreds of exercise, rather just a handful of good ones. However, provided the exercises are working on the actors' instrument, then hundreds of good ones can be of great benefit. There isn't only one exercise to work the bicep in the gym, and yet some people will do only one exercise their entire life. A good personal trainer can show you numerous ways to work the bicep. The other thing to be aware of is that the bicep has different parts of the muscle that need to be hit. To work the bicep effectively, you have to engage different bicep exercises. This is also true in knowing how to continually shock the muscle. You may have used one exercise all your life to work your concentration muscle. This is fine, and yet there are different elements that make up concentration that can be approached in different ways. Is it better to have one good exercise or ten good exercises? It is up to each individual actor to decide what works for him. If you are deciding intellectually, without actually experiencing exercises, then your argument becomes futile. However, it is also worth remembering that one good exercise is infinitely better than ten bad ones.

213. Nonverbal Party

Have your actors bring food and games and have a class party. The difference is that the entire party should be nonverbal. Not one word should be spoken between the actors the entire time. They should play games together. They can eat food and mill about the room socializing. They can converse nonverbally with other actors in the room. This should be like a regular party, except that there is absolutely no verbal communication. This is from the moment they enter the room until the moment the party is over. This should be followed up by a discussion. If your class is short on time, save the discussion until you next get together.

Purpose

To utilize nonverbal communication skills

This exercise is all about utilizing nonverbal communication skills. In a way, it will feel like a performance, except for the fact that the party is real. Perhaps you can have this party before Christmas or the New Year. In every performance an actor will give, they will know that it is not a real setting. However, his character should not. If his character does not believe he is by a lake instead of on-stage, then neither will the audience. For technical reasons, such as to avoid falling off the stage, the actor must know he is in a world of make-believe. However, the character lives in a very real world, where everything is happening at that precise moment in time.

Industry Connection

Raise the following points with your actors:

INSTRUCTOR: Most of your communication at an audition is nonverbal. You may think this was not the case at auditions you have attended because of the amount of dialogue that occurred. The dialogue was the superficial part. What was said beneath the surface was far more powerful than verbal language will ever be. There was a communication dance that took place between you and those at the audition, whether you realized it or not. It is up to the actor to become an expert in nonverbal communication skills.

214. Charade Twister

Tell everyone to take out a small piece of paper, or provide some. They will want to cut their piece of paper into three pieces. On one piece of paper, they should write down the name of a famous person whom everyone will know. On the second piece of paper, tell them to write down a well-known destination, such as the Eiffel Tower, Buckingham Palace, or Yellowstone National Park. On the third piece of paper, ask them to write the name of an occupation, such as a vet or a musician. Instruct the actors to fold up their three pieces of paper, remembering which is which. Go around the room and collect the papers separately and put them into three hats, buckets, or containers. At this point, divide the group into two teams. Have the teams play so that all the normal rules of charades apply, but with a slight twist: Instead of having only one sentence to look at, the actors have to pick a piece of paper from each hat. They should end up with a famous person, a location, and an occupation. This means that an actor may have to act out Harry Potter, the White House, and a gardener. The actor who is going to have to portray Harry Potter works at the White House as a gardener. If team one goes first, they will send their actor up first. Team one will have two minutes to guess the correct answers. If they get them right in under a minute, they get five points. If they get them right in less than two minutes, they get three points. If they do not discover the answers, team two will be given one guess to obtain three points. Remember that the actor must mime the whole thing without any words being spoken. I have not set out the rules of charades here, but if you do not know them, I guarantee that most of your students will. You can play for a certain amount of time or until the winning team has reached a certain number of points.

Purpose
To communicate in a clear and concise fashion
In this activity the actors have to be able to communicate clearly. They cannot speak and so they have to send direct forms of nonverbal communication. They also have to work in a concise fashion. They are not trying to communicate one thought, but three separate ones. For instance, in the example given above, if the audience guesses that the famous person is Harry Potter, that success does not help them realize that he is a gardener. The actor will either have to combine the three thoughts together, or work efficiently at moving from one clue to the next. He will have to move rapidly between thoughts. In a play, an actor has to communicate his thoughts the first time around. He cannot go back and do another take if he feels he failed to communicate part of the story. The nonverbal communication a character uses is as important, if not more important, than anything he could have to say.

Industry Connection

The teams have more clues than they might think. Between the teams, they have recorded every possible scenario that could come up. To ignore this important fact will make their task harder. When actors are auditioning in Los Angeles, there are certain pieces of information that they already have. If they have done their research, they may have some information about the casting director. Looks do matter. Parts are usually cast according to type. This does not mean they have to be the best looking. It means that they have to create the image that the casting director is looking for. The good news is that the casting director does not always know what he is looking for until he sees it. If the actors ignore this important concept, they will be putting themselves at a disadvantage.

215. Boxed In

This exercise is very popular in mime-based classes. Have your actors sit as the audience. Bring one actor into the performance space. Tell him that he is trapped in a big box, six feet by six feet, high enough for him to stand up in. His aim is to break out of the box. The challenge is that as time passes, the box starts shrinking. The actor has a number of objectives:

1. To escape from the box
2. To show the audience how he escaped from the box
3. To mime the scene
4. To clearly show the different stages of the box getting smaller and smaller as he is trapped inside

This is a lot for the actor to take on. If an actor cannot justify escaping from the box, he should not escape. Change the actor to allow different actors to take a turn.

Purpose

To work with numerous objectives

One of the actors' objectives is to escape from the box. This is obviously their main objective. However, it is not their only one. They also have to show the audience that the box is getting smaller. If the audience does not see it, they will not believe that the box has changed size in any way. In a play, some actors fall into the trap of one objective. It is true that their character may have one *main* objective, but there will be many smaller objectives to help them achieve this. For instance, let us say Bob wants to marry Marissa. Let us say that this is his main objective. To reach this goal, Bob comes up with a lesser objective, which is to become wealthy. He figures that if he has money, Marissa's family will give him their blessing. The actors will want to consider the many smaller objectives that get them to their main aim.

Industry Connection

The actors are virtually boxed in. They have to find a way to break out of the box before it crushes them. This is a fairly dramatic way of putting it, but some actors feel they are trapped inside the industry. They want to act, but they have to make money to pay their bills, get headshots, take classes, buy clothes, create a demo reel, and so on. Some actors say they feel trapped for years in an industry that does not reward them. It seems that to live in a world in which a person feels trapped cannot be fulfilling in any way. It is up to the actor to reframe the world in which they live so that it becomes more acceptable to them. A person who is trapped is being held against his will. Actors living in Los Angeles, London, or New York have not been forced to go there or stay there. They are there of their own free will. The glorious thing about being actors is that they are able to do everything and anything. They will have to learn to embrace their journey or find something else to do with their lives.

216. In a Word

This exercise is in my book, *Acting Games for Individual Performers*. It has been adapted here for group work. Tell the actors to sit as the audience. One actor should come into the performance space. Explain in the following way:

INSTRUCTOR: I want you to choose a word that, in a moment, you will act out in pantomime style, without speech or voice. Some examples of words are: America, statue, greed, poverty, freedom, or adolescence. Your task is not to simply define your word in a literal sense, but to explore its wider meaning. For example, if you were going to explore the word *America,* you might create a scene of someone rushing to get dressed, rushing to eat breakfast, rushing to get in his car, rushing to get to work, rushing to get into his office. Finally, when he makes it to his office, he puts his feet up on the desk and twiddles his thumbs in boredom. At first glance, this activity appears to be a simple one, yet to define the greater meaning of your chosen word is going to be a more complex task. You do not need to tell us your chosen word ahead of time.

Once the actor has finished, ask the audience to discuss which word they believe the actor was portraying. They will want to offer specific reasons for their observations. Let different actors come up and work with the meaning of different words of their choice. These scenes are not thirty seconds long, but should last three to five minutes. Remind your actors that they need to portray the bigger picture of the meaning behind the word.

Raise the following questions to your actors: Why did you choose that particular word to interpret? Did your scene really explore your chosen word in its entirety? Because you had an audience, were you more tempted to make the scene entertaining? Why did you choose to interpret the word in that way?

Make sure you feel the actors can justify their answers. Take time out of an exercise to delve in the discussion portion. While it is true that "acting is in the doing," it is equally true that for the doing to have any value, it needs to be explored through the discussion process. Encourage your actors to start "doing" things and not just showing them.

Purpose

To find the deeper meaning of the words given by the writer

What is it that the writer wants to say? What are the messages he is attempting to get across? I like to give the actor this activity with just one word because it can make a far-reaching point. If one word can have so much meaning, and so much depth, and have so much to say, then it becomes impossible to look at a script without attempting to find the deeper meaning behind the words. As Hamlet said, "Speak the speech, I pray you, as I pronounced it to you, trippingly on the tongue."[56] If actors do not know the meaning of a word or understand its background, how are they going to be able to interpret a word the way it is intended to be used? I will be the first to admit that there are a number of poorly written scripts that offer the actor very little to work with. However, this activity plants a seed suggesting that words are not just words, but have a deeper meaning when fully explored.

Industry Connection

If you took the word *freedom* and had two people interpret it in a scene, you would end up with two different scenes. One person might interpret freedom by recreating a scene from a slave ship, breaking free from his shackles, jumping off the boat, and finally being free from the shackles that bound him. Another person might create a scene of a rich woman driving a beautiful Mercedes Benz while stroking her chinchilla fur and sipping chilled bottled water. Both scenes are legitimate, yet they represent vastly different interpretations of the word *freedom*. Actors pursuing their career use words to describe their lives on a constant basis. They say things like: it's tough, I'm barely surviving, I'm hanging in there, I can't get a decent break, or there's just no work. These are the out-of-work actors who get what they focus on. There are other actors who say: I'm getting there; things are moving in the right direction; life is an adventure; or the harder I work, the luckier I become. These are the actors who are more likely to succeed. It is important to realize that our interpretation of the words we use in our daily lives is only constrained by the limitation we put upon them. Each actor will want to aim to find freedom in every character they play.

---

56. William Shakespeare, *The Complete Works of William Shakespeare* (London: Abbey Library, 1978), 863. Hamlet, Act III Scene II/1.

Chapter 26
Motor Skills

217. Eye Tag

Bring two actors forward to work on this exercise. They will already need to have a memorized scene prepared. Have the rest of the students sit as the audience. Have your actors work on their scene much as in the Don't Blink exercise, but this time have them lead with one eye. Remind the actors that they are performing this scene as if it is for a close-up camera shot. This means that whichever eye leads, they need to stay with that eye and not change focus. They have to hold the other actor's attention but cannot change eyes or change focus. If they are working opposite a partner, have them work close together.

Variation

You may want to take this to a more specific level. If an actor is talking to another actor and you tell him that the camera is over the left shoulder of the other actor, the actor facing the camera should lead with his left eye looking at the other actor's left eye. This is because it will bring his face around to the lens in a strong position. If the camera is over the right shoulder, then just reverse everything to the right eye. I would recommend bringing in the Michael Caine series, *Michael Caine Acting in Film*. It is also available to watch online if you prefer your students to see it that way. If you have a camera you may want to film your actors so they can see for themselves the results.

Purpose
To explore technical aspects of acting

This is purely a technical exercise. Your actors are not going to be given a motivation for why they are leading with one eye, but they may certainly find one. Speaking clearly and being understood is also a common demand of actors for which they will be given little praise. It is the technical aspects of your actors' work that will give them the freedom to go in any direction they choose. I have heard world-famous actors say that technique counts for nothing, while in the same breath talk with a beautiful, clear, and resonated voice. They know how their body feeds itself oxygen. This may be a technical exercise, but if your actors can master it, they may appear to be a stronger actor to the audience. As the famous actor and director Michael Chekhov says, "I worked with Stanislavski, Nemirovich-Danchenko, Vachtangov, and Sulerjitsky. In my capacity as actor, director, teacher, and finally, head of the second Moscow Art Theatre, I was able to develop my methods of directing and formulate them into a definite technique."[57] If an audience is unfocused, it is never, ever their fault. It is always the responsibility of the actor to hold the audience's attention.

---

57. Michael Chekhov, *To the Actor* (London: Routledge, 1953), Introduction.

Industry Connection

Michael Caine says, "When you are the on-camera actor in a close-up, never shift your focus from one eye to the other. During a close-up, be especially careful not to change which eye you are leading with."[58] This exercise applies quite specifically to close-up camera work. He goes on to point out that it is the close-ups that will eventually sell the actor in the movie. This is powerful information for your actors to be aware of. It will probably not be that much use to them for a Broadway show. It is important for your actors to know what they will use and where and how it is applicable to the job at hand. Let us say they are shifting their eyes from one to the other, it is unlikely that the director will correct it. He may do a few more takes. He may just accept what he's got and edit around it. The reason is he has so many things going on and he may not be paying attention to the acting in the same way a theatre director may. This is why the demands for the actors are very high and they must be prepared. Some directors will use every trick imaginable to get what they want. They know film grammar and they know how to tell a story. A film is like a patchwork quilt that has to be stitched together scene by scene. A good editor will edit first and foremost for the performance. A film is little tiny pieces on mosaic that are spliced together. It is creating a moment to propel another moment. It's these moments that every actor wants. It is better to have had them than to have played it safe. If actors are being immortalized on the silver screen, let's hope it is work they can be proud of. A theatre performance is for one night only. A movie performance lasts forever!

218. Cat and Mouse

This is a children's game. Have your actors sit in a circle, but leave a small space between each one. Choose one actor to stand at the outside of the circle. He is going to go around the circle quite fast in a clockwise direction and tap each actor on the head as he passes them. Each time he taps an actor on the head, he will say "mouse." When he feels inclined, he will tap one actor on the head and say "cat." At this point, the actor who is tapped will jump up and chase the other actor (mouse) once around the circle. The mouse is going to try to get all the way around the circle and back to the open space and sit down before he is caught by the cat. If he can do this, you will now have a new mouse. If the mouse is caught by the cat, the activity continues as before. The reason you want a little space in between each actor is so that the cat can jump up at any moment without injuring another actor. It is also important that the cat and mouse run clockwise around the circle and not start chasing each other around the room. They also need to be spatially aware so that they are not colliding with all the other actors sitting in the circle. It is not fun to get kicked in the back. If you feel this exercise is too dangerous, adjust the rules so that the cat and mouse can only walk around the circle at a fast pace and not run.

---

58. Michael Caine, 59.

Purpose

To help the actor become more coordinated

In order for the cat to catch the mouse, he is going to have to be fast, athletic, coordinated, and agile. To be a good actor, it is not necessary to be fast, but it is important to be coordinated. There are two-hundred-and-fifty-pound actors who tower above us, yet they can move with grace and finesse. They have worked their instrument so much that it has become muscle memory. They have developed a coordinated instrument and now have the ability to manipulate it into any direction they choose. If actors slump their shoulders out of habit and bad posture, that is their choice. The challenge is that it is not necessarily the choice of their character. Just because the actors have bad posture does not mean it has anything to do with the breeding of the part they are playing. The challenge is that unless they work on their physical body, they will have no real control over it whatsoever. They will be completely at its whim, and all the characters they play can potentially become one generic blur. Have your actors have a discussion about well-known actors who they feel are, "Exactly the same in every role." Then ask them to talk about actors who they feel are able to, "Transform themselves in every role they play." Ask them to discuss their convictions and what enables these possibilities to arise.

Industry Connection

Explain the industry connection to your actors in the following way:

INSTRUCTOR: This activity is a great metaphor for an acting career. It says that if you are not careful, you are going to spend your time running around in circles. Even if you run very fast and very hard, if you are not careful, you will still be running around in circles and ending up back in the same place. A cat or a dog may enjoy playing the game of trying to catch its own tail. Unfortunately, a number of actors will spend their short-lived careers doing the same thing. They need to take a note out of the mouse's toolbox. You are going to have to plan your career. You are going to have to be highly adaptable to the challenges that will come your way. In *Artaud for Beginners,* Gabriela Stoppelman makes reference to a performance by Artaud. "At the end of this memorable event, the audience remained silent. They had been in the presence of a man who had been brutally beaten but was not yet burned out from his pain and suffering. Artaud had extracted a vital force that paralyzed his audience."[59] In Artaud's performance, his audience could almost hear the sound of his pain. You are going to have to be tough, resilient, smart, and savvy to stand even a chance of making your living as an actor. You will want to embrace all of these things because you are choosing to follow your passions and do what you want with your life. Most people will never get to do or say that, but the catch is it's going to come with a price. There is only one journey, and that is your journey. You want to fully experience the journey of the actor. Good actors take us on an emotional journey in such a compelling way. Your path is the right path, if you learn to adjust and adapt to every challenge and opportunity that comes your way. If you don't, you will simply be running around in circles chasing your tail.

---

59. Gabriela Stoppelman, *Artaud for Beginners* (New York: Writers and Readers Publishing, 1998), 140.

Note

You may be asking yourself the question as to why children's games are being played in an acting class. It is important to remember that a game can be turned into an advanced exercise depending on the approach it is given. The more experience and knowledge you and your actors have, the more advanced the exercise can then become. It is also worth remembering that children hold the key to some of the most important tools an actor can have. A couple of examples are vivid imaginations and few or no inhibitions. Imagine how much more productive companies would be if the employees were compelled to play games together for ten or fifteen minutes every morning before beginning their work?

219. One Knee

For this exercise, have your actors find a partner and find their own space in the room. Each pair should face each other and stand about four or five feet apart. Each pair will need a ball — tennis ball or juggling ball. Explain in the following way:

INSTRUCTOR: In a moment you are going to play a game of catch with your partner. There are a number of rules you must follow. Here is what you must do if you drop the ball:

First time: one arm behind back

Two times in a row: one arm behind back and kneel on one knee

Three times in a row: one arm behind back and kneel on both knees

Four times in a row: one arm behind back and sit on floor

Five times in a row: one arm behind back and lie on your belly on the floor

Six times in a row: both arms behind back and lie on your belly on the floor — you're out!

The interesting part of this exercise is that you can redeem yourself. If you drop the ball, you now have one arm behind your back. If the next round you catch the ball, you can now go back to using both arms. If you are down on both knees, and the next round you catch the ball, you can then go back to being on one knee. In theory, this activity can go on forever. Please remember that you are surrounded by other teams who are also playing this game. This is going to add to the complexities and challenges of this activity. You can begin when you are ready.

If your actors appear confused, then you can start off with a brief demonstration. After awhile, have the actors work with a new partner.

Purpose

To enhance motor skills

In this exercise the actors have the opportunity to enhance their motor skills. Their hand-eye coordination becomes a key factor in order for them to stay competitive. During a scene, you might have to do many things that involve hand-eye coordination. Some examples are: pouring a cup of coffee, ironing a shirt, tying a shoelace, counting out some money, putting a necklace on. In real life, an individual might fumble with a necklace and drop it. In the play, the actor's character is supposed to put it on his wife the first time as it rekindles their romance. The pressure to "get it right" has just been intensified. The actor has to have enhanced motor skills in order to cope with the demands put upon him.

Industry Connection

Let's talk for a moment about the pragmatic approach to putting on the necklace. I saw a movie star who had to put on her own necklace. She could not do it without fumbling. She demanded that the director "do something." So what the director did was film the shot of her taking the necklace off. In the next shot she already had the necklace on. If you are a movie star, you can make these demands. If you are not, then you better know how to put that necklace on in one take!

Note

Some actors die an untimely death at such a young age. Had they lived they may have become such big stars. In these premature cases it is possible that their best work was yet to come.

220. Circle of Hands

Have your actors sit in a circle and explain in the following way:

INSTRUCTOR: I would like you to start by crossing your arms with the person sitting on either side of you. Both of your hands should now be overlapped with two other people. Both of you should also have your hands palms down on the ground. In a moment, we are going to go around the circle and each hand in turn must tap the ground. If one of the hands misses its turn, that hand is out. If your hand is out, then it must be removed from the circle. You will still have one hand left in. The person with the last hand left in is the winner.

You may never get down to just one hand, so use your judgment as when to stop. If the actors are finding this exercise too easy, have them speed up the hand tapping. It may be the case to where you have your actors tapping at a rapid pace. If they find it too difficult, then you can slow down the pace. You can also choose to switch from clockwise to counterclockwise at any moment to confuse the actors.

Purpose

To develop motor skills

In this exercise the actors have to use their hand-eye coordination. It is challenging in that they can become confused as to whose hand is whose. Actors who are involved in a stage fight have to become experts on hand-eye coordination. They have to appear to hit the other person when, in fact, they are sometimes only hitting through the air. An actor has to become a master of his own body, but also has to be sensitive to his surroundings.

Industry Connection

Raise the following discussion points with your actors:

INSTRUCTOR: In this exercise, looks can be deceiving. You can think it is your turn because your hand is overlapped. The fact is that another actor has to tap his hand first. The industry you are in can also be deceiving. You will meet a number of people who will appear friendly and kind. This may be their initial approach. You will shortly discover that a number of them want something from you. It may be your money, your connections, or what they believe you can do for them. They will come in the form of other actors, agents, directors, casting agents, producers, grips, and a whole array of others who have nothing to do with the industry. Unfortunately, the deceiving aspect of the industry is a very real one. Now that you know this, you can guard against it at all times.

Note

I want to clarify this a little bit further. It is commonly accepted that in Hollywood, New York, and London most of the aspiring actors are out of work. It is also the case that there are workshops galore offered to these actors to become the next star. The statistics tell us this is a virtual impossibility. It is not that an actor cannot become a star, but that the prime motivator of most of these workshops and seminars is to make the instructor or organizer a lot of money. Their motivation is very rarely to make the actor a star. There is nothing wrong or illegal about this, provided that we recognize it. It is not called the "town of love and art." It is called the "industry," and it is called this for a very good reason. It is also worth noting that many free workshops are given in Hollywood. Some of these workshops bring in amazing actors, directors, and producers who are looking to give something back to the industry. A colleague of mine owns a theatre in Hollywood. He phoned me the other day to tell me that he had just had an interesting phone call, to say the least. He said this man had called from another state to say he wanted to put on a workshop in Hollywood on how to get into the Hollywood movie business. My colleague asked him when he was last in Hollywood. The man told my colleague he had never been. "He wants to put on a workshop on how to get into the Hollywood movie business and he has never set foot here!" Encourage your actors to part with their money cautiously.

221. 9-Ball

You are going to need a soft sponge ball about the size of a tennis ball for this game. Have your students spread out around the room. Explain in the following way:

INSTRUCTOR: In a moment, I am going to throw this sponge ball into the middle of the room. Your aim is to get out of the way. If the ball hits one of you, that person will lose one point. Each of you has nine points to start with. If you are hit with the ball, you will start the next round. If no one is hit by the ball, the first person to pick it up will start the next round. No one is allowed to attempt to move out of the way until the ball is actually thrown. The thrower is not allowed to pretend to throw the ball and bluff. If a person is hit in the face with the ball, the thrower will lose three points and the person it hits will lose none. This is done because even though we are using a sponge ball, it is no fun to be hit in the face. Please be spatially aware of those around you as you move around the room. The aim is to be the last person left in, or to be the person who has the most points left. (This will depend on whether or not you have a time limit for the game.)

Purpose

To create a physical and gut response

The purpose for this exercise is to create a physical and gut response. This is the reason why the actors are not allowed to move out of the way until the ball has been thrown. We want to create a reaction that is so visceral it affects every cell in the actor's body. When we see a performance of poor acting, we are often looking at a delayed response. Instead of responding through his gut, the actor is busy trying to remember his next line. He put on a big smile to tell us through his external actions that his character is happy. A good actor will respond in such a way that it is almost as if he has no idea what he is going to say. It is as if he is speaking those words for the first time. It is that reflex, knee-jerk reaction that is an example of this.

Industry Connection

In this activity, the actors are hit by the ball on numerous occasions. Each time they are hit by the ball, they lose a point, but they are not out. They have numerous opportunities to recover. After seven rounds, a player may be in last place and still go on to finish ahead of everyone else. The actor is going to have to learn to take many knocks along way. Think about this for a moment. How many professions are there where every month, every week, every day they are told, "No!" It may not be said to the actor's face, but the rejection from the audition may feel like it. Remind your actors that they are going to have to learn to take these knocks and, with each one, allow it to strengthen their resolve. They are going to have to learn to keep their chin out and their head held high. When the actor is hit by the ball, he may learn a lesson. He may say to himself, "I know I was not fully focused in that round, but I will be ready for the next round." He has hopefully learned a lesson and will adjust accordingly. If you talk to successful working actors, you will find they are masters at adaptation. If something doesn't go their way, they are always willing to learn and try something else. Encourage your actors to become as flexible as a reed, rather than a dried-out old stick.

222. Penny Up the Wall

You are going to need a number of coins of small value for this exercise. Divide your actors into groups of three to six players. It is best if you have no more than five teams. If you have five teams, you will need five coins. Explain in the following way:

INSTRUCTOR: This is a game I used to play as a kid growing up in England. It was one of our favorite playground games. In a moment, I am going to divide you into teams that are going to stand next to each other with a gap between each team. The members of each team will want to stand one behind the other. I am going to give each team one coin. Each team is going to face the back wall and you are going to be standing ten feet away from it. The first person from each team is going to throw their coin towards the wall. The aim is to get the coin as close to the wall as you possibly can. You can only throw your coin once. We will go in order so that team one will throw first, then team two, and so on. To be fair, in different rounds I will change the team order for throwing. The team that gets its coin closest to the wall wins. The winning team will receive two points. The first team to get to ten points is the winning team. There is no rolling or sliding the coin. The only way you can get the coin to the wall is by throwing it. It is where it finally lands that counts as your end mark.

KYLE: What happens if there is a tie?

INSTRUCTOR: This does sometimes occur. If two or more teams tie for first place, each team will receive one point.

DALE: Can the same person go twice?

INSTRUCTOR: After every round the person who threw must go to the back of the line. It is possible that they will be able to throw again, depending on how many rounds are played. After each round, the players have to rotate.

As kids, we would play this game for money. The winner would take all. For our purposes here, you are going to be playing for points. This is a basic exercise that your students will love. Think of ways to make it more challenging. You can change the distance from which the actors have to throw the coin. If it is too easy, perhaps each team member can be blindfolded when it is their turn to throw. Think of ways to heighten the stakes in this game. If you want to, you could have a double-or-nothing round.

Purpose
To utilize motor skills
As the actors throw their coins toward the wall, they are utilizing their hand-eye coordination. They are utilizing their motor skills in order to do this. Mind and body are intertwined in this activity. As actors we are constantly tapping into this connection. As the actors throw their coins, they learn to adjust the force they use depending on the previous result. Just as the coin bounces off different stimuli along its path, actors bounce their interpretations off different stimuli to form decisions. After reading *Richard III,* an actor might decide to interpret the main character in a physically grotesque manner. The actor in this situation is choosing to utilize the mind-body connection. Also, the actors are becoming more aware of their bodies and how they work as they strive to enhance their motor skills — their hand-eye coordination.

Industry Connection
It is winner takes all. The closest coin to the wall wins. There are no points for second place. As a street game, the winner literally takes all the money. It is the same way for the actors when they are going for a part. Let's assume there is only one part. This means there is only one job. An actor may give a fine performance and be the second choice, but in reality he did not get the part. It went to the actor who was the first choice. Actors believe that there are no prizes for second place. This is not entirely true. Perhaps the actor is remembered by the casting director and will be called in for other auditions. An actor will want to find a way not to focus on the past but to live in the present. No matter what, the actor must give it his all.

223. Needle and Thread
This exercise is not for the fainthearted. It is also not going to be for all your students. Split your students up into teams with four or five members in each. Give each team fifteen needles and fifteen pieces of thread. The first team to thread all of their needles is the winner. They also have to knot each thread separately to complete the exercise. Of course, there is a potential that students could prick their fingers. This means you have to look at the maturity of your students and decide whether this is the right exercise for them. Please make sure you use new needles or that you clean and sterilize used ones. To make this exercise extra challenging, you can instruct your students to close their eyes as

they thread the needle. I am not saying you should do this, but it is an option. I do not use this activity with every group. Please use your discretion as to when to use this exercise.

Purpose

To bring about coordination within the body

The purpose behind this exercise is for the actors to engage their motor skills. In order to thread the needles, the actors have to develop good hand-eye coordination. At first, threading the needle may appear easy, but if this coordination is not well developed, the actors may find themselves struggling. Coordination is an ongoing process, and we are not highly coordinated in all that we do. During a performance, the actor has to be able to coordinate thought, energy, and action. During a performance, the actor creates coordination between his muscles and his emotions. This exercise aims to bring about coordination within the body.

Industry Connection

I am going to use the needle as a metaphor in terms of the industry connection here. Statistically, actors have as much chance of being discovered as of finding a needle in a haystack. Before actors can be discovered, they have to discover themselves. They have to work on themselves in terms of their instrument. They have to work on themselves in terms of believing in themselves. They have to market themselves so they can move out of obscurity. I have a colleague who is now in his eighties who loves to say, "If they don't know about you, they can't hire you." He only started acting in his early seventies and is now a working actor. If you think about the phrase "waiting to be discovered," you will quickly realize this is a contradiction in terms. If you talk to working actors, they will tell you they don't wait for anything. They never stop working on themselves and their careers. They have talent and perseverance. Like a butterfly, they are discovering the chrysalis of their talent. Remind your students that to be a professional actor, they are going to have to be willing to put in time and effort on a continuous basis.

224. The Cannon Ball Runner

You will need a soft ball about the size of a soccer ball for this exercise. Explain in the following way:

INSTRUCTOR: I am going to divide you into two groups. I would like the first half to form an inner circle. I would like the second half to form a larger, outer circle that leaves about a four-foot space in the center. I would like the inner circle to face outwards and the outer circle to face inwards. Both circles are now facing one another. At this point I am going to put this ball between the two circles. Now I would like you to kick the ball in a clockwise direction between the two circles. Please be careful not to kick each other. (Give the students a couple of minutes to get used to doing this.) In a moment, I am going to tap one of you on the shoulder and your aim is to run clockwise between the lines of the circle. You have to get back to your place in the circle before the ball catches up and hits you.

SIMON: Can we throw the ball at the person?

INSTRUCTOR: The only way to catch them is to kick the ball around the circle until it catches up with them.

NATALIE: Can you tap a person when the ball is right next to them?

INSTRUCTOR: That is a very good question. I will not tap a person who is directly next to the ball, but they may be close by. The ball runner can come from either circle. As a reminder, please be careful not to kick each other or the person who is running around the circle.

This is not a competition between teams. It is only a competition between the ball and the ball runner. If the player gets hit by the ball then the teams in the circles have achieved their objective. It is important to note that this game is not a competition, and there is no winning team at the end. Please use a soft or light ball to avoid injury.

Purpose

To develop motor skills

As the ball travels around the circle, the actors have to use foot-eye coordination. They have to use exact coordination or they will either kick each other or miss the ball entirely. Their motor skills have to be highly developed because of the number of people and the potential pandemonium that may follow. An actor on-stage has to have very good motor skills. An actor may be in a scene in which he has to pick up a book. In another scene, he may have to place a teacup back on a saucer. These are both simple and straightforward tasks in everyday life. The challenge is that the actor performing in front of an audience has to get these tasks right the first time. He has to deal with the fact that an audience is analyzing his every move. If he drops the book or knocks over the teacup, the dynamics of the scene will now be shifted. Actors need to have highly developed motor skills.

Industry Connection

Let's use this exercise as an industry metaphor. As the actors run around the circle they are constantly being chased by the ball. As they try to get back to their destination, the ball is constantly at their heels. This is the way it feels to many actors as they pursue their acting careers. Money, or lack of it, is like the ball attempting to stop them getting to their destination. They want to go to auditions, but they need to have "the other job" to pay their bills. They want to take an acting class, but they don't have the money right now. They want to get a new headshot, but it is an extra expense they cannot presently cover. Some actors feel that if they were independently wealthy, everything would be OK. They would have all the time they need to focus on their acting career. As it happens, this is rarely the case. The actor has to find a way of dealing with the ever-chasing ball so that he can pursue his dreams. Discuss with your actors the importance of pursuing dreams. Many people talk about their dreams but very few people actually pursue them.

225. Ambidextrous

You can let all your students work this exercise at the same time. Bring up a volunteer first to show them what you would like them to do. Explain in the following way:

INSTRUCTOR: Lance, please come help demonstrate this exercise. Please hold your left arm in the air and point it forward. I would like you to make twenty circles in a clockwise direction. (Lance makes twenty circles successfully.) I would now like you to drop your left arm and do exactly the same with your right. (Lance raises his right arm and successfully makes twenty circles in a clockwise direction.) This time, I would like you to raise both arms together. With your left arm you are going to make circles in a clockwise direction. At the same time, you are going to continuously draw crosses in the air with your right hand. (Lance attempts the exercise but ends up drawing circles with both arms.)

LANCE: That's tough.

INSTRUCTOR: It's harder than it looks. Now, everyone should find a partner and spread out around the room. One partner will begin while the other one watches. If it is too easy, I would like you to speed up the activity. After a few minutes, you can change over and the other person will take a turn. Please follow the same protocol that I used with Lance.

Once the actors have attempted this exercise, bring the whole group together. See if there was anyone who found they could complete the exercise successfully. Let them demonstrate to the whole group.

Variation

See the Center of Gravity exercise in *112 Acting Games*.

Purpose

To work with bilateral function

The actors have to work with both sides of their body at the same time. If they are not in control of both sides of their body, this will be a virtually impossible exercise for them to complete. Most of us do not have good bilateral function in our bodies. The way you can tell this is to look at an individual's posture. If one side of the body is not in symmetry with the other, it means that that individual does not have bilateral function. To play any character, an actor has to have command of his body. While he wants to look at the similarities between himself and the character, he also wants to look at the differences. Perhaps the character moves with his head jutted slightly forward, which comes from having an inquisitive and intellectual mind. Perhaps the character moves from his pelvis to highlight his sexuality. To manipulate his body to suit the needs of the character, the actor has to control his body. To do this well he has to have bilateral function.

Industry Connection

This exercise is a good challenge. Statistically speaking, it is highly likely that the majority of your actors will fail. This is in tandem with an acting career. Statistically, most people who want an acting career will never have one. However, this does not mean an acting career is impossible. In our exercise, there may be one or two actors who can successfully rise to the challenge. There are usually one or two others who will come back months later and demonstrate that they have conquered the task. Some actors may have contacts and get a lucky break. This can help them get a foot in the door, but it will only keep that door open if they are good at their profession. Other actors may struggle for a long time. If they are persistent and work hard, the law of averages begins to move in their favor.

Note

I want to be clear that working hard also means working smart. Some actors get away from the business from time to time to recharge their batteries. A man goes to the doctor and says, "I am still getting the headaches." The doctor replies, "Are you still banging your head against the wall?" The man says, "Yes. But I am taking the prescription you gave me and it is not working!" The doctor says, "Here is a new prescription. I want you to follow the instructions closely. Stop banging your head against the wall!" The actors who continue to hit their head against the wall will continue to get the same results. Encourage your actors to look at what is working and what is not working. The actor must know when it is time to adapt and make changes.

Chapter 27
Nonverbal Communication

226. Heavy, Yet Light

Have your students sit as the audience. Have one student come forward to work this exercise. Give an actor an imaginary bucket or a real bucket and tell him he is going to carry it from one place to another. Tell him that the bucket is filled with feathers, leaves, rocks, water, cow manure, or you can come up with your own item. If the item is heavy, the students must adapt their movements accordingly. You can also set the scene if you choose such as, "You have gathered just enough water from the well for your family. If you spill any on the journey home, some of them will go thirsty." Switch out the actors and finish with a discussion on the observed work. A discussion or observation can happen at any time, not simply at the end of each exercise.

Variation

Have the actors stand in a large circle. Make it large enough so that each student has to walk one or two steps to reach the students on either side of them. Have an imaginary bucket passed around the circle. As the bucket gets passed from one student to the next, change the item that is inside the bucket. This can happen in a number of ways. You can call out loud a new item as the bucket gets passed from student to student. Another way is to have the students make the choice for themselves as they receive the bucket.

Purpose

To express oneself physically

The actors are going to tell us, through their body language and nonverbal communication, what is in the bucket. There should be a big difference in their movements and actions in terms of carrying feathers or cow manure. If the character gets covered in feathers, that is one thing, if they get covered in cow manure, that is something altogether different. The stench and smell may stay with them for many hours. This means that for the actor a bucket of cow manure raises the stakes. Each actor has to learn to play the stakes. Even though the items are carried in the same object, their weight can vary dramatically. It is up to the actors to be aware of this and convey it to the audience through their actions.

Industry Connection

Whenever an actor tells me, "this exercise has no industry connection," I ask him to think a little bit deeper. Here is an example of how you might respond:

INSTRUCTOR: You are on a movie set and you are playing a police officer. You are given a plastic gun to use because of budgetary and safety issues. A real gun can be quite heavy, yet your gun weighs next to nothing. You gun doesn't feel anything like a real gun and yet you are going to have to convince us that the plastic toy could actually kill. Perhaps the prop guy has made your job more difficult, but you will be the one to look ridiculous if you are unable to convince us that you have a real weapon and not him. Suddenly the actor begins to see the deeper value of the exercise as it relates to the world of the professional actor.

227. Building Rapport Exercise

Tell your actors that in a minute you are going to ask them to find a partner. Explain in the following way:

INSTRUCTOR: What I would like you to do is name yourselves A and B. In a moment, A is going to start a conversation about why they believe acting is the only career for them. B should join in the conversation and can also ask questions of A. At this point, I am going to ask the As to leave the room for a minute so that they are out of earshot. (Wait for As to leave the room.) At the same time as this is happening, Bs, you have another objective. Your aim is to mirror As in every way you can. If they sit down and cross their left legs over their right, then at some point you want to do the same thing. This means if A sits down and there is only one chair, you are going to have to excuse yourself and go bring over another chair. If they use their hands for expression, then you want to mirror this behavior. If they are smiling a lot, you want to be smiling a lot. If they are nodding their heads, then you want to be nodding your head. If they speak in an excited and rapid pace, then you want to speak in an excited and rapid pace. If they lower their voices, then you want to lower your voice. So your aim in this exercise is to mirror your partner's behavior. You want to do this without drawing attention to yourself. This means you don't want to do something the second that they do it. Do not highlight their action, but mirror it in a more subtle way. It also means you may end up mirroring sixty or seventy percent of the behavior, but not all of it. Try to do this in as subtle a way as possible, without telegraphing. So if you cross your legs, do it in a matter of fact way. Today's situation is a little artificial, because the actors have been sent out of the room. This means that when they come back, they will be looking for something. Make a mental note of any discoveries you make. (Group A is brought back into the room.)

OK, guys, I would like you to find a place in the room and As, begin a discussion about why you believe acting is the only career for you. You can stand or sit for this activity, it is entirely up to you. (Give the actors about five minutes to have the discussion.)

After this, bring the group back together. Have a discussion and get some feedback from group A first. Ask them questions like: Was your partner a good listener? Did you feel his responses were beneficial? What was it you liked about talking to your partner? Did you enjoy talking with your partner?

Before switching, explain to group A about the rapport exercise and what was going on. Find out if any of them could tell. Now have group B talk about what it felt like to mirror their partner. When group B takes over the conversation, they can talk on any topic they choose. The reason group A had to talk about acting was to try to take their focus off their partner. Of course, group B will know they are being mirrored, but it will still be a good experience for both partners. Once they have finished, bring the group back for a final discussion.

Purpose

To highlight the importance of body language

This exercise encourages the actor to become aware of the power of body language. It has been shown that well over seventy percent of communication is done without saying a word. It is important for the actors to understand that when they are on-stage, everything they do is being read by the audience. Even if they cross their legs because of nerves the audience will make a mental note of it. It does not mean they will discuss it with the person sitting next to them in the theatre. It does not even mean that they are consciously aware of it. Subconsciously it has been registered as being part of the makeup of your character. Let us say an actress is playing a lady of some means in 1920s England. While on-stage she has a scene where she is sitting in a chair and she crosses her legs because of a nervous habit. She is not even aware she is doing it. It is interesting to note that in the 1920s in England it was considered bad form for an English woman to cross her legs for fear of showing too much leg. Even if the audience has no idea of this, it does not matter. The actor has to know that anything his body is doing on-stage is because he has decided it should be so.

Industry Connection

Here is a little secret you can share with your actors:

INSTRUCTOR: When you go for an audition, you want everything possible to go in your favor. You may only have five minutes, so it is imperative that you build some kind of rapport with the casting director. When you leave the room, you want him to say, "I don't know what it is, but there is something about him that I really like. Let's bring him back for a recall." When you mirror the behavior of another person, they will generally like you. They see a little bit of themselves in you. They do not necessarily know this, but it is OK that you do. This may be considered a form of manipulation, but you are doing it to get the job. The only reason an actor goes to the audition is to get the job. Another term for building rapport with others is called *networking*. It is another absolute skill for those looking to break into the industry. You may already do these things to some extent subconsciously. This exercise allows you to do them on a conscious level. Eventually, mirroring will become so natural for you, that you will do it automatically.

228. Subtext

Choose between two and four actors to come into the performance area. Have the other actors sit as the audience. Explain this exercise as follows:

INSTRUCTOR: In a moment you are going to act out the following scene. David, you are going to be the doctor. Sarah, you are going to be the nurse. Marc, you are going to be the man with the broken left toe. Claire, you are going to be the administrator of the hospital. Marc, you had an affair with the administrator of the hospital last year. It ended on a sour note when she found you cheating with her best friend. That is as much detail as I am going to give you. In a moment, you will start your scene and at some point I will say "freeze." Any time you hear "freeze" you have to do so immediately. At this point I am going to point to one of you who is then going to say the subtext of what your character is really thinking. For instance, the hospital administrator might say to the patient, "It's nice to see you again." The subtext might be, "I hate your guts you lying, cheating bastard!" Remember that while the actors hear the subtext, the characters do not. This means that no character will want to react to the subtext he hears. As soon as the character has spoken their subtext, the scene automatically continues until the next freeze.

You can choose the scene or you can have the audience set the scene. Allow time for questions and clarification before you begin. Some students may be struggling with their understanding of subtext. This exercise is going to be an excellent way to help them with the importance of the subtext.

Purpose
To find the subtext behind the spoken word

We are not simply interested in the words a character says, but the hidden meaning behind those words. If an audience was simply interested in listening to the words, they could buy the book. It is the actors' job to find the subtext of what their character is thinking. It is up to the actors to find their relationships with the other characters. Subtext is one of the main reasons we are able to go see the same play on ten separate occasions. Each actor will want to rethink it, reinvent it, and make each role his own. When an audience sees a new actor in a role they may say, "I never thought of the character like that before. He showed me things I have never seen in Romeo. His interpretation was quite different from anything else. Her performance as Juliet was quite mesmerizing." The audience is not talking about what was said, but rather what was left unsaid. They are talking about the subtext.

As your actors begin to understand subtext they will be able to take their work to a deeper level. In the play *A Streetcar Named Desire* by Tennessee Williams, Blanche says, "You must be Stanley. I'm Blanche." Part of the subtext before this line as written for Stanley says, "He sizes up at a glance, with sexual classifications, crude images flashing into his mind and determining the way he smiles at her."[60] Without this information Blanche may say her line very matter-of-fact. After being on the receiving end of the nonverbal communication being sent from Stanley, there may be a whole other subtext when she says, "You must be Stanley. I'm Blanche." An actor cannot afford to ignore the subtext. It is the actor's job to teach the world to listen.

Industry Connection

Raise this discussion with your actors in the following way:

INSTRUCTOR: Next time you audition for a casting director, see if you can figure out the subtext of what they are saying. If they say, "Nice to see you," the subtext might be, "This one's too short." If they say, "That was great!" the subtext might be, "What a lousy performance!" If they say, "Thanks for coming," the subtext might be, "She is the one!" If you listen to the words that come out of their mouths, you are most likely wasting your time. Listen to the way they say it. Pay attention to their nonverbal communication, then you may be onto something.

Some of your actors are in junior high, high school, or college. They may say that at present they have not auditioned for a casting director so this does not apply to them. Any actor who has tried out for a school play can apply this approach in exactly the same way.

---

60. Tennessee Williams, *A Streetcar Named Desire* (New York: A Signet Book, 1969), 29.

Note
A producer has to have a good reason to put on a production that has already been done well before. One reason might be because the material is more relevant today than when it was originally produced.

229. Greetings
Start off by having the actors sit as an audience. Bring up two actors into the performance space. Tell them that you would like them to walk over to one another and shake hands. At this point ask for a scenario from the audience. Have the actors act out a number of different scenarios given to them by the audience. The catch is that there is no dialogue, and every greeting can *only* be done through a handshake. After each handshake, have the audience discuss what they read into it. Did they find it believable? You can choose to work with another set of actors. You can rework a scenario if the audience does not buy into the believability. The audience can make observations and critique a performance. You can also have everyone spread out around the room and work this exercise separately.

A few scenarios could be:
1. You bump into an ex of yours, whom you haven't seen for two years. He or she cheated on you with your best friend.
2. You meet your real father for the first time.
3. You greet your neighbor's two-year-old daughter.
4. You meet a prospective employer at the first job interview.
5. You have just met someone whom you find attractive.

Variable
To vary this exercise you can allow the actors to greet each other in any way they see fit. There is still no dialogue allowed. Your actors should learn to trust in a thought or a look as much as they do in the dialogue.

Purpose
To convey thoughts and feelings
This exercise asks the actors to convey all of their thoughts and feelings through a single handshake. In the case of the ex-girlfriend she may want to say, "I hated you for cheating on me! I hated the way you made me feel, but now I have moved on with my life and am stronger for it." She cannot say this verbally. She cannot say this by punching him in the stomach, and yet it can still be said. All her pent-up feelings and emotions must come through that handshake and the subtext. Through that one handshake, her ex will know exactly how she is feeling, without a word even being uttered. There are many times in a performance where actors are on-stage without dialogue when a look, a stroke of the cheek, or kneeling on one knee says it all. As Stansilavski says, "If you want to convey feelings in a role, you have to understand them."[61] An action in itself is not enough. It is the intention behind it that will really drive the scene.

---

61. Constantin Stanislavski, *An Actor's Work*, (New York: Routledge, 2008), 28.

Industry Connection

This exercise leans heavily on nonverbal communication because it demands that the actors tell us what they are saying without actually saying anything. One interesting aspect of film is the different angles directors like to shoot from. Sometimes they like to shoot from overhead or perhaps a shot of the actor's back. Sometimes they might choose a close-up of hands. Even though the words may sound convincing enough, is the actor's body telling the same story? It can only do so if he is fully engaged in the scene. If he is not really present, his audience will say, "He was good, but something wasn't quite right." They might also say, "Her performance was OK," or "She's not bad." Notice that an audience isn't necessarily going to be specific. However, they know when they are being cheated out of a performance. Discuss with your actors the importance to find it within themselves to drive the story and stay connected to the scene at all times.

Note

Make sure your actors are constructive in their critiques of each other. To say, "That sucked," is not only tactless, it is also pointless. It gives the actors nothing of value from which to glean. Have your actors get specific and constructive in their critiques. For instance, an actor can say, "David, you were so softly spoken I lost half of your words. It would be better if you could project more in the future." David now has a clear understanding of what wasn't working and how he can move forward. The same concept should apply with any positive critiques that your actors give. To say, "That was good," holds little water. To tell the actor, "I enjoyed your work because I felt that at every moment you justified each and every action." This is much more specific and again allows the actor involved to realize the strengths of his performance.

230. Scene One

This exercise is one that is popular in improvisation workshops. Have your actors sit in the audience. Choose two actors to come up into the performance area. Explain in the following way:

INSTRUCTOR: In a moment, you are going to perform a scene that is between two and five minutes in length. The challenge is that only one line of dialogue can be spoken in the entire scene. It does not matter which actor says the line, provided it is only one sentence. For the rest of the scene you have to communicate using nonverbal communication. I will hold up my hand when you have one minute left. The line can come at any point in the scene. Do not speak the line until you feel compelled to do so.

You can give the actors a scene or take suggestions from the audience in order to set up the given circumstances for the actors. Once the actors are finished, follow up with a discussion and then move on to another pair. You might want to work a scene with four or five actors. The same rule of one sentence would apply.

Purpose

To use nonverbal communication

This exercise teaches players what can be communicated using nonverbal communication. I have seen an actress on-stage for an entire play without a word of dialogue. Her face and body language conveyed so much that she blew me away. She had a great deal of dialogue inside of her but she chose not to say it. She was able to leap to her self-created inner text. In this exercise, the actors are asked to hold back the dialogue until they absolutely have no option but to speak the words. The actor has to trust what a thought or look can portray. There are many occasions in life when you want to speak, but choose not to. An actor might be playing a character who is being reprimanded by his boss. The character might want to tell his boss where he can shove it, but he chooses not to.

Industry Connection

This exercise reminds us that sometimes less is more. An actor may be working with a director on a television series. He may feel the director is incompetent and feels the urge to tell the director so. Instead, the actor holds back the impulse and takes onboard his suggestions while using his own justifications for his character's actions. If an actor feels that he absolutely must raise the issue, then he must do so in an efficient, concise, and courteous manner. The last thing the actor wants is to get into a big argument that causes tension and ill feeling between him and the director. This is especially true if he wants to work again.

231. The Writing's on the Wall

Have two actors demonstrate this activity before splitting up the group into pairs. For this exercise, all actors will want to be wearing only one top layer of clothing, such as a T-shirt. One actor is going to turn with his back toward the other actor. The actor behind him is going to write a word on his partner's back using his index finger only. He is going to write the word one letter at a time and very slowly. An example is the word "dog." The aim is not to trick the partner. The aim is to see if he can help his partner work out what word is being written on his back. Ask the actors to split into pairs and work on this. Ask them to start off with easy three-letter words. Once they have mastered this, let them move on to four-, five-, and six-letter words. Have the actors change over after every word. Walk around and observe the actors working. If a person is struggling to guess a particular word, see if you can help out. Perhaps the writer is going too fast. Perhaps the person doing the guessing is not focusing correctly. Give the actors ten or fifteen minutes to work with their partners. Bring the actors back together and follow up with a group discussion.

Purpose
To heighten the senses
For the actors to comprehend what is being written on their back, they are going to have to fully engage their senses. They are going to have to become tuned into their sense of touch. They are also going to have to use their sense of sight to visualize in their mind what is being written on their back. The actor needs to heighten his senses to a much greater degree than the average person. This is because the actor often has to use his senses to create imaginary circumstances. Some stage actors believe that film actors don't have to use their senses in the same way because they are often on location. Film actors are as likely to be in the studio, if not more so, as they are to be on location. The logistics and costs of being on location mean that if a director can shoot in the

studio, he probably will. Let's say a film crew goes on location to a castle in Scotland. In the movie, there is also a dragon, which attacks our lead actor. Because dragons are not an everyday event, this dragon is created through computer graphics. In other words, the actor is never going to see the dragon. He is going to have to use his imagination and his heightened senses to create this reality. He has to see the dragon, hear its ferocious roar, smell its foul breath, and feel the heat from the fire it breathes. An actor who is not in touch with his senses cannot do these things with any credibility.

Industry Connection

In an on-camera close-up, the camera is going to catch everything. If a character caresses his wife's cheek in the last scene, the camera is going to catch every moment of it. Now multiply this by the fact that it is on a large screen and is magnified a thousand times. As Andrew Biel says in his book, *Trail Guide to the Body*, "The fingertips are one of the most sensitive areas, with up to 50,000 nerve endings every square inch."[62] If an actor makes this gesture carelessly, the camera is going to tell that story. Ask your actors to think about what happens when they put their hand on a friend's shoulder. They are able to make certain observations about them. Sometimes, from simply putting their hand on the shoulder they will say, "Are you alright? Is everything OK?" This is because, through their sense of touch, they have understood something about their friend. It is important that your actors do not disregard their sense of touch because the camera will not ignore it.

232. Prison Breakout

I first discovered this exercise at an acting comedy workshop in London. You are going to make a circle of chairs. You will need half the number of chairs to the number of students. So if you have twenty-five students, you will need thirteen chairs in a circle. You will want to work with an odd number of students for this exercise. If you do not have an odd number, join in yourself.

Tell the students to find a partner. One of them should sit on a chair and the other should stand behind it. One student should be left standing behind an empty chair. The students who are sitting in the chairs are the prisoners. The students who are standing behind the chairs are the guards. The guard who has no prisoner has a special task. His aim is to entice a prisoner from another guard into the empty chair. The way he can do this is by nodding at a prisoner or winking at him. He can do anything to get the attention — except he cannot talk to him. Once a prisoner has been given a signal, he can attempt to run to the empty chair. As he attempts to run, the guard has to lightly tap him on the shoulder. If he is tapped on the shoulder he has to stay in the prison. Once a prisoner escapes, there will be a new guard who has to entice prisoners. There is a very important rule: A prisoner cannot attempt to escape unless the guard with the empty chair signals him to do so. A guard can signal more than one prisoner if he chooses. It is also worth noting that a prisoner does not have to run the moment he is signaled. Once he has been given the order, he will want to wait for the right moment. To make it more challenging, instruct the guards to stand with their hands behind their backs at all times — except to stop a prisoner

---

62. Andrew Biel, *Trail Guide to the Body* (Colorado: Books of Discovery, 2005), 17.

escaping. Make sure the prisoners are sitting back in their chairs and not leaning forward or sitting on the edge to get a head start. These rules may sound somewhat sterile, but they are in place to make the exercise more challenging.

Purpose
To comprehend nonverbal communication signals
This exercise involves a good deal of nonverbal communication. The guard without a prisoner communicates nonverbally in order to gain the attention of a prisoner. The guards who are behind the chairs cannot see the faces of their prisoners. They have to watch for signs such as tension or flinching in the muscles to help them attempt to work out when their prisoner is about to run. A character in a play may say, "There is something about her I do not trust." There may not be any dialogue that makes this statement a fair judgment. The actor playing this character is still going to have to find a way to justify why his character has made this assumption. If it is not in the dialogue, it has to be through nonverbal communication. So many signals are given via the unspoken word. Encourage your actors to pay attention to nonverbal clues in their day-to-day lives.

Industry Connection
The prisoners are trapped. In order to break free, they are going to have to think outside the box. They are going to catch their guard off-guard. Some actors who are trying to develop their career also feel trapped. They feel as if they are simply going around in circles. Every time they try to get an agent, they are turned down. Every time they go to an audition, they do not get the part. If actors do exactly the same thing every time, they will achieve the same result. If the actors send their headshot out to agents and the headshot is poor, this is going to count heavily against them. If the actors simply rely on their own judgment, they may never discover this fact. Perhaps if they had asked an acting instructor or a casting director what they thought of the headshot, they might have been given an honest answer. If the advisor has nothing to lose or gain, he may be only too happy to give an honest opinion. If an actor throws all his energy in the wrong direction, he is going to remain trapped in a self-created prison. Each actor has to learn how to think, breathe, and live outside the box. By doing so, he will be able to problem solve pragmatically.

233. Picture Perfect
This exercise has been adapted for group work from my book, *Acting Games for Individual Performers*. For this activity, I would like you to obtain a number of different types of magazines. One might be a fashion magazine, while another might be about housekeeping, and one on gardens. You can get these very cheap at a thrift store. Used bookstores often sell them. I am especially keen on you finding magazines that contrast with each other in some way. I would also like you to make sure that each of these magazines has plenty of pictures of people in them, including people in some form of advertisement. Divide your actors into groups of between two and six students. Explain in the following way:

INSTRUCTOR: I have given each group a selection of old magazines to work with. Go through the magazines and look at pictures of people. You need to decide what they are really saying. For instance, you might find an advertisement

314

in which the man is smiling and supposedly saying, "I am happy because I use such and such a product." If you look more closely, you might find that his smile does not turn up at the edges, his eyes look slightly glazed and dull, and his smile appears forced, rather than soft and warm. In other words, whichever pictures you choose, you are going to analyze for authenticity. Instead of being genuinely happy, you might decide that this man in this advertisement is saying, "They have asked me to hold this pose forty times now and I am really fed up with it." You can do this assignment with any pictures in a magazine that involves people — it does not have to be an advertisement. In fact, it might be quite interesting to compare pictures in advertisements with pictures of regular people. Do you feel the regular people look more genuine, or perhaps they are nervous being in front of the camera and it shows? It is very important that you are specific in the way you define each picture. To say, "I don't believe his expression," is not specific enough. Look at his eyes, his mouth, his arms, his shoulders, his feet, and the tensions in his handshake and make your observations that way. See if you can find three pictures that you feel are quite genuine, and three that seem fake, then explain why. I would like you to cut out each picture and stick it on a piece of poster paper. Beside each picture you will want to write comments as to what you think is really being said. I have asked you to use contrasting magazines for balance and to take away any biases you might find in one magazine over another. Afterwards, you are going to share your findings with the group.

Purpose
To read body language
Raise the following points with your actors:

INSTRUCTOR: You are paying particular attention to the nonverbal clues given to you by these pictures. In day-to-day life, people are giving off nonverbal clues all the time. In any character you play, you will want to access your nonverbal clues. This activity allows you to see the importance of body language not only for your own good, but as it applies to others. I want you to get used to the idea of looking at other people and understanding what it is they are saying and not what they think they are saying. It is a very important distinction for you, as an actor, to make because you can be in a scene positive you are giving a certain performance, when in fact the other actors and the audience are reading it quite differently. By understanding and interpreting the body language of others you will be far more able to understand your own body language and what it is saying about you.

Industry Connection
The actors are asked to look at pictures and make judgments based on what they see. There are various people involved in the industry who sometimes work this way. A casting director may look for a physical type to play the younger version of the lead. In this instance, he is going to have a specific physical appearance in mind. The strongest actor may not get the part if he does not have the right look. This is not always the case, but sometimes it is. A casting director may invite an actress to audition for her. She may be impressed by the actress, but decides she already has too many medium-height brunettes. Actors cannot control every aspect of their career, but they will want, at the very least, to do their best to understand each element of it.

Chapter 28
Thinking outside the Box

234. A Day in the Life Of

For this exercise you can have all of the students working at the same time. Explain in the following way:

INSTRUCTOR: For this exercise I want each of you to choose an occupation. It can be any occupation that you like: nurse, lawyer, teacher, bank manager, bartender, garbage collector, or musician. I want each of you to choose your own occupation. It can be one that was just mentioned or you can come up with a totally different one. Each of you will then find your own space in the room. You are then going to live out a day — twenty-four hours — in the life of this person. We are going to do this in three-hour increments. Each three hours will be covered in one minute of actual time. This means the entire exercise will last eight minutes. We are going to start the day at midnight. That means that whatever your character would be doing between midnight and three a.m. is what you will want to be doing.

DERECK: If I am a teacher, I guess I would be sleeping at that time.

NADIA: If I play a nurse, I might be changing bed sheets.

INSTRUCTOR: Exactly. Your occupation will determine on what you should be doing. Let us say you choose a lawyer. Does that mean you should be sleeping at 6 a.m.?

MEL: It would depend on your personality. Even if you didn't have to be at work you might want to go to the gym first.

INSTRUCTOR: Exactly. I want you to think outside the box a little for this exercise. While taking into account the occupation of your character, I also want you to consider their personality. One schoolteacher doesn't have exactly the same routine as another. However, they will both be in the classroom throughout the day. I am going to ask you to mime this exercise without any dialogue. Any questions?

JANE: Since we only have one minute for each three hours, should we be acting at an extra-fast speed?

INSTRUCTOR: That is a very good question. You are only acting out a small moment of each three-hour period. You will want to do this at a pace and rhythm fitting to your character.

BILL: Can I change occupations halfway through?

INSTRUCTOR: It's an interesting concept, Bill. For the purpose of this exercise I am going to ask you to keep the same occupation throughout. Please find a space in the room. As you act out these scenes I want to remind you that there is to be no interaction with each other. If you come across another person, ignore them and stay focused on your own scene and what you are doing.

If a student asks a question that you feel is redundant there is no need to put the student down. The idea is to encourage your students to ask questions and not to discourage them. Being an actor sometimes requires that he ask himself questions that he would prefer not to know the answers to. We are looking to ignite their imaginations. Remind the students that each time period covers three hours. So if you call out "midnight," the time period is midnight to three a.m. If you call out "three a.m.," the time period is three to six a.m. Make sure you call the new time every minute. Walk around and observe the students. If you prefer, you can have half the class perform the exercise while the other half observes. At the end of the exercise the groups reverse roles.

Note
It is very important that you allocate enough time for each activity. Let us say because of time you stop in the middle of this exercise. You tell the students you will pick up where you left off next time. Unfortunately, it will lose some of its edge. The students' first visceral response to each exercise is an important one. Always plan more time than you think you will need. Always have backup material in case you finish ahead of schedule. If it is up to your students to plan and be prepared, then it is also up to you to do the same thing.

Purpose
To gain a sense of rhythm and tempo
In this exercise the actors are made aware of time. Time has its own sense of rhythm and tempo. The time of day will often affect the way we think and the way we feel. It is also this way for the actors' character. Some people are early birds while others are night owls. Time is a factor to be considered in terms of a character's behavior. Ask your actors to observe their own life and see how their behavior and actions change as the day progresses. It is the actor's job to understand human behavior. The actor cannot live a passive existence but must take life in completely. Some people might say this is over analyzing or being too picky. Guide your actors so that they leave no stone unturned and get specific in detail. Preparation and research are a privilege for the actors. The more specific they are in their preparation the more freeing they will be in their work. Some actors base a character they are playing on someone they know. Your actors will want to become experts in human behavior. The actors will want to know how to completely utilize the rehearsal process. The rehearsal process is almost considered a luxury in film. It is important that they do their homework, but they will not want the homework to show in the performance. They will want to throw it all away when they show up on-stage or on-set. In reference to preparation, Chaliapin said the following in a conversation with Maxim Gorky, "Prepare as I might, study and strive as I might, I never once walked on the stage with the feeling of mastery. That was something that grew in the act itself; and the reward and the knowledge arose out of my performance. It was this living of the role that, with each production, I broadened and deepened the character."[63]

Industry Connection
This exercise highlights the importance of time. Many people have nine-to-five type jobs. Actors do not have a job, but a lifestyle. They could get called in for an audition at 8 p.m. The next day they might be shooting a film at 1 a.m. The following morning they might be back on-set at 9 a.m. Some of this may happen because a director says, "We have to get this shot and this is the only opportunity we will have to get it!" It is at times like these that cast and crew are expected to pull together. If your actors have any doubt about the type of hours

---

63. Maxim Gorky, *Chaliapin* (London: Columbus Books, 1988), 130.

317

they will be working, tell them to watch any interview with a famous actor about the making of a movie. It is not enough that the actor arrive on-set at these times. Remind them that they have to be fully functional and be able to give everything they've got no matter what time of day or night it is.

235. Dance Tag

For this exercise, choose one of the actors to be the tagger. Everyone else should find a dance partner. When you start the music, the partners should be dancing in any style they choose. At any given moment you should change the music, and at this point the actors must find a new partner. Any time an actor is looking for a new partner and is dancing on his own, he can be tagged. The only time anyone can be tagged is when he doesn't have a dance partner. Anyone can find a new partner at any time he chooses, but when the music changes he has to immediately break and find a new partner. If he does not break, he can automatically be tagged and a new tagger takes over. There is no rest period in this exercise, so the actors will be dancing the entire time.

Purpose

To use creative thinking

The purpose behind this exercise is to get the actors to use creative thinking. It is to get the actors to use their upper levels of cognition. When actors create, they get a little adrenaline rush. Let us assume an actor has just got tagged. If he wants, he can attempt to tag someone else immediately. There is nothing in the rule book that says he cannot do so. In order to do this, he is going to have to think outside the box. He is going to have to have a vivid imagination. If actors took a play and simply read it out loud, no one would come to see them act. The audience could go to the library and read the play by themselves. It is the actor's interpretation of the character that is of interest to the audience. Actors have to wear the shoes of their characters. It is the way the actors lift the words off the page that grabs our attention. In order for this to happen an actor must possess a vivid imagination. An actor needs to have a childlike fascination with the world.

Industry Connection

In order not to be tagged, the actor has to be immediately aware of his surroundings. The music could change at any moment and the tagger could be dancing right next to him. This means that each actor has to strategize and, to the best of his ability, plan ahead. The actors will want to look around and attempt to plan what they are going to go to next. Do not tell them this before the exercise, but see if they can figure it out for themselves. You can always follow up in a group discussion at the end. For actors pursuing a career in the competitive world of acting, they will want to constantly be preparing their next move. They should constantly be on top of networking, mail outs, thank you cards, reading up on industry-related topics, and numerous other things. Instead of waiting for things to happen, the actors will want to encourage them and preempt at every turn. Great hockey players say, "I didn't go for the puck, I went where I thought the puck was going." Discuss with your actors that they will want to stay one step ahead of everyone else so that they can catch the train before it has even arrived.

Note
To tag a fellow actor is to tap a fellow actor. It should never mean slapping, pushing, kicking, or grabbing. It sounds obvious, but in the heat of the moment it does not always appear to be.

236. Chicken Blast
Have your actors find a space in the room. Tell them that in a moment you would like them to mill around the room as chickens. Tell them that you would like them to be as authentic as possible. They should move like a chicken, scratch like a chicken, eat like a chicken, and so forth.

Pause the activity for a moment and bring the actors back together. Tell them that at some point a bomb is going to go off in the chicken coop and all the chickens will die. It is very important that you do not allow any questions or discussion at this point. Give them a good ten minutes to explore as chickens and watch their behavior. See if anything has changed with this new knowledge.

Here is the underlying part of this exercise: The actor knows a bomb is going to go off at some point, but the chicken has no idea. Any actor who creates a panicky chicken, or shows desperation of sorts, is doing so as the actor and not as the chicken. Allow this to happen without comment. Do not allow questions before the actors begin this exercise. The reason is you do not want anyone to raise this topic beforehand. During the group discussion, you can highlight which actors intellectualized the exercise and which ones were simply being a chicken.

Purpose
To work from the character's worldview
Intellectually, the actor knows a bomb is going to go off, but the chicken has no idea. You give the actors the information about the bomb in order to trick them. The actors have to learn to separate their own knowledge from that of their character's, to a certain degree. If an actor is playing Romeo, then he will know that both Romeo and Juliet are going to die. As an actor, he will already know this the first time he ever sets eyes on Juliet, but Romeo does not. Romeo will give everything to be with Juliet forever. The actor cannot play what he knows intellectually because the character has not made the discoveries yet to come to the same conclusions. Juliet is not dead, but merely asleep. The actor knows this, but Romeo has no idea. Tell your actors to be careful not to go above and beyond their character's boundaries.

Industry Connection
This exercise looks at perceived knowledge over actual knowledge. Many other actors are going to be happy to share their advice and knowledge. Some of it will be good, some of it will be misinformed, and some will be given to sabotage. Actors are going to have to be highly selective of whom they accept as a good advisor and what they accept as good advice. "Talk is cheap" is a good phrase to take onboard. If every actor had good advice, then every actor would be working. We know that statistically this is far from the case. Raise the following points with your actors:

INSTRUCTOR: Be selective. Pick out the good advice and disregard the rest. If the actor you are talking to arrived in LA last week, their advice may be limited.

If the actor arrived in LA ten years ago and they have never booked a job, their advice may also be limited. Find those who you hold in high regard, and then use your intuition. Only take onboard selective advice as it applies to your situation and your needs.

237. Magnetism

To start this exercise, bring an actor into the performance space for a demonstration. Have the actor clasp his hands together as if he is making one fist. His fingers should now be interlocked. Now have him point out his fingers to make a gun-like gesture. Have him take those two fingers and separate them so that they are about one inch apart. You, the instructor, should now take your forefinger and quickly move it between the actor's two fingers. This should last about ten seconds. Ask the actor to close his two fingers and then separate them about an inch apart once more. Move your finger between the actor's two fingers one more time. The actor should still have his two fingers one inch apart. What I would like you to do is place your hands on either side of the actor's hands. Be as close to his fingers as possible without actually touching. Now, put your thumb and forefinger together on each side. Make small, circular clockwise motions. You should find his fingers start to close in together all on their own. You should be doing this simultaneously on both sides of his hands. The actor will most likely find his two fingers appear to involuntarily move together. As he sees his fingers closing, the actor may try to fight it, but he will have little success.

Once the demonstration is complete, have the actors split into pairs and work this exercise on their own. Walk around the room and observe to make sure they are doing it correctly. Have the actors change over so that they both get the experience. Come back together as a group. Have two actors demonstrate the exercise for the entire group. See if they remembered it all, or if they forgot some key parts. Finish up with a group discussion.

Purpose
To heighten the imagination
If you are the instructor leading this exercise, you probably don't know why it works. What is important is that you come across as congruent and have an air of certainty about you. If you come across as nervous, or as if you are about to do something silly, the exercise might not work. An actor may walk out onto the stage, which is supposed to be on the beach. He knows it's not the beach and the audience knows it's not the beach. If he walks out apologetically as if to say, "I'm sorry that this is really just the stage," he has suspended all belief. From then on he has lost his audience. In order to heighten their imaginations, the actors have to heighten their own. They have to walk out as if they are going to the beach, and as if you are truly on the beach. If, through their imaginations they are congruent in their beliefs, the audience and their imaginations will soon follow.

Industry Connection
Have the following discussion with your actors:

INSTRUCTOR: Each time you do this exercise with someone, you keep your fingers crossed that it is going to work. As if by magic, it seems to work almost every time. The fascinating part and the exciting part of acting is that, even if you did everything that everyone ever said you should do, it does not guarantee that you will make it as an actor. At some point, you will need a little luck and a little magic. It might be a day-player role where you get noticed by the casting director. Perhaps you are in a soap opera for two years and a producer wants you for her movie. Now you are able to make the transition to movie acting. Talent and hard work are a big part of what will get you where you want to be. Due to the long hours on-set, it is beneficial for the actors who adore working. This is in part because of the emotional drain that can take place. On occasion actors will be pushed to their physical and mental limit. To reach their goals, actors have to be willing to dig deeper. The actors have to create a different frame of reference from the civilian. A little bit of luck and magic will also have to play their part.

Note
In terms of magic, we are not talking about trickery. We are talking about things that cannot be explained. There are performances that are so wonderful we are left speechless. Sometimes all the odds are against you and yet something will still go in your favor. As Anne Bogart says, "Magnetism in art is the force that draws people towards it."[64]

238. Body Parts
For this exercise, have all the actors begin by walking around the room. At any given moment, shout out a set of instructions such as, "three noses." At this point the actors have to get into groups of three and touch noses. The actors start wandering around the room until a new group is formed. Whenever a body part and number are called, the actors have to create a new group. Here are some other examples: seven big toes, five ears, ten knees, eleven fingers, nine feet.

This exercise is not a competition but can be turned into one. For instance, if an actor does not move fast enough, he may be left out of a group, at this point he may not be able to complete the task. In this situation, he would be out. Remind the actors that they have to touch these body parts together. If the actors are asked to create "four arms," they could do this with only two people, but if they choose to, they could form a group of four people and get the same results. If they had to do seven big toes, they would have to take off their shoes. If they half-perform this exercise, they will only get half of the results.

Purpose
To become aware of your environment
In this exercise the actors are immediately becoming aware of their environment. If they are asked to form "seven big toes," they will have to form a group of anywhere between four and seven to achieve this. While two actors may be involved in a romantic love scene on a bench in the park on-stage, their characters may become acutely aware of every passerby. The situation at hand may make them more aware of their environment.

Industry Connection
This exercise has an element of problem solving. If you have the actors create "nineteen fingers," there are a variety of ways to achieve this. Your students'

---

64. Anne Bogart, *And Then, You Act* (New York: Routledge, 2007), 65.

acting career is going to involve a good deal of problem solving. I am often concerned by acting coaches who say, "There is only one way!" Each actor's journey is different, in that it is a sum of his own experiences. Actors will face numerous challenges in their acting career and will sometimes have to find creative ways to solve them. The only time an individual's life will be problem free is when he is six feet under. Until that time, embrace your challenges and move on!

239. Hug the Cup Holder

For this exercise you will need a cup and a cup holder. I use a cup holder that is wooden and can carry about six cups on it. As long as you have something similar, that is fine. Explain in the following way:

INSTRUCTOR: To start off with, I am going to send five of you outside the room. You may be there for awhile, so please be patient. (Five students go outside.) There is a reason I sent the students out before explaining this exercise. As you can see, I have just placed a cup holder in the center of the room. Gillian, will you hold this cup, please? (Explain the following in a quiet voice.) In a moment I will bring in one of the students and tell them that they have three minutes to hug the cup holder. I will also tell them that unfortunately they must do this without actually picking it up. It cannot move off the ground in any way. I will also tell them that the audience may shout out suggestions and help. One suggestion that you will want to shout out again and again is, "Hug the cup holder." Of course, this exercise is a bit of trick, because the person who wins is the one who hugs Gillian — the cup holder. Please do not look at Gillian or indicate her in any way. I am not going to take questions because I don't want those outside to become suspicious. I am going to bring the first person in.

The reason you have people outside is because that means you can watch five different people perform. Once a group has played this activity you can never play it again with them because they will already know how it works. After three minutes, if the student does not hug "the cup holder," he is out. At this point do not send him out of the room. You do not want him discussing with the others what has just happened. Instead, have him become part of the circle. Eventually, there will be just one person left outside waiting his turn. This exercise may last up to fifteen minutes because each student has three minutes. You may find that a student catches on really quickly and hugs the cup holder (Gillian) almost immediately. For each round you can change the cup holder. It is important that the students don't indicate the cup holder. It is so much more fascinating to watch the person in the middle struggle and crawl around. Tell the participants you cannot answer any questions once they enter the room.

Purpose
To live outside the box
This exercise encourages the actors to think outside the box and move away from literal thinking. If the actors take this exercise literally, they will never be able to complete it. If they think literally, they will not even consider hugging the person holding the cup. This means that at any given moment they are only looking at half the picture. An actor may be playing the part of a character who he believes is a "very good" person. He takes this literally and makes every thought, every action, and every nuance good. He feels he is doing the role

justice, whereas the audience feels he is watching a caricature. Ask your actors to think of the kindest person they have met. Then ask them if they think that individual has ever told a white lie in their lives. You want your actors to see their characters as rounded, rather than one-dimensional. Human beings are not perfect. We come packaged, warts and all. This may sound negative, but it is not. It will help the actors justify why sometimes their characters appear to act in an unpredictable way.

Industry Connection

Actors may give a role everything they've got. For three minutes they may work so hard that they are sweating by the end of it. They may use all their focus and concentration, and intellect and knowledge, yet come up empty. The challenge is that they only looked at the exercise from one perspective. Unfortunately, a number of actors treat their career in the same way. They take their headshot and resumé and send it out to fifty agents. They don't get any response, so they send it to another fifty. They still get no response, so this time they send it to one hundred agents. They work faster, harder, and spend more money. They run around like a headless chicken. The point is that they were not willing to look at the situation from all sides. The punctuation on their resumé was full of errors. Their headshot was done by a friend and is grainy with bad lighting. These challenges alone will lead any agent to believe that this is the work of a careless amateur. In his mind, they are an indicator of the actor's talent, or lack of it. Encourage your actors to look at all sides of an equation instead of just the obvious.

240. Answer Back

For this exercise you are going to need a black or blue felt-tipped pen. You will also need enough blank stickers for one per student. Explain in the following way:

INSTRUCTOR: In a moment I am going to ask you to stand in a big circle facing inwards. At this point, I will come around and place a sticker on the back of each of you. Everyone will have a sticker with a different animal on it. When I say "go," you will all begin moving around the room. Your aim is to discover what animal you are. The way you do this is by asking one question of everyone you meet. You can ask any question you like. The challenge is that the person you ask can only answer yes or no. A question might be, "Do I climb trees?" If I am a deer, the answer will be "no." This means you have to ask further questions.

DAISY: Do you both get to ask a question?

INSTRUCTOR: Each of you gets to ask one question of the other, at which point you will want to move on.

LANA: What if you think you know what animal you are?

INSTRUCTOR: You have to have asked at least five questions from five different people before you can make a guess. If you are wrong, you have to ask five new questions before you are allowed to guess again. If you get the answer right, the person will tell you. The aim is to discover your animal as quickly as possible, and not be the last person left in.

In this example I used animals, but the stickers can say anything you want. For instance, the students could all have different countries on their backs. You could alternatively make each sticker something random. I would advise you have this part already prepared ahead of time. Remind the students that the person answering them can only answer yes or no. He is not able to answer in any other way or give hints or clues. It is up to the students to play fairly. If a student whispers the answer to his colleague, the exercise becomes pointless. I mention this to remind the students that there is nothing to gain from this approach.

Purpose
To build on the information given
The purpose of this exercise is for the actors to build on the information they are given. Every time they are told "yes," they have made a discovery. They have learned something about their animal. Every time they are told "no," they have also learned something. Some of the actors may only pay attention to the "yes" answers. This means they will be losing fifty percent of the information they are being given. If an actor knows his animal cannot climb trees, he has valuable information with regards to future questions. Sometimes, when actors are researching their characters in a play, they look at everything their characters say for clues. What they forget to do is look at everything everyone else says or does in connection with their character. For instance, perhaps the playwright has a stage direction in his script. The note says, "Rebecca walks straight past Tom, ignoring him." There could be multiple reasons why Rebecca might act this way. The director may choose to cut the direction. However, it is still a clue for the actor as to how Rebecca feels about Tom. It is up to the actor to build on the information he is given. It is up to the actor to be interested in the characters and the plot line. Famous actors are given access to allow them to do significant research on a character if they choose to do so. A good play will ask a lot of tough questions. It will hold a mirror up to the audience and ask them to reflect.

Industry Connection
Let's say an actor is meeting with an agent and he wants to ask a question or two. If he is going to ask his question successfully, he has to establish a connection between himself and the person from whom he is inquiring — that is the actor's responsibility. He needs to make sure he is looking in his direction, as opposed to the floor or the ceiling. The actor has to state the question slowly and clearly. Imagine if he is asking irrelevant questions. Not only is he of little value, he is wasting his and the agent's time. One thing that people in the industry never have enough of is time. Before the actors can ask a question, they have to learn how to ask a good question. Most actors will acknowledge they have many more questions than answers. Tell your actors to create one new question on acting every week. In this way, they are learning to ask a better question.

241. Walk the Line
This exercise comes from my book, *Acting Games for Individual Performers,* and has been adapted here so that it can be used with the group. You are going to instruct the whole group to work this exercise at the same time. Let everyone find their own space in the room. They will want as much of a gap between themselves and the next person as possible. This exercise should be done without talking, as if there is only one actor in the room. Explain in the following way:

INSTRUCTOR: I would like you to start by finding an open space in the room. I want you to picture an imaginary line that goes from one end of the room to the other. I would now like you to walk along the imaginary line in a comfortable way. When you have finished, note how you are feeling as you prepare to walk again. This time, I would like your imaginary line to be a tightrope that is four feet in the air. You are going to walk along the rope with the knowledge that it is four feet off the ground. With this information, I want you to use the caution that is needed to walk along the rope at this height. When you have finished, I want you to note how you did things differently from the time before. Take a moment and walk around the room to regain your composure. When you come back, I want you to imagine now that your rope is thirty feet in the air. I want you to walk along the rope with the knowledge that if you fall, you will drop thirty feet. As you proceed, do so with the honesty and commitment that you feel is required. When you have finished, pay attention to what has just been going on in your body and see if you notice any differences from the previous two occasions. Take a few minutes to walk around and regain your composure. Do not stop to discuss the exercise with anyone else. Imagine you are the only person here. This is the fourth and final time you will be asked to walk along the rope. It is going to be the most challenging of all. This time, I want you to imagine your rope is two hundred feet above the Grand Canyon. There are shards of rock, razor sharp like glass, soaring skywards in your direction. If you fall, you will certainly meet a grisly death. An enormous fire is roaring behind you and you only have three minutes to make it across before the flames engulf you. You are the sole breadwinner for your family and if you die, your family will lose their home and all their possessions. Before you begin, prepare yourself for a task such as this. When you start, remember this part has enormously high stakes and that there are time constraints to bear in mind. Once you have finished, review how you coped with this final part of the exercise and what was going through your mind. It is quite possible that you could have fallen at any stage, in any section of this activity. If you found that you fell in the first or second parts of the exercise, the consequences would have been fairly minor. However, if you had fallen in the third or fourth stages, the results would have been severe. When you have finished the exercise, let everything sink in. Have you just conquered the Grand Canyon, or did you meet your doom trying?

Follow up with a group discussion. There is no rush to complete this exercise. As the challenges increase, so should the gaps between them. The final stage should come after a good few minutes time for the students to prepare themselves.

Purpose

To commit to your objectives

Make the following observations with your actors:

INSTRUCTOR: The further you go in this activity, the more important it becomes to commit to your objectives. As the stakes become higher, the necessity to succeed is intensified. As an actor, you want to commit to your characters' objectives at every turn. Objectives do not always have to be complex or clever. However, they do need to be executed by the actor. Let us say you are playing a judge in a court scene. Your objective might be to wrap the case up, because you have had a long day and you want to relax in front of the television. This may be the overall objective, and within the scene you may have mini-objectives, such as putting the prosecution in his place, because he is being brazen. Be sure that your objectives have a purpose when you choose or find them. If you said, "My objective is to play the judge," this is more of a fact than an actual objective. If you have no clear objectives, your work will become clouded, gray, and muddled.

Industry Connection

Make the following observations with your actors:

INSTRUCTOR: In this activity you are always on the ground, yet through your imagination you end up two hundred feet above the Grand Canyon, threatened by flames. This activity takes a creative imagination to simulate a feeling of realism. Time and again in your acting you are going to have to use your imagination to create truths that are not given. All we know is what is true to us. Let us say you are on a studio floor that is supposedly a beautiful beach. The floor is hard, lights are shining in your face, camera men, the assistant director, producers, are all running around in the background, and you have to create the appearance of being on a beautiful, secluded beach. It is going to take all your powers of concentration and imagination for you to believe this scenario, but if you do not believe in it, how can you expect your audience to do so? Look for opportunities throughout your day to work with and explore your imagination.

Chapter 29
Unlimited Possibilities

242. Third Time's a Charm

Have your actors sit down with a pencil and paper. Tell them you are going to play a song for them. Tell them to make notes on whatever feelings, emotions, or images that particular song brings up for them. You are going to play the song for them three times. The song will need to be by a different artist. For instance, you might bring in three different versions of *Imagine*, by John Lennon. You might bring in three different versions of *New York, New York,* by Frank Sinatra. It doesn't matter which song you choose, provided you have three different versions of it. As the actors listen to each song, have them close their eyes for the first minute. Tell them at what point they are allowed to open their eyes and start writing. Do this for all three songs. After hearing all the songs, follow up with a group discussion. Have the students read some of their notes out loud to the group.

Purpose
To be open to different possibilities

The plays, *Romeo and Juliet, Death of a Salesman,* and *Cat on a Hot Tin Roof* have all been produced thousands of times. So why is an audience willing to go and see the same play again, and again, and again? Each time each play has been produced it has been by a different company or theatre. Each production has most likely put its own slant on the material in some way or another. Sometimes you will hear someone say, "We went and saw *Romeo and Juliet* for the eighth time because we wanted to see what they were going to do with it." Perhaps the set design is different. Perhaps the actress playing Juliet sees her in a slightly different light than previous performances. If the three versions of the same song sounded exactly the same, no one would listen to them. It is because there is something slightly different, or perhaps dramatically different, that grabs our attention. *Romeo and Juliet* has been around for hundreds of years and yet audiences still go fresh faced and eager to find out what is going to happen. Each play has its given circumstances, but around that, the rest is left to the actor for interpretation. Actors must not approach a play as if it is an open-and-shut case. They should not approach their character as if everything is already decided, leaving them with nothing of value to offer. They will want to look to discover the internal life of their character. An actor should be open to try anything. It is precisely because they have something to offer that audiences want to come.

Industry Connection

While we often see classic movies remade, it is usually only once or twice. However, it is the actors on television or film who have to deal in repetition. They may have to perform the same take ten or fifteen times. Then they will have to do it again, so the cameras can film them from a variety of angles. The director is going to want the same things in terms of continuity. If an actor drank the wine on a certain line, then they are going to have to match it each and every shot. Some directors may tell an actor to do what he likes and that it will all be taken care of in the editing room. However, in each take the actor may bring something ever so slightly different to the table. Every take is different. Good actors do this because it keeps everything alive, fresh, and impulsive for them. They arrive on the set ready to play. If a performance is stale for the actor, then it is also stale for the audience. Only an actor with a creative imagination will be able to do the same scene twenty times, as if each version is the first time. The three songs allow the actor to realize that what first appears the same can still be quite different.

Note

I have just been watching *The Wizard Of Oz,* and I was once again reminded of the concept of timing. There are many reasons as to why this movie is considered a classic, and I will not explore those, but I would like to explore the historical birth of this movie. *The Wizard of Oz,* was released in 1939 by Metro-Goldwyn-Mayer. The movie as we all know is aimed at children and explores topics such as hope, courage, determination, friendship, fun, problem solving, and overcoming obstacles. There are also many other topics covered in the film, but I leave that to you to figure out. What is interesting is that the same year this movie was released World War II broke out. This may not necessarily have influenced the film's success, but it could have. Look at some of the topics explored in the movie and think about what becomes extremely important in people's lives during wartime: hope, courage, determination, friendship, fun, problem solving, and overcoming obstacles. You might comment on the fact that this is a children's movie, but who do you think takes the kids to the movies? Perhaps my observation seems a little far-stretched or perhaps not. You may say, "Who cares?" It is the actors' responsibility to care, it is their task to continuously ask questions about any area or topic that influences their craft and resolve to get to the bottom of it. There is a laissez-faire attitude in the acting world that just does not wash. I remember reading about a famous acting instructor who once asked the acting world if it wanted to be taken seriously. I think we are still asking the same question.

243. Movie Mayhem

Choose two actors to come into the performance area. Have the audience come up with a storyline for a movie that, in a moment, the actors are going to have to act out. Have the audience also come up with characters for the actors. Before the actors begin, tell them that you are going to have them act out the movie in three separate scenes. The scenes are being shot out of sequence. For instance: middle, beginning, end; or end, beginning, middle. The scenes will want to be mixed up so that the actors have to work out of sequence. Movies are often filmed out of sequence, and so the actors will get a taste of that here. It is quite uncommon for a movie to be shot in continuity. Allow each of the three scenes to last about two minutes. Give the actors about a minute break between each scene. Remind the actors that in their three scenes they must cover the entire movie.

Purpose
To know what came before
In this exercise, the actors are asked to act out the entire movie. Even though it is performed out of order, they need to have a beginning, a middle, and an end. In a play, a scene may start in the middle. For instance, as the lights come up a character may be in the middle of a phone conversation. The audience will not

know what was said before, but the actor must. Perhaps he has just had an argument and is now calming down. Perhaps the other character told him a very funny joke. The dialogue may start in the middle, but for the actor, a scene can never start in the middle. A scene must always start from somewhere.

Industry Connection

Actors who have only performed in theatre all their life will be used to a logical progression in the story. A play will go from the start to the end. A movie will almost certainly shoot out of sequence. This is not to trick the actor, but is usually related to issues such as shooting on location. If a film is on location at a hotel for two days, then the director will get every shot that he needs to shoot at the hotel within that time. If he likes the shot, he will say, "print that." Some of those hotel scenes may be at the beginning of the movie and some may be at the end. Actors playing these scenes have to take into account the changes and transformations their characters may have made during this time. They have to take into account the transformations their characters may have made in regards to relationships with others. The challenge is that an actor may shoot the scenes one immediately after the other. It is interesting to note that in the early days movies were shot somewhat in sequence.

244. Do You Love Me, Honey?

This exercise has been around for many years. For this exercise, have your actors sit on the floor in a circle. Explain in the following way:

INSTRUCTOR: In a moment we are going to go around the circle in a clockwise direction. We are going to start with Kayla, who is going to turn to the person sitting to her left and say, "Do you love me, honey?" The person sitting to her left is going to respond: "Yes, I love you, honey, but I just can't smile." Kayla will then have thirty seconds to see if she can make the second person smile. The second person must do everything in their power not to smile. The only things the second person cannot do are: look away, talk, or close their eyes. The second person will then turn to the person to their left and the process continues until we have been around the whole circle.

This is not an exercise where a person is out because she smiled. We do not want every exercise to be about being a winner or a loser. It is the process and the discoveries that we are really interested in.

Purpose

To explore contradictory behavior

Raise the following points with your actors:

INSTRUCTOR: This exercise contradicts itself. While one person says they cannot smile, the other person has to do everything in his power to make him smile. How are you going to stop yourself from smiling? What techniques are you going to use to assist you in this? You might be playing a wife who turns to her husband and says, "But of course I love you, darling." In reality, she hates his guts and is planning to leave him. The words she speaks contradict her thoughts, as well as the actions that eventually follow. Many of us use contradictory behavior all the time. It is up to you as an actor to understand the motivation behind these actions.

Industry Connection

We might want to call this section "Industry Contradiction." Actors will find a number of occasions where they are told one thing, only to find it is not the case. Here are some examples:

Casting Agent: The part is yours! (The part goes to someone else.)

Director: Great scene! Let's do it again! (It was not good enough.)

Fellow Actor: You really look the part. You're sure to get it. (I hope you fall flat on your face. I want the part!)

Acting Coach: You should definitely sign up for my advanced acting course next. (I want to make as much money as I possibly can from you. I am running a business.)

Producer: Do we really need the airport scene? (We cannot afford to go on location. We do not have that kind of money in our budget.)

These are not facts I am giving you here, but they are potential scenarios. I am sure you can come up with hundreds more.

245. Everything but the Kitchen Sink!

For this activity you are going to need to come up with a whole array of items. Split the students up into teams of six to eight players. Ask them to sit down in their teams. By doing this, it will become easier for you to introduce the exercise in a controlled environment. Explain in the following way:

INSTRUCTOR: For this exercise you are going to have to be creative and put on your thinking caps. In a moment, I am going to give each group fifteen items. These items will vary enormously. At this point, I also want to inform you that each team is stuck on a desert island. Obviously, we are not really on a desert island, so using your imaginations is going to be necessary. You are going to have to figure out how to get from the desert island — one side of the room — back to your homes — the other side of the room. Unfortunately, the ocean is between you and the safety of home. The rule is that your feet cannot touch the floor. If they do, it means that that particular individual has "drowned." If this happens, the whole group has to take responsibility for it. You have to work out a way to get your entire team off the desert island. The other challenge is that you have to use every single item you have been given and explain its use on the journey.

ANNA: Does a pencil have to stay a pencil?

INSTRUCTOR: Excellent question, Anna. You do have some leeway in that you can designate an item as anything you want, provided you can justify it. For instance, you can turn a towel into a flotation dinghy because it is large and covers a good surface area. You cannot turn your pencil into an elephant because there is no clear connection between the two. I am going to give each group twenty minutes to work out how to involve every item on your journey. After that twenty minutes we are going to get together and watch each group perform. Your aim will be to take your entire team to safety within five minutes. Each group will need to explain their choices. You have a limited amount of time, so you will need to work together as a team. This is not a competition. The only people you are competing against are yourselves.

While the students are brainstorming, you may want to walk around and observe. If they are totally stuck, see if you can give then a nudge in the right direction.

Some examples of items are:
Chair
Book
Umbrella
Piece of string
Blanket
Ball
Stick of gum
Balloon
Pack of crayons
Large piece of cardboard
Here are some questions for discussion:
In what way does the participant have to focus?
What were the unexpected results in this activity?
What about the importance of the group for this activity?
Are there any benefits for acting from this activity?

Purpose

To stretch the imagination

The actors have to be able to problem solve together. When the students first start this exercise, they may have a preconceived idea of what is going to work, but the longer they continue, the more varied their ideas become. Without a strong imagination, the students will struggle with this exercise. Stella Adler, a renowned actress, trained with Lee Strasburg and Stanislavski. Adler comments that, "Ninety percent of what you see on-stage comes from the imagination."[65] This exercise is an excellent way to stretch the imagination.

Industry Connection

It is important to ensure that the students extract the Industry Connection from this exercise.

The actors are not in competition with the other groups, even if they feel they are. This exercise is purposely organized in this fashion. Down the road, a number of your actors may choose to move to Hollywood, London, or New York. When they go to an audition, they may choose to tell themselves, "I am competing for the part against all these other actors." Technically, they are correct. In reality, this is not the case at all. They need to be reminded that the only person they are competing against is themselves. When they walk into the room, the auditors are looking at their performance. It is up to the individual actors to campaign for the part and show why it should go to them. If they give it their all, this is the best they can do. If they do not get the part, they can still be satisfied with the knowledge that they gave everything they had. By taking competition out of the work, the actors can learn to focus on their own performance. They can learn to put their energy to good use, instead of wasting it unnecessarily.

---

65. Stella Adler, *The Technique of Acting* (New York: Bantam Books, 1988), 17.

246. Get Knotted

To begin, have all your male students stand at one side of the room and all the female students at the other. Ask everyone to take off their shoes and put them somewhere out of the way. If anyone is wearing items such as necklaces, bracelets, or rings, these should also be removed. Explain in the following way:

INSTRUCTOR: To start this exercise, I need all the male students to find a space on the floor. I would like you to lie down and when you do, stay fairly close to each other. What I would like you to do next is link your arms and your legs (calves and below) to each other. This means that each student lying on the floor should be physically linked to other students. You want to make sure that you are linked as securely as possible. It is also important that you are not uncomfortable or putting your body into a compromised position. It is very important that you practice safety first.

PHIL: Can we also link hands?

INSTRUCTOR: It's a good and specific question, Phil. You will want to link arms, but you are not allowed to link hands. (Give the guys one or two minutes to do this.) Ladies, you get the fun job. In a moment you are going to move around the room unlinking your male counterparts who are lying on the floor. Please do not yank them or hit them, but you have to find a way to pry them apart.

STEPHANIE: Can we tickle them?

INSTRUCTOR: Now that's using your imagination! Gentlemen, once the women have unlinked an arm or a leg, it stays that way. You cannot then link it up again. The aim for you ladies is to unlink all the men's arms and legs. You have a time limit of four minutes. If one leg is still linked, the gentlemen win. If all arms and legs are unlinked, the women are the winners. I want you to remember that safety comes first. There are many ladies moving around the room. You are being asked to move efficiently, but not to run. I am sure none of the gentlemen would like your foot in their mouth. Gentlemen, you cannot grab or push back. If your arm is unlinked, it must stay that way. Safety first!

This may sound obvious, but in the excitement and with high-energy levels, it's easy to forget the basics. The ladies are given four minutes, but you can adjust this to anything between three and six minutes, depending on the needs of the group. This exercise may seem sexist, but that is not the intention. Men are generally stronger and for them to do the pulling or unlinking is more likely to cause injury. Again, I make suggestions here, but you will want to work to the specific needs of your students.

Purpose

To communicate clearly

Communication is the key component. If a student on the floor feels his arm is becoming detached, he will want to communicate this to his partner, since when his arm becomes detached, so does his partner's. As the ladies are moving around, they may find one guy who is particularly strong. By communicating with each other, they can work together to get the job done more efficiently. Everything about the actor's work revolves around understanding how to communicate with others. Actors on-stage have to communicate with one another. The actor also has to be able to communicate the story to the audience. It is the actor's level of communication with everybody that is of great importance. Encourage your actors to become good communicators at all levels.

Industry Connection

If the ladies want to succeed in their task, using their imaginations is an important part of the exercise. While it is possible for them to unlink the men using force alone, it is unlikely. Notice that in the exercise explanation, one student talked about the tactic of tickling. If the students use their imaginations, they will be able to succeed with a limited amount of effort. We have talked on numerous occasions about the importance of imagination for the actor. We have talked about how it is vital for any actor on-set to be able to use imagination. What we have not explored a great deal is the importance of vivid imagination with regard to living in an acting hub. In London, Paris, New York, and Los Angeles, actors are going to have to use their imagination with regard to their "other job." They may not want to get one, but unless they are independently wealthy, it is most likely they will need some means of supporting themselves. If they work for fifty hours in a retail store, how much time will they have left over for their acting? How much creativity will they have left at the end of the day? When will they have the time to audition? Using their imaginations and creativity, they will be able to work towards another job that complements their acting career. This may not happen overnight, but this is what they are working towards. Eventually the aim is that they can support themselves on their acting income alone.

247. Jokers Wild

This activity is not for the faint of heart. You will need two cards for this exercise. I like to use the jokers. Explain the following:

INSTRUCTOR: Will two volunteers who are feeling adventurous today come forward? OK, Edward and Ron, why don't you two come forward? Edward, I'm going to give you this joker playing card. I want you to take this playing card and put it to your mouth. I then want you to pass it to Ron. The challenge is that the only way you are able to keep it on your mouth is to suck on it, using your lungs. If Edward runs out of air, the card may fall to the ground. The only way you are then able to pass it to Ron is by blowing it to Ron. At the same time as Edward is blowing out air, Ron, you actually have to be sucking air in. (The two students try and actually pass the card successfully the first time. Be prepared for the class to laugh.) Great job you two! Please take a seat. In a moment, I am going to divide you into two teams. We are going to have a race. Each team will receive a playing card that they have to pass from one end of the line to the other, without dropping the card.

ANDREA: What happens if we drop the card?

INSTRUCTOR: I am glad you asked. Actually, a couple of things happen. If the card is dropped, it goes back to the beginning of the line. The other challenge is that if you are not careful, two of you may actually end up kissing. (Be prepared for laughs or screams with disgust.) This means you are going to need an extra degree of focus for this activity.

WILL: Can we rest the card on our chin?

INSTRUCTOR: Provided you do not use your hands in any way, and the card stays on the face area, you are allowed to pass the card in any way you can. Remember that you then have to find a way to pass the card to the next person.

I am not ordering you to use this exercise with your students. It is a lot of fun and has some great benefits, but it is not for everyone. You are the teacher and instructor and it is up to you to decide what will work best with your actors. If students prefer to sit this one out, you will want to allow them to do so. I am merely giving you suggestions to work with. Make sure the cards are clean before you begin. If a student has a cold or cough, he should sit this one out.

Purpose

To problem solve

The purpose behind this exercise is for the actors to problem solve. At first, they may find that the card keeps falling on the floor. They may also find that they run out of air before they can pass the card. The actors will then have to problem solve. Problem solving does not mean persisting in doing what does not work. Problem solving means finding new ways that do work. Actors are constantly having to problem solve during the rehearsal process. Perhaps the director does not like what they are doing, but is unable to articulate what he wants. It is up to the actors to problem solve to find what it is the director is looking for. This is going to take actors who are willing to go through trial and error. It is going to take actors who are willing to take a pragmatic approach. This is a fun exercise that usually has everyone laughing. It is also valuable in having the actors use their problem solving skills.

Industry Connection

When you start explaining this activity, a number of the actors are going to look at you as if you are joking. They are not going to want to do the exercise. As I have said, it is not for every group. Once they are engaged in the activity, the actors will forget what they were inhibited about in the first place. They are too busy looking to find a way to help their team win to care about anything else. At various points in their career, actors are going to be offered a number of roles that give them a knee-jerk reaction. Perhaps an actor is asked to play the role of a life-sized duck who can talk. The actor may feel too embarrassed to take on such a role. He may feel it will ruin his career. If a famous director is behind the project, perhaps his embarrassment will quickly vanish. An actress may be offered the role of a call girl. You may feel I have no right to mention something like that in this book. It is worth remembering that Julia Roberts played such a role opposite Richard Gere in *Pretty Woman*. It was a role that turned her into an international superstar. I am not saying actors will want to take on every role they feel uncomfortable about. I am saying they will not want to immediately turn down offers until they have explored all their options.

248. The World's Worst

Send your students to sit in the audience space. To start with, tell two volunteers to come into the performance area. You can have some stage props, such as a table and chairs, if you wish. Let the audience provide a scenario for the actors. An example would be a father and son having breakfast at the kitchen table. Tell the actors that the scene has to begin in silence for at least one minute. At this point, only one sentence is to be spoken by one of the actors. It does not matter which actor speaks. The challenge is that what they say must be the world's worst possible thing to say in that moment. Let's take the scenario given here of the father and son having breakfast. Just as the father is about to finish, the son says, "It's a good thing I found those month-old eggs in the dumpster, or they would have been wasted." Continue in this way with other students and other scenarios. You can work with more actors if you prefer. Remind the students that there is no back-and-forth conversation going on here. In terms of spoken dialogue, there should only be one sentence spoken by one actor. As mentioned, it has to be the world's worst possible thing to say in the given situation. Remind the actors there should be at least one minute of no dialogue before the sentence is spoken. It is also necessary that the actors say something that is credible. The scene does not end once the sentence has been spoken. We want to see how the actors react to what has been said and what happens next.

Purpose
To find the logic of the illogical
The actors have to come up with an almost illogical remark. They have to make the world's worst possible comment at the precise moment it should not have been made. If a play script is written logically, this could never happen. The challenge is that human beings do not always act in a logical way. All of us can remember a time when we have said to ourselves, "Why did I just say that?" In part, it is because the impulsiveness of human nature allows us to make such blunders. In a play, the actors have no say in the dialogue their character speaks. What they can do is play the character in such a way that they could potentially say or do anything. It is the unpredictable aspects of human nature that an actor must discover in a role. On a side note, it is unfortunate that new plays have become rarer and rarer. This is in part due to funding and because of the lucrative temptations of becoming a screenwriter.

Industry Connection
How many times has an actor walked out of an audition and said, "What was I thinking? Why did I just say that?" At that precise moment, many actors feel as if they have said the worst possible thing in the world. Nerves often cause us to act and speak in ways that are not normal for us. The challenge is that actors are often placed in high-stakes situations. A one-to-one interview with a casting director is not a normal, everyday event. The novice actor may become tongue-tied, as if the words can hardly come out. Actors have to find normality in the situation. They have to keep a conversational manner with the agent, rather than putting him on a pedestal. I have spoken to actors who have been cast in certain roles who have said, "I can't believe I got the part. I went into that audition as if I didn't even care." If you translate that, the actor may have appeared as if he didn't have a care in the world. The refreshing part for those watching the audition was that the actor had unwittingly stripped away all his barriers.

249. Arm Extensor

This exercise has been adapted for group work from my book, *Acting Games for Individual Performers*. All your students can work this exercise at the same time. Explain in the following way:

INSTRUCTOR: For this exercise, I would like you to find a nice, comfortable space where you can lie down on the floor. Make sure your space has a pretty smooth surface and your back is able to be almost flat against the floor. Please make sure your legs are straight out, and not at a forty-five degree angle. I would like you to close your eyes and take your arm up ninety degrees towards the ceiling. Your biceps should now be by your ears, and your arms should be straight, but not locked at the elbows. What I would like you to do is, keeping your arms straight, slowly start to take them backwards towards the floor behind you, in the same direction they would be going if you were doing the backstroke. The key to this exercise is to move very, very slowly. When you think your fingertips are just about to touch the floor, I would like you to hold that position for thirty seconds. I would then like you to continue to move your arms backwards until they actually touch the floor.

When you have done the exercise, review your findings. Your students may be surprised by the results. It is quite common for the students to stop considerably sooner than they had intended. Follow up with a group discussion. Another way to work this exercise is to ask half the group to perform the exercise while the other half observes. When they have finished, the groups reverse roles.

Purpose
To expand your perceptions and understanding
Many actors find, when exploring this activity, that they felt they were about to touch the floor, though in fact there was still a long way to go. They often comment that it felt as if their arms were going way beyond where they perceived the floor to be. In other words, their physical and mental perception of reality differed from actual reality. Let's say an actor is performing a play that is supposed to be set in a castle. The set designer has done a great job, yet the castle is still made of cheap wood that is then painted with a brick design. Logic tells the audience that this is not a real castle, yet through strong acting and stimulating their imagination, an audience can be persuaded to suspend logic for a new perception and understanding. Actors can transport their audience anywhere they want to, if they can transport themselves there first. Acting can happen anywhere.

Industry Connection
The actors usually imagine that their arms have gone beyond their perceived belief structure. Actors working in the industry have to learn how to do the same thing. If they thought logically, based on the statistical possibility of their getting work, they would pack their bags, turn right around, and leave. Actors who can only think in conventional terms are unlikely to hang around for long. Actors will want to believe they can be anything they want to be. They will really want to strive to understand and embrace the human spirit. To think unconventionally and outside the norm is a practical approach for the actor.

250. Balancing Act
Tell your actors to stand in a circle. Place a paper bag, such as one from a grocery store, in the center of the circle. The bag should not be flat, but standing upright and open. Choose an eager student to go first. Tell him his objective is to pick up the bag. The challenge is that he can only do so using his mouth. The other challenge is that only one foot can be touching the ground while he attempts this. He can raise it in the air or he can put one foot on top of the other foot. Allow each actor to try two or three times. You are also going to need a pair

of scissors for this activity. If a student gets his mouth on the bag but cannot pick it up, you will want to cut off that piece of the bag for hygiene reasons. This means that the bag is going to get lower and lower, which adds to the challenge. Go around the circle until someone can pick up the bag. If the group finds this too easy, turn the bag on its side or use a smaller bag.

Purpose
To develop coordination
Actors who are flexible may be able to pick the bag up by bending forward. In order to be able to do this on one leg, they are going to have to be well-coordinated. Their flexibility alone may not be enough and may cause them to fall over. Actors have to take on many different roles in their lifetime. Many of their characters do not move as the actors do. One character may be a sophisticated duchess who carries herself with dignified posture. Two years later the same actress may play a drunken character with a limp. She is going to need a well-coordinated instrument to take onboard the challenges she faces with these characters. While I have mentioned physical aspects here, coordination applies to all aspects of the actor's performance.

Industry Connection
This activity is a balancing act. If the actors cannot balance, then their flexibility is not going to count for much. The actors' career is a balancing act. Some aspiring actors say, "I am just going to focus on my acting and disregard everything else." At first glance this seems admirable and commendable. The question that needs answering is: How are they going to pay their bills? Perhaps it would be better to say, "Acting is going to take up the majority of my time." In *Acting for Love & Money,* Paul Gleason and I talk about the Pie Exercise. The concept is that the actors will want to work towards putting as much time as possible into their acting and their career. This is something that actors can work towards, rather than accomplish overnight.

Chapter 30
The Storyteller

251. Poetry in Motion

Choose five actors to go into the performance area and line up side by side. Explain this exercise in the following way:

INSTRUCTOR: In a moment, the five of you are going to make up a poem one sentence at a time. David, you will give the first sentence and immediately, Claire, you will give the second sentence, and so on. Here is a really bad example:

ACTOR 1: It was a cold and dreary day in the merry old month of May.

ACTOR 2: The chickens refused to come out to play.

ACTOR 3: Inside, inside, inside, they decided to stay.

There is no pausing, and the poem will want to move as if it is one fluid piece. The poem should be as long or as short as you choose to make it.

After the actors have told one poem, they can switch the order and make another. Switch actors to allow others to work with this exercise. The poems do not have to rhyme. In regards to hearing poems out loud, John Timpane says, "Not reading a poem aloud is like not living in a house after you've built it. Why would you do that to a poem? Just leave it sitting there, silent, a bunch of marks on the page?"[66] Have your actors bring their poetry to life.

Variable
You could also vary this exercise by having the actors perform it as a rap.

Purpose
To engage in interpretation
Just like this exercise, acting is a form of poetry. If five people hear the same poem, they may each come away with something very different. If five people go to see a play, each one will have his own interpretation. Each one will come away with something slightly or enormously different from the next. One person may say, "I loved it," while another may say, "It was awful." Like poetry, acting is subjective and often comes down to preference. A person who hates war movies may see a brilliant performance and still say it was a bad movie. This is why actors must always take reviews with a pinch of salt. Some movie stars take their negative reviews and frame them on the wall as encouragement.

Industry Connection
In this exercise, the actors start with nothing. If they put their trust in the exercise, they may end up with a pretty decent poem. An actor who moves to Hollywood usually does so armed with little more than some training, a few credits, and hopes and dreams. There is no guarantee that he will have an acting career. The statistics say it is almost certain that he won't. Hard work and perseverance are extremely important, but they are not enough. Actors also have to trust that things will happen. They have to be aware of their place in the bigger picture. If you are a doctor, you can work your way up. A lawyer can do the same thing and

---

66. John Timpane, *It Could be Verse* (Albany: Boaz, 1995), 11.

become a partner in a firm. An actor can be a movie star one year and out of work the next. Actors have to trust and believe that next job will always arrive.

Note

If you want your actors to be prepared, then, as an instructor, you will also want to be prepared. Review all of these exercises well before each workshop and make any necessary adjustments and adaptations that you need to. A word of caution: If you do adapt an exercise, make sure your changes have a valid purpose. A good exercise can very quickly become pointless if there is no real purpose behind the adaptations.

252. Get Off

Bring up six players into the performance area. Have the audience give them each a character and set the scene for them. When this has been established, explain in the following way:

INSTRUCTOR: The six of you now know who you are and the outline of the scene. Your scene can last up to two minutes, at which time you will be cut off. The audience will then vote one of you out. This is going to be based on who they think gave the weakest performance. If you are in the audience, you are going to have to justify your answers. You cannot say, "I want to vote Derek off because his acting was bad." You have to tell us why his acting did not work for you. After an actor has been voted off, the scene is played out again in the same way. Those of you remaining are somehow going to have to incorporate the actor who was voted off. At the end of the scene one of you will be voted off again. The final performance will be given by the last actor remaining. It will be given in the form of a monologue. Remember, you are not acting out a new scene each time. It is the same scene but with fewer and fewer actors.

SARAH: How can we incorporate an actor who is not there?

INSTRUCTOR: Use your imagination and find a way.

Purpose

To communicate the story
Raise the following points with your actors:

INSTRUCTOR: You may feel you are giving a wonderful performance, and yet you might be the first one voted off. How can this be? Perhaps you feel you are giving a wonderful performance, but it is all drawn into yourself. The technical aspects of theatre demand that you are seen and heard. If you are mumbling away in the corner, this is very likely to go against you. If you are ever watching television where the volume is too low, you either turn it up or quickly lose interest. Make sure that your audience does not lose interest in you! Perhaps you are making the audience laugh, but nothing you are doing had any justification. It is true that you may entertain the audience, but it does not mean they believe anything you are doing. In this exercise we are looking for strong and believable performances.

Industry Connection

In this exercise an actor is voted off because something about his performance didn't convince the audience or was not believable. When the audience goes to the movies, they vote actors off much in the same way. They say, "Her performance was so fake." They tell this to their friends who then tell this to their friends. As a result, the movie does poorly at the box office. This is not if two people decide this, but if there is a general consensus amongst the public. An audience more often than not is going to see their favorite actor, as opposed to the movie itself. If their favorite actor ceases to be convincing, perhaps he will also cease to be their favorite actor.

253. Monologue Marathon

Have your actors stand in a circle and explain in the following way:

INSTRUCTOR: I would like a volunteer to step into the center of the circle. Thank you, Diana. What I would like you to do is to make up a monologue of your choice. You are to improvise the contents of the monologue. At some point, I would like another actor to come into the center and take over the monologue. This should happen without discussion. The person who takes over should continue immediately, without pause. The person taking over is not starting a new monologue, but continuing from where Diana left off. Diana, you will go back to your place in the circle without comment. This cycle can proceed with seven or eight actors continuing the same monologue. It is worth noting that even though it is part of the same monologue, you can take it in any direction you choose.

This is a great exercise, but can be challenging to do accurately. One of the challenges is that some actors will totally lose sight of the original monologue. It is important to remind the actors that they must continue in the spirit of the original monologue. I have not said that the actors must continue with the original character. I have left this as a gray area. The character may not be clearly established. It is also possible to continue the same monologue, yet transform the character.

Purpose

To transcend the monologue

A powerful part of this exercise is that the original monologue can transcend itself in many different ways. The original actor can say things he would never have dreamed of saying. By having seven or eight actors take over the monologue, it opens up a whole new set of possibilities. Let us say an actor has performed in the same play for a year. It has become old and boring and he is simply going through the motions. This is going to show in his performance and may stick with him in future performances. It is up to the actor to rekindle his enthusiasm in every performance. It is up to the actor to ignite his imagination and see where it takes him. Only good actors are able to do this. Bad actors do not even bother to try.

Industry Connection

I always find it a bitter pill to swallow when I hear an actor say, "Film acting is easy." Some directors will watch you do a scene and say, "Try something else." This is an immensely difficult piece of direction to take, because it is giving the actor very little to go on. What it does tell the actor is the director was not satisfied with the take he just did. Some actors say this is not the case and that they just want another shot to be safe. This is certainly a possibility, but when a director asks for another take it is almost certainly because he hasn't seen what he is looking for yet. If an actor is in a play, the director might allow him to go home and come back the next day and show the director his thoughts on the scene. In a movie, the director might give an actor three minutes. This is not because he is being inconsiderate. It is simply because he needs the shot. Actors have to be able to think fast on their feet. They have to be able to handle the demands and requirements of their industry.

254. Bull's-Eye

For this exercise you are going to need to put two chairs facing each other in the performance area. Choose two actors to come forward. Explain in the following way:

INSTRUCTOR: Lorraine, I would like you to sit in the chair on the left, and David, you are going to sit in the chair on the right. You are going to sit facing each other with your knees practically touching. In a moment, I am going to ask Lorraine to close her eyes. David, at the same time, you are going to look towards the ground. After a few moments, David, I want you to look up and immediately focus on one of Lorraine's eyes. It does not matter which eye, provided it is just one. I am going to ask you to do this for sixty seconds.

LORRAINE: Are both my eyes still closed?

INSTRUCTOR: Yes. You keep your eyes closed the entire time. After the minute is up, I am going to ask you to guess which eye you think David is focusing on. That is the whole exercise.

STEVE: What if David isn't focusing properly? Won't that throw Lorraine off?

INSTRUCTOR: That is a very good observation. David is going to have to remain extremely focused at all times. If he is looking in the direction of one eye, but not really focusing on it, Lorraine is going to receive mixed signals. At the same time, Lorraine has to stay focused to pick up the signal David is sending. David's aim is for Lorraine to guess correctly. He has to do everything he can to make this happen.

Once one pair has finished, begin to work with another pair. It is very important that the audience sits in silence during this exercise.

Purpose

To use clear channels of communication

Actors have to develop the ability to communicate clearly, both to one another and to their audience. The actor who is looking at one eye has to send a strong signal. If he is looking at one eye, but thinking about other things, he is not communicating a clear signal. He has to put all his energy into the one eye he is focusing on and communicate that to his partner. The partner with his eyes closed will only receive that channel of communication if he is open to it. We are constantly in the process of communicating with others. Sometimes we communicate clearly, at other times we attempt to send false signals of communication. For instance, a student might tell his English teacher, "I really love your class!" His motivation for saying this might be because he wants a good grade, although actually he cannot stand the class. The teacher may already know this through awareness of the student's nonverbal communication signals. Even if one character is sending confusing signals to another character, the actor must still be able to send clear signals to the audience. The other characters may sometimes be kept out of the loop, but not the audience.

Industry Connection

What is the actor's bull's-eye? Some actors may see it is as their ultimate goals. Actors may say their bull's-eye is to become a movie star. This is a noble aim, but it is also one that puts an enormous amount of pressure on the actors. Let us say after five years of hard work, an actor landed a small role on a soap opera. His friends and family see this as an amazing achievement. The actor sees it as a failure, because he is still not a movie star. While going for the bull's-eye, actors have to allow themselves to enjoy the journey. What if this actor finally became a movie star after thirty years of trying? When he finally got there, he suddenly realized that it was not all he thought it was reputed to be. He has now wasted thirty years of his life being miserable for nothing. Discuss with your actors the following topic: It is great to have grand ambitions, provided you allow yourself to enjoy the journey that gets you there.

255. The Fortune-Teller

Set up two chairs in the performance area. Send one student outside of the room. Choose another student and name him as a famous character in history. Some examples are: Marilyn Monroe, Abraham Lincoln, Mahatma Ghandi, Albert Einstein, and Florence Nightingale. Tell the student secretly, or with the help of the audience, the name of a famous person. Tell the student outside — the fortune-teller — to come back into the room. Ask both students to sit on the chairs. At this point, the fortune-teller is going to make a series of statements and assumptions about the client. It is as if he is reading his fortune. In reality, he is trying to work out who the client is. Let us say we had told the client he is Abraham Lincoln. The fortune-teller might guess, "You were born a long time ago." This would be a fairly accurate statement. If the fortune-teller said, "You went to a women's school." The client could respond, "I don't think so." Try to have both performers steer clear of absolutes. For instance, if the fortune-teller said the client is definitely a woman, this would be inaccurate. Advise the fortune-teller to make more general and subtle statements. You can either give the fortune-teller a limit of twenty questions, or you can come up with a time limit. Within the specified limit, he can make subtle guesses, provided he keeps them within the context of the exercise. For instance, he might say, "Thank you for coming, Mr. Armstrong." If the customer is not the famous astronaut, the scene continues. If the client is Mr. Armstrong, he might say, "It was nice to meet you." They should then leave the scene in character. Allow the fortune-teller a maximum of three guesses. Once the scene is complete, change the players to two new ones.

Purpose

Asking a good question

The fortune-teller has to be able to ask a good question. It is not enough to make unsuitable guesses. He has to be able to ask good questions while keeping the credibility of the scene going. By stating, "You were born quite a long time ago," the actor has made a general statement that will give him some important information. If he said, "I think you were born in the last twenty years," this is a poor statement in that it is statistically likely to be inaccurate. In a play, the actors have to constantly ask themselves questions with regard to their character. "Why does my character appear to hate her best friend at this point? What has motivated her to feel this way?" It is not enough for the actors to just say the lines. They have to understand what motivates their characters to do the things they do. Actors cannot change the lines in the play. It is the writer's job to make sure the story is well-crafted. The actors can invent a backstory that makes their choices and motivations subtly different from another actor playing the same role. This is what brings the audience back to see the same play year after year. They want to see what another cast or actor has done with the play.

Industry Connection

The fortune-teller does not know who the customer is. He is going to have to use his creative imagination to figure things out. He is going to have to get into his creative mode. He is going to have to put his trust in the fact that he can find the right answer through his observations and statements. The aspiring actors arriving in Hollywood sometimes think they know everything there is to know. Shortly after arriving, they usually find out the hard way that this is not the case. Even if they are a very well-trained actor, there are many aspects of the industry that they will have to learn. Some actors say, "I don't live by the rules." Actors cannot break the rules if they do not know what the rules are. It is not necessary to have all the right answers before they arrive. There are things they can learn, and will learn, as they gain more experience. They can also take workshops and courses to further their industry knowledge. When actors presume to know everything, their work becomes stagnant. It is the actors who ask a better question of themselves and others who have the potential for growth. The great actors are always questioning and have an appetite for life.

Note

If one hundred of the finest actors were put together in the same room and asked to talk about their acting process, they would most likely continually contradict each other. One of the reasons for this is that acting is more of an art than an exact science. When great actors are interviewed about their own acting process, quite often they are not able to articulate what they do. This is because many actors do what they do, but have not analyzed it clearly in their own minds. It is very important that your actors are aware of this to avoid confusion and contradictory advice. In the end, each actor has to develop his own technique and do what works for him.

256. Poetically Speaking

Have your actors sit as the audience. Bring two actors into the performance area. Ask the audience to outline a scene for them to improvise, or they can come up with their own. Instead of simply speaking the lines, the actors are going to converse with one another using poetry. Not only do they have to talk in poetry, but they must talk in *rhyming* poetry.

Here is an example:

ACTOR 1: How are you today? Are you coming out to play?

ACTOR 2: I can come soon. Let me go get my balloon.

ACTOR 1: I love to watch them fly way up in to the sky.

ACTOR 2: You are right. It is great to watch them take flight. Shall we get some food? It always puts me in a good mood.

This is a pretty bad, short example of how a scene may go. The actors need to continue to alternate with each other. It does not have to be every line, but have the actors keep their responses fairly concise. The reason is that you do not want one actor to give a long soliloquy while the other actor responds with one-liners. Allow the scene to play out for a few minutes then change to another pair of actors. If you want to, you can have a three- or four-person scene. It is going to be tough for the actors to respond to one another without pauses, yet they should aim to respond as if in prose conversation. The audience will probably do a great deal of laughing. We do not want to see laughing on-stage unless it is character-motivated.

Purpose

To work in the moment

The actors cannot prepare their responses in advance. The reason is that they have no idea what the other actors are going to say. The only way each actor can respond is at that moment. This is supported further by the fact that the actors are asked to keep their pauses to a minimum. We live in the moment. If a person calls out our name, we usually turn and respond. Even if we do not turn, we usually react and respond. The challenge is that bad actors miss a vital piece of their acting. They never react to anything because they already know what is coming. They already know what their fellow actors are going to say so they respond without reacting. The reaction can tell the audience a great deal as to how the character feels about what has just been said. To work in the moment and react in the moment takes an actor of some experience. It takes an instinctive actor to perform this way. It can also only happen when an actor has trust in his own work and ability. Guide your actors towards reacting in the moment.

Industry Connection

The actors are given specific instructions. They are told to talk in poetry. They are also told that their poetry has to rhyme. Some of your actors will automatically do this, while others will ignore or forget most of what you have said. The challenge comes when the same thing happens in the audition situation. Actors who receive sides or the scene ahead of time will hopefully put a good deal of work into it. They may make choices as to how they want to play the scene at the audition. They go through what they want to do and all their blocking. When they arrive at the audition the director asks for something totally different. The actors still feel in their hearts that they want to show the director "what I can do!" They ignore the director's suggestions and play the scene their own way. Even if they do a great job, it is highly unlikely they will get the part. Here is the challenge: At the back of his mind, the director will be saying, "This actor is very good, but he cannot follow direction." An actor who cannot follow direction may cause many extra takes. This could add a good deal to production costs. No producer is going to be happy with such a situation. Some of your actors may point to famous actors who are demanding and stubborn. Remind your actors that when they are bringing in multiple millions at the box office, they may also be able to behave in this way. However, it is not for supporting actors to behave unprofessionally. I have made this point purely to explain why certain actors are able to get away with it.

Note

I often start out my exercises with two actors. I do this in order to establish the premise of each exercise. It can be cleaner and more efficient to start out with two actors. It is not a rule, and you should feel free to work in any way that suits the needs of your actors. Some actors may find doing numerous takes frees them up. Just because the director says, "action" does not mean the actor has to "do" something. An actor does not want to let the camera catch him changing gear.

257. Moment by Moment

Have your actors sit as the audience. Bring five actors into the performance space. Have one actor sit downstage, far left. Have the other four actors stand behind him in the performance space. The actor sitting at the front is going to improvise a story. If you want to, you can create a premise for the story with the help of the audience. The actors are going to act out the storyteller's tale. They need to act it out in as literal a fashion as they can. The storyteller may say, "She ran across the road to catch the bus." At this point, one of the actors will want to run across the road and another should become the bus. All four actors do not have to be involved in every scene. It is also important to note that the actors do not have to be human in every scene. They could be a bus, or a cat if need be. It is also worth reminding the storyteller that if there are four actors, he will want to take this into consideration. The storyteller will only want to give one or two sentences at a time, which are then acted out. The storyteller is at the front corner and cannot see what is happening behind him. After a few minutes, change over to another group of actors and a new storyteller.

Purpose

To act in the moment

The actors have to act in the moment because they have no choice. They have no idea what the storyteller is going to say next and therefore cannot plan ahead. To act in the moment is one of the hardest parts of acting. Actors in a play already know the script. They know their lines, and they have rehearsed each scene so many times, they could perform it in their sleep. It is therefore a challenge for the actors when their characters should appear surprised, confused, or uncertain. A good script is something that an actor can work *with* and not *on*. When actors are intimately familiar with the story, they are certain of everything. The challenge for the actors is to separate what they know from the reality of their character. It is one thing to talk intellectually, but another for the actor to achieve it in performance. This exercise forces the actors to be in the moment, whether they want to or not.

Industry Connection

The storytellers cannot see the results of the story they are telling. They have to trust that it is all coming together. When actors are in a movie, they have to trust that the final product will create the entire vision. When filming their scenes, they will get a small idea of audience reaction in terms of the crew. However, the crew members are not clear barometers, as they may see the same scene eleven times. The actor cannot see the movie he is making until it has been sliced and diced in the editing room. Just like the storytellers, he has to trust in what he is doing. This is not always easy for many of us who are wired to immediate gratification. Actors have to trust in their own ability to bring the very best they can to each scene. If they can do this, the rest is out of their hands. If they don't do their share, they only have themselves to blame when the final product reflects poorly on them.

258. Tangled Web

You are going to need a big ball of yarn for this exercise. Before your students arrive, unroll the ball of yarn and make single knots at intervals throughout. Make the same number of knots as there are students in the group. When you have finished, rewind the ball of yarn. When your students arrive, ask them to sit on the floor in a circle. Tell them that they are going to create a story together. Hand the ball of yarn to the first person. Tell him that when he begins the story, he is also to begin unraveling the ball of yarn, using two hands. He is not allowed to put the ball on the floor and roll it out. As soon as he comes across a knot, he is to pause in the story and pass the ball to the next person. He is to continue the story from where the last person left off. He is also to continue unraveling the yarn until he comes across a new knot. By making him do the unrolling manually, it will take longer, and it will also demand his skill and concentration. If he is not paying attention, he may miss a knot. It is also important that he continues the story while he is unraveling the yarn. He should not be doing either one or the other, but both things simultaneously. It is important that a student does not bring the story to an abrupt end. You want to keep it going around the circle. Before playing this activity, I would advise working with One-Word Story and Story Time, both of which are in *112 Acting Games*. You can also work with other similar exercises you are familiar with. I mention that because this is a more advanced version of the story exercises.

Purpose
To move rapidly between thoughts
We could say that the actors are multitasking. They have to make up a story and they have to unravel a ball of yarn. We might also say they are doing two things at once, although, in fact, what they are doing is moving rapidly between one activity and the other. The more proficient they are, the more it will appear as if they are doing two things at once. During a performance, actors can appear to be doing multiple tasks at the same time. This is in part because fine actors are able to turn some technical aspects of their performance virtually over to their subconscious. They are experts at moving between thoughts. Alternating between thoughts at a rapid pace opens the pathway to heightened imagination. They are training their mind to be open to a constant flow of thoughts, which in turn creates a flow of ideas.

Industry Connection
Many people involved in the industry have learned to move rapidly between thoughts. Just spend a couple of days in Los Angeles and you will know what I mean. People appear to be doing fifty things at once. A director on-set can be talking to an actor while also conversing with her assistant director. At the same time, she could be on the phone to the producer and signaling the sound crew for something else. An agent can be on his computer or phone and auditioning

a prospective client, all at virtually the same time. Some actors look to retain a sense of isolation on-set. Actors have to learn to move rapidly between thoughts for their acting, but they also have to be able to do it for their career. They have to learn how to keep up with all the other people involved in the industry. This is easier said than done. Like everything else an actor desires, it can be done, but it comes after hard work and practice.

259. Sound F-X

You are going to need a number of short children's stories for this exercise. Split your actors up into groups of between four and six. Give each group a children's story that takes three to five minutes to read. Each group is going to choose a narrator who will read the story. This individual must be good with expression. The rest of the members of the group are going to create the sound effects to go with the story. They are going to have to look through the story to see where they can best add sound effects. For instance, there may be a line that says, "A steam locomotive passed by." This would be an ideal time for the actors to create the sound effects for the train. They would also want to take into account that it is a steam train. Give each group twenty minutes or so to work on this. They can divide the sound effects as they like. Now bring the whole class back together. Tell each group to perform their story while the other groups sit as the audience. The only person who should be seen on-stage is the narrator. The rest of the group should not be seen, but only heard. Follow up with a group discussion, either after all groups have performed, or following each performance.

Purpose
To direct the story
The actors are asked to create sound effects themselves. In a sense, they are being asked to direct themselves. Some actors believe that they will never have to direct themselves. This is sadly a little naïve. A director may tell an actor to "make it bigger." This really has very little practical meaning for the actor. The actor would then have to direct himself to justify his next action. A famous actor may receive even less direction. In this case, some directors are afraid to step on the actor's toes. The director says things like, "What do you think you would like to do at this point?" It is over-simplistic to say actors never have to direct themselves.

Industry Connection
Each group is asked to create the sound effects that relate to their story. They are not going to have to do this for a movie, but the exercise highlights a complementing factor of the actors' work. Henry Mancini was considered by many to be a master at composing television and film scores. His scores added an extra cohesiveness to the overarching story. If the technical aspects of a movie are not strong, the overall impact of a movie will be weakened. If the acting is not strong, the technical aspects will have less impact. How many times have you heard someone say, "The special effects were great, it's a shame the movie was so poor"? Actors are not expected to become technical experts in all aspects of a film. They are, however, expected to understand that there are many elements that go into making a good movie, of which sound effects are but one.

Chapter 31
The Audience

260. Order, Order!

Split your actors into two groups. Once they know who is in which group, they can mix up with the whole class again. Instruct all your actors to mill around the room. Without warning, call out an instruction such as, "Line up your teams in order of height." As quickly as they can, the actors must join their team, then line up from shortest to tallest. They can do this by talking or by any means of communication necessary. The first team to do so correctly gets a point. After each round, have the actors walk around the room again until the next order is called.

Other instructions are:
1. Line up in order of age.
2. Line up in order of shoe size.
3. Line up in order of hair color from light to dark.
4. Line up in order of number of cars you own from the most to the least.
5. Line up in order of the number of vacations taken over the past year, from the fewest to the most.

By the way, just because a team has lined up first, does not mean they get the point. This exercise requires checks and balances. Make sure that their answers are accurate. It is also recommended to keep away from areas that are too personal or too offensive. Such as, "Line up in order of thin to fat." This would be considered in poor taste. It is true that it may be useful in terms of releasing inhibitions in your actors. However, there are plenty of other ways to do this, without attempting to make the actors feel worthless.

Purpose
To use effective forms of communication

In this exercise the actors have to be able to communicate effectively with one another. The actors also have to be able to communicate effectively with the audience. They have to have a desperate need to communicate. If an actor is giving an honest and heartfelt performance, and no one can hear what he is saying, he will lose his audience. If he is on-stage and profiles his entire performance because of lack of stage awareness, he will lose his audience's attention. To hold the audience the actors have to make sure they communicate with them. Of course, there are times when it is acceptable to turn your back on the audience. There may be times in a scene where a voice is softer and yet it is still projected. These are artistic and directorial choices, as opposed to lack of technique. It doesn't matter if actors are performing in front of five or five thousand, they still have to communicate the story! The actor is a storyteller.

Industry Connection

This exercise requires the actors to communicate in an efficient and effective manner. If they don't communicate effectively, they will always be the runner-ups. Raise the following points with your actors:

INSTRUCTOR: A colleague of mine once said, "If they don't know about you, they can't hire you." You may be a fine actor, but if no one knows you exist, you are not going to work. To put your name on the map, you are going to have to remind agents, casting agents, directors, and producers that you exist, on a regular basis. You can do this through mail-outs, emails, thank you cards, text messages, your own website, Facebook, Twitter, a blog, YouTube, networking events, and a whole variety of other methods. You may feel this is beneath you and has nothing to do with acting. Please note that the title of this section is "Industry Connection." If you want to work in the industry, then you have to play by its rules, while creating a few of your own. It does not mean you have to like it, but you may as well embrace it and push ahead full throttle. The actor will want to learn to march to the sound of his own drum,

261. Corners

For this exercise, have the actors sit outside of the performance space. Choose four actors who stand one in each corner of the room. Bring a fifth actor into the center of the room, and explain in the following way:

INSTRUCTOR: The objective of this exercise is not to be in the middle. The people in the four corners can communicate with each other only by making eye contact. At any given moment, two of them should try to switch places. The objective of Nigel, who is in the middle, is to steal a corner. He can only do this while two or more actors are crossing from one corner to the other. If he succeeds, a new actor will be in the middle. A rule for this exercise is that once an actor has left their corner, they cannot run back to it. As always, please use safety first and be spatially aware of others. All four actors can change corners at the same time if they choose.

Purpose

To remain fully alert

In this exercise the actors have to be fully alert at all times. Good actors can rely on their training and give an average performance. In order to give a good performance that engages their audience, they will have to remain fully alert at all times. They will want to fully engage the other actors in the scene and be aware of everything that is happening around them. Their performance must be so unbelievably fluid. While rehearsals require a certain amount of planning, there must be room for the actor to react to the moment.

Industry Connection

To get out of the middle, the actor will have to seize the opportunity as it arises. Perhaps one of the actors slips, or is a really slow runner. When the opportunity comes his way he has to be ready for it. There may be an occasion where he doesn't even run because he knows it is not worth wasting the energy. If an actor is consistently working toward his acting goals, opportunities will arise. The challenge is they may be few and far between. He has to be alert enough, and prepared enough, to seize them. An acting career is not a part-time job. It is a way of life! It is a way of looking at the world.

262. The Hot Seat

Have your actors sit in the audience. Put a chair in the center of the room and have an actor come up and sit in it, facing the audience. The audience is going to spend the next ten minutes asking the actor any questions they want in regard to his acting career.

Example questions:

Why do you want to be an actor?

How long have you studied acting?

What will you do if you fail?

What makes you think you have got what it takes to succeed?

How do you support yourself?

How do you feel about all of the competition out there?

When the actor has answered a question, members of the audience can challenge him if they see holes in his answer. To be in the hot seat takes guts. Acknowledge the fact that the actor who takes the seat is laying himself open. Each actor should be in the hot seat for ten minutes. Aim to work with three or four actors in this way.

In this exercise, the audience has many questions they wish to ask the actor. In a play or film, the audience will have many questions they want to ask your character:

Why did you cheat on your girlfriend?

Why did you rob the bank?

Why are you full of hate?

Why did you tell your mother you never want to speak to her again?

Why did you leave your coffee untouched?

This is not an exercise to use with your beginning actors. It is better to work with a group who has been together for a period of time.

Purpose

To be able to answer questions

In this exercise the audience learns to ask a good question. The actor in the hot seat has to learn to answer a question clearly and effectively. The character cannot step off the stage or screen to answer these questions. The actor is going to have to predict these questions and answer them through his interpretation of the text. In terms of the text, Sanford Meisner says, "The text is like a canoe, and the river on which it sits is the emotion."[67] When the audience leaves the theatre, they want to do so with all of their questions answered.

Industry Connection

The actor is in the hot seat every time he steps into an audition room. He is in the hot seat every time he meets with producers, casting directors, agents, etc. Perhaps he is being considered for a current project or perhaps for a project in the near future. The actor is always in the hot seat, because the actor always has to prove himself. No actor is immune to being in the hot seat. A-list actors have made a couple of box office failures in a row, never to be heard of again. They become banished to the B-movie graveyard.

---

67. Sanford Meisner and Denise Longwell, *Sanford Meisner on Acting* (New York: Random House, 1987), 115.

Make the following observations with your actors: Each time you get up in front of an audience you are putting everything on the line again, and again, and again; actors live in the hot seat!

263. Body of Evidence

To start this exercise, ask one of your actors to step out of the room. Pick six actors to come up to the performance area. Have one of the actors stand in the middle. The other five have to stand around this actor. Using only their bodies, they have to shield him as best they can. The other actor is then brought back into the room. He is going to walk around the huddled group and try to work out who is in the middle. Perhaps he can see a shoe or a piece of clothing sticking out. He can get down on all fours if he wants to and really peer at the one in the middle. The actor can have a maximum of two guesses. This is not an exercise in which he should guess right away. He should take his time. One of the actors surrounding the one in the middle may scratch his nose and give something away. Perhaps he gets an itchy left knee and he has to move. The observer may want to play the waiting game to some extent. The rest of the class should be allowed to observe the exercise, but they need to do so from a distance. The reason for this is that you don't want the observer to figure out who is in the middle by using the power of deduction. You might also tell him not to look at the audience. The more discrete and out-of-the way the audience is, the better. You can work this exercise with different actors in the middle and follow up with a group discussion.

Purpose
Audience participation
In this exercise the audience has to be discreet and out-of-the-way. If the audience does not play its part, then this activity will be over before it has begun. The observer will automatically know who is in the middle by the power of deduction. When an audience comes to a play, it is also their responsibility to participate. They have to arrive on time, sit quietly, and pay attention to what is happening on-stage. Of course, if the play or acting is poor, these things may not happen. The audience must have theatre etiquette or be advised on it. I have seen elementary teachers coach their actors on theatre etiquette before taking them in to a show.

Industry Connection
In this exercise the actors have to cover the person in the middle at all times. In other words, they have to stay consistent the entire time. In actors' careers, they also have to remain consistent. There are actors who move out to Hollywood, London, and New York full of excitement and enthusiasm. For six months they work really hard to make things happen. When they find that things are not as easy as they thought, they start to slow down. They begin to become bitter and frustrated and they slow down even more. Eventually they are doing virtually nothing for their acting career, and yet they wonder why they don't have one. Encourage your actors to move away from saying "no" to their lives and learn to embrace "yes."

Note

You will see similar topics mentioned in this book again and again. This is not done by accident. Repetition is an important part of the actor's work. Instead of giving you fifteen exercises, this book contains hundreds of them. They work the same muscles as the fifteen exercises, only with slight adjustments each time. I am not telling you one is better and one is worse. Actors must do what works for them and their instruments. My advice is use what works and disregard the rest.

264. Body Double

Have your actors get into groups of three and find a space in the room. Explain in the following way:

INSTRUCTOR: In a moment, one member of your group is going to contort their entire body in any way they choose. Another member of the group is going to emulate their body position as close as possible. In order to do this, you will need to get as close to them as possible, without actually touching them. This is not a mirroring-from-the-front exercise. For this exercise, you are going to have to work from behind the other actor. You are not back to back, but standing directly behind them, without touching. The third member of the group is the observer. Your job is to make sure that the actor who is emulating does so as accurately as possible. If they have not quite achieved an accurate copy, tell them to keep going. If they are still having challenges, coach them on what they specifically need to do to look identical to their partner. Once the actor has assumed a pose as identical as possible to his partner, have both of them hold that position for about a minute or so. At this point, both of the actors should whisper to the observer what they are thinking about at that precise moment in time. The observer should then share what was said with both actors. See if there are any similarities between what the actors are feeling. When you have completed the activity, switch roles with your partner and start the process again. Obviously, the new actor will mold their body into a totally new position. Please do not feel the need to rush this exercise. If the third actor has a cell phone with a camera, you can take a picture from a side view. At the end of the exercise you can share it with the two participants.

Walk around and observe the groups working. Offer advice only if you feel it imperative. It is better to allow the actors to make the discoveries for themselves. When people are in physical unity, you will sometimes find their thoughts become very similar also.

Purpose

To remember there is an audience

In this exercise, there are two performers and then there is the audience. Actors must never forget that it is an audience for whom they are performing. This does not mean while they are on-stage or in the middle of a scene. Without an audience there is no theatre. If an actor and a colleague act out a scene and there is no audience, that is not theatre. In this exercise the actors have checks and balances. If they do not achieve the required results, the observer will tell them. If an actor is not up to par, the audience will tell him. It may be through word of mouth or box office ratings, but the audience will let the actor know what they think.

Industry Connection

In this exercise the actor's aim is to form his body in exactly the same way as the other actor. He is looking to create continuity. When an actor is on-set, he may have to do the same scene many times over. The director will be looking for continuity in the scene, so that he can use it in the editing room. If the actor drank coffee in one take, but decided not to in another, the take now becomes worthless. In a sense, actors have to learn to mirror themselves. The actors have to be able to recreate what was already created.

265. Toilet Roll Nightmare

For this exercise, pick three volunteers. Ask the three volunteers to wait outside the room. Tell the rest of the group to remain seated and talk amongst themselves. Go outside to the group and inform them that in a minute they are going to come into the room, one at a time. They are going to sit down in the chair that will be placed in the middle of the room and act out a scene. Tell the students that you want them to act the whole scene sitting in the chair, because this is the challenge of the exercise. Do not tell them the name of the activity. Once they have finished their scene, they are to exit the room and the second person is immediately to come in and act out a different scene. The third person will follow in the same way. You are going to need to give each of the actors a situation to act out.

Some example situations:

1. You are riding a wild horse that is out of control. Every time you think you have got him back under control, he starts to go wild again.
2. You are submersed in water up to your nose. The only way you can survive is to hold your breath as long as you can and then take a big deep breath and keep repeating the process.
3. You are going through the steps of an entire tap dance routine. The tap dance starts off slowly and quietly. As you keep going, the moves become faster and more aggressive, until they virtually explode.

Tell the students that they cannot use any dialogue and that all this must be done through nonverbal communication. It is very important that you remember to explain this part. Say you will come back outside in a moment to tell them when to begin. Go back to the class and explain the following quietly:

INSTRUCTOR: I need everyone to focus now, as I am going to explain this to you very quietly. In a moment the three people outside are going to come in, one at a time. They are going to sit on this chair (The chair should be in the center facing towards the audience) and they are going to act out a scenario. Each of them is going to act out a different scenario. Your aim is not to guess their scenario. Your aim is to use your imagination. I want you to imagine, whenever you see one of them performing, that they are on the toilet. No matter what they are doing, I want you to imagine that they are using the toilet. You are not allowed to indicate this aloud. Do not say, "Haha, you look so funny on the toilet." In their minds, they are acting out their scene. If you give anything away, it will ruin it for the rest of the exercise. So remember, your job is to imagine they are on the toilet, but you must not indicate this in any way. I am not going to take any questions, because I do not want to make the students outside suspicious.

Go to the students and remind them to come in one at a time. It is important to remind them that their objective is to perform the whole scene sitting in the chair. You will also want to remind them that at the end of their scene, they must leave the room and the next person will automatically want to follow. At the end of the exercise bring the three actors in and follow up with a group discussion.

Discussion

Explain to them that the students in the audience were not really interested in what they were doing in the scene. Explain to them that the audience had to imagine they were sitting on the toilet. Tell them that the class will now make comments based on their observations, not to poke fun, but to share their discoveries with the students. At first, some of the students may appear offended, but this should quickly dissipate. Start with the first person who performed and have the audience make observations.

Once you have gone through the observations about all three people, ask them for their own comments:

Were you aware something else was going on?

What made you suspect something?

What motivated you to keep going with the exercise?

If you were an audience member, how easy would it have been to use your imagination?

How easy or difficult was it to tap into your imagination, even when you knew the scene had nothing to do with what you were imagining?

Purpose

To see the audience's perspective

The actors are given a scenario to act out during this exercise. At the end of this exercise they discover that the audience had a totally different objective. They discover that the audience's perspective of the scenes is quite different from their own. This may seem like an exercise that is just for a laugh, but there is more to it than that. I remember once watching an actor perform a monologue that he thought was really heartfelt and meaningful. His aim was to move the audience and literally have them in tears. He wanted them to feel real pathos for his performance. He did have them in tears, but they were tears of laughter. The audience thought the piece and the actor were hysterical. At first he was devastated. After giving it some thought he realized there was some humor in the piece — he had just never seen it that way before. The audience was not mocking him, and indeed his performance was heartfelt. What was happening was precisely the same thing. The audience was looking at it from their own perspective. The audience brings with them more imagination collectively than any solo performance, and they beg the actors to let them use it. Studios will often test screen their movies with audiences months in advance of their release date. The actor will want to engage his audience at every turn.

Industry Connection

Each performance has a double meaning. It has meaning for the actor and meaning for the audience. Actors in Hollywood, London, New York, or Paris may attend numerous auditions. Their agent may text them and say, "Here is a role you are perfect for." The actors look at the breakdown and wonder why their agent is sending them to an audition for which they are in no way suited. At the audition the actors read for the part, and the director says, "You are not really suited for this part." The actors feel vilified and think they will tell their agent what they really think of him. As the actors are about to leave, the director continues, "We do have another role that we would love to hear you read for." The actors went in auditioning for one role and through their performance, look, etc., the director saw something else in them. The director saw them as a totally different character. Encourage your actors to broaden their horizons so that they are open to all possibilities. The actor who decided not to go to that audition would have missed a golden opportunity. This is not necessarily something that happens all the time, but it most certainly happens some of the time.

Note
Big studios are often seen as the big bad wolf. It is also worth pointing out that directors often desire the backing of big studios. It is these studios that have the ability to create worldwide distribution of a movie.

266. Body Mechanics

Tell your actors to sit as the audience. Call up seven actors to begin with and explain in the following way:

INSTRUCTOR: In a moment, what I would like you to do is move as one unit and as one body. Debby, you are going to be the left arm. Nick, you will be the right arm. George, you will be the left leg. Loraine, you will be the right leg. Paul, you will be the brain, and Sylvia, you will be the eyes. There are obviously other body parts, but for this first round we are going to start with these. Please stand as close together as you can. Let's have the brain and eyes in the middle. The left arm and leg should stand on the left. The right arm and leg should stand on the right. Jane, you are going to instruct the body as to what you want it to do. If you tell the body to take two steps forward, the body has to discuss it. The way this works is that the body can talk. The brain may tell the eyes, "You need to look in front of you." The eyes may then tell the left leg, "Take one step forward." The left leg may then tell the right leg, "Take one step forward." I have begun with these six body parts, but after working for awhile, you may choose to add more body parts. Once the order has been given, the body has to work together to follow the instructions.

As shown in the example, the body can talk. Every time the body is going to follow through with an action, it is going to have to talk to the brain first. Don't allow the actors to skip steps. Instruct the body to discuss the situation if it feels steps are being missed. Once you have worked with one group of actors, change over to another. The person telling the body what to do can only give one order at a time. Once the body has followed the instructions, it can move on to another set of orders.

Purpose
To be part of a team
One body part cannot move without the approval of and communication with another body part. If the actors do not communicate, the body will move in an illogical fashion or it will become stuck. This can happen even if three of the six body parts are moving really well. It only takes one body part to break the cycle for challenges to follow. It only takes one actor in a play to break the audience's

355

imagination. If an actor breaks character in the middle of a play and says, "I am sorry, I just forgot my line," this is what the audience will remember. Even if the rest of the play and the actors are excellent, this is what the audience will remember. Their imagination will be affected as this break in character will bring the audience abruptly back to reality.

Industry Connection

The actors have to follow through with every step. They are not allowed to skip a step. If the body wants to move, then it has to go through the brain first. If the left leg moves, then the right leg has to follow. Every step must be taken for the actors to complete this exercise effectively. Some aspiring actors would prefer to skip many of the steps necessary to pursue a professional career. I have mentioned this before, but it is so important that I am mentioning it again. They say things like, "I want to be in a television show during my first year," or "Within two years, I want to make enough money from acting to live on." These are often people who have virtually no training in acting. It is not a bad thing to be positive, but it is a challenge for actors to want to skip many of the steps. Many of the aspiring actors who make these statements find themselves giving up their supposed dreams very quickly. It takes the average actor three to five years just to get his feet wet. Remind your actors that they have to be willing to follow through with every step to be ready to have a shot at a professional acting career.

Chapter 32
Performance

267. Through the Lens

This exercise is inspired by an exercise called The Fourth Side by Uta Hagen. Talk to your actors a week in advance about this exercise so that they can come to the session prepared. Explain in the following way:

INSTRUCTOR: In a moment, I would like one of you to come up here and perform your monologue. There is a slight twist to this. Instead of looking at the other character or characters in the scene as if they were around you, you are going to talk directly to the camera lens. This means that the person or persons you are talking to are through the lens of the camera. (You can film this exercise and the actor will have an actual lens to reference. If you prefer not to use a camera, then give the actors a clear reference point to work with.) At no time are you to take your eyes off the camera lens. All the meaning of the piece will want to be there and all the subtleties it entails. The only difference is that you are communicating through the lens and you have to know who is on the other side. Perhaps it is your boss, your lover, your father, your school children. This will obviously depend on your scene and its given circumstances. If it is not clear who you are talking to, then use your imagination.

A way to vary this exercise is to have your actors talk directly to the audience. The actors can also do as Uta Hagen's exercise does and have them communicate through the fourth wall. These are three different choices. Only allow your actors to choose one of them. It would also be useful to discuss movies where actors work directly with the lens. A couple of examples are Mathew Broderick in *Biloxi Blues* and Michael Caine in *Alfie*. Watch two or three actors and have a discussion after each one or at the end, if you prefer. Where necessary, work with the actors on their scenes in this exercise.

If your students do not have a monologue learned, then you can have them improvise a scene for the camera. The important part is that they do not take their eyes off the lens.

Purpose
To develop a specifically vivid imagination
A vivid imagination is necessary for good acting and for great acting. Very occasionally an actor is born with a vivid imagination. Almost all children have a vivid imagination. Most adults do not have a vivid imagination. Their imagination is limited and constrained in many ways. It is most likely that your actors are not one of the select few. They must use the tools and exercises at their disposal to constantly ignite their imaginations. All great acting teachers, past and present, have looked for ways to guide actors into firing up their imaginations. They look to give their actors as many tools as they can possibly give them. Some of the greatest actors of our time have been taught or affected by Stella Adler, Lee Strasberg, and Sanford Meisner. Each of them had their own approach in regards to acting technique. All of them were doing something right. All of them were looking for the same truths at the end of the line. The fourth wall does not exist without a vivid imagination. The audience can never become the actors' best

357

friends in the world without a vivid imagination, a free imagination. Here is the kicker. Some actors read an exercise and say to themselves in an intellectual way, "Yes, I must have a good, vivid imagination." They feel that because they have read about it, and vocalized it, it is now a given reality. The challenge is they have done nothing to develop this muscle. They are doing absolutely nothing to create this reality. As Lee Strasberg says in his book, *A Dream of Passion,* "The training of the senses to respond to imaginary stimuli becomes part of the basic training of the actor; and the possession of this capacity to respond to imaginary stimuli is what characterizes the nature of the actor's talent."[68] The actor will want to make a study of human nature. If actors want a vivid imagination, then they are going to have to work at it on a regular basis. There is a Buddhist proverb that says, "When the student is ready, the teacher appears." This is an important lesson for your actors to comprehend. If they want to be good actors, then they have absolutely no choice but to work on their imagination. Good actors have immediacy about their work. Some of your actors may take issue with you here. They may say, "So and so is a very famous and successful actor and they don't seem to have a good imagination." Help your actors to recognize the difference between a financially and commercially successful actor and a good actor. While they can be one in the same, it is not always the case. An actor who falls into the financial rut of success may cease to grow. A famous actor is not necessarily a good actor. This is another great topic of discussion you can raise.

Industry Connection

There are not going to be many roles where the actor has to work directly through the camera lens, but there may be some. This can make the scene even more challenging for the actor. Instead of being able to create a world of make-believe and as ifs, they are now faced with the stark reality of the camera lens. Yet the camera lens has to transform into the actors' scene partner. The camera lens has to be the actors' best friend, their worst enemy, their mother, their church congregation, or whoever the lens is supposed to be. If the actors do not buy into this, then neither will their audience.

Some actors have a dream of what they imagine it will be like to be on a Hollywood set. In their dream it is a glamorous and romantic world. The reality will let them in for a rude awakening. It does not mean that they will not meet nice people and enjoy working on-set. It means as any professional actor can tell them it is a lot of hard work. They will need to be a stickler for professionalism. Each of your students will one day have to decide if they are going to follow their heart to Hollywood. If a person lies down, then people will always step over him. When an actor is on-set, he is there to work. All the glitz and glamour is saved for another day, but on-set he works. There is very little glamour and a lot of hard work to do on the set. Help your actors to be aware of this so that they are not in for a rude awakening.

Note

Your actors will want to have a variety of contrasting monologues they can perform at a moment's notice. If they do not have any monologues, then help them to get some. They should also have scenes from television and film they

---

68. Lee Strasberg, *A Dream of Passion* (New York: Plume Printing, 1987), 71.

can perform off the bat. A great little exercise is to have your actors pay attention to the television shows they watch at home. Ask them to make mental notes of the type of roles actors or actresses who look similar to them get cast in. For instance, as a generalized statement, police and crime dramas set in New York are more likely to cast dark-haired actors over blonde-haired actors. This might sound like a ridiculous statement to make, but if you watch crime dramas set in New York, you will find that it is a statistically accurate statement. It is important for actors to know what type of actor gets cast on what type of shows. It is part of the working actor's job to know. A show that is on at seven p.m. on Wednesday night might eventually appear at nine p.m. on Thursday night. This is in part because the networks are constantly involved in a ratings war.

268. Cut!

Have your actors sit as an audience. Choose two actors to come into the performance space. Have another actor set a scene for them by using the following circumstances: who, what, when, where, why. Then ask the actors to begin the scene. At any point the actor who set the scene can shout, "Cut!" He is now the director of the scene. The actors are now his raw material. At this point, the actors will pause and be given direction changes. The director can shout, "Cut!" whenever and wherever he feels it is necessary. An example would be, "Felicia, when he strokes your cheek, this time express disdain and repulsion, rather than enjoying the moment." To keep everybody on their toes, allow the audience to have a total of three rebuttals. This means that once the director has reset a part of the scene, if a member of the audience disagrees with the director, he can shout "Rebuttal!" He then goes on to explain how he would direct that moment. If the majority of the audience agrees with him, his version is played out instead. Only allow the audience a total of three rebuttals. This is so that the director gets a chance to actually direct the scene.

Allow a scene to continue for about three to five minutes, and then switch out the actors and director and start a new scene. Some directors will have their actors go beyond what they know is the cut. This is because the moment after may turn out to be the most vital. Premature cutting can stifle the actors' creativity and the development of the scene. There is a whole array of languages available to a director in regard to film.

Purpose
Accountability and the actor
This exercise raises the issue of accountability. In this exercise, the actors are accountable to the director, and the director is accountable to the audience. Actors in a play will want to recognize what they are and are not accountable for. They are accountable for giving the finest performance they can possibly give. They are not responsible for running the lights, checking the sound, other actors' performances, and selling all the tickets. If this is the case, then one would assume they are also the director, producer, and stage manager of the show. If this is the case, then perhaps they are spreading themselves too thin. There are theatre companies such as cooperative theatres where the actors are expected to do some of the jobs mentioned above. This is fine as long as these expectations were discussed prior to the production.

Industry Connection

Raise the following discussion with your actors:

INSTRUCTOR: Are you only going to work with one director for your entire life? If the answer is yes, then you may want to ignore this exercise. The chances are you are going to work with a large and varied assortment of directors. Some will be actor-friendly and some will not. Some will be hands-on, and some will be hands-off. Some will speak an actor's language, and some won't have the faintest clue. You are going to have to know how to adapt and embrace all of these. You might say, "When I work with a professional director, it will be different." You may live to regret this statement. There are a number of directors whose main thrust of direction is giving you your blocking and very little else. They will say things like, "Move to the right a little. You have to have finished the line by the time you pass the oak tree." You have to be able to take this direction and find the justification behind it. You have to do the work and you have to have a fully-functional instrument in order to be able to do so on a constant basis. You have to find a way to be emotionally and physically free between the moment of *action* and *cut*. During a performance, some actors choose to leave their own personalities at home. Benoit-Constant Coquelin is considered one of the greatest French actors of all time. In twenty-two years (1864-1886) he performed forty-four lead roles for the Comédie-Française. In regards to the actor's instrument, Coquelin said, "The instrument of the actor is himself. The actor must have a double personality. The first self works upon the second self until it is transfigured. Thence, an ideal personage is evolved in short until from himself he has made his work of art."[69] Actors are sometimes accused of having eccentric and curious personalities.

Note

There are some theatres where an actor will pay a monthly or yearly membership fee. These are quite common in LA. They will also be expected to sell a certain number of tickets for each performance and donate a certain amount of time to help run the theatre. In return, they will get to perform a little or a lot. It is up to each actor to decide the value of this type of theatre. The producer may argue that without a membership fee they would have to shut up shop. They may well be right. It is worth noting that a school for producers is hard to find. To find an excellent producer is not necessarily an easy task. Some producers sit up higher to make them look taller and more in control. For some producers, artistic talent is something that is bought and sold. What the actors have to decide is what is in it for them. What are they getting out of being in a cooperative theatre? As long as the pros outweigh the cons, they are on the right track. The actor will want to be careful of expectations. Expectations can lead to disappointment. The only people who are going to hold themselves accountable for their acting careers are the individual actors.

---

69. Constant Coquelin, *Harpers New Monthly Magazine Volume LXXIV,* (New York: Harper and Brothers Publishers, 1887), 894.

269. Scene Mutation

Start off by having your actors sitting as the audience. Explain as follows:

INSTRUCTOR: Virginia, please come and join me in the performance area. In a moment, I would like you to begin a scene of your choice. An example could be a student studying for an exam. At some point, and without discussion, I would like another actor to come up and interact with Virginia and start a new scene. This means that both actors are now different characters. There should be no pausing and no discussion. Then, another actor should come up and start a different scene, this time involving three actors. Each scene should be continuous and mutate from one to the next. There should be no pausing between scenes and no discussion. All of these scenes are mimed without dialogue. Do not rush to go up. I only want you to go up when you have a new scene to begin. Each time a new actor appears, they have to be the one to establish the new scene. If there were five people and David went up, he might establish himself as the history teacher while everyone else becomes his students. It is also important that those of you already on-stage are aware each time a new actor enters the performance space. You also have to be alert to adapt to each new scene.

Keep going until you feel the exercise has reached its limit. I have worked this exercise taking it up to ten actors on-stage. If you have ten actors who have not worked yet, change the actors. These scenes should now involve dialogue. This time, start with ten actors on-stage. Each time an actor leaves the stage a new scene should be established. Because no one new is entering, the new scene can be started by any of the remaining actors. Remember that this must happen in a smooth and seamless fashion. In the end, you should be left with only one actor on the stage.

Purpose

To react to and justify each and every moment

In life we are constantly responding to our environment. If a person is driving down the road and a car pulls out in front of him, he has to react instantaneously. In this exercise, the actors also have to be in the moment. They cannot plan for the next scene if they are already on-stage because they have no idea what the next person is going to establish. Not only do they have to instinctively go with it, they also have to be believable in their new role. The audience has to buy that the character is authentic and that his actions and reactions are justifiable. When it is written down on paper it sounds easy and obvious. In order for actors' performances to be instinctual, they have to do a lot of work. It is not a process of natural selection. For the actors to give honest performances it is also going to take a tremendous amount of hard work on their part.

Industry Connection

This exercise has a large degree of unpredictability. The actors on-stage never know what is going to happen next. Explain the following to your actors:

INSTRUCTOR: You could plan your acting career down to the last detail and yet it can change at every turn. One day you might be the lead in a show and the next day the show may get cancelled. One year you might be a virtual unknown, and the next year you could be an Oscar-winner. You might say these are exaggerations and that these examples are not realistic. Both of these examples are based on real circumstances. An acting career will be full of unpredictability and change. This is fine, provided you are able to adapt and embrace each and every moment. Don't become wooden and inflexible, rather become vibrant and alive.

270. Never-Ending Movie

Have two to five actors go up into the performance area. Have the audience give them a scene to improvise. Also have the audience give each one of them a character breakdown, a mini-biography, and some personality traits. Allow them to spend two to three minutes on each character. Once this has all been discussed and decided, have the actors begin the scene. After a few minutes, pause the scene and switch out all the actors. The new actors are to take over exactly where the scene left off. Each one of them is to replace one of the characters and play precisely the same character as the previous actor. As they take on the character, they should bear in mind the bio and character traits that were discussed at the beginning. Have the actors continue the scene from where it left off. After a few minutes, pause the scene and bring in a new set of actors in the same fashion. This whole exercise should involve one continued scene with the same characters. The only continuous change is the actors playing the characters. Follow up with a group discussion.

Purpose
To build on the given circumstances

Before the actors begin the scene they are given information about their character. When the scene is played out, the audience expects to see some of that detail. If nothing in the performance resembles the given circumstances, then the audience will be left confused and unconvinced. When actors play a role, they often like to make the character their own. This is commendable, but good actors will always find the essence of the character. They will not disregard everything they know about the character, but use it to their advantage.

Industry Connection

This scene is disjointed in that it stops and starts a number of times. Just as the actors are getting familiar to the scene, they are pulled out and a new set of actors are brought in. On a film set the director will start and stop the scene with each take. One scene might be three-fourths of a page. In a play, one scene might be forty-two pages long. The actor has to be able to get used to this transition from theatre to film. The director also may choose to direct the last scene first, and the first scene last. The dysfunction of this exercise fits the dysfunction of the film medium. This is not a criticism, but a challenge the actor has to embrace.

Note

Do not tell the group that there will be pauses where new actors take over the roles. It will add to the challenge if they do not know ahead of time. It will also show who is focused, alert, and paying attention.

271. Conversation Bites

Have all your actors write a sentence on a small slip of paper that you have given them. Have them fold up the piece of paper and throw it onto the stage or performance area. Pick between two and four actors to come up onto the stage. Have the audience suggest a scene and a scenario for the actors to improvise. The scene should be performed to the best of the actors' ability, with one difference: Every time you clap your hands, one of the actors has to pick up a piece of paper from the floor, and immediately integrate what's written on it into the conversation. They have to say the line exactly as it is written. They have to justify what they are saying and why they are saying it. They have to justify bending down to pick up the piece of paper. Keep going until every piece of paper has been picked up and integrated into the scene. It is not necessary that the actors pick up the pieces of paper in order. In other words, the same actor is allowed to pick up two pieces of paper before another actor has a turn. I would limit each actor to twice in a row. Once the scene is finished, bring up another group of actors.

Purpose

Saying the line for the first time

The actors have no idea what is written on the pieces of paper, and yet somehow they have to convince us that this was their next thought. Actors in a play have gone over the lines on numerous occasions in the rehearsal period. They still have to convince the audience that when the say the line, it is the first time that thought occurred to them. This is one of the greatest challenges facing actors. They have to know how to make the material fresh again, and again, and again. It is true that in this exercise the actor has never seen the sentence before, and yet he still has to convince the audience that it came from his thoughts. It is a luxury not to know what is coming next.

Industry Connection

The actor who will likely be the strongest in this exercise is the functioning actor. An actor with raw talent may also do well in parts, but be lacking in other areas. This is not an easy exercise to do credibly, without having some sort of training. It is an important point to make. Some of your actors will be good entertainers. They will be able to make the class laugh. The challenge is that no one for a minute believes anything they are doing. They are choosing to be a celebrity rather than an actor and in this they are selling themselves short. The actor who has the best chance of succeeding in London, New York, or Los Angeles is the prepared actor. The actor who has no training and has put no time into learning the ropes of the industry is likely to sink as opposed to swim. If an actor marries a famous movie producer, then he may feel what I just said does not apply to him. It is true that she can get her husband a part in a movie or a television series. The challenge is that if the audience doesn't like the actor, and the ratings don't like him, then she can't and won't be able to hire him for very long. The only way around this for any actor who wants longevity is to become a good actor!

272. Finger Puppet Frenzy

Instruct your actors to sit in the audience. In the performance area, set up a small table, or two chairs facing upstage and away from the audience. Pick two actors to come forward. Have the audience set the storyline. Allow the audience to choose up to six characters. Tell the actors that they are now going to go behind the table or chairs and kneel down. You can give them cushions to kneel on, if you like. You can also drape the table with a blanket or sheet to hide the view of the actors. They are now going to perform their story using their fingers. In other words, they are going to act out a finger puppet play. Tell the actors that they should not be looking toward the floor when talking. They need to look forward and project their voices. They also need to keep their heads hidden at all times. The only parts of their body that should be in full view are their fingers. The two actors will be playing the roles of up to six characters using only their fingers. If one of the characters is quite old, they will want to bend their finger to show this. If one of the characters is supposed to be a small child, perhaps that finger will move around faster and more inquisitively. The actors will also want to adapt their voices for each of the characters. Give the pair two to three minutes to perform their play. Once they have finished, repeat the process with a new pair.

Variation

You can vary the number of actors whom you put in the finger puppet show. If you want to, you can take this exercise a step further. Split your class into four or five groups. Give each group fifteen minutes to come up with their own mini-play and create costumes for their fingers. They can do this with paper, scissors, and some colored pencils or felt pens. Watch each group perform their finger puppet plays.

Purpose
To work with physicality

The actors in the play have to enable all their characters' movements to be portrayed through their fingers alone. If a character wants to sit down, they have to find a way to show this with their finger. If another character is tired and wants to go to sleep, they also have to show this through the use of their finger. It is through the subtlety of the actors' fingers that the characters' physicality will be portrayed. For this to happen, the actors have to be familiar with physicality. Let us say an actor is playing a character who is supposed to be seventy, but the actor is only seventeen. While he is unlikely to be cast in this role in professional theatre, it is quite possible in a high school theatre production. The actor will want to understand that older people sometimes have scoliosis, which leads to curvature of their spine. Even without scoliosis, a seventy-year-old will, generally speaking, hunch slightly forward with a rounding at his shoulders. This is not always the case, but it is a greater potential reality. If the actor playing the role has not done his research or observed any older people, he is going to have a challenge playing the role with authenticity. The actor will want to connect himself to reality to enable him to disconnect. Encourage your actors to understand the physical makeup of their characters.

Industry Connection

It is unlikely that any actor is going to make his fortune doing finger puppet shows. Although having said that, a number of years ago there was an actor in England who did do this with a character called Finger Mouse. The finger puppet performance allows the actors to show their versatility. An actor on-set may be asked to do a number of things that he was not aware of before he arrived. This is not because the director is playing a cruel trick. It is because as he starts filming, the director will get an idea or two and want to see how the actor looks. The director may ask an actor to "roll over" or "jump over the bucket." If it is a stunt, there will be a stunt person to do those things. I am talking about quirky behaviors or actions that may be performed by the actor. A star may refuse to do these, or even try. An up-and-coming actor is unlikely to protest, provided that what he is being asked to do is not potentially dangerous or against union rules. Remind your actors that they have to be versatile and ready to handle every challenge that comes their way.

273. Space Filler

Ask two actors to come into the performance area. Give them a scene suggested by the audience, or tell them to work with a scene they have previously presented. What you are going to do is tell them to work within a designated space. You may choose to use a third, half, or the entire stage area. At some point during the scene, the actors have to cover the entire designated space. Not only do they have to cover the area, but they have to do so in a way that is justified by the scene. If an actor decides to go and sit in a chair at the corner of the stage, he has to find a reason for doing so. As mentioned, you can adjust the stage area from very small to very large. Whatever the size of the designated area, the actors have to work with the entire space.

Purpose

To understand the importance of blocking

We live in a world where people are used to seeing fast moving images on the screen. There was a time when seeing a static play was completely acceptable to the audience. This has become less acceptable with each generation. A way of showing this is to know that while the majority of professional shows in the West End of London used to be plays, there has now been a role reversal. The vast majority of shows are now musicals. The audience wants to see something that moves them visually as well as emotionally. When the blocking of a play is static, it can often lead an audience to switch off. We do not have the patience that generations before us had. Theatre has to find ways to adapt to today's environment. Part of this picture is to keep the play as a visually interesting spectacle for the audience.

Industry Connection

The actors have to get used to working with the entire space. They cannot just place themselves in the middle of the stage and stay there. Some actors like to go to an audition and literally glue themselves to the spot. This may. make sense in certain film auditions where they are filming a close-up only. An actor who is auditioning for stage work may want to command a larger amount of space. In some film and TV auditions the director will say something like, "Go wherever you want to and the camera will follow you." This is an obvious indication that he does not want the actor to glue himself to the spot. This does not mean that he wants the actor to frantically run around the room without a purpose. It means that when the scene calls for it, the actor must be able to command the space.

274. Topsy Turvy

This is quite a popular activity in improvisation circles. *Topsy turvy* is an English term that means everything is upside down or jumbled up. Its meaning fits nicely with this exercise. In the performance area, set out two chairs, slightly turned in towards one another. Instruct your students to sit as the audience. Explain in the following way:

INSTRUCTOR: Jessica and Marcus should join me for this activity. Jess, you're going to be interviewing Marcus on a well-known news channel. I will ask you to use your imagination to decide which one. We are going to need a topic from our audience. (The audience provides potential topics for the interview and character traits.) Jess, you are going to interview Marcus on the topic you have been given. The challenge is that you are going to have to do everything backwards. In other words, you are going to start with the end of the interview and finish with the beginning.

ADAM: Are all the sentences literally backwards so that they don't make any sense?

INSTRUCTOR: This is a great question. The answer is no, the interviewer might begin with, "Thanks for watching. Good night." They might end with, "Welcome to ABC news channel." The words are forwards, but the sentences are backwards. Marcus, you also have to answer the questions in the same style.

The interview can be any topic your group decides on. Make sure your students have their characters well-defined. The interviewer will want to sit upright, with good posture, as a news reporter would.

Variation
See the activity Expert in *112 Acting Games.*

Purpose
To think on your feet
In this activity there is no time to go through the motions. The actors are having a conversation. If they pause at every opportunity to figure out what they should be saying next, the sentences will seem false and abrupt. It is the same concept as when novice actors are going over their lines during a scene, instead of responding to what is being said. The challenge in this activity is to keep the conversation natural and flowing, even with the complexities involved.

Industry Connection
In this activity the actors are being asked to work out of sequence. It is a practical example of how they have to work in the industry. It is very rare for a movie to be made in sequence. A good director will have his macro-preparation worked out. It is much more likely that the movie is shot in order of location. All the scenes that take place by the beach may be shot over the course of a couple of days. This may be the case, even though the beach scenes occur at the

beginning, middle, and end of the movie. Actors have not only to get used to shooting out of sequence, they also need to be able to connect the dots in the characters' world at any particular time.

275. The Soothsayer

Ask three actors to come to the performance space. Tell them that in a moment you are going to ask them to get into a Buddha-like pose, one behind the other. For instance, the first person should be sitting on the floor. The second person should be kneeling behind him, and the third person should be standing behind the second person. Have the actors stagger themselves slightly so that their faces can be seen. Tell the audience that in a moment they will be able to ask questions, which the soothsayers will then answer. The only trick is that the actors must answer the question one word at a time — each person taking a turn to add a word to the sentence. For our purposes, the audience can only ask questions that are related to the field of acting. You can vary this if you like.

An example would be:

AUDIENCE: Oh, wise and wonderful soothsayer, how does an actor get the part?
SOOTHSAYER 1: The
SOOTHSAYER 2: most
SOOTHSAYER 3: important
SOOTHSAYER 1: part
SOOTHSAYER 2: of
SOOTHSAYER 3: the
SOOTHSAYER 1: audition
SOOTHSAYER 2: is
SOOTHSAYER 3: to
SOOTHSAYER 1: show
SOOTHSAYER 2: up.

The soothsayers do not have to stick to an order in answering the questions. Each round, a different soothsayer can begin to answer the question. The essential rule is that they can only answer one word at a time. After a few rounds of questions, change the soothsayers.

Purpose
To learn about the field of acting
The soothsayers are told to answer questions on acting. This is of benefit to the actors. It will allow them to acknowledge to themselves whether they have any idea how to answer the question. An actor who knows little about acting can still give a good performance. An actor who knows the history of acting inside out may give a poor performance. However, isn't a doctor expected to understand how the body works? Isn't the pilot expected to know how to fly the plane? Isn't the basketball player expected to know how to dribble the ball? So why, then, shouldn't the actor be expected to know about acting? If he doesn't, it's high time he did.

Industry Connection
The soothsayers have to be actively listening to each other in order to answer the questions with conviction. If they are simply playing around, their answers will most likely be utter nonsense. Let us say there is a scene in a movie in which an

actor has very few lines, yet he is on-stage the entire time. Every time the camera cuts to him, the audience wants to see that he is actively listening. They want to see the cogs turning. They want to see that the actor is listening to what is being said and planning his next response. If his response is to say nothing, then the audience wants to see this. The actor will want to get the most intense attention from his audience.

Chapter 33
Monologues

The following monologues are from my book, *Reality Driven Monologues*.

1. Forshizzling

The scene takes place in the bedroom of Meagan, who is Clarissa's best friend.

CLARISSA HAMMOCK: So anyway, you know that player I told you about? He asked me to go hang and I was like, that's tight. So he picks me up in these really rad wheels and I'm like, what a player! So we were just talking and forshizzling and I'm thinking, this boy is actually pretty fly. So he told me that some of his peeps were in a band and that we could mozy over there and just chill and I was like, whatever dude, because I was playing way cool. So we hanged for a few beats and I got my groove on. Anyway, I was like, "Dude, time is burning, let's be slick and chow down." So we went to this really rad joint and the food was really forshizzling. I mean it was just tight, you know what I'm sayin'? He wanted to chat about his thrash metal band and his homies and I was down with that. At one point he was talking a lot of smack, but I was chill. We went back to his place and he tried on a few moves and I said don't go there fly boy. I said, "I'm not down with your mac-daddy image," and he got all Buffy the Vampire Slayer on me. And I said, "Play it cool, honey. You're not on *The Jerry Springer Show*." Anyway, he took me back to my pad and was all like, for reals? And I was like, for reals. Anyway, I haven't seen him again since, but it's fly because I met this ultra-retro dude who is just the forshizzle king. So we're going to hang next week. Isn't that just electro, forshizzle?

Character Breakdown

Clarissa is five feet, two inches tall. She has a Mediterranean complexion with dark hair and brown eyes. She has a great smile that turns many boys' heads. She is sixteen years of age. Up until about four years ago she spent a good deal of time going out with her mother. She used to love it when her mother took her shopping and to the movies. Once she reached the age of thirteen everything changed, and it became embarrassing for Clarissa to be seen out with her mother. In other words, she was developing her own attitudes and becoming a teenager. Her best friend is Meagan, and they spend most of their time together. They love to go to each others' houses and talk about boys. Clarissa is the more outgoing of the two and will say anything to anyone. Meagan finds her friend really funny and loves to be around her. Clarissa loves to be the center of attention. This month, she has started to talk in her own form of slang. Meagan and Clarissa like to go everywhere and talk to people in this slang. When they go to the food court at the mall, they get a lot of blank stares from the people behind the counter. In about a month's time, they will probably tire of this and come up with some other way to amuse themselves. Clarissa is very intelligent but thinks that education sucks. She spends most of her time rubbing her teachers the wrong way. By constantly trying to be the center of attention, she gets herself into a lot of trouble. She thinks that it's worth it, because she finds it makes school more interesting. It is quite likely that she will have a promising future because she is so outgoing. She believes that life should be fun and in this respect she is way ahead of most people.

2. Toilet Roll Terror

The scene takes place in the kitchen of a shared house.

KATIE ARMENTA: Derek, can you come in here for a minute. I think we need to talk. Last night I noticed that someone had been using my toilet paper. Over the last six weeks I became suspicious that my toilet rolls were being used unusually quickly, so last night I marked my toilet roll with a red marker. When I checked this morning, the piece of paper with the red marker was gone. I spoke to Mark and Janet about it, but they both assured me it was not them. Derek, have you been using my toilet paper? I can see a look of guilt on your face, so I'm going to take that as a yes. I'm very disappointed in you, Derek. How can I trust you if you take my toilet roll? Everyone recognizes my toilet roll, because it is the extra soft type. Toilet rolls aren't cheap you know, and I don't make a lot of money. This morning I started to label all my items, to avoid any future confusion. When you open the fridge you will see *Katie's milk, Katie's cheese, Katie's bread, Katie's cottage cheese*, and all the other things that belong to me. I have also amended the bathroom situation so that you will now find, clearly identified, *Katie's toilet rolls*. I hope you realize that I am very upset with you, Derek, and I'm not sure the trust will ever be the same again. I'm going to bed. Don't use my toilet rolls!

Character Breakdown

Katie is dressed in Mickey Mouse pajamas. She is eighteen years of age. She has long, frizzy ginger hair. Her face is covered in freckles. She is of average height and very skinny. She is a college student and shares a house with three other students. She is a first-year psychology student. Everything in her life turns into a drama. Even when a situation should be resolved fairly simply, it never is. She likes to make a mountain out of a molehill. Katie moved in with Derek, Mark, and Janet at the beginning of the year. They met at a freshman induction meeting and none of them had previously been friends. At the beginning everything was going well. Then Katie started imposing her list of rules. It has come to the stage at which no one in the house wants to live with her, but there is nothing they can do until the end of the school year when their contract is up. Katie likes to speak her mind and if other people don't like it, that's their problem. When she lived at home, she was always being told what to do and her opinion was not considered important. Now that she has left home, she is making up for it tenfold. She believes in laying down a firm set of ground rules so that everyone is on the same page. Katie has a boyfriend named Nick, who pretty much does as she says. One day, Katie plans to set up her own practice, because she feels there are a lot of dysfunctional people out there.

3. I Hate You

The scene takes place in the hallway, just outside a theatre arts classroom.

KATIE ERIN: I hate school and I hate you! Give me another referral. I really don't care. You've already given me five, so what's one more. I hate this class! I thought it was supposed to be fun, but all the projects you give us are so boring. You're going to phone my mother? Do you really think I care? That's the funniest thing I ever heard. Go ahead and phone her. You probably won't be able to get hold of her, and she won't care anyway. She's always too busy. She doesn't care about anything I do. Why do you always blame me for everything? What about Liz and Courtney? They mess around about as much as I do, but you always blame me. It's because you hate me that you blame me for everything. Just because I speak my mind and tell the truth about your class, you hate me. Don't tell me you don't hate me, because that would be a lie. Go ahead and give me a referral, and when you do, I'll tell them how much I hate this class and get a transfer. I love referrals. It's like having free time, and you get to just sit there and do nothing. If you think I'm going to apologize or change my attitude, you're wrong. It's not my fault you're a bad teacher and don't know what you're doing. It's not my fault you can't find a real job instead of baby-sitting us. So go ahead! Give me a referral!

Character Breakdown

Katie is five feet, four inches tall. She has straight, brown hair that she ties back in a ponytail. She has a slim build and a pretty face. She is fifteen years of age. She is wearing a khaki skirt and a lime green T-shirt. Katie is a high school freshman. The only thing she enjoys about school is going to see her friends. Although she gives her teacher a hard time, it is not so much because of the subject matter. Katie feels she gets ignored at home and that her mother never has time for her. Her parents divorced three years ago, and that put an enormous amount of pressure on her life. Her mother works long hours and rarely feels able to spend quality time with her daughters. As a result, Katie began to rebel at school to get some attention. School is the one place where she knows her teachers cannot ignore her actions. Katie's teachers know she is intelligent and can pass most of her class work with ease, if she puts her mind to it. Most of them do not feel giving referrals is the best approach, but have run out of options as far as Katie is concerned. Without being able to tackle the bigger picture, they feel there is very little else they can do in Katie's case. Katie loves her cell phone and keeps it with her wherever she goes. Even though the students are not supposed to have them in class, Katie always does. Katie spends every other weekend and a month each summer with her father. Her father really spoils her and lets her do pretty much as she pleases. He still considers her as daddy's little girl. Even though Katie's mother tells him there are problems, he refuses to acknowledge them. Katie loves to listen to Nirvana, and Kirk Cobain is her hero. She loves the idea that he just rebelled against everything and showed life as it really is.

4. Hairy Man Theory

The scene takes place in the apartment of Billy Levy's good friend Mitch.

BILLY LEVY: Listen, Mitch, I'm telling you it's a proven theory. The hairier you are, the safer you are. Take me for example. I've spent many years of my life being hairy and always felt perfectly safe. Do you remember a few years ago when I worked in a restaurant? Remember how I never used to get out of work till at least one o'clock in the morning? Do you remember that? Because I only lived about a mile from home I used to walk back. And in the two years that I walked, never once was I mugged, never once did I get threatened — nothing. And all because I'm hairy! There's something about hairy people that just puts people off. It's probably the fact that they're hairy. It stops people wanting to go anywhere near you. Have you ever been to the swimming pool and seen a man with a hairy back? What happens? Everybody clears the pool. There could be a packed pool, but you can guarantee that the hairy guy will have a space all to himself. So my idea is that we get all of the hot chicks to hire a hairy guy to be their protector. You know what I mean? Let's say they need to go out one night to do some last minute shopping and they feel a little unsafe on their own. Take a hairy guy. It's an absolutely guaranteed form of safety. Now the only downside of being hairy is that it is more than likely you will be stopped by the police. One year I got stopped four times by the police while riding my bicycle because they thought I was a burglar. I think it relates back to Darwinism where the criminal always had large bushy eyebrows that joined together. I have to admit, though, that when you weigh it up, there are more benefits to being hairy than not, and I'm not shaving for no one.

Character Breakdown

Billy is five feet, eight and a half inches tall. He has dark brown hair and hazel eyes. He has hairy arms and legs, but is hair-free on his back. He has an athletic build, although he is still striving for that elusive six-pack. He loves sports, but finds he does not have the time for team activities. He likes to run around the lake and do the four-mile loop. On his first attempt to run the loop this year he hurt his knee and the run took him over two hours. He finds that a great motivator is looking at attractive women as he runs. His friends enjoy his sense of humor, which they say is sarcastic. When he explains his hairy man theory, he does so with a degree of sarcasm, although he believes there is a lot of truth in what he says. He really was stopped by the police four times for being a potential burglar. He has a big problem with commitment, which any girl who's been out with him can vouch for. His friends say he is too picky and that he is going to be left on the shelf. He is a very picky person with just about anything, from food to women. He is not the sort of person who could go to a music festival, because he would not enjoy it, unless he knew and liked all the bands that were playing. He is not concerned about being hairy and often makes jokes about it. He did decide that if he ever gets a hairy back he will have laser treatment. He does not believe any person should have to live with that.

5. The Hot One

Paul and his friend, Michael, are scouting out girls at a bar. The bar is packed and it is difficult to see over all the heads.

PAUL COFEY: Is she looking at me? No, not the ugly one, the hot one with the blue top. Don't make it obvious! Make it look like you're looking at the clock or something. Well, what do you reckon? She's looking at me, isn't she? What do you mean, *no*? You probably missed it, I bet she's a little shy and she doesn't want to make it obvious. Look again. Make it slow. Don't do any sudden moves. Well? What do you mean, *nothing*? Yes, what? You got something? She looked? Her friend is not looking at me. I saw her looking in this direction before, but I think she was looking at the clock or something. She was looking to the right of me and a ways above me, so the ugly one wasn't looking anywhere near me. There it was again, the hot chick just looked right at me. Did you see it? You must have seen it, man. She wants me. Come on! I know you saw it that time. There is no way you missed that. Look, if you're jealous, just say so, but there's no need to act all dumb like. Whoa! Did you see that? Did you see the ugly one? She looked straight at you, man. She's got the hots for you! That's why you didn't see the hot one looking at me, because you were too busy playing eye tag with the ugly one. You are such a player! I'm gonna go over in a minute and speak to the hot one, just as soon as she looks at me one more time. As soon as she looks at me one more time, and gives me the sign, I'm going over. Any minute now.

Character Breakdown

Paul is twenty-one years of age. He is five feet, nine inches tall and weighs one hundred and fifty-five pounds. He has short black hair and hazel eyes. He is a junior in college, studying history. He loves to exercise on a regular basis and has what is known as an athletic build. He has a slight inferiority complex as far as women are concerned. He feels that many of the good-looking girls have really ugly boyfriends. He finds this really frustrating and believes that a lot of girls lie when they say they are looking for a nice, funny guy. In Paul's opinion, girls prefer to go out with jerks who cheat on them. Paul has had a few girlfriends, but has always wanted to go out with someone beautiful. His friends say that he is shooting out of his league. He believes that a good personality is important, but that being attracted to the person is an absolute must. Paul lives away from home and speaks to his family once a week by phone. He loves them dearly, but does not feel the constant need to talk to them. He talks on the phone more out of a sense of duty than a feeling of necessity. Paul is a very independent person and quite content with being that way. He loves to go off on long walks by himself. He loves it even more when he gets lost and has no sense of his bearings. He finds this quite exciting and loves the sense of adventure it gives him. He never travels with his friends because he believes that this will only lead to arguments. He lives by himself and loves the sound of silence. His New Year's resolution was to date a really hot chick. So far, this goal has not been accomplished. He is a very bad dancer and has what his friends call *Caucasian rhythm*.

About the Author

Gavin Levy is currently organizing acting workshops in Austin, Texas. He instructed for a number of years at the American National Academy in Studio City, California. He also worked alongside Paul Gleason at the Paul G. Gleason Theatre on Hollywood Boulevard. He has led guest workshops at a number of organizations including for the Creative Actors Alliance. He has also led master classes, some with colleague Paul Gleason, for the organization Women In Film. His first book, *112 Acting Games*, was published by Meriwether in 2005. Meriwether also published his second book, *Acting Games for Individual Performers*. His third book, *Reality Driven Monologues*, was released in 2008. His latest book, *Acting For Love & Money* was co-authored with Paul Gleason.

Levy is a native Londoner who came to the United States in 1999. He received his ALAM from the London Academy of Music and Dramatic Arts and is also a graduate of the Academy of Live and Recorded Arts. From October 1992 through July 1995, Levy studied theatre at the world-renowned Academy of Live and Recorded Arts. ALRA recognized the need for a new kind of training, one that enabled students to grow into fully-rounded professionals ready to meet the differing challenges of the stage, screen, and broadcast industries. Since that time, the ALRA has been training some of the best and brightest in the industry.

Levy became involved with Theatre in Education and in the Dragon Drama Theatre Company in London. He also wrote scripts for the various workshops, directed plays, and was an instrumental force in after-show workshops that were designed to educate students. As an active member of the Dragon Drama Company, Levy continues to educate students through theatre by teaching them skills through acting and improvisation as well as organizing and coordinating acting workshops.

Gavin Levy has over twenty years of theatre experience, including acting, instructing, directing, and writing. Levy's desire is to share his knowledge in learning the craft of acting in ways that adapt to the needs of our modern culture and audience.

Contacting the Author

Gavin Levy wants you to get the most out of this book. If you have a question about the work or simply want to pass on your discoveries, feel free to drop him a line. Gavin offers visiting master classes. You may also contact him with questions about teaching workshops at your school. You can also contact his colleague, Paul Gleason, in regards to questions in relation to acting and workshops.

Gavin Levy: gavlevy@yahoo.com or www.gavinlevy.com
Paul Gleason: pgg@acmt.org or www.acmt.org

www.ingramcontent.com/pod-product-compliance
Lightning Source LLC
Chambersburg PA
CBHW070644150426

42811CB00051B/613